AND I

The Faith
of the Early Church

TRINITY
AND INCARNATION

The Faith
of the Early Church

BASIL STUDER

Translated by Matthias Westerhoff
Edited by Andrew Louth

T&T CLARK
EDINBURGH

T&T CLARK LTD
59 GEORGE STREET
EDINBURGH EH2 2LQ
SCOTLAND

First Published 1993

ISBN 0 567 29244 4

British Library Cataloguing-in-Publication Data
A Catalogue record for this book is available from the British Library

Typeset by Buccleuch Printers Ltd, Hawick
Printed and bound by Page Brothers, Norwich

Contents

v

CONTENTS

Part Two: THE NICENE TURNING POINT

Foreword to the English Edition

It is not quite ten years since I wrote the book, *Gott und unsere Erlösung im Glauben der Alten Kirche*, which was published by Patmos-Verlag, Düsseldorf, in 1985. In it I was concerned to make clear how, in the first Christian centuries, the doctrine of the Trinity and Christology had developed in a complementary interaction. Certainly it may seem obvious today that the Church's faith in the eternal Trinity was only apprehended from the Easter mystery of Christ. That, however, the intimate connection between *theologia* and *oikonomia* – as the post-Nicene theologians were accustomed to describing these two realms – must be allowed for in an historical exposition, because it affected the actual development itself, is often overlooked even by those who are concerned with introducing the history of Christian doctrines. My long concern with the soteriology of the Fathers of the Church – prompted by an invitation to provide the relevant section of the *Handbuch der Dogmengeschichte* – has led me to the conviction that it is not possible to separate the exposition of the doctrine of the Person of Christ (Christology) from the treatment of the work of Christ (soteriology). After I had published 'Soteriologie in der Patristik' (HDG III/2a) in 1978, it was ever more strongly impressed on me through my lectures in the following years at S. Anselmo and the Augustinianum in Rome, as well as at the seminary at Rolduc, that the treatment of the historical unfolding of the doctrines of the Trinity and of Christ may not be separated. It became clear to me that the baptismal faith, as already expounded in the Apostle Paul's Epistle to the Romans, contains within itself both a confidence in the death and resurrection of Jesus Christ as well as confession of Father, Son and Holy Spirit, and that it must therefore be always regarded as a whole.

This trinitarian-Christological approach to the history of dogma is certainly already given recognition in a preliminary way in the classical manuals. Yet even Josef Barbel is alarmed about drawing out its full consequences in his study *Jesus Christus im Glauben der Kirche* (1976). It was not however granted him to work out a corresponding synthesis of early Christian doctrine. Even in my case, as I freely acknowledge, I have only partially succeeded in demonstrating how much in the course of the early centuries the ways in which trinitarian and Christological questions are put depend on each other and searches for solutions, both terminological and real, are always mutually connected. At all events the title I chose for my exposition – Gott und unsere Erlösung im Glauben der Alten Kirche (God and our Redemption in the Faith of the Early Church) – cannot be regarded as a happy one. It does not express clearly that according to the Fathers of the Church the history of salvation is to be traced back to that eternal life, in which the almighty Father is one God with the Son and the Holy Spirit. So for the English translation I have preferred the title, *Trinity and Incarnation: The Faith of the Early Church*. Nevertheless there can easily be drawn out of my detailed discussions of Justin, Irenaeus, Origen, and above all, Augustine my understanding of the close historical connection between the doctrine of the Trinity and Christology.

If discussion of this formulation of the question is not yet closed, one thing is certain: that my attempt to provide an introduction to the early Christian history of the doctrine of the Trinity and of Christology has found an echo with many a colleague and with many students. This is shown in particular by the, indeed, partly critical, but throughout appreciative reviews by M. Simonetti (Rome) in *Augustinianum*, H. D. Hauschild (Osnabrück-Münster) in the *Theologische Revue*, M. Slusser (Pittsburgh) in *Patristics*, A. de Halleux (Louvain-la-Neuve) in *Revue Théologique de Louvain* and E. Ferguson (Abilene) in *Church History*. It is also borne out by the Italian translation of my book, which appeared in 1986 from Borla, Rome, and its French translation, which appeared in 1989 with Le Cerf, Paris. I may also, to be sure, take it as recognition, if *Gott und unsere Erlösung im Glauben der Alten Kirche*, as more than one of my reviewers hoped, now makes the journey into the English-speaking world. I therefore sincerely thank the editors of the publishing house of T&T Clark, Edinburgh, for including my study in their programme of publications. And I express my especial thanks for the distinguished English translation.

S. Anselmo, Rome
before Easter, 1993
BASIL STUDER

Preface

In undertaking to present an overall view of the early history of trinitarian doctrine and christology, under the title of 'Trinity and Incarnation: the faith of the early Church' we are undoubtedly meeting an urgent concern of contemporary theology. For it is a matter uncontested today that access to the mystery of the Trinity is to be sought in the Easter mystery. This connection, however, is already obvious from the history of Church doctrine. When I was asked by the editors of the *Handbuch der Dogmengeschichte,* published by Herder, Freiburg im Breisgau, to give a summary of the soteriology of the Church Fathers, it was already clear to me, from the very beginning, that christology in the narrow sense, i.e. the doctrine of the person of the Redeemer, contrary to the concerns of the above-mentioned handbook, must be kept in mind. The close link between christology and soteriology in the present study, in which 'our salvation in Jesus Christ' is under discussion, will, accordingly, always be taken into account. Further, it was only natural to take up thoughts and even formulations from that first introduction to the patristic teaching on salvation for this new summary with its wider scope. In a more comprehensive context they, accordingly, get a more solid foundation, thus leading to a deeper insight into the mystery of salvation. In my further studies I realized more clearly that the Church Fathers' holistic christology must not be separated from early Christian trinitarian doctrine. For the saving activity of the son of God incarnate appears in the faith of the early Church as the revelation of the eternal Trinity, in which it had its beginning and in which it will find its fulfilment. Not without reason was the basic experience of salvation in baptism in the death and resurrection of Jesus Christ from the very beginning bound up with the faith in Father, Son and Spirit. So I was happy, when in the course of my teaching profession I had the opportunity of placing the historical development of faith in Jesus Christ, our Lord and Saviour, in a trinitarian perspective, i.e., in line with the creeds of the early Church, of linking *oikonomia* with *theologia.*

Like my 'Soteriology of the Church Fathers' this attempt at tracing the early history of trinitarian doctrine and christology from the aspect of their mutual

xiii

interrelation has also grown out of my lecturing at the theological faculty of S. Anselmo in Rome, and out of a year of theological studies at the Abbey of the *Dormitio* in Jerusalem and seminary of Rolduc in the Netherlands. This outward circumstances may here and there have had a detrimental effect. The concern for my hearers of very different backgrounds has, however, certainly helped me to bear in mind the present situation of the Church. At any rate I am grateful to my students from all over the world for their attentiveness, for their many suggestions and criticisms. In any case, I want fraternally to dedicate to them this summary of the origin and the transmission of our common creed.

There remains for me the pleasant duty of expressing my sincere thanks to all those who have contributed to the publication of this introduction to patristic theology. I am especially indebted to the Patmos Verlag, above all to Dr K. Pichler of the Lektorat Theologie for all his efforts in this connection. Further, I wish to thank my young fellow brethren of the abbeys of Gerleve and Muri-Gries, and especially Fr Markus Muff of my own monastery of Engelberg for all their editorial work, for the proof-reading, and for their compiling of the indexes. Finally, my thanks goes out to all who have encouraged me during the last few years with their friendly concern for my labours and my efforts.

S. Anselmo, Rome
Easter 1985

Abbreviations

ACO	*Acta Conciliorum Oecumenicorum*
AThR	Anglican Theological Review
AugMag	Augustinus Magister
BAug	Bibliothèque Augustinienne
CChG	Corpus Christianorum, series Graeca
CChL	Corpus Christianorum, series Latina
COecD	G. Alberigo *et al.*, ed., *Conciliorum Oecumenicorum Decreta*, Bologna, [3]1973 (reprinted with Eng. tr.: N. Tanner, ed., *Decrees of the Ecumenical Councils*, 2 vols., London and Washington, 1990).
CPG	*Clavis Patrum Graecorum*
CPL	*Clavis Patrum Latinorum*
CSChO	Corpus Scriptorum Christianorum Orientalum
CrSt	Cristianesimo nella Storia
CSEL	Corpus Scriptorum Ecclesiasticorum Latinorum
DS	H. Denzinger and A. Schönmetzer, *Enchiridion Symbolorum, Definitionum, et Declarationum de Rebus Fidei et Morum*, Rome, [36]1976
DSpir	*Dictionnaire de spiritualité ascétique et mystique*
DThC	*Dictionnaire de théologie catholique*
EEC	A. di Berardino, ed., *Encyclopaedia of the Early Church*, Cambridge, 1992
EstTrin	Estudios Trinitarios
EThL	Ephemerides Theologicae Lovanienses
EvTh	Evangelische Theologie
FzPhTh	Freiburger Zeitschrift für Philosophie und Theologie
GCS	Die griechischen Christlichen Schriftsteller
Greg	Gregorianum
Hahn	A. Hahn, *Bibliothek der Symbole und Glaubensregeln der alten Kirche*, Breslau, [3]1897
HDG	M. Schmaus *et al.*, eds., *Handbuch der Dogmengeschichte*, Freiburg, 1952 ff

HerdKorr	Herder Korrespondenz
HistWPhil	*Historisches Wörterbuch der Philosophie*
HKG	H. Jedin, ed., *Handbuch der Kirchengeschichte,* Freiburg, 1962 ff
IrTheolQu	Irish Theological Quarterly
JThSt	Journal of Theological Studies
KerDog	Kerygma und Dogma
LThK	*Lexikon für Theologie und Kirche*
MelSR	Mélanges de Science Religieuse
Mirbt	C. Mirbt and K. Aland, *Quellen zur Geschichte des Papsttums und des römischen Katholizisimus,* Tübingen, [2]1967
MG	J. P. Migne, *Patrologiae Graecae*
ML	J. P. Migne, *Patrologiae Latinae*
MySal	*Mysterium Salutis*
NRTh	Nouvelle Revue Théologique
NTest Stud	New Testament Studies
OCP	Orientalia Christiana Periodica
PO	*Patrologia Orientalis*
PWK	*Paulys Real-Encyclopädie der classischen Altertumswissenchaft,* ed. G. Wissowa *et al.,* Stuttgart, 1893–
QuDisp	Quaestiones Disputatae
RAC	*Reallexikon für Antike und Christentum*
RBén	Revue Bénédictine
RBib	Revue Biblique
RchAug	Recherches Augustiniennes
RchSR	Recherches de Science Religieuse
REAug	Revue des Etudes Augustiniennes
RFilosNeoscolast	Rivista di filosofia neo-scholastica
RHE	Revue d'Histoire Ecclésiastique
RQ	Römische Quartalschrift
RSLR	Rivista di Storia e Litteratura Religiosa
RsPhTh	Revue des sciences philosophiques et théologiques
RThLouv	Revue Théologique de Louvain
SChr	Sources Chrétiennes
StudAnselm	Studia Anselmiana
StudPatr	Studia Patristica
StudTheol	Studia Theologica
ThDNT	*Theological Dictionary of the New Testament*
TheolPhil	Theologie und Philosophie
ThGl	Theologie und Glaube
ThPrQ	Theologisch-praktische Quartalschrift
ThR	Theologische Revue
ThSt	Theological Studies
TRE	*Theologische Realenzyklopädie*
TrThZ	Trierer theologische Zeitschrift
TThQ	Theologische Quartalschrift
TU	Texte und Untersuchungen

Introduction

1. 'Theologia' and 'Oikonomia'

'If the Spirit of him who raised Jesus from the dead dwells in you, he who raised Christ Jesus from the dead will give life to your mortal bodies also through his Spirit which dwells in you' (Rom 8:11). With these words the apostle summarizes his message of new life granted to all who trust in God alone. In essence John states the same when he has Jesus saying: 'This is eternal life, that they know thee the only true God, and Jesus Christ whom thou hast sent' (John 17:3).

These and similar words from Scripture clearly express how closely interrelated God and our salvation in Jesus Christ are. And this interrelationship holds as much in the faith and theology of the post-apostolic Church as it does in the apostolic message. Therefore, if someone retraces the beginnings of the history of Church dogma and the theological doctrine about the Trinity and the saving incarnation of the Son of God, he will always have to consider how the churches of early Christianity reached the confession of faith in Jesus Christ, our Lord and Saviour, and in that the confession of faith in the triune God. To put this in more concrete even though more restricted terms: he will ask the question as to how far the first Christian generations accounted for the fact that any believer is to be baptized not only into the death of Christ (cf. Rom 6:1–4) but also in the name of the Father, the Son and the Holy Spirit (Matt 28:19).

God and our salvation in Jesus Christ: here a twofold problem seems to be announced. On the one hand the Father, the Son and the Spirit, the one God is in question. More precisely, it is very tempting to work out how these three co-operate in history according to the faith and teaching of the first Christian centuries, how they form an *economic* Trinity, and how they reveal that they have always lived as Father, Son and Spirit, have always been an *immanent* Trinity. On the other hand, the person of Christ is contemplated in *christology* proper as well as Jesus' saving action in *soteriology*. It is necessary to address the question of how the second person of the Trinity has become man in order to lead all men to divine life.

1

In essence this twofold formulation of the question amounts to one question, or at least it is a matter of two points of view, which are intimately interrelated. Certainly the distinction between the question about the triune God and the question about salvation founded in the Son of God made man goes back to the times of the early Church itself. From the fourth century onwards one encounters in theological thinking and even in certain creeds the antithesis of *theologia* and *oikonomia* as it was developed subsequent to the creed of Nicea (325).[1] The roots of this basic distinction reach back even further, in that one finds from the very beginning christological as well as trinitarian credal formulae.[2] Whereas the first range of formulae above all underlines the fact that salvation can exist only in the name of the Lord Jesus, and precisely in this soteriological sense was of particular interest for the apologetical orientation of second-century theology; the second expresses – even if this is not extended further, but simply confessed in the liturgy – that Father, Son and Spirit have always been the fulness of life.[3] It has also to be admitted that the division between the doctrine of God and the doctrine of salvation worked out since the fourth century has proved in the event to be extremely productive. It underlies the patristic syntheses which then led to the scholastic summas.[4] Accordingly the modern history of dogma is largely determined by this distinction.[5]

Nevertheless it would be better to speak of a single formulation of the question. In fact no one can remain ignorant of the fact that the eternal Trinity is in the end only revealed in the historical mystery of Easter. In the cross it became apparent that the Son has always given himself to the Father, and in the resurrection it was shown that this surrender of the Son, intended by the Father, has always been performed through the Holy Spirit. This is why the first Christians were forced to the realization that baptism, in which according to their conviction they were taken into this mystery, must be accomplished in the confession of faith in Father, Son and Holy Spirit.[6]

What burning actuality is summed up in such a history of trinitarian and christological doctrine, the following three notes may make even clearer.

The doctrine of the triune God as well as that of our salvation in the Son of God made man are generally acknowledged to stand at the centre of our partaking in the eternal life of the Trinity, which has been granted to us in Jesus Christ. In that God condescended to man to be his salvation he has revealed himself as the Father who lives with the Son in communion with the Holy Spirit. This central

---

[1] Cf. esp. Gregory of Nyssa, OrCat prol. 5f and 5.1; Theodoret, Eranistes 2: MG 83, 149 AB; Fides Damasi: DS 71f, and the Symbolum Quicumque: DS 75f; also A. Grillmeier, 'Vom Symbolum zur Summa', *Mit ihm und in ihm*, pp 585–636, esp. pp 592–7, 618ff.

[2] Cf. J. N. D. Kelly, *Early Christian Creeds*, London ³1972.

[3] Cf. Irenaeus, AHaer III 1.2 and IV 33.2, and I 10.1 and Demonstr 3; also J. Moingt, *Tertullien*, pp 75–86.

[4] Cf. A. Grillmeier, art. cit.

[5] This is also true of the most recent histories of dogma and theology: C. Andresen, ed., *Handbuch der Dogmen – und Theologiegeschichte* I, Göttingen 1982, and K. Beyschlag, *Grundriß der Dogmengeschichte* I, Darmstadt 1982.

[6] Cf. esp. Rom 6–8 and I Cor 12, where Paul speaks of baptism in a trinitarian context. Also R. Kerst, '1Kor 8,6 – ein vorpaulinisches Taufbekenntnis?', ZNW 66, 1975, pp 130-9. See also 1 Cor 6:11 and Jude 20ff.

mystery of the Christian faith deserves to be looked upon as the heart of all theological thought, all the more so as it is in danger today of being forgotten or of being called in question.[7] How many Christians do not know what to do with faith in the triune God? How many, too, are hardly aware that faith in the real incarnation of God forms the distinction between Christianity and the other religions, above all Judaism and Islam? On the other hand, is there not here and there in theological literature a tendency which results in neutralizing the eternal distinctions of Father, Son and Holy Spirit and at the same time viewing Jesus simply as a man filled by God?[8] It is also the case that the view that the early Christian formulation of faith in the Trinity and the incarnation is a mere hellenization of the Christian faith, and therefore a more or less far-reaching distortion of the gospel, has not at all yet been ousted.[9]

The attempt to treat the historical development of trinitarian and christological doctrine together corresponds further to a really basic concern of modern theology. That is to say, it takes all the more seriously the requirement that Christian faith in the Trinity can only be understood and established through the mystery of Easter.[10] The history of doctrine, however, has not come to grips with this urgent matter of concern to systematic theology. It has remained a mere desideratum until now.[11] It is high time, at least, to make an attempt. Christology is clearly understood here in a comprehensive sense as the doctrine of the person *and* the work of Christ. Yet in the field of history of doctrine there are very few attempts to take this seriously, although the requirement that christology be not separated from soteriology has been emphasized for a long time.[12]

Finally, reference should be made to the hermeneutic interest that a description of the early Christian history of trinitarian doctrine and of salvation in Jesus Christ ought to attract. It is well known that the concepts of orthodoxy and of Christian dogma have been developed primarily in this context. What is more, the creeds, which for the Christian churches have remained until now the sign and expression of the *communio fidei*, to a large extent emerged from the fight for the true faith in the Trinity and the incarnation of the Son of God. Therefore, the rules of theological hermeneutics are to be verified especially in this context. From the first it becomes clear, particularly in the development of trinitarian and christological doctrine, how the gospel of God's salvation has been transplanted from its Palestinian native soil to new conditions. It is apparent here how, for apologetic and pastoral reasons, Christian teachers transmuted the original

[7] For the present situation concerning this issue cf. U. Ruh, 'Das unterscheidend Christliche in der Gottesfrage', HerdKorr 36/4, 1982, pp 187–92.

[8] Cf. the declaration of the German bishops' conference 'Das Glaubensbekenntnis von Nizäa', HerdKorr 29/11, 1975, pp 558ff.

[9] Cf. the essay on this subject by A. Grillmeier, *Mit ihm und in ihm,* also R. Hübner, *Der Gott der Kirchenväter und der Gott der Bibel.*

[10] Cf. W. Breuning, 'Trinitätslehre, wissenschaftstheoretisch', LThK 10, 1965, 360; K. Rahner, 'Yesterday's History of Dogma and Theology for Tomorrow', *Theological Investigations,* vol 18, London 1984, pp 3–34, esp. p 17; E. Jungel, *God as the Mystery of the World,* Edinburgh 1983; P. Schoonenberg, 'Denken über Chalcedon', TThQ 160, 1980, p 301: '. . . a trinitarian doctrine that is independent of christology is impossible.'

[11] Cf. the (not implemented) approach of J. Barbel, *Jesus Christus im Glauben der Kirche,* pp 235ff.

[12] Cf. B. Studer, *Soteriologie,* pp 56ff (notes).

3

preaching, though remaining strictly faithful to it, into current forms of preaching and theology. In short, it becomes clear in the course of history, how the Christian religion passed from Jewish surroundings into Greco-Roman culture.

Furthermore, the early Christian development of the doctrine of God and our salvation shows us that it is impossible to understand or to adhere to the apostolic tradition without knowledge of later ecclesiastical tradition. In other words: the early history of the central core of the Christian confession enables us to understand particularly clearly just to what extent the preaching of the early Church is still the norm of faith for Christians of today, even though a *norma normata*. That this is still a burning problem is shown by the discussions which are being held about the integral retention of early Christian creeds[13] and particularly about the lasting obligation to the faith of Chalcedon.[14] Finally an unprejudiced Christian cannot pass over that incessant, even dogged struggle in which the first Christian generations endeavoured to express in a genuine way their faithfulness to the inherited apostolic faith and strove not to lose anything with which, through Christ, the faithful, the whole of humanity are related to God. In this way he may feel all the more strongly that all human talk about divine matters falls short of reality itself, that all ecclesiastical paraphrasing of the faith only defines the boundaries within which Christians may find themselves in prayer and reflection, and never sounds the depth of the faith which the churches confess.

2. The basis of a historical and at the same time theological answer

'Trinity and Incarnation: the faith of the early Church'. A theme like this naturally demands a historical perspective. The first task is to grasp unambiguously the roots of the history of trinitarian doctrine and christology, which are basic to their whole development. It is however beyond our scope here to give a full account of the theology of the biblical writings, let alone of the events of revelation of which they tell.[15] It is necessary though to recall at least summarily the biblical basics without which the development of ecclesiastical doctrine cannot be comprehended. This is all the more obvious as the Church Fathers themselves in their doctrine of *theologia* and *oikonomia* not only drew practically the whole

---

[13] Cf. e.g. G. J. Békés and H. Meyer, eds., *Confessio fidei. International Ecumenical Colloquium (Rome, 3–8 Nov. 1980),* Rome 1982, and K. Lehmann and W. Pannenberg, eds., *Glaubensbekenntnis und Kirchengemeinschaft. Das Modell des Konzils von Konstantinopel (381),* Freiburg-Göttingen 1982. See also S. M. Heim, ed., *Faith to Creed. Ecumenical Perspectives on the Affirmation of the Apostolic Faith in the Fourth Century,* Grand Rapids, Michigan, 1991.

[14] Cf. among others A. Grillmeier, 'Moderne Hermeneutik und altkirchliche Christologie', *Mit ihm und in ihm,* pp 489–582, and A. de Halleux, 'La définition christologique à Chalcédoine', RThLouv 7, 1976, pp 3–23, 155–70.

[15] Cf. among others M. Hengel, *Son of God, Origin of Christology and the History of Jewish-Hellenistic Religion,* Philadelphia 1976; H. Merklein, Zur Entstehung der urchristlichen Aussage vom präexistenten Sohn Gottes, QuDisp 87, Freiburg 1979, pp 32–62; C. Colpe, 'Gottessohn', RAC 11, 1981, cols. 19–58; C. Colpe, 'Neue Untersuchungen zum Menschensohn-Problem', ThR 77, 1981, pp 353–72, and the relevant chapters in MySal II and III/1–2, Einsiedeln 1967–70.

time from Old and New Testament testimonia, but also saw themselves as under obligation to the prophets and the apostles, not intending to be anything other than *tractatores Sacrarum Scripturarum.*[16]

The starting point of the trinitarian doctrine and christology of the early Church is the religious experience of Jesus and the early Christian community. In this original experience the basic foundation is the faith of Israel in the one God who has created all and continually governs the history of mankind wisely and powerfully, as well as faith in the pouring out of the Holy Spirit, as foretold by the prophets.[17] At the very heart of this experience is the Easter certainty of God's final salvation, by which Jesus has been fully acknowledged as the Son of God and established as the Saviour of the world, this certainty being prepared through contact with Jesus, and powerfully confirmed in the communication of the gifts of the Holy Spirit. In short: according to the early Christian experience which is founded on the apostolic preaching to which the New Testament writings bear witness, Jesus Christ, the saviour sent from God, is himself true God, although he is not identical with the Father, and as such is fully and completely present to his people only in the Holy Spirit. This faith in God, who through his Holy Spirit has glorified Christ as his Son and still glorifies him, is however always preached in the context of faith in the God of the patriarchs, i.e. in the faith in God's salvation which in the last days should find its fulfilment in the pouring out of the Holy Spirit. It is impossible to neglect this connection with the faith of Israel, all the more so as the scriptures of the Old Testament, the most forceful testimony in this regard, remained *the* Holy Scriptures until the middle of the second century.

Setting out from this starting point of trinitarian doctrine and salvation one finds that it is necessary to differentiate the early Christian experience of God's salvation from the apostolic tradition as its expression. Certainly the experience of faith and its proclamation must not be separated, as the former is accessible only through the latter. Nevertheless, a certain differentiation is extremely helpful in this connection.

The *experience,* in which the early Church attained the certainty that God through the power of the Holy Spirit has fulfilled and confirmed Jesus' messianic claims in spite of suffering and death, took place in the encounters of the chosen witnesses with the risen Lord, in the joy of the breaking of bread, in the success of preaching, in the disciples' steadfastness before the Sanhedrin and the people, in the miraculous cures and the charisms, and not least in the persecution of the community.[18]

However, the *apostolic tradition,* which has survived for posterity mainly in the New Testament, expresses the eschatological experience of the presence of God, effected through Christ in the Holy Spirit, that is, the coming of the kingdom

---

[16] Cf. above all Augustine, Trin I 2.4; I4.7; and, for the theme in general, A. Benoit, *L'actualité des Pères de l'Eglise,* Neuchatel 1961.

[17] Cf. above all Isaiah, the 'gospel of the OT' and the messianic psalms.

[18] Cf. P. Pokorny, 'Christologie et baptême à l'époque du christianisme primitif', NTest Stud 27, 1981, pp 368–80.

of God in a threefold way: First it moves within an apocalyptic climate[19] as was already the case with Jesus himself, so that faith in the Lord's resurrection is combined with the expectation of the second coming of the Son of Man: the whole of the earthly saving event is regarded as a revelation of celestial realities.[20] It goes back even further to the sayings of Jesus, to the *logia* in which he himself expressed his unity with the Father, and which were rethought anew in the post-Easter situation. Finally the apostolic tradition interprets the mystery of Jesus in the light of the Old Testament as it was then understood by Judaism and also by Jesus himself.[21]

Despite these manifest facts – here, however, represented in a simplified way – it would be wrong to try to derive the faith in Father, Son and Spirit as well as in the divine sonship of the Redeemer which is involved here, from contemporary Jewish, and especially, apocalyptic, concepts. These rather constituted the mere forms of expression with which the early Church formulated her Easter conviction of faith, which was itself rooted in the messianic experience of Jesus himself, in her prayer and confession, in her proclamation and exhortation.

This Easter experience of the original community, unique though it appears to be, did not however simply peter out. Rather it lived on in the post-apostolic communities, particularly in the baptism of converts,[22] and the Eucharistic celebration,[23] in the experience of the newness of Christian life[24] as well as in martyrdom[25]. The continuing experience of God's salvation had its deepest roots, however, in the original experience of Jesus, and of the post-Easter community. In fact the later generations, too, were incessantly confronted with the mystery of the suffering Messiah, with the stumbling-block of the crucified Son of God, which can only be accepted through the power of the Holy Spirit, and is tolerable only through its very own comfort. All this happened, however, in an indirect way. Obviously the later Christians had not lived with Jesus and had not seen him hanging on the cross. They learnt of this only through the Gospel accounts. However, they had their own very personal experience of Jesus' mortal suffering in the misery of their own lives, and particularly in the affliction of Christ in the members of his persecuted Church.[26]

At the same time the post-apostolic communities expressed their experience of faith in which they knew themselves to be following Christ and the

[19] Cf. among others K. Koch and J. M. Schmidt, eds., *Apokalyptik: Wege der Forschung 365*, Darmstadt 1982, and R. Pesch, 'Zur Entstehung des Glaubens an die Auferstehung Jesu', FZPhTh 30, 1983, pp 71–98. See also P. Grech, in A. di Berardino and B. Studer, eds., *Storia della Teologia* I, pp 88–92.

[20] Cf. the themes of the seven spirits and the lamb in Rev 1–3 and 5, as well as the term mysterion in Mt 13:11 (cf. 11:25) and 1 Cor 2:1, 7.

[21] Cf. Jesus' use of the messianic psalms, and the traditions which were fundamental to the Apostle in 1 Cor 10: 1–13; Gal 3–4.

[22] Cf. Clement of Alex., Protr 10.94.2; also P. Stockmeier, 'Offenbarung', HDG I/1a, pp 60f.

[23] Cf. Justin, Apol I 65ff.

[24] Cf. Justin, Apol I 14, and also R. Minnerath, *Les chrétiens et le monde*, pp 289–307: on the community of the first Christians.

[25] Cf. MartPolyc 14 and 19, and the letter to the congregations of Lyons and Vienne, which mentions charismatic experience: Eusebius, HE V 1.3–3.4, esp. 3.3f; 1.9f.

[26] Cf. above all Justin's theology of the cross, e.g. Dial 35.7; Apol I.35.

apostles by means of the sayings of Jesus and the forms of prayer and confession of the early Church. Of course they were not satisfied with this, rather they found new forms of expression of their own. From their personal experience they extended the traditional invocations and confessions and reshaped them; even the old forms of expression they interpreted in the light of a new understanding of Christian life. This appears most clearly in the tradition of baptismal faith as testified in Matthew 28:19f and Didache 7. It did not only point the way for the shaping of baptismal liturgy, but had a normative effect also on the interpretation of other credal formulae, and did this without any sense of a new interpretation.[27] It is characteristic as well that the formulae which include the terms Lord (*kyrios*) and Son of God should gain another meaning in new surroundings.[28] Incidentally the post-apostolic communities, like the primitive Church before them, went back for their own formulations of their experience of Christ to the sayings of Jesus as recounted in the gospels, to Jewish conceptions and to Old Testament testimonia. In this, however, they went beyond the first Christians. They not only included forms of expression from the above-mentioned sources, but increasingly took over images and categories from the hellenistic environment. Thus the later generations, even more than the earlier ones, had to strive to bring into line the perhaps too disparate, at least seemingly contradictory, terms of confession.[29]

The development of the apostolic doctrine of God and salvation in Jesus Christ is therefore first to be explained as a mutual engagement between the experience of Christian faith and the traditional forms of prayer and confession; at the same time it is to be conceived as an exchange between traditional and new forms of expression. In any case, for a full understanding of these extremely complex historical developments, the main spheres of the Christian life, which have also been more or less effective in the formation of the apostolic tradition, need to be surveyed.

First the role of *worship* needs to be considered. The need to respond to the proclamation of God's salvation with a confession of faith and at the same time to commend all spiritual and bodily concerns to God's mercy resulted in the formation of new forms of prayer and confession. It is above all in the celebration of baptism and the eucharist that the Church sought to adapt doxology and epiclesis to its own conditions. Furthermore, the continual impulses of *Christian spirituality* must be taken into account. The enthusiasm for Christ which is to be found particularly in martyrs such as Ignatius of Antioch; the desire for union with God, which in circles marked by Platonic traditions became the ideal of 'deification'; and the charismatic movements which kept alive the memory of the original spiritual outpouring: all these in their own way promoted deeper reflection about divine salvation. Under the influence of the great New Testament theologians Paul and John, Christian life was understood above all as a way back

---

[27] Cf. Justin, Apol I 6, 1f; 61, 3.10. Irenaeus AHaer I10.1f; Demonstr 6. Also J. N. D. Kelly, *Early Christian Creeds*, pp 70–82.

[28] Cf. IClem 16.2: kyrios meaning the pre-existent; Ignatius, Eph 20.2: son in the sense of descent. Also A. Grillmeier, *Jesus Christus*, pp 40–57, 88–96.

[29] Cf. B. Studer, 'Zur Entwicklung der patristischen Trinitätslehre', ThGl 74, 1984, pp 81–93.

to the Father to be trodden with Christ in the communion of the Holy Spirit.[30] Moreover, the main concern of the *human intellect* must be taken into account, which seeks to understand the significance of the whole of reality. The circles open to Greek ways of thinking tried to formulate the mystery of the Trinity and the incarnation according to the laws of the then prevailing logic. They endeavoured to grasp it more fully by ruling out inadequate or false explanations. They relied upon a scientific exegesis of the texts, as developed by the rabbis and above all by the Alexandrian philologists.[31] Trouble was taken to bring home the doubtless offensive proclamation of the cross and the resurrection to people who found it difficult to come to terms with because of education and sensibility.[32] Finally, the external circumstances should not be overlooked: the growing co-operation of the Church and the Roman empire, and bound up with that the political resonance of the Christian message; the need to translate the gospel into more and more languages, involving opportunities for new forms of expression;[33] and last but not least the new ways of thought that sprang from the genius of particular individuals, such as Origen, Gregory of Nyssa and Augustine.[34]

Whoever tries to trace the early Christian history of the doctrine of God and our salvation is confronted with the task of considering more fully the question as to how the apostolic proclamation, in which the primitive Christian experience of God's salvation is expressed, has come to clarify that experience, in which the Christians of the first centuries relived through their own prayer, faith and action the original Christian experience of the presence of Father, Son and Spirit. In short, he is confronted with the question as to how the New Testament revelation of God in Christ has become the faith of the Church and Christian theology.

In undertaking to sum up early Christian history of trinitarian and christological doctrine further problems are involved. First and foremost it is not easy to discover the inner coherence between *theologia* and *oikonomia*. Even if it is granted that the threefold divine action in the history of salvation – the economic Trinity – reveals the divine life, triune from eternity – the immanent Trinity – it is nevertheless not entirely clear how a more precise understanding of Christ's person and work has influenced conceptions of the eternal relationship of Father, Son and Spirit. So, for example, the development of a common terminology for trinitarian and christological doctrine, as initiated by Apollinaris of Laodicea, is rather complicated. To meet these difficulties the following guidelines are particularly to be observed.

First, the twofold doctrinal development should not be dealt with separately, but within a single comprehensive account. Thus the councils of Nicea

---

[30] Cf. among others Ignatius, Eph 9.1; MartPolyc 14; Irenaeus, Demonstr 7; AHaer IV 33.7.

[31] The influence of ancient exegesis in particular affects the development of the concept of person in the trinitarian and christological context. Also C. Andresen, 'Zur Entstehung und Geschichte des trinitarischen Personbegriffs', ZNW 52, 1961, pp 1–39.

[32] Cf. P. Stockmeier, *Glaube und Kultur*, Düsseldorf 1983, pp 60–105.

[33] Cf. A. Adam, *Dogmengeschichte*, pp 92–105: 'Linguistic presuppositions of dogmatic thinking in the Church'.

[34] Cf. O. Gigon, *Die antike Kultur und das Christentum*, Gütersloh 1966, pp 7f.

(325) and Chalcedon (451) will constitute the chief landmarks. Even though Nicea has more to do with trinitarian doctrine, and Chalcedon with christology, each council has still been of basic significance for the other point of view, at least in retrospect. This is true particularly of the council of Nicea; without its determination of faith the later development of christological doctrine cannot be accounted for, historically speaking. For the rest the two most important councils of the early Church mark to a large degree the changes in the history of the churches and theology. Therefore, so far as the context of the fundamental determinations of faith is concerned, they are to be considered as constituting decisive caesurae in the history of dogma itself.

Even if during certain periods the interrelation may seem to be only an outward one, it has to be pointed out that trinitarian and christological doctrine have developed in the same ecclesiological context, the same historical context of theology and exegesis, as well as of spirituality. So detailed consideration of the theological situation during each period will enable us to state in one way or another an inner coherence between trinitarian and christological doctrine. Thus it can be seen how the apologetic orientation of the theology of about the year 150 determined, in similar ways, both the doctrine of God and that of salvation in Christ, by the introduction of the concept of the Logos. However, this does not require a purely chronological procedure, but rather a typological one. In this way individual phenomena of doctrinal development are dealt with within the framework of the period of which they are most characteristic.

So the doctrine of *redemptio,* of redemption, may be considered within the context of second-century theology, in which dualism, and belief in demons, were particularly well developed. In the same way the treatment of the creeds can be located right at the beginning, because their development can be examined particularly well at the very point of transition from apostolic tradition to that of the Church.

The principle of concentrating on both doctrinal developments at the same time allows, of course, one or other to predominate at different times. This corresponds to some extent to the historical development itself. Even though in the whole of early Christian history *theologia* and *oikonomia* must never be divorced from each other, the difference between them, especially from the time of Nicea onwards, must not be overlooked. It may very well be conceded that the trinitarian aspect was in the ascendant between 325 to 381, whereas from the end of the fourth century the question about the one Christ pressed to the fore. However, it cannot be denied that both threads of doctrinal development were interwoven, as the first beginnings of christological discussion had already occurred around 360, at the time, therefore, in which the trinitarian controversy entered its second and final phase.

What matters first to anyone who undertakes to give an account of the historical development of trinitarian and christological doctrine is to work out from the critical examination of the sources what Christians of the first centuries believed about God and salvation in Jesus Christ. Historical impartiality must not, however, leave him there, but should rather enter into his theological perspective.

It must not simply be his concern to make a historical survey – neutral in itself – of the confession and thought of the Church of former times, which could constitute preliminary work for a contemporary systematic theology. It is not even sufficient to reckon on the fact that there is no historical examination of trinitarian and christological doctrine which would not set out from a certain theological bias, which thus determines the question, and even many of the answers. A historical introduction to the world of faith of the early Church should also be theology in the proper sense.

A fairly old, and perhaps somewhat simplistic, distinction may explain more closely what this basic concern is about. In theology three functions can be differentiated, an apologetic, a dogmatic and an interpretative one.[35] The apologetic function is about demonstrating the rationality, or better, the non-irrationality of Christian faith. A dogmatic statement is expected to judge what is to be regarded in Christian doctrine as the norm of faith for all who want to belong to the fellowship of the Church. The third function can be understood as *intellectus fidei,* as a deeper understanding of the mysteries of faith. These three basic theological functions should now be brought to bear on our current historical survey.

As far as the apologetical function is concerned, two main points of view are to be taken into account: On the one hand the relevant traditions of the early Christian theologians can help to elucidate, to some extent, for the human mind, the mysteries of the Trinity and God's salvation, as they themselves had to deal with objections to the rationality of ecclesiastical teaching which differ very little from modern objections; on the other hand, and this is even more important, a historical consideration of the doctrine of God and of salvation in the early Church can show us to what extent she has been faithful to the gospel of Jesus Christ despite all accommodation to the Greco-Roman environment. Thus it will be confirmed that, in dealing with the Church's faith in the Trinity and the incarnation, something genuinely Christian is involved. The dogmatic function comes into its own to the extent that the historical past yields up to the Church of Christ what it is to believe concerning God and his salvation. It is not, however, enough to prove that the dogmas of today's Church have their roots in the apostolic tradition. There must rather be concern that the totality of the faith of the early Church is brought into consideration, as it is possible that not the whole of what the forefathers confessed and venerated in their faith has been preserved in the spiritual life of their descendants.[36] Finally, a believer cannot deal with early Christian theology without himself being involved, because he is always being encouraged to progress further in his *intellectus fidei,* in his own understanding of the doctrine of God and salvation. There is no doubt that not only the labours of the Fathers of the Church in establishing a true confession of faith, but also all their endeavours to draw closer to God can be invaluable in helping to orientate and enlighten any Christian who is prepared to get involved.

[35] Cf. Y. Congar, 'Théologie', DThC 15/1, 1946, cols. 341–502.

[36] Cf. K. Rahner's allusion to 'forgetting' in the history of dogma, e.g. in 'Forgotten truths concerning the sacrament of penance', *Theological Investigations* vol. 2, London 1963, pp. 135–74, esp. pp. 135f.

PART ONE
The Pre-Nicene Period

BIBLIOGRAPHY

J. Lebreton, *Histoire du dogme de la Trinité, II. De s.Clément à s.Irenée,* Paris 1928.

G. Kretschmar, *Studien zur frühchristlichen Trinitätslehre,* Tübingen 1956.

J. Daniélou, *The Theology of Jewish Christianity (A History of Early Christian Doctrine before the Council of Nicea,* vol. 1), London 1964.

C. Andresen, 'Zur Entstehung und Geschichte des trinitarischen Personenbegriffes', ZNW 52, 1961, pp 1–39.

H. Jedin and J. Dolan, eds., *History of the Church* vol. 1, London 1980.

A. Bsteh, *Zur Frage nach der Universalität der Erlösung. Unter besonderer Berücksichtigung bei den Vätern des 2. Jahrhunderts,* Vienna 1966.

R. Cantalamessa, *L'omelia 'in S. Pascha' dello Pseudo-Ippolito di Roma. Ricerche sulla teologia dell'Asia Minore nella seconda metà del II secolo,* Milan 1967.

F. Normann, *Christos Didaskalos. Die Vorstellungen von Christus als Lehrer in der christlichen Literatur des 1. und 2. Jahrhunderts,* Münster 1967.

H. von Campenhausen, 'Die Entstehung der Heilsgeschichte', Saeculum 21, 1970, pp 189–212, now collected in *Ges. Schriften,* Tübingen 1979, pp 20–62.

J. P. Martín, *El espiritu santo en los origenes del cristianismo,* Zürich 1971.

W.-D. Hauschild, *Gottes Geist und der Mensch,* Munich 1972.

W. Maas, *Unveränderlichkeit Gottes,* Munich 1974.

B. Lonergan, *The Way to Nicea,* London 1976.

J. Daniélou, *The Origins of Latin Christianity (A History of Early Christian Doctrine before the Council of Nicea,* vol. 3), London 1977.

G. May, *Schöpfung aus dem Nichts,* Berlin 1978.

A. A. 'Lo Spirito nella riflessione della Chiesa prenicea', Augustinianum 20, 1980, esp. pp 471–83, 655–69, 671–86.

See also:

F. Courth, *Trinität in der Schrift und Patristik* (HDG II/1a, Freiburg 1988), pp 31–109.

E. Dassmann, *Kirchengeschichte I. Ausbreitung, Leben und Lehre der Kirche in den ersten drei Jahrhunderten,* Stuttgart 1991.

1. A Survey of Pre-Nicene Christological Proclamation

BIBLIOGRAPHY

L. Goppelt, *A History of the Christian Church: Apostolic and Post Apostolic Times*, Göttingen [2]1966.

G. Kretschmar, 'Der Weg zur Reichskirche', Beihefte zu 'Evangelische Theolgie' 13, 1968, pp 3–44.

R. Cantalamessa, *Dal Cristo del Nuovo Testamento al Cristo della Chiesa: tentative di interpretazione della cristologia patristica: Il problema cristologico oggi*, Assisi 1973, pp 143–97 (bibliography).

R. Minnerath, *Les chrétiens et le monde (Ier and IIe siècles)*, Paris 1973.

G. G. Blum, 'Apostel, Apostolat, Apostolizität II. Alte Kirche', TRE 3, 1978, pp 445–66.

I. THE PRE-NICENE PERIOD IN GENERAL

In the year 325 the emperor Constantine the Great summoned a general synod at Nicea, close to his residence, to settle a theological controversy which had flared up in Alexandria, the empire's cultural centre, between Alexander, the bishop of that city, and his presbyter Arius on the issue of Jesus Christ's divinity. The mere fact that political authority was so deeply concerned with peace in the Church arouses the suspicion that at that time a new era for Christianity had dawned.

In fact, with the first ecumenical council the era of ecclesiastical freedom commenced, the era, which today is labelled as the period of the State Church.[1] That the Church and the Roman empire were, to an increasing extent, in a state of coexistence, altered ecclesiastical life in almost every sphere. The form of worship as well as of preaching were determined by the Christians' sense of also belonging to the empire. The now almost universal and ever-growing openness towards imperial culture had its impact above all in theology and exegesis. The council of Nicea itself, which announced this new era, through its confession gradually determined the whole of theological work and the whole of Christian

---

[1] On the concept of the 'State Church' cf. G. Kretschmar, 'Der Weg zur Reichskirche', Beihefte zu 'Evangelische Theologie' 13, 1968, pp 3–44; C. Andresen, *Die Kirchen der alten Christenheit*, pp 325–32; H. Jedin and J. Dolan, eds., *History of the Church* vol. 2: *The Imperial Church*, 1981, pp 89ff.

spirituality. From that time on, Christ, the Lord and Saviour, stood at the centre of Christian believing and thinking.[2]

If Nicea could be regarded as the symbolic start of a new epoch of Church history and history of theology, this implies that the preceding three centuries constitute another period, namely the pre-Nicene one. But there remains the task of discovering in what, exactly, that singularity consists. From the social and political aspect the Christians of that time lived in the restricted situation of a religious minority.[3] Even if outward pressures and persecutions did not always oppress them, nor everywhere to the same extent, they nevertheless felt misunderstood by the masses and in their habits of life separated themselves to a large degree from the pagan environment. Concerned though they were for the salvation of all men they did not simply identify with Roman citizenship. Accordingly the whole of their spirituality bore the mark of an élitist and martyr's mentality.[4] So their conditions of life were not very different from those of the Jews of the diaspora. In fact the early Christians lived in more or less close proximity with them in many places.[5] Therefore in many instances they were regarded as a Jewish sect and quite often shared the privileged role which was granted to the Jews. However, from the socio-political point of view Christianity fairly soon broke away from Judaism. Already by about 130 the final break had been effected. This certainly contributed to an even greater openness towards religious and cultural influences from the Greco-Roman environment. Not without reason, then, it is exactly at that time that the rise of antijudaistic and hellenophile gnostic trends is alleged. Christian theology began gradually to draw away from Judaic tendencies. In particular, apocalyptic conceptions, which at first had completely dominated Christian thought, weakened. In the course of separation from the Synagogue and of rapprochement with the pagan world, theology itself became more open towards the thinking of antiquity with its scientific methods. This is particularly evident in the exegesis of Holy Scripture in which the chasm separating it from rabbinic methods broadened and deepened, whereas the ancient art of interpretation as it was exercised especially in Alexandria gained the upper hand.

For a full understanding of the first Christian centuries it is not sufficient to define them in relation to later Nicene times. Within this framework a distinction must be made between primitive Christianity and early Christianity. The line is not easy to draw, though. The dividing line between canonical and non-canonical writings, drawn at a later stage, certainly cannot serve as the deciding factor, as it is only later that these two groups of primal sources were

---

[2] Studer, *Soteriologie*, pp 121–5, 144–56.

[3] Cf. R. Minnerath, *Les chrétiens et le monde,* esp. pp 163–75.

[4] H. Jedin and J. Dolan, eds., *History of the Church* vol. 1, London 1980, pp 288–306. R. Minnerath, op. cit., pp 309–19.

[5] L. Goppelt, *A History of the Christian Church: Apostolic and Post Apostolic Times,* pp 117–23; J. Speigl, *Der römische Staat und die Christen,* Amsterdam 1970, esp. pp 4–42, 82–90; J. Maier, *Geschichte des Judentums im Altertum,* Darmstadt [2]1981, pp 95–120.

differentiated in that way; and they overlap anyway.[6] The main reason for differentiation must rather be seen in the fact that towards the end of the first century there began a harking back to the origins, regarded as the apostolic era. Testimonies to the effect that the first period of Christianity is to be regarded as fundamental now frequently occur.[7]

To view this from a more theological perspective, the difference between primitive and later Christianity may be defined more precisely as follows:[8] in primitive Christianity the revelation of the mystery of Christ was *constituted* within a historical framework which was still determined by the direct consequences of Jesus' religious experience, by the experience of Easter, by apostolic thought and feeling, and by the Christian understanding of the Old Testament. In later Christianity, however, this revelation continued only to the extent that the original experience of Christ was realized, and that partly under similar, and partly under new conditions: under the indirect influence of the experience of Jesus, in an ever less apocalyptic and ever more hellenistic context, in connection with a more deeply Christian exegesis of the Old Testament, and through the continuation of the apostolic preaching. Even if such a differentiation between primitive and later Christianity is basically true for all times, it will always be particularly valid with regard to the first three centuries. In other words: Seen from a theological perspective the pre-Nicene period, especially its first beginnings, can be considered as the time of the beginning of the continuous revelation of the mystery of Christ.

II. THE ESSENTIAL FEATURES OF THE PRE-NICENE PROCLAMATION OF CHRIST

The preceding reflections on the pre-Nicene *period* are especially justified with regard to what is nowadays called trinitarian and christological doctrine. This dogmatic aspect, which could be called the proclamation of Christ in a narrower sense, corresponded at first to that of the apostolic period in its form and content alike. But gradually it deepened and broadened according to new missionary and ecclesiastical demands.

To put this in concrete terms: The Christians of the post-apostolic era (90–150) appropriated the original Christian proclamation according to which God has established his rule in Christ through the power of the Holy Spirit. However they did not expound this doctrine in writings that took the form of

---

[6] See the chronology of the first Christian writings, e.g. in K. Aland, *Noch einmal. das Problem der Anonymität und Pseudanonymität in der christlichen Literatur der ersten beiden Jahrhunderte*, festschrift B. Kötting, Münster 1980, pp 127–30.

[7] Cf. G. G. Blum, 'Apostel, Apostolat, Apostolizität II. Alte Kirche', TRE 3, 1978, pp 445–66, esp. pp445f.

[8] On the concept of the 'constitution' of the revelation see K. Rahner, *Inspiration in the Bible*, Edinburgh/London 1961. See also W. Trilling, *Bemerkungen zum Thema Frühkatholizismus*: CrSt 2, 1981, pp 329–340.

treatises. Their taking over of the apostolic kerygma is evident rather in occasional writings which are in part quite similar to the apostolic letters. In the apologetic and anti-gnostic confrontation with hellenism (150–200) Christian theologians and preachers reinterpreted the apostolic faith through a comprehensive vision of salvation history, which expressly involved not only mankind, including even the pagans who had lived before Christ, but also material creation. In a still greater openness towards the ancient world Origen attempted to base the *regula fidei* which stemmed from apostolic tradition on a new scientific explanation of the world (220–300).

More precisely, the deepened and developed proclamation of Christ of the first three centuries led to a thorough reflection on the relationship of Christ – now especially called Son and Logos – to the Father on the one hand and to the man Jesus on the other. To put it even more precisely: The stronger emphasis on a christology of pre-existence which had become necessary for apologetic reasons and because of the need to defend the resurrection of the flesh (*salus carnis*) at the same time entailed that theologians had to pursue sooner or later the question of the *one* Christ, true God and true man.[9] Still more urgent was the problem as to how Father and Son could be differentiated while maintaining biblical and philosophical monotheism.[10]

III. THE CULTURAL BACKGROUND OF THE PRE-NICENE PROCLAMATION OF CHRIST

This somewhat brief survey of the developing proclamation of Christ permits us to describe its early development as a defensive advance. The defence is to be explained by fidelity to the apostolic tradition. The advance, on the other hand, is to be linked to the change of cultural background.

The change of cultural background itself involves primarily the gradual emancipation from an apocalyptic conception of the world. In this latter vision of salvation history 'this aeon' is contrasted with the 'aeon to come'. 'This aeon' being understood as a sin-dominated and therefore transitory world, the 'aeon to come' is conceived as the celestial world, completely governed by God. According to the Christian understanding of this apocalyptic view, in the resurrection of Christ the world to come has already dawned. What is still lacking is the fact that the already revealed mystery of God's will will be disclosed completely in the parousia of the Son of Man. This apocalyptic vision of salvation slowly retreated. There are two reasons for this. First, the Christian community between 66 and 135 separated from those Jewish circles who had used this apocalyptic vision in an attempt to rid themselves of Roman rule. Secondly the Christians gave up their original expectation of an imminent parousia, because of

---

[9] Cf. Justin, Apol I 13.4; Irenaeus, AHaer III 21.4; Tertullian, Prax 29; Origen, Cels III 28; IV 18; Colo 32 (25).321–26; 19.2.6.
[10] Cf. Justin, Dial 62; 128; Tatian, Graec 5.7; Theophilus, Autol II 22.

the ever-growing extension, spatial and temporal, of the Church.

Slowly emancipating itself from an apocalyptic perspective of salvation, early Christianity at the same time moved increasingly within the horizon of the hellenistic world view. This is marked by a dualism of another kind. According to this view the derivative world of the senses stands over against the true, intelligible world. The salvation of man himself consists in liberation from the corporeal world, the soul's prison, and in a return home through a purifying spirituality. According to the Christian reception of the hellenistic explanation of the world, through his ascension to the true world Christ plays the role of the mediator, who just as he has called all things into multiplicity, also leads them all back to unity.

It would doubtless be wrong to set apocalyptic soteriology over against hellenistic soteriology in a stark contrast. On the one hand the apocalyptic view, even after 130, still exercises a more or less powerful influence on Christian thought for a long time, quite apart from the fact that the linear conception of history underlying it is taken from the Old Testament writings, which in Christianity will always live on, thanks especially to the defence of the prophecies which point to Christ. On the other hand, the hellenistic way of thinking will never dominate.[11] It will always be subject to Christian criticism, above all with respect to the faith in God who has created all and continually governs human destiny in a sovereign way.[12] Despite all reservations about a too simplistic differentiation between apocalyptic and hellenistic explanations of salvation, the retreat of the first and the growing importance of the second still have to be taken into account as they led to a change in the cultural background in which Christ has been proclaimed. Nor has all this been without consequences involving a conspicuous change of emphasis.

It is immediately obvious that the proclamation of Christ gradually took place in a different historical setting. In an apocalyptic context Christians reckoned with the final invasion of the kingdom of God, which, after a long past history in Israel and its immediate preparation in the life and death of Jesus, would happen soon. They admittedly soon extended the distance between Christ's resurrection and his second coming, filled it up, as it were, with the historical existence of the Church. But according to their consciousness it still remained God's own history in which through the Son's saving activity he would subdue the whole creation. In a hellenistic context, though, Christians reduced the act of salvation to the reversion of the many to the One. Thus history as God's activity was almost eliminated. Under the influence of the biblical concept of history the return of the many was perhaps identified as an education on the part of God or as the divine reconstitution of all things. But essentially that return was more like a natural process than a constant operation of God, inspired by wrath and love.[13]

---

[11] Cf. A. Grillmeier, 'Hellenisierung – Judaisierung des Christentums als Deuteprinzipien der Geschichte des kirchlichen Dogmas', *Mit ihm und in ihm,* pp 423–88, esp. pp 487f.

[12] Cf. R. Hübner, *Der Gott der Kirchenväter und der Gott der Bibel;* B. Studer, 'God', EEC 1, 1992, pp 354–6.

As a result of a less historical view of salvation, salvation history was seen more in a moral and individual way. According to this, individual man had to strive towards perfect virtue, of which Christ served as teacher and example. Perhaps this also referred to responsibility before the judge of living and dead. Less emphasis was placed on the return of the already glorified Son of Man who is to renew earth and heaven. This moralizing and individualistic way of explaining salvation is noticeable in some of the writings which are ascribed to the so-called apostolic fathers.[14] It will be far more pronounced in the Alexandrines, Clement and Origen. In spite of all their concern for the hellenistic cohesion of macrocosmos and microcosmos, of the world's salvation and that of the soul, emphasized particularly by the gnostics of the second century, these two writers are wholly concerned about spirituality, and are interested primarily in the salvation of the individual, whom the Logos, the true pedagogue, will lead back to the unity of all things.[15]

The growing influence of hellenistic thought, for which salvation essentially consists in the *reductio omnium ad unum* implies that the Christians increasingly regarded God and the world as a hierarchy of various levels of being. They also conceived of things as entities, which in a gradual declension from ultimate truth fall short of being, truth and goodness. It is against this background that they also came to understand the relationship of God and the Logos, the Logos and Jesus. In other words: Christian thought increasingly operated by means of ontology.[16] This is already noticeable in the writers of the beginning of the second century who no longer understood the words 'Son of God' and 'Son of Man' in an apocalyptic sense, but rather related the two concepts to their origin – 'out of God' and 'out of man'.[17] This tendency to see things in their ontological context emerged still more clearly when in the middle of the second century the fact that the Messiah belonged to a different aeon was related to the creation of all things. Important, too, for the establishment of the *ante constitutionem mundi* was however the biblical theme, according to which the Word and the Wisdom, identified with Christ, on apologetic grounds, had always been with the Father and were therefore before all things.[18] In a comprehensive ontological transformation of the understanding of faith, the supreme being, according to Greek philosophy, was finally

---

[13] The difference between the more salvation historical theology of Irenaeus and the more philosophical theology of Origen is very significant in this respect. Cf. AHaer V 36.1–3 and PA I 6, both discussing 1 Cor 15:25–28.

[14] Cf. B. Studer, *Soteriologie*, p 61.

[15] On the theme in general see, B. Studer, *Soteriologie*, pp 91f, and esp. W. Völker, *Das Vollkommenheitsideal des Origenes*, Tübingen 1931; id., *Der wahre Gnostiker nach Clemens Alexandrinus*, Leipzig 1952.

[16] It is to be noted in this context that the significance of the incarnation of Jesus increasingly overshadows that of his baptism. On the general issue of Christian faith being reinterpreted in ontological terms see J. Liébaert, *Christologie*, pp 19–34, and esp. R. Cantalamessa, *Dal Cristo del Nuovo Testamento al Christo della Chiesa: Il problema cristologico oggi*, Assisi 1973, pp 143–97, esp. pp 144–55.

[17] Cf. esp. Ignatius, Eph 7.2; Justin, Dial 85.2; 100.3f; Melito, De Pascha 8 (cf. 70).

regarded as utterly unchangeable. Accordingly the Word, the 'second God', could only have been generated and was therefore visible.[19] This generation had, however, to be differentiated from that of the creation, a consequence which the apologists were already labouring to explain.[20] On the other hand, that irrefutable philosophical axiom inevitably brought about an ontological distinction between the divine and the human in Christ: Logos and sarx. Tertullian and Origen clearly recognized this. Influenced by anti-gnostic polemic against all who distinguished the Christ above from the earthly Jesus, but also because of the *regula fidei,* they did not fail to lay stress on, and to explain the unity of, the two *ousiai* or *substantiae.*[21]

Finally, to avoid misrepresentation of the gradual transition from the apocalyptic to a more hellenistic conception of God and salvation, it must clearly be kept in mind that the cultural change in the background of the pre-Nicene proclamation of Christ did not simply imply a break from the original gospel, or some straightforward scientific progress in pre-Nicene theology. Apart from the fact that the apocalyptic explanation of God's saving act has never completely vanished from the theological scene and that the hellenistic theory of the reversion of all things to the One has never been adopted indiscriminately, the advantages and disadvantages of both theological conceptions must not be overlooked. In the apocalyptic view it was easier to understand salvation as an act of God showing no longer wrath, but mercy. However, there was a lurking danger of restricting to Israel, as the natural descendants of Abraham, the historically powerful election by the creator of heaven and earth, or even to misuse it in a political way. The hellenistic conception of the world, on the other hand, involved the risk of conceiving of salvation not as a historical but a cosmic process and of sacrificing Christ's saving death on the cross for the mediation of the eternal Logos. On the other hand the hellenistic conception of the world opened up a perspective within which the universalistic approach, which was already present in the Bible, could be taken quite seriously. In consequence early Christian reception identified the Father of Jesus Christ with the creator of all things in such a way that salvation now stood wide open to all men, who had come forth out of his hand (cf. already 1 Tim 2:4f).

The presentation of the pre-Nicene proclamation of Christ will show adequately that, as its cultural background was changing, a never-ceasing struggle as to the appropriate expression of the true faith was engaged. On the other hand, it was by no means an easy task to draw out from the cultural limitations of preaching about God and salvation in Christ in the context of apocalyptic those statements that would have validity not just for the children of Israel but for all men and women.

---

[18] Cf. esp. Theophilus, Autol II 10; 22 – also M. Simonetti, 'Sull'interpretazione patristica di Proverbi 8,22', *Studi sull'Arianesimo,* pp 9–87; P. Nautin, 'Genèse 1,1–2 de Justin à Origène', P. Vignaux, ed., *In Principio,* Paris 1973, pp 61–94.

[19] Cf. B. Studer, *Zur Theophanie-Exegese Augustins.*

[20] Cf. Justin, Dial 128.4; 61.1; Tatian, Graec 5.7; Athenagoras, Suppl 10; Theophilus, Autol II.22.

[21] Cf. Tertullian, Prax 27.11; 29.2; Origen, Cels III 41; VII 16f; CoIo I 28.191–200.

2. The Mystery of Christ in Prayer and Exhortation

BIBLIOGRAPHY

A. Stuiber, 'Doxologie', RAC 4, 1959, 210–26.

J. Laager, 'Epiklesis', RAC 5, 1962, 577–99.

J. A. Fischer, *Die Apostolischen Väter,* Darmstadt 1964.

A. Hamman, 'Die Dreifaltigkeit in der Liturgie und im christlichen Leben', *Mysterium Salutis II,* Einsiedeln 1967, pp 132–45. See other studies by the same author in his bibliography: Augustinianum 20, 1980, pp 11–17.

J. Liébaert, *Enseignements moraux chez les Pères apostoliques,* Gembloux 1970.

H. von Campenhausen, 'Das Bekenntnis im Urchristentum', ZNW 61, 1970, pp 126–44, now collected in *Ges. Schriften,* Tübingen 1979, pp 217–72.

P. Vielhauer, *Geschichte der urchristlichen Literatur. Einleitung in das Neue Testament, die Apokryphen und die Apostolischen Väter,* Berlin and New York 1975.

A. Wörner, *La formula de fe 'Creo en el Espiritu Santo' en el siglo* II, Santiago, Chile 1980.

K. Wengst, 'Didache', 'Barnabasbrief', 2. 'Klemensbrief', 'Schrift an Diognet', *Schriften des Urchristentums* II, Darmstadt 1984.

See also:

S. Tugwell, *The Apostolic Fathers,* London 1989.

The apostolic heritage of faith was adopted in the post-apostolic Church primarily in connection with liturgical prayer, and exhortation and instruction. This everyday way of Christian confession may be called proclamation of Christ in a (subjectively) narrower sense, or Christian kerygma. The kerygma, however, is not to be separated from extended reflexion, from theology. For a certain reflexion precedes any professing or proclaiming. On the other hand any new liturgical or kerygmatic expression can lead to a rethinking of traditional faith. So already the choice of words or motifs in prayer and confession presupposes a certain amount of reflexion.

In the same way the credal formulae that are sanctified by tradition provide more food for reflexion. Further, in that interplay of proclamation and reflexion living experience must not be overlooked. The different forms of proclamation are above all received by the faithful in worship, and their meaning is realized in the daily testing of Christian life.[1]

---

[1] Cf. G. Kretschmar, 'Christliches Passa im zweiten Jahrhundert und die Ausbildung der christlichen Theologie', RchSR 60, 1972, pp 287–323.

In kerygma itself different forms are to be distinguished, most of which are already prefigured in the apostolic proclamation.[2] According to the witness of the New Testament this takes a narrative form (*narratio*), the narration of God's great deeds, which serves to awaken faith and to motivate Christian action. Also invocation (*epiclesis*) and praise (*doxologia*) of God's name are encountered. These basic kerygmatic forms live on in the post-apostolic Church, but they have now developed considerably and are adapted to the new circumstances. Generally speaking they have remained influential to the present day: above all in the Apostles' Creed which harks back to these forms and had already reached a distinct outline by the end of the second century.

Although these remarks on the forms of early Christian proclamation are relevant in a certain sense for the whole of the further development of Christian doctrine, they are particularly relevant to the first two centuries. This general statement comprises three points: First, if the expositions of trinitarian and christological kerygma are placed at the beginning of this study, this is not simply on chronological grounds. This is rather to provide a lasting foundation for proper theological reflexion. Secondly, regarding the liturgical and paraenetic character of post-apostolic christological proclamation, it is difficult to place its principal features in any definite order. Therefore it will be appropriate to expound the doctrine of Father, Son and Holy Spirit and of our salvation in Jesus Christ with regard not to their different content but rather to the different kerygmatic forms. Thirdly, as far as the chronological point of view is concerned, it must be remembered that the early Christian conception of the apostolic kerygma was still to a large degree determined by the Jewish-apocalyptic context. This is true also of the forms of expression which are almost entirely taken over from Judaism.

I. NARRATIO

Before 150 there are a fair number of relatively unsystematic writings: letters to congregations, letters of a more personal character, exhortations to repentance, ordinances for congregational life, writings of consolation etc.[3] In these, references are quite often to be found to the life, death and glorification of Jesus, to God's saving act performed in his Christ, as well as to the saving work of the Three who are named in baptismal faith, to Father, Son and Spirit. These, however, are not meant to be far-reaching considerations of the significance of the story of salvation. They are just fragmentary hints which are to motivate an appeal to trust, an exhortation to repentance, to virtue or to unity, or words of consolation. Because these texts contain just a simple recollection of the divine acts of salvation it is certainly not erroneous to label them as *narratio*. In order to evaluate this kind of proclamation properly it has to be kept in mind that in the

---

[2] On the connection between the apostolic and postapostolic time see G. G. Blum, 'Apostel, Apostolat, Apostolizität, II. Alte Kirche', TRE 3, 1978, pp 445f.

[3] Cf. P. Vielhauer, *Urchristliche Literatur,* also J. A. Fischer, *Die apostolischen Väter;* and K. Wengst, *Schriften des Urchristentums II.*

Bible as well as in ancient writing stories are told for edification: for admiration and imitation.[4]

As with the New Testament writings, so the other writings before 150 refer in a particular way to *Jesus' saving deed*. They present his suffering and death as an example of patience and obedience.[5] In this they also underline that Jesus is the true teacher who did not point out the way for men with his words only but has gone before them with his powerful example.[6] At the same time they see in his resurrection the beginning and the pledge of our resurrection.[7] It would not be correct, however, to take into account only the references to Christ as example and thereby overlook the formula *pro nobis*. Even if this formula is not explained any further, still its frequency clearly indicates that for the early Church Christ's saving deed possessed saving power in itself.[8]

Of still more importance, particularly in 1 Clement, are the references to the saving deed which God has accomplished through Jesus Christ. As already in the Old Testament, God, the creator of all things, is considered to be saviour in the strict sense.[9] Certainly he saves men by Jesus Christ. It is through him that they can approach God.[10] But it is always God who in the end elects and saves.

Even though not so frequently, there occur also texts in which the *narratio* includes Father, Son and Holy Spirit. These texts are even less to be disregarded as they possess a certain solemnity and are to be found in decisive passages. So 1 Clement gives an account of the foundation of the Church in a clearly trinitarian form. According to this the apostles, commissioned by the risen Christ in the power of the Holy Spirit, proclaimed the kingdom of God and also appointed bishops and deacons for the future believers.[11] In the same way Ignatius of Antioch asserts the Christians' value by saying that they have been set up as God's edifice with the cross of Christ serving as a pulley and the Holy Spirit as a rope.[12]

It is clear that the apocryphal gospels and the apocalyptic writings of consolation are still further dependent on the *narratio*.[13] Just for this reason they are to be regarded as theological reflexion rather than simple proclamation. In any event, here we have to do with texts that through more or less traditional formulae

[4] Pleasure (delectare) and moral usefulness (prodesse) form the baselines of ancient historiography. Cf. already IIMacc 2:25; and esp. Theodoret, HistEccl prol. Also P. Meinhold, *Geschichte der kirchlichen Historiographie* I, Munich 1967, pp 123ff.

[5] Cf. esp. IClem 16.

[6] Cf. Polycarp, Phil 8; also F. Normann, *Christos Didaskalos*.

[7] Cf. IClem 24.1; also T. H. C. van Eijk, *La résurrection des morts chez les Pères apostoliques*, Paris 1974.

[8] Cf. Ignatius, Rom 6.1; Smyrn 2.1, Polyc 1.2; also B. Studer, *Soteriologie*, pp 62f. On the theology of Ignatius in general see H. Paulsen, *Studien zur Theologie des Ignatius von Antiochien*, Göttingen 1978, on the recently reconsidered issue of authenticity and date of the letters of Ignatius see esp. B. Dupuy, 'Aux origènes de l'épiscopat', Istina 27, 1982, pp 269–77.

[9] This theocentric concept of salvation is characteristic esp. of IClem. Cf. IClem 59ff. as well as Ignatius, Eph 19.1–3; also A. Bsteh, *Zur Frage nach der Universalität der Erlösung*, pp 42–5.

[10] Cf. IClem 36.1–5; 61.3; 64; Ignatius, Eph 19.3–20.1; also A. Bsteh, op. cit. pp 64f.

[11] IClem 42.1–3; cf. IClem 46.6 and also Heb 2.1–4.

[12] Ignatius, Eph 9.1; cf. Eph 17.3–18.2; Magn 13.1–2; also P. Stockmeier, 'Offenbarung', HDG I/1a, p 34: explanation of Magn 8.2.

[13] Cf. A. Grillmeier, *Jesus Christus*, pp 157–84 (=*Christ in Christian Tradition*, pp 53–76).

refer to salvation and in this way contain an element of exhortation without resorting to reflexion of their own. This still does not diminish their value. For they testify precisely through their formal character how much the work of Father, Son and Spirit meant for the believer of that time a divine act of salvation and to what extent the life and death of Jesus were completely included in this saving act.

II. DOXOLOGY

Whereas *narratio* refers to the *magnalia Dei* in order to edify or to exhort to virtuous behaviour or to responsibility in the congregation, doxologies and eulogies (blessings) represent the response in which the believer himself acknowledges and praises God's great deeds. Believing in God's salvific mystery preached to them they respond by the glorification of God whom they sense in their own lives in the power of the Spirit of Christ. In it they glorify and bless God and also conclude their prayers with God's praise.[14]

Such doxologies or benedictions, formal in character, some closing with *Amen,* are to be found above all in 1 Clement,[15] the greater part of which is simply addressed to God. Some add that God receives glory through Jesus Christ (58:2, 61:3). Certainly in one instance the doxology is addressed to Christ himself (20:12, cf. 50:7). Finally it is interesting to note that one of these doxologies appears in a trinitarian context (58:2). In the *letters of Ignatius* the theme of glorification is also very important. However, no formulae of benediction in the proper sense occur here. Nevertheless, the letter to the Smyrneans (1:1f) commences with a sort of christological doxology. In this Ignatius praises Christ as God who has made the Smyrneans so wise, and thus commemorates Jesus' birth, baptism, death and resurrection.[16] Elsewhere he interprets the worship of the community as a matter of giving thanks to God and glorifying him.[17] This markedly eucharistic connection is even more evident in the eucharistic prayers of the *Didache.*[18] Here, as in 1 Clement, the fact is emphasized that God, who is revealed by Jesus Christ, receives glorification through him (9:4). This eucharistic emphasis finally comes to its clearest expression in Justin who while describing the eucharist stresses that the president of the community offers praise and glory to the creator of all things through Jesus Christ and the Holy Spirit, and in saying this proves that the believers do so in all their love-feasts.[19] In

---

[14] On the whole issue see A. Stuiber, 'Doxologie', RAC 4, 1959, 210–26, with many references, as well as A. Quacquarelli, 'Sulla dossologia trinitaria dei Padri apostolici', VetChr 10, 1973, pp 211–41, and J. Mühlsteiger, 'Exomologese', ZKTh 103, 1981, pp 1–32, 129–55, 257–88.

[15] Cf. A. Stuiber, 'Doxologie', RAC 4, 1959, cols. 215f.

[16] Cf. also Ignatius, Eph 2.2, and IIClem 20.5.

[17] Ignatius, Eph 13.1, Phld 10.1.

[18] Didache 9 and 10. Also W. Rordorf and A. Tuilier, *La doctrine de douze Apôtres:* SChr 248, Paris 1978, and A. Tuilier, 'Didache', TRE 8, 1981, pp 731–36.

[19] Justin, Apol I 65 and 67; also V. Saxer, 'Le Saint-Esprit dans les prières eucharistiques des premiers siècles', S. Felici, *Spirito Santo e catechesi patristica,* Rome 1983.

later tradition this conception of the eucharistic prayer as a doxology will always remain vivid.[20] In fact, the trinitarian use of the different doxologies by tradition will become in the fourth century a crucial issue in the Arian controversy.[21]

If the above-mentioned writings give the glorification of God such an important place, they will obviously give an idea of the conception which the Christians around 100 AD had of worship, even of the whole Christian life.[22] If in these or other contemporary texts genuine formulae of doxology with *Amen* occur, it is probable that these are reminiscent of the language of prayer as then used in liturgy.[23] The eucharistic prayers handed down by the Didache make this clear. The letter by Pliny the younger may also be relevant here. He reports to the emperor Trajan in 112/13 that the Christians in Asia Minor in their early morning services would sing songs of praise to a certain Christ *quasi Deo.*[24] But above all this is proved by comparison with Jewish use according to which benedictions of God or the divine name (*berakha* = *eulogia*) filled the whole day.[25] Among Jewish examples the so-called Eighteen-prayer deserves most attention. For it is structured according to the following scheme: God creates, saves and administers grace.[26] Christians, however, cannot have started extending Jewish doxologies in a Christian way only from about the end of the first century. They had certainly done it far earlier, as is made especially clear by those New Testament writings which reach back to the middle of the first century. According to these, benedictions were already addressed quite early on to God as the Father of Jesus Christ, and indeed through Christ himself (cf. Rom 1:8; Heb 13:15). What is more, Christ himself was addressed (cf. Rom 9:5, 2 Pet 3:18).[27] 1 Clement adds to this only the double *dia.* Christ is the mediator of the Christians' benediction, and through him praise and glory are imparted to the Father.[28] The extension of the doxology to the Holy Spirit as well, however, is testified to first by Justin, even though earlier testimonies do not lack a certain trinitarian colouring.[29]

To this context the *Sanctus* also belongs, even though it appears more as an acclamation than as a doxology.[30] In the Jewish liturgy Isaiah 6:3 is part of morning prayer. There is also evidence of this use by the Christian congregation of Rome at the end of the first century.[31] Irenaeus and Origen show that the

---

[20] Cf. TradApost 4: ed. Botte 12, and Origen, Orat 33. Also A. Hamman, *Du symbole de la foi à l'anaphore eucharistique: Festschrift J. Quasten* II, Munich 1970, pp 835–43.

[21] Cf. esp. Basil, Spir 29.71–75.

[22] Cf. IClem 62.2; IIClem 20.5; Barn 19.6.

[23] Cf. G. Krause, 'Amen II.1: 2nd – 4th cent.', TRE 2, 1978, pp 391–94.

[24] C. Plinius min., ep. X 97.7.

[25] Cf. A. Stuiber, 'Doxologie', RAC 4, 1959, cols. 211f, as well as J. Ponthot, 'La signification religieuse du nom chez Clément de Rome et dans la Didache', EThL 35, 1959, pp 339–61.

[26] Cf. A. Adam, *Dogmengeschichte,* pp 121ff; also the texts in J. Bonsirven, *Textes rabbiniques* II, Rome 1955, pp 143ff.

[27] Cf. also the doxologies to the lamb in Rev 5:9–14; 7:10ff; 16:2ff.

[28] IClem 61.3; 58.2.

[29] Justin, Apol I 65; 67.

[30] Cf. A. Adam, *Dogmengeschichte,* pp 117–20, and esp. G. Kretschmar, 'Abendmahlsfeier I', TRE I, 1977, pp 244f.

[31] Cf. IClem 34.6, also Rev 4:8.

Sanctus did not take on a trinitarian sense without the influences of Jewish tradition.[32] For the Christians identified the Seraphim, who sing 'Holy', with the Word and the Spirit as the mediators of our praise.[33] In later tradition Word and Spirit themselves receive the worship of creation. So in the Christianization of the Sanctus we possess a typical example of the development of a liturgical form to express the experience the early Church had of salvation. This liturgical and exegetical tradition is not to be seen however as the beginning of trinitarian doctrine.[34]

III. EPICLESIS

In the worship of the congregation and on other occasions faith in God's saving activity is also expressed in *epiclesis*. This has much in common with doxology.[35] But it does not mean primarily the acknowledgement of divine power and divine action in history even though it embraces all this just as doxology does. Epiclesis is rather a matter of invoking God. In it God is called to the present with his helping power. What matters here more than anything else is that the one who is praying knows the name of the one invoked. Only in this way will the being that lies behind the name be present with its help.

This correlation between invocation and name already shows that this form of prayer is derived from the Old Testament and Judaism.[36] Here too we are faced with a Christianization which goes back to the primitive Church. Instead of simply invoking God, Christians address the Father through the Son and the Spirit, or address the Son and the Spirit themselves.[37] Incidentally this Christianization did not affect only the invocation of the name, but also the other uses of names, as phrases like 'to suffer in the name of Jesus', to 'bear the name of Jesus' show.[38] Particular attention in this context is merited by the trinitarian reinterpretation of the Old Testament formula of swearing in 1 Clement: 'For as God lives and the Lord Jesus lives and the Holy Spirit also.'[39]

The most important and best attested epiclesis is without doubt found in the *baptismal liturgy*.[40] Like Matthew 28:19, *Didache* 7:1 emphasizes that baptism is performed in the name of the Father, the Son and the Holy Spirit.

---

[32] Cf. Irenaeus, Demonstr 10; Origen PA I 3.6; also J. Lebreton, *Histoire du dogme de la Trinité* II, pp 631–4.

[33] Cf. also Justin, Apol I 65.

[34] Cf. J. P. Martín, *Espiritu santo*, pp 341ff.

[35] Cf. J. Laager, 'Epiklesis', RAC 5, 1962, cols. 577–99. On the coherence between doxology and epiclesis see Hermas Vis II 2.

[36] Cf. K. L. Schmidt, 'epikaleo', ThDNT vol. 3, pp 496–500, and W. O. Oesterley, *The Jewish Background of the Christian Liturgy,* Oxford 1925, pp 220ff.

[37] Cf. IClem 60.4 with IClem 64.

[38] Cf. H. von Campenhausen, 'Taufen auf den Namen Jesu', VigChr 25, 1971, pp 1–16, esp. p 2f.

[39] IClem 58.2. The context speaks about the all-holy and glorious name.

[40] Cf. also H. von Campenhausen, art.cit. (with his bibl.), R. Kerst, '1Kor 8,6 – ein vorpaulinisches Taufbekenntnis?' ZNW 66, 1975, pp 130–9; G. Lohfink, 'Der Ursprung der christlichen Taufe',.TThQ 156, 1976, pp 35–54 (with bibl.); F. Courth, 'Die Taufe "auf den Namen Jesu Christi" in den Zeugnissen der Dogmengeschichte bis zur Hochscholastik', ThGl 69, 1979, pp 121–47.

That this order of the Lord was heeded,[41] is revealed by the witness of Justin,[42] Irenaeus[43] and Tertullian.[44] Even though it is not certain when this custom of baptism in the name of the Trinity appeared – certainly before the end of the first century – and even though it is hard to distinguish it from 'baptism in the name of Jesus', it is without doubt an epiclesis. Father, Son and Spirit are invoked as present at baptism. Thus the candidates to be baptised are made subject to them, and they are granted salvation, which can come only from the Father, Son and Spirit. To this dedication and promise of salvation a whole range of texts refers, particularly in the *Shepherd of Hermas*.[45]

The trinitarian formula, as it is quoted by the aforementioned texts, is, however, not to be understood simply as a ritual formula. As is known from *Tertullian*[46] and particularly from the *Traditio Apostolica*,[47] baptism was rather performed in a kind of dialogue. Nevertheless, the names must presumably have been pronounced in some way or other, invoked, as it were. This is alluded to by James 2:7 as well as by the *Shepherd of Hermas*.[48] In any case, certainly at the latest from the end of the first century a close connection was maintained between the performance of baptism and the faith in Father, Son and Spirit. This is clearly emphasized later on. Irenaeus, for example, rejects gnostic baptismal rites and demands baptism according to the true faith.[49] And according to the *Traditio Apostolica*, not only the baptismal bath but also other rites of the baptismal liturgy, such as the post-baptismal anointing and the laying on of hands as well as the rites of dedication, are performed with trinitarian formulae.[50]

To what extent the *eucharist* was also celebrated in the form of an invocation, is not so easy to discover. Certainly the eucharistic prayers of the *Didache* contain a prayer for the unity of the Church, which is, however, only directed to the Father. They also pray for the coming of Jesus.[51] Perhaps in the case of *Justin* as well it is not only possible to speak of a doxology but also of a Logos-epiclesis.[52] In this case it should strictly speaking be thought of as an epiclesis, whereby the eucharistic gifts are assigned to Christ and therefore are no

[41] On the significance for history of dogma of Matt 28:19 cf. J. Lebreton, *Histoire du dogme de la Trinité* I, pp 553–64.

[42] Justin, Apol I 61.3.

[43] Irenaeus, AHaer III 17.1; Demonstr 3. Cf. AHaer I 21 inc. various epicleses.

[44] Tertullian, Bapt 6.1; Prax 26.9.

[45] Cf. Didache 9.5; IClem 46.6; Barn 16.8. Hermas. Vis III 7.3; IV 2.4; Sim VIII 6.4; IX 12.4f, 18; esp. Sim IX 13.2–5, where the Holy Spirit is alluded to as well, whereas elsewhere mention is made only of the names of the Lord or the Son of God.

[46] Tertullian, Bapt 6.2.

[47] TradApost 21: ed. Botte pp 48ff.

[48] Cf. Hermas, Sim VIII 6.4. Also Justin, Apol I 61.10. Note that epilegein, which is used here, means 'invoke' as well as 'agree'. The later Syrian tradition also points in the same direction. Cf. G. Kretschmar, *Die Geschichte des Taufgottesdienstes in der alten Kirche: Liturgia* 5, Kassel 1970, pp 123–7.

[49] Cf. Irenaeus AHaer I 21; Demonstr 6f; 99.

[50] Cf. TradApost 4: ed. Botte p 10; 6–8: ed. Botte pp 18–26; 21: ed. Botte p 52.

[51] Didache 10.6; cf. 16.7. Also G. Kretschmar, 'Abendmahlsfeier I', TRE 1, 1977, pp 232–5.

[52] Justin, Apol. I 66.

longer just ordinary food.[53] With *Irenaeus* things are clearer. He not only argues against the epiclesis as certain gnostics perform it in the eucharist, but also states in explicit terms that bread and wine become the eucharist through the work of God.[54] Neither Justin nor Irenaeus, however, speaks of a trinitarian epiclesis. They rather, with a hint of a Logos-epiclesis, bring the eucharist in relationship to the incarnation of the Word. As the Word appropriates the flesh in the incarnation, so in the eucharist bread and wine become by the invocation of the Word the body and blood of Christ. This parallel in particular seems to have brought it about that from the fourth century in the Eastern liturgies the transformation of the gifts has been ascribed to the Holy Spirit.[55] As far as the link between epiclesis and eucharist is concerned it would be interesting, too, to examine how the Fathers interpreted Ps 50 (49):14, which speaks of the 'sacrifice of thanksgiving' and the invocation of the name.[56]

It should be added that the trinitarian epiclesis in the second-century baptismal liturgy is not subject to theological reflection. This happens only later, to some extent already in Tertullian, above all, though, in the fourth century with Basil and Ambrose.[57] Nevertheless, the Christianization of the invocation of the name of God in the liturgy has contributed to the establishing of trinitarian consciousness in the Christian communities of the second century. In this context two issues in particular are to be noted. First, the use of the baptismal formula of Matthew 28:19 contributed to the preference, from among the different names of the three actors in salvation history, of the names of Father, Son and Spirit.[58] On the other hand the close connection between baptism as conversion and reception into the community, and faith in the Trinity, proves that this faith was regarded from a fairly early time as the distinguishing characteristic of the Christian. This is confirmed by the historical hypothesis that the formula 'in the name of the Father and the Son and the Holy Spirit' was introduced simply in order to be able to distinguish Christian baptism, baptism in the name of Jesus, from other Jewish baptisms.[59]

IV. THE BEGINNINGS OF THE BAPTISMAL CREED

In relation to the above-mentioned connection between baptism and faith in the Trinity, a word on the beginnings of the baptismal creed may be appropriate, even

---

[53] Cf. J. Laager, 'Epiklese', RAC 5, 1962, col. 592: on the discussion of the meaning of logos: word of prayer, word of institution, Logos of God?

[54] Irenaeus, AHaer I 13.2; V 2.2f.

[55] Cf. J. Laager, 'Epiklese', RAC 5, 1962, cols. 590ff.

[56] Cf. IClem 5.23. Also J. Laager, art. cit., 580f: on the invocation of the gods at sacrifices and banquets.

[57] Cf. Tertullian, Prax 26.9; Basil, Spir 10.24; 17.43; 29.75; Ambrose, Spir I 5.73; II 8.71f (indebted to Basil).

[58] See the even less definite definition of baptismal faith in Justin, Apol I 61.

[59] Cf. G. Kretschmar, *Der Heilige Geist in der Geschichte,* QuDisp 85, Freiburg 1979, pp 127ff.

if this only goes back to the end of the second century at the earliest.[60] It may be presupposed that a knowledge of faith in the Trinity was expected of the baptismal candidates from an early stage, and that it was therefore felt necessary to compile for them the doctrine of the three names, i.e. of the three articles of faith.[61] This was given extended treatment in the so-called *regulae fidei* and more summary treatment in the creed. The concern to communicate the true faith to the new converts, was, however, not the only reason for a formulation of the faith in the Trinity, and indeed in the Trinity as acting in salvation history. Another motive was the need to be able to present and defend faith in the Trinity against outsiders.[62] The need to ground the proclamation within the Church on a firm credal formulation proved to be even more important towards the end of the second century.[63] Above all, from the very beginning, the intention behind the development of a clearly defined baptismal faith was to praise and glorify the salvation of the triune God through the confession of faith.[64] This correlation between the confession of the true faith and the praise of God later on found a particularly solemn expression in the Te Deum.[65] It is also worthwhile noting that the more eirenic texts show a trinitarian structure, whereas polemic expositions are restricted to God and Christ.[66]

The early Christian confession of faith in the triune God and his salvation in history, as it is expressed in the prayers and exhortation of the first Christians is on the whole to be regarded, from the point of view of form as well as of content, as essentially a taking over of the primitive Christian faith in God's salvation. In formal terms this confession has undergone a development which has in the end led to the formation of the baptismal creed. In the course of this development certain Jewish forms of prayer were of particular importance. They could easily be used to define more precisely the three names. So far as content is concerned, too, the early Christian confession has obviously developed. More and more clearly the tendency to grant the three actors in salvation history an equal status or at the very least to distinguish them from creatures, comes to the surface. In the same way 'Kyrios' and 'Son' gained increasing prevalence, when Christ was to be confessed. Of some significance also is the intention to outline in a more detailed

[60] Cf. the fundamental work of J. N. D. Kelly, *Early Christian Creeds*, and A. Wörner, *La formula de fe;* also L. D. Holland, 'Credis in Spiritum Sanctum et sanctam Ecclesiam et resurrectionem', ZNW 61, 1970, pp 126–44; H. von Campenhausen, 'das Bekenntnis im Urchristentum', ZNW 63, 1972, pp 210–53, P. Smulders, *The 'Sitz im Leben' of the Old Roman Creed,* StudPatr 13 (=TU 116), Berlin 1975, pp 409–21. See also the references in DS 10ff.

[61] Cf. Irenaeus, Demonstr 6; also EpApost: DS I and TradApost: ed. Botte pp 48ff.

[62] Cf. Justin, Apol I 6 and 13: countering the charge of 'atheism', which was raised against the Christians; Apol I 65.3; 67.2: description of the Christian service.

[63] Cf. esp. Irenaeus, AHaer I 10.1; Tertullian, Praescript; Virg Vel 1; Prax 2; Origen, PA I, praef 4f; also B. Häegglund, *Die Bedeutung der regula fidei als Grundlage theologischer Aussagen:* StudTheol 12, Lund 1958, pp 1–44, and for Irenaeus in particular A. Benoît, *S. Irénée,* Paris 1960.

[64] Cf. Ignatius, Smyrn 1.1–2: christological doxology with the mysteries of Jesus.

[65] On the liturgical confession of faith in general see A. Hamman, 'Die Trinität in der Liturgie und im christlichen Leben', MySal II, pp 132–44, and esp. for the Te Deum E. Kähler, *Studien zum Te Deum und zur Geschichte des 24. Psalms in der Alten Kirche,* Göttingen 1958.

[66] Cf. J. N. D. Kelly, *Early Christian Creeds,* pp 13f. 64f, and J. Moingt, *Théologie trinitaire de Tertullien,* pp 75–9.

manner the story of salvation in its various phases from birth to ascension.[67] The Holy Spirit himself is increasingly considered to be God, and communicates himself both in prophecy and exposition of scriptures as well as in the sacramental and the ascetic renewal of humankind. This development in the form and content of the early Christian creed is above all to be understood from the biblical and Jewish context. This is fairly easy to grasp, if it is considered that this development took place in a liturgical context which was still entirely determined by Jewish tradition, in which doxology and the invocation of the name play a prominent part. A determining influence from outside, from Greek mythology and philosophy is not, however, worth considering as a possibility.[68] This further development of the primitive Christian creed on the whole remains within its proper kerygmatic framework. It does not represent a deepened theological reflexion on God and his saving work, even though it actually contains new elements – as compared with the primitive Christian tradition – which could promote more profound reflexion. So it does not touch the question as to how traditional monotheism and the adoration of Son and Spirit are to be reconciled, although Father, Son and Spirit are granted an equality of status more often than before. In the new formulations of confession the question as to how Father, Son and Spirit are interrelated does not occur either,[69] although they indicate more clearly than before that there is a fixed order for the three. Finally they fail to tell more precisely in what the incarnation of the Son of God consists, although his divinity and humanity are worked out more clearly.[70]

[67] Cf. A. Grillmeier, *Jesus Christus*, pp 168–85 (=*Christ in Christian Tradition*, pp 64–76).

[68] Cf. J. P. Martín, *Espiritu Santo*, p 340.

[69] An approach to this question appears in the prepositions which are used with a certain preference for each of the three persons, esp. ek, dia, en. This, however, will only later be a matter for consideration. Cf. esp. Basil, Spir 2.4–8.21.

[70] Cf. Ignatius, Eph 7.

3. The Beginnings of Theological Reflexion on God and his Salvation

BIBLIOGRAPHY

G. Kretschmar, *Studien zur frühchristlichen Trinitätslehre*, Tübingen 1956.

J. Daniélou, *The Theology of Jewish Christianity (A History of Early Christian Doctrine before the Council of Nicea*, vol. 1), London 1964.

H. Opitz, *Ursprünge frühchristlicher Pneumatologie. Ein Beitrag zur Entstehung der Lehre vom Heiligen Geist in der römischen Gemeinde unter Zugrundelegung des 1.Clemensbriefes und des 'Hirten' des Hermas*, Berlin 1960.

R. N. Longenecker, *The Christology of Early Jewish Christianity*, London 1970.

J. P. Martín, 'La Pneumatologia en Ignacio de Antioquía', Salesianum 33, 1971, pp 379–454.

G. Brunner, *Die theologische Mitte des ersten Clemensbriefes. Ein Beitrag zur Hermeneutik frühchristlicher Texte*, Frankfurt 1972.

H. B. Bumpus, *The Christological Awareness of Clement of Rome and its Sources*, Cambridge Mass. 1972.

H. J. Vogels, *Christi Abstieg ins Totenreich und das Läuterungsgeschehen an den Toten*, Freiburg 1976.

H. Paulsen, *Studien zur Theologie des Ignatius von Antiochien*, Göttingen 1978.

S. Zañartu, 'Les concepts de vie et de mort chez Ignace d'Antioche', VigChr 33, 1979, pp 324–41.

F. Manns, *Bibliographie du judéo-christianisme*, Jerusalem 1979.

Before the middle of the second century the apostolic kerygma undoubtedly lived on chiefly in the liturgy and the exhortations contained in a few occasional writings. According to these too the Christians of the post-apostolic generations confessed faith in a threefold divine work in the mystery of Jesus, which had been prepared by Israel's history. Theological reflexion on God and his salvation seems, however, only in an early stage of development at that time. At any rate the early Christian writings, as compared with the early New Testament, extended the so-called *testimonia* and also deepened the understanding of them. In the same way the titles of the Lordship of Jesus are found to be enriched. At the same time, however, they emphasize more strongly certain New Testament epithets of Jesus. Furthermore they lay more stress on Jesus and the Holy Spirit as mediators. Finally, certain soteriological conceptions, the victorious ascension of the Saviour, the value of the blood and the cross of Christ, become more prominent in their importance.

This still somewhat timid theological reflexion took place in a world of thought, which was still to a large extent dominated by Judaism. Certainly Jewish Christianity after 135 separated from Judaism, which had by that time become entirely rabbinic.[1] By then Christians had almost entirely lost connection with the Jewish congregations, which connection had become tenous enough as it was. But the Jewish heritage continued to prove decisive. Apart from the fact that the Old Testament writings were held to be *the* Bible well into the second century, Christian authors in other respects too remained unambiguously within the confines of Jewish ancestry. Nevertheless the influence of apocalyptic thought was weakening markedly, particularly where pagan influence had already become stronger. In other words: anyone who intends to trace the beginnings of Christian theology must always bear in mind that the first attempts to deepen the apostolic proclamation of Christ took place entirely within the horizon of Judaism, and to a large extent were determined by apocalyptic conceptions: by the distinction between the two aeons, by the correlation between beginning and end, by the kingdom of God which is set up in Christ. The question must not, however, be ignored as to why and to what extent this apocalyptic way of thought was already less effective than it had been around the middle of the first century.[2]

I. THE PERSPECTIVE OF THE HISTORY OF SALVATION IN GENERAL

At the very heart of the gospel according to the New Testament scriptures stands the mystery of Christ. The 'Good News' deals with Jesus Christ, the Son of God (Mark 1:1; Rom 1:1–6 etc.). In early Christian writings, too, 'gospel' simply means the Christian message, the proclamation of the salvation which has come in Christ.[3] Nevertheless in these writings, which are still entirely rooted in Jewish tradition, God appears as the Redeemer. In his salvation he reveals his mercy towards his creation. The condescending loving-kindness of God is proved above all in the sending of Christ, his life and glorious passion, but also in all that God had done beforehand in the history of the whole of mankind. The completion of his creation, however, God effects through Jesus Christ, his mediator. Through him it is that he elects and saves. In him man has access to him who is at the beginning of all things.

---

[1] Cf. L. Goppelt, *A History of the Christian Church: Apostolic and Post Apostolic Times,* pp 117–23, and J. Maier, *Geschichte des Judentums im Altertum,* Darmstadt ²1989, pp 95–110.

[2] On the problem of the so-called Jewish-Christian theology see A. Grillmeier, *Jesus Christus,* pp 138–44 (with a long bibliography) (=*Christ in Christian Tradition,* pp 37–41). Also F. Manns, *Bibliographie,* pp 9–15.

[3] Cf. IClem 47.2; Ignatius, Phld 5.1f; 9.2, with the annotations of J. A. Fischer, *Die Apostolischen Väter,* also P. Stockmeier, 'Offenbarung', HDG I/1a, p 35.

This theocentric perspective is characteristic above all of *1 Clement*, according to which the creator himself stands at the beginning of the Christian order of salvation.[4] Even the *letters of Ignatius,* which talk so much about Christ and name him as God more often than the earlier writings, are determined by this perspective.[5] The proof-text is above all the famous one, from *Ephesians,* which is still entirely inspired by an apocalyptic conception and which deals with the revelation of the three mysteries which have been brought about in the silence of God: Mary's virginity, her childbearing and the death of the Lord.[6]

A theocentric perspective does not, however, imply that God alone is at work. He is beginning and end. But his salvation he performed, as was mentioned before, through his mediator, Jesus Christ. 1 Clement leaves no doubt about that.[7] 2 Clement introduces Christ in its own way as the God-sent redeemer and leader to immortality.[8] For the *Shepherd of Hermas* he is the gate which alone leads to the Lord (God).[9] But even though the early Christian writings continually underline the mediatorship of Christ, particularly through the use of the preposition *dia,* and even though they increasingly view Christ as God, they are very little concerned in their soteriology, which is still mainly derived from the Old Testament theology of deliverance, with the question as to how far the work of Christ itself has been saving and liberating. Nor is the question why the renewal of the world was necessary within their horizon.

Nevertheless, the mediatorship of the Son of God is developed in a way that particularly involves the *pro nobis* of his suffering and death. Neither are there wanting allusions to the second coming at which Christ will judge living and dead.[10] No less impressive are the statements about the present reality of salvation. According to them Christ is the origin of teaching and order, the source of faith and love, the hope for life eternal. Therefore, according to 1 Clement, the community as well as the individual believer acts and lives in and through Christ.[11] In the same way Ignatius' letters emphasize the importance of the Eucharist as being the body and blood of the Lord, the correlation between the earthly and heavenly Church, as well as martyrdom as union with the crucified Lord.[12] For all early Christian authors Christ lives as teacher and master in the community, who has lived out beforehand what he now teaches.[13] This implies that neither the present nor the future of salvation can be understood without its

---

[4] IClem 59ff. 36.1–5; 64. Also A. Bsteh, *Zur Frage nach der Universalität der Erlösung,* pp 42ff.

[5] Cf. Ignatius, Eph 1.1; 15.3; 18.2; Smyrn 1.1; also J. A. Fischer, *Die apostolischen Väter,* p 124, and E. Stauffer, 'theos', ThDNT vol 3, p 107.

[6] Ignatius, Eph 19.1: 'And there have remained hidden from the prince of this world Mary's virginity and her giving birth, as well as the Lord's death; three mysteries proclaimed, which have been worked in the silence of God.'

[7] IClem 61.3; 64 etc. Cf. J. A. Fischer, *Die apostolischen Väter,* p 13.

[8] IIClem 20.5.

[9] Hermas, Sim 12.1–3.7.

[10] Cf. IClem 23–27, 34.3; 50.4f; Didache 16, Ignatius, Polyc 3.3; IIClem 17.4; Barn 5.7; 7.2; 15.5.

[11] IClem 36.1–5, 48.4; 59.2f.

[12] Ignatius, Smyrn 7.1; Eph 20.1; Trall 3.1; 11.2; Magn 6.1; Smyrn 8.2; Eph 11.2; Smyrn 4.2; Rom 6.3.

[13] Cf. IClem 13.1; 21.8; Ignatius, Magn 9.2; 13.1; Barn 2.6; also F. Normann, *Christos Didaskalos* pp 78–98.

past. In this way, accordingly, Ignatius defends the reality of the incarnation and death of Jesus.[14] Neither do the two letters of Clement lack interest in the mystery of Christ.[15] Above all, the numerous references in the early Christian writings to the blood of Jesus, even to the blood of God, cannot be overlooked. So 1 Clement exhorts: 'Let us look to the blood of Christ and let us realize how precious it is to God and his Father; for, shed for our salvation, it has brought the grace of repentance to the whole world.'[16] Similarly the theme of the 'wood' is remarkable. *Barnabas* in particular compiles – together with other Old Testament types of the death of Jesus – every possible allusion to the wood of the cross.[17] According to the early Christian writings, as well as to the New Testament, it is clearly God who has reconciled the world in Christ (cf. 2 Cor 5:11–19). Three points are unmistakeable: The perspective on the history of salvation of the so-called Apostolic Fathers has taken into account, more than before, the saving presence of Christ in its different aspects, especially the sacramental and martyrological. In the same context the reality of the birth and death of Christ is even more strongly emphasized. Finally, in this perspective, Jesus appears mainly as teacher and example for the individual.

II. THE VICTORIOUS ASCENSION OF THE SAVIOUR

Whereas the *pro nobis* of the salvation in Jesus Christ, which is taken over by the apostolic proclamation, is not on the whole extended any further in the early Christian writings, this is not true of some apocryphal writings, which at least partly reach back to the first half of the second century and are usually counted in with Jewish-Christian literature. These writings entertain conceptions of salvation, which in some way presuppose the scheme of the descent and ascent of the redeemer. According to this scheme Christ is a pre-existent being, who first lives in heaven, then, sent by God, descends to this world to perform here his task of salvation, liberating mankind from death and the powers, or to reveal the God who is utterly other, and finally returns to heaven to be enthroned there as victorious redeemer.[18]

The first signs of this model are visible already in the New Testament writings and in the letters of Ignatius.[19] It became more fully developed,

---

[14] Cf. Ignatius, Magn 11; Smyrn 1–2; also H. Kessler, *Die theologische Bedeutung des Todes Jesu,* p 30f: 'identification with the suffering of Christ as the criterion of orthodox doctrine in Ignatius.'

[15] IClem 24.1, resurrection of Christ, IClem 16.1–17, with Isa 53:1–12; IIClem 1.2, suffering of Jesus; IIClem 14.1–5, incarnation and Church.

[16] IClem 7.4. Other texts in J. A. Fischer, *Die apostolischen Väter,* p 275, under the heading of haima.

[17] Cf. Barn 8.1; 12.1–7; also H. Kessler, op.cit. p 28, and for the period following Justin, Dial 86; 138.2f.

[18] Cf. B. Studer, *Soteriologie,* pp 67ff.

[19] For the New Testament cf. R. Bultmann, *Primitive Christianity in its ancient setting,* London 1956, pp 196ff, and R. N. Longenecker, *The Christology of Early Jewish Christianity,* pp 58–62. For Ignatius cf. H. Schlier, *Religionsgeschichtliche Untersuchungen zu den Ignatiusbriefen,* Gießen 1929, esp. pp 32–81.

however, only later on. The first writings to describe the descent and ascent more closely were the *Ascension of Isaiah,* the *Epistula Apostolorum,* the *Odes of Solomon* and other writings. According to these the heavenly redeemer during his descent had to pass through the spheres of heaven. In this process he continually changed appearance and therefore remained hidden from the heavenly powers. After descending as far as death, even to the underworld, he returned in his glorified humanity before the astonished angels as king of glory.[20]

In so far as this scheme was carried out fully, it expressed two ideas: First the universal meaning of salvation is acknowledged: the whole world is concerned. On the other hand it shows that the superhuman redeemer is clothed with humanity and accordingly lifts man up with him into heaven.

This basically apocalyptic conception of salvation is backed up by the simpler statement of the exaltation of Jesus, who is appointed Messiah and Kyrios (cf. Acts 2:36). Jewish Christian circles never forgot this original christology of exaltation. This is true even of the Jewish Christians, mentioned by Justin[21] and still more of the Ebionites who are referred to in Irenaeus.[22] In so far as these circles connect Jesus with a pre-existent Spirit, they come very close indeed to the full scheme of descent and ascent.[23] Later, too, this christology of exaltation will still exert an influence in all the circles for which the example of the obedience of the man Jesus is the crucial point.[24]

In this soteriological context another theme must be taken into account, namely the theme of the descent into the underworld. According to this the redeemer's descent does not end on earth but in sheol, which he is able to reach by taking on the appearance of the angel who is guardian of this part of the tripartite cosmos.[25] The theme of the *descensus ad inferos* indeed covers several motives: the preaching to the just of the Old Testament, the remission of sins in connection with the necessity of baptism, the victorious liberation from the power of death. Always in some way it is a matter of the universality of salvation. Christ has become redeemer also for those people who lived before his advent or else died without baptism in his name.[26]

---

[20] AscIs 10f; EpApost 13ff; OdSal 42; HomSPasch, with the explanations of R. Cantalamessa, '*In S. Pascha*', pp 265–8, as well as G. Kretschmar, 'Christliches Passa im 2.Jh. und die Ausbildung der christlichen Theologie', RchSR 60, 1972, pp 287–323, esp. pp 310ff.

[21] Justin, Dial 47f.

[22] Irenaeus, AHaer I 26.2. Cf. Ebionite gospel frag 6: R. McL. Wilson, ed., *New Testament Apocrypha*, vol 1, p 158; Tertullian, Carn 14.5; Eusebius, HE III 27.1–6.

[23] Cf. Hermas, Sim V 6.4–7, Ps.Clement, Hom III 20.2; Recogn I 43.1f. Also P. Smulders, 'Christologie', MySal III/1, pp 392–8, and A. Grillmeier, *Jesus Christus,* pp 179–84 (=*Christ in Christian Tradition,* pp 73–76).

[24] Similarly with the Arians and the so-called Antiochene theology. Cf. below p 104 and pp 196f.

[25] Cf. AscIs 10.8ff. Cf. already IPet 3:18ff, and EpApost 27(38); Hermas, Sim IX 16ff; OdSal 17.8–11; 42.3–20.

[26] Cf. A. Grillmeier, *Jesus Christus,* pp 179–82 (=*Christ in Christian Tradition,* pp 73–5), and esp. H. J. Vogels, *Christi Abstieg ins Totenreich und das Läuterungsgericht an den Toten,* pp 183–235.

III. THE THEOLOGY OF THE NAMES

The above-mentioned Jewish theme of the names was widespread in early Christian literature. The name of God features prominently there, and scarcely less the name of Jesus. This is true particularly of those texts which contain some sort of invocation. The frequency of the theme allows us to infer that it was a point of theological reflexion.

In fact, the names attributed to Christ experience a marked enrichment in this context. He receives new names which come either from biblical *testimonia,* Jewish tradition or pagan religious language. In particular divine names, even *theos,* are increasingly conferred on him. In this way the credal formulae which were taken over from apostolic tradition became more precise and were extended. The same also happened to the titles of Father and Holy Spirit. So it is striking that Justin, in recording the baptismal faith, puts 'Father of all things, Lord and God'[27] or even 'Father of all virtues without sin' instead of simply 'Father'.[28] He is also fond of speaking of the 'prophetic Spirit' instead of merely the Spirit, and even calls him gift *(charis).*[29]

Circles strongly influenced by Judaism developed a peculiar theology of names.[30] This attributes to Christ fully Jewish titles such as name, law, covenant, beginning, day.

The designation of Jesus as *name* is derived without doubt from Jewish tradition as well as the New Testament and early Christian usage of 'name of the Lord' and 'name of Jesus' (cf. Acts 2:21; Rom 10:12; John 17:5f; 1 Clem 60:4, PolycPhil 10:1–3). It is especially evident in the Evangelium veritatis.[31] According to this the name points back to the unspeakable essence of God which is revealed through the Son. The Son is to receive the title of 'name' because he is so closely related to God that he is able to reveal his life, which is in itself hidden. When furthermore the *Shepherd of Hermas,* the *Kerygma Petrou* and *Justin* name Christ as *law* or *covenant,* they compare him to the Torah, which, according to Jewish interpretation, is not only to be understood as the revelation of the will of God and the communication of salvation, but is also to be attributed real pre-existence.[32] Finally, with reference to Rabbinic exegesis, 'in the beginning God created' (Gen 1:1) is referred to Christ by

---

[27] Justin, Apol I 61.3.

[28] Justin, Apol I 6.1.

[29] Cf. Justin, Apol I 6.2, 13.3; 61.13, and Apol II 13.6; Dial 87f. On the name charis J. P. Martín, 'Il rapporto tra pneuma ed Ecclesia nella letteratura dei primi secoli christiani', Augustinianum 20, 1980, pp 471–83, esp. p 481.

[30] Cf. J. Daniélou, *The Theology of Jewish Christianity,* pp 147–72; A. Grillmeier, *Jesus Christus,* pp 144–7 (=*Christ in Christian Tradition,* pp 41–4), as well as J. Fossum, 'Jewish-Christian Christology and Jewish Mysticism', VigChr 37, 1983, pp 260–87.

[31] Evangelium veritatis 35–40; also J. Daniélou, *The Theology of Jewish Christianity,* pp 157–60, and other texts, such as Hermas, Sim IX 14.3–6; Justin, Apol II 5 (6); Clement of Alex., Excerpta ex Theodoto 26.1.

[32] Hermas, Sim VIII 3.2; Kerygma Petrou: Clement of Alex., Strom I 29; Justin, Dial 24.1 (note variant reading C); 43.1; also J. Daniélou, *The Theology of Jewish Christianity,* pp 163–6.

Christian authors.[33] According to his explanation, *Theophilus of Antioch* strikingly names Christ the *'beginning'*.[34] In a similar way Justin, Clement of Alexandria and Hippolytus of Rome speak of the Logos as the *day* or the *light,* in a protological as well as eschatological sense.[35]

The early Christian authors, and the apologists in their wake, made use of these names and titles of Jewish provenance, apparently in order to describe Christ as above all revealing God, mediating creation and the source of salvation. It cannot be denied, though, that these soteriological designations entail the acceptance of the pre-existence and divinity of Christ. This is true even more of the themes to be dealt with below, which concern the Holy Spirit, as well as Christ.

IV. EARLY CHRISTIAN CONCEPTIONS OF PRE-EXISTENCE

In the early Christian writings which are still strongly influenced by Jewish tradition, a christology is encountered which is to be located within the context of a fully developed angelology. It is called *angel-christology*.[36] In this Christ appears as an angel and, accordingly, receives the traditional angelic names, such as Michael and Gabriel. Yet he is not treated as their equal. He towers above them with his colossal stature and appears as their Lord who sends them and is going to mete out judgement some day with their help. Such ideas are to be found above all in the *Shepherd of Hermas,*[37] in 2 Enoch[38] and the *Recognitiones* of Clement.[39] Of particular interest is the *Epistula Apostolorum* in that it identifies the angel of Annunciation of Luke 1:35 with the Logos.[40]

This angelological description of Christ's salvation of course presupposes the biblical idea of the angel of the Lord. A tradition which understood Christ mainly as revealer of the invisible Father obviously identified him with that angel who appeared to the patriarchs and proclaimed to them the will of God. Justin, for whom all theophanies are to be ascribed to the Logos, explicitly makes this identification.[41] Even though he is not here dependent on Philo, he is nevertheless

---

[33] Cf. Kerygma Petrou: Clement of Alex., Eclogae 4.1; also P. Nautin, 'Genèse 1.1–2 de Justin à Origène', P. Vignaux, ed., *In Principio,* Paris 1973, pp 61–94.

[34] Theophilus Autol II 10. Cf. Justin, Dial 61.1; Tatian, Graec 5.

[35] Cf. Justin, Dial 100.4; Clement of Alex., Eclogae 53.1; Hippolytus, BenedMos: PO 27.171; also J. Daniélou, *The Theology of Jewish Christianity,* pp 166–72.

[36] Cf. J. Barbel, *Christos Angelos;* J. Daniélou, *The Theology of Jewish Christianity,* pp 117–46; A. Grillmeier, *Jesus Christus,* pp 150–7, with bibl. (=*Christ in Christian Tradition,* pp 46–53).

[37] Hermas, Sim V 4.4; VII 1.1f; VIII 3.2f; IX 6.1; IX 12.7f.

[38] IIEnoch 22.4–9: ed. Bonwetsch 21. J. Daniélou, *The Theology of Jewish Christianity,* p 125.

[39] Ps.Clement, Recogn II 42; Hom 18.4.

[40] EpApost 13 (24)–14(25): R. Mc.L. Wilson, ed., *New Testament Apocrypha,* vol 1, pp 197ff. Cf. Christ. Sibyls VIII 456–61; Irenaeus, AHaer I 15.3.

[41] Justin, Dial 75; 125f.

compatible with the Jewish exegetical tradition and at the same time takes over notions from middle Platonism.[42]

In the same context the Holy Spirit is viewed as an angelic being. This is especially true as far as the *Ascension of Isaiah* is concerned, according to which the Spirit stands at the throne of God and worships the highest God together with the Lord.[43] In a similar way the *Shepherd of Hermas* speaks of the angel of the 'prophetic spirit', while *Elchasai,* according to Hippolytus' testimony distinguishes a giant male angel from a female angel, the Spirit.[45] This identification of Spirit and angel is not devoid, though, of reference to certain formulations in Acts (cf. 8:26, 29) and in the Apocalypse of St. John (1:4; 3:1; 4:5; 5:6).[46]

To an even greater extent early Christian literature, influenced by obviously Jewish traditions, describes Christ as Spirit. Thus the term *spirit-christology* has been coined.[47] For an understanding of this pneumatological conception of Christ it has to be borne in mind that *pneuma* (spirit) is a quite ambiguous term. *Pneuma* is understood as: the breath of life, the higher part of the soul, the cosmic soul, the grace imparted to man, the divine being, the divine element in Christ, the Holy Spirit of the baptismal faith.[48] The term *pneuma,* as applied to Jesus, carries the meaning of something divine, of wisdom, or even of the Son of God. In this way Jesus is declared to be filled with the Spirit, this fulness being regarded either as indwelling by a higher being of the man Jesus or as identification with such a being. In any case, Jesus is placed close to God.[49] Even though the importance of this spirit-christology must by no means be underestimated, to speak of binitarianism would not be correct. The Trinity may retreat from the limelight in such a context. But it is not thereby excluded. Quite apart from the almost ubiquitous trinitarian formulae which occur in connection with the baptismal faith, the statements about the prophetic Spirit must not be overlooked. For this is called pneuma precisely because he is understood to stand close to God and at the same time to be God's self-communication to mankind. This second point of view is of particular importance in those texts which refer to the Holy Spirit in the context of the Christians' anointing or the unity of the Church.

In this context those passages in 2 Clement and the *Shepherd of Hermas* which affirm the pre-existence of the Church should be considered. Thus, the Church is practically identified with the Spirit, who reveals himself in the history

---

[42] Cf. J. Michl, 'Engel', RAC 5, 1962, cols. 65–69, 84, 140ff, and B. Studer, *Zur Theophanie–Exegese Augustins,* pp 53–69ff.

[43] AscIs VII 22ff; IX 27; 36; XI 4; also G. G. Stroumsa, 'Le couple de l'ange et de l'esprit: traditions juives et chrétiennes', RBib 88, 1981, pp 42–61.

[44] Hermas, Mand XI 9.

[45] Cf. Hippolytus, Refut IX 13.2f: GCS 26, p 251.

[46] Cf. W.-D. Hauschild, *Gottes Geist und der Mensch,* pp 78–83.

[47] Cf. P. Smulders, 'Christologie', MySal III/1, pp 395–8, and A. Grillmeier, *Jesus Christus,* p 160, with bibl. (=*Christ in Christian Tradition,* p 56).

[48] Cf. J. P. Martín, *'Espiritu Santo',* pp 333ff, and M. Simonetti, 'Note di cristologia pneumatica', Augustinianum 12, 1971, pp 201–32.

[49] Cf. Ignatius, Eph 7.4, Barn 7.3; 11.9; IIClem 9.5; Hermas Sim V 5.2f; V 6.4–7; IX 1.1; Melito, Pascha 32; 44; 66f.

of the community of the earth.[50] Even more interesting is the formula, transmitted by a gnostic text: God – Son – Church.[51] Even if this formula does not sound quite orthodox, it is, nevertheless not very far from the content of the third article of the primitive creeds (cf. DS 1–10).

Among the testimonies which contain angelological or pneumatological conceptions, those which speak of *two angels* or *two spirits,* which stand next to God or act in the name of God, are without doubt especially worthy of mention. For an understanding of these texts the following Jewish themes are to be taken into account: the distinguishing of two witnesses or paracletes who know the plans of God and take part in his judgement; the juxtaposition of Michael and Gabriel; the doctrine of the two divine measures, the one of justice, the other of mercy; the notion of two hands or creative powers.[52] Also those passages in Philo are to be referred to here in which he explains the apparition of the three men at the oak of Mamre (Gen 18), the two cherubim on the ark of the covenant (Ex 25:22) and the two seraphs in Isaiah's vision (Isa 6).[53] The Jewish doctrine of the two hands takes on a special significance in the late second century. Theophilus of Antioch associates the two hands with Logos and Wisdom, whereas Irenaeus, in accordance with the baptismal faith, understands them as Son and Spirit.[54]

Although these angelological and pneumatological explanations primarily refer to the role of Christ and the Spirit in creation as well as in the history of salvation, they unmistakeably place the two close to God and ascribe to them, with more or less clarity, pre-existence over against creation and mankind. In order to appreciate these more or less clearly expressed statements of pre-existence three points are to be borne in mind: First it has to be fully acknowledged that the beginning of trinitarian reflection was made because of the Easter experience, understood in apocalyptic terms. For the primitive Church, which like the apocalyptic tradition correlated beginning and end, Christ was able to enter the other aeon only because he had always belonged to it. Jesus, who has become *Kyrios,* has in fact always been *Kyrios* (cf. Phil 2:5–11). Furthermore, it has to be taken into account that conceptions of pre-existence were very widespread in Judaism. According to Jewish traditions the Torah, repentance, paradise, hell, the throne of glory, the heavenly shrine, and the Messiah's name were created before the beginning of the world.[55] To be more precise, the Torah and the throne of glory, at the very least, did not exist merely in God's thought but were really created before the world. These widespread conceptions of pre-

---

[50] IIClem 14.2ff; Hermas Vis I 3.4; II 4.1; Sim IX 1.1f etc.

[51] TractTripart 57.33–59.5. Cf. J. P. Martín, 'Il rapporto', Augustinianum 20, 1980, p 472.

[52] Cf. AscIs 9.27–42; 11.32–35; IIEnoch 20ff: ed. Bonwetsch pp 18–21; Irenaeus, Demonstr 5 10, Hippolytus, Refut IX 13.2f: GCS 25, p 251; Origen PAI 3.4; IV 3.14, CoRom III 8; IsHom I 2; also J. Danièlou, *The Theology of Jewish Christianity,* pp 134–40, and G. G. Stroumsa, 'Le couple de l'ange et de l'esprit: Traditions juives et chrétiennes', RBib 88, 1981, pp 42–61, and J. Fossum, 'Jewish-Christian Christology and Jewish Mysticism', VigChr 37, 1983, pp 260–7, esp. pp 276–80.

[53] Cf. G. Kretschmar, *Trinitätslehre,* pp 82–91.

[54] Theophilus, Autol II 18, Irenaeus, AHaer IV 20.1; V 1.3; Demonstr 11. Cf. H. J. Jaschke, *Der Heilige Geist,* pp 193f.

[55] Strack-Billerbeck IV, p 435.

existence which get fleshed out in Proverbs 8:22, a text continually cited in the Christian tradition, make it quite plain how easily heavenly, pre-existent beings were accepted by contemporary Judaism. It is apparent, too, how problematic such conceptions of pre-existence could be. Finally, it has to be taken into account that in the relevant texts, at least in the later early Christian texts, a hellenistic tradition became noticeable, albeit already partly adopted by Jewish circles, according to which the Logos, the second and visible God, existed before all creation. Quite apart from this, numerous Old Testament statements, according to which God has created the world by means of speech, easily suggested the pre-existence of the Logos.[56] The same may be true of the Stoic doctrine of pneuma. Hellenistic ideas of this sort without doubt modified the Jewish heritage to a large extent.

Although the early Christian writings serve merely to restate the apostolic kerygma, they by no means lack a certain reflexion, mainly determined by Jewish tradition, on the baptismal faith. It is primarily salvation history in general that is of concern. Like the New Testament writings, the early Christian writings are wholly orientated towards the mystery of Christ, to the gospel. In spite of this they reveal a soteriological vision, the central core of which is God. He constitutes beginning and end, even though he performs his salvation through the mediator Jesus Christ, as well as through the prophetic Spirit.

The mediatorship of Christ is more closely defined by allusions to the judge who is to come, to the Lord who lives and acts in the Church, as well as to the act of salvation performed once for all, to the shedding of the blood and salvation through the cross. Christ will save mankind, he saves them even now, because he has already saved them. Certain writings, strongly influenced by apocalyptic conceptions, explain Christ as mediator with a mythical scheme of descent and ascent. This entirely universalistic scheme of redemption presupposes the primitive christology of exaltation which has been more or less combined with concepts of pre-existence.

In the still relatively undeveloped reflexion of the early period, the theology of the names has a particular importance. To this context, also derived from Judaism, the enrichment of the names of Christ, but also the names of God and the Holy Spirit, belong. As regards the christological titles, the designations of name, law and covenant, beginning and day are especially worthy of consideration. For these titles express that Christ is not only the revealer of the Father, but also that he stands in the place of God himself. Similar ideas, such as the revelation of the invisible God and close union with him, are basic also to the so-called angel-christology. The so-called Spirit-christology, however, is intended to emphasize God's self-communication in Christ to men. Insofar as these two concepts are extended by the Holy Spirit of the baptismal faith and, by a development of Jewish traditions, indicate two heavenly beings, a quite attractive illustration of the conviction of a genuine trinitarian faith is effected. It is quite evident here to how great an extent Christ and the Holy Spirit, even when

---

[56] Besides the texts referring to wisdom see also Judith 16:14ff.

their pre-existence is not sharply distinguished over against creation, are placed wholly in the heavenly sphere, in close proximity to God.[57]

It is not so easy, though, to form an opinion about the dogmatic value of these rather modest beginnings of theological reflexion. First of all the precarious situation with regard to the sources makes it necessary to be careful. Even though it should be taken into account that under the influence of the Arian controversy many early Christian texts about God and his salvation ceased to receive attention, which is not, in any case, certain; it could be the case that it was precisely those statements that sound strange today, especially in gnostic sources, which were regarded as being of only marginal importance right from the beginning. On the other hand, the faith of the Church in the divine threefold work of salvation and in the mystery of Jesus can certainly not be traced back to Jewish traditions of teaching, even though these latter provided Christian thought with invaluable possibilities of expression. Those first theological attempts therefore present nothing else than a transposition of the experience of salvation, as had already happened in the apostolic communities. They depended on the apostolic tradition not only so far as kerygma was concerned, but also in their theological concepts. As an attempt to express the post-apostolic experience of salvation in contemporary terms, these theological considerations almost entirely moved within the realm of the *oikonomia*. The trinitarian and the christological questions proper, as to how the three actors in the history of salvation are to be clearly distinguished from creation, as to how they are mutually related, or as to the inner reality of the incarnation of the Son of God, still remained outside their scope of reflexion. Nevertheless, by giving equal status with the Father to the Son and the Spirit, and by emphasizing the divine and the human in the salvation worked through Christ, such questions were bound to arise sooner or later.

---

[57] Cf. P. Smulders, 'Christologie', MySal III/1, pp 398f.

4. The Soteriological Vision of the Greek Apologists

BIBLIOGRAPHY

R. Seeberg, 'Zur Geschichtstheologie Justins des Märtyrers', ZKG 58, 1939, pp 1–81.

C. Andresen, *Logos und Nomos. Die Polemik des Kelsos wider das Christentum,* Berlin 1955.

H. Wey, *Die Funktionen der bösen Geister bei den griechischen Apologeten des 2. Jahrhunderts nach Christus,* Winterthur 1957.

G. Aeby, *Les missions divines de s. Justin à Origène,* Fribourg 1958.

A. Orbe, *Hacia la primera teología de la procesión del Verbo* (=Estudios Valentinianos I/2), Rome 1958.

W. Pannenberg, 'The Appropriation of the Philosophical Concept of God as a Dogmatic Problem of Early Christian Theology', *Basic Questions in Theology,* vol. 1, London 1971, pp 119–83.

B. Reinhold, 'Trinität und Inkarnation bei den griechischen Apologeten des zweiten Jahrhunderts', thesis: Bonn 1961.

A. Orbe, *La teología del Espiritu Santo* (=Estudios Valentinianos IV), Rome 1966.

L. W. Barnard, Apologetik I. Alte Kirche', TRE 3, 1978, pp 371–411 (with bibl.).

B. Studer, *Der apologetische Ansatz zur Logos–Christologie Justins des Martyrers,* Festschrift C. Andresen, Göttingen 1979, pp 435–48 (with bibl.).

J. P. Martín, 'Il rapporto tra Pneuma ed Ecclesia nella letteratura dei primi secoli cristiani', Augustinianum 20, 1980, pp 471–83.

W. Rordorf, *La Trinité dans les écrits de Justin Martyr,* Festschrift A. Hamman, Augustinianum 20, 1980, pp 285–97.

G. Tavard, 'Dämonen V. Kirchengeschichtlich', TRE 8, 1981, pp 286–300.

See also:

S. Lilla, *Introduzione al Medio Platonismo,* Rome 1992.

E. Osborn, 'L'ingresso del mondo greco', *Storia della Teologia,* pp 99–144 (with bibl.).

Around the middle of the second century Christian theology faced a new situation. This new situation was characterized by the concerns which impressed themselves upon the ever-growing Church, which was at the same time threatened in her very existence. In any case, the writings preserved from that time are directed to such an extent towards propaganda and self-assertion that they may appropriately be summed up under the heading of 'Greek apologetic of the second century'.

The authors of these writings, the so-called apologists – Aristides, Justin, Tatian, Athenagoras and Theophilus –, however, were not the first to defend the Christian religion and to adapt it to a different audience. Their questions were largely similar to those with which the early Church and Judaism, too, felt they were faced. As against the Jews they had to defend Jesus as Messiah and to establish that claim as scriptural.[1] In the dispute with the pagans, Jewish monotheism and the superiority of Moses over against the philosophers were debated.[2] The old questions, however, had grown in importance with the much more intense contact with hellenistic culture, which led to the conversion of an ever-growing number of intellectuals, and at the same time more learned attacks against Christianity. It was now time to justify the providence of the one God in face of persecutions, to which the Christians were subject – and this in an environment which ascribed all evil to demons.[3] On the other hand, it was increasingly difficult to explain why the Messiah, foretold in the Scriptures, had to suffer, while Christians were displaying an ever-growing veneration of this Messiah as divine in their worship (and elsewhere),[4] and furthermore had adopted from Greek philosophy the idea of the impassibility of God.[5]

The so-called apologists of the second century had to give an intellectually satisfying answer to three questions in particular: How can the universality of salvation be upheld by a religion which reaches back no further than 150 years? How can the scandal of the cross, of the suffering Messiah who at the same time is God, be accepted? How is the power of the demons in pagan worship and in the persecution of the Christians to be reconciled with the providence of the one, merciful God? The answer to these three burning questions may be summed up briefly as follows: According to Holy Scripture there is one history of salvation embracing the whole of creation, in which the Logos, through whom God has created everything, reveals him to all men. Through this revelation, which is accessible to the whole of mankind, Jews and Gentiles, the Logos has triumphed over darkness and brought light to the world. This victory he has already achieved in his incarnation, his first, humble advent. It will be perfected, however, only at the parousia, his second coming in glory.

This concept of the Logos encompassing the whole of the history of salvation, which is especially prevalent in Justin, proves to be an essentially salvation–historical theology. At the same time it includes further reflexion of a more philosophical kind, in which the revelation of salvation through the Logos is understood to be the act of the visible, second God, whose relation to the Father is described as that of spiritual generation. The extent to which the Holy Spirit, too, which the apologists also confess, played a part in this historical revelation of salvation, is, however, not pursued very far.

[1] Cf. Justin, Dial.
[2] Cf. Justin, Apol; Tatian, Graec.
[3] Cf. H. Wey, *Die Funktionen der bösen Geister.*
[4] Cf. Justin, Apol II 13.
[5] Cf. Justin, Apol I 13; also W. Maas, *Die Unveränderlichkeit Gottes,* pp 65–76, on Middle Platonism.

I. THE SALVATION-HISTORICAL VISION
OF THE LOGOS-THEOLOGY

1. The Logos who has always spoken to all men

In disputing with Judaism and the pagan world, second-century Christianity introduced itself as the true law, as the true covenant, as the true Israel, as well as the true philosophy.[6] This aspect is represented above all by Justin. As against their two classes of opponents, the Christians claimed to possess the only true religion worthy of mankind. This assertion necessarily evoked a strong reaction from Jews and pagans alike, as they considered tradition to be fundamental. In their view, therefore, a *new* religion could not possibly be the true one.[7] The absolute newness, on which Christians insisted, also led to a quite existential question: If Christ is to be the sole source of salvation for the whole of mankind, what is one to think about the fate of those who had lived before him? Why did this unique saviour of the whole of mankind enter the world at so late a time?[8]

The answer to this urgent question is foreshadowed in the beginning of Hebrews (Heb 1:1–3): God has always spoken to human beings, first through the prophets, finally through his Son. As he has created the world through his Son and continually keeps it in order through his Word, so he has liberated humankind from all guilt through Christ. This basic answer was developed by the apologists, above all by Justin, in two respects. On the one hand Justin extended the historical perspective of Hebrews from the history of Israel to universal history. On the other hand he and the other apologists identified Christ with the Logos in a more decided and thoroughgoing way.[9] The Logos, however, is not understood so much as the mediator of creation and the principle of knowledge in the hellenistic sense, as God's speech in the biblical sense.[10]

This second point, the identification of the saviour with the Logos, is more important in that it gives a theological ground for the theory of a universal history of salvation. For this identification enables emphasis to be placed on Christ's pre-existence. Because God has created all through his Word, it is clear that this Word was present from the beginning, and therefore able to speak to all men. In so far as the Logos may be regarded as the principle of all knowledge, it is possible to explain the mode in which the Logos has always spoken. He was in fact active in all the just, in Jews and pagans, in Moses as well as in Socrates, even if this only became fully clear to Christians. It would be wrong to exaggerate this second point, thus ending up with a hellenization that distorts the gospel. Justin, as well as the

---

[6] Cf. M. Simon, *Verus Israel: Study of the Relations between Christians and Jews in the Roman Empire, 135–425 AD*, Oxford 1986, and A. M. Malingrey, *Philosophie. Étude d'un groupe des mots dans la littérature grecque, des Présocratiques au 4e siècle après J.C.*, Paris 1961.

[7] C. Fredouille, *Tertullien*, pp 235–300.

[8] Cf. Justin, Apol I 46, and esp. Diognetus 9: SChr 33bis, pp 72ff, with commentary by H. I. Marrou; also K. Wengst, *Schriften des Urchristentums* II, pp 297f, with the texts in note 75.

[9] Cf. J. Lebreton, *Histoire du dogme de la Trinité* II, pp 434–38.

[10] Cf. B. Studer, *Der soteriologische Ansatz zur Logos-Christologie Justins des Märtyrers*, Festschrift C. Andresen, Göttingen 1976, pp 435–48.

other apologists, did not intend from the first with their Logos-theology to present Christ as the principle of creation and through this to explain the origin of the world. They were far more concerned to emphasize the Logos as WORD, as God's speech, as the principle of revelation and education.

This thoroughly soteriological orientation of the doctrine of Logos appears to be worked out most clearly in Justin. As regards the objection that men before Christ were not able to exercise their personal responsibility, he meets it by stating that it was possible for all to participate in the Logos, to live according to the Logos and therefore to resist the demons.[11] It is also remarkable that he compares the Son of God with Hermes, thus interpreting the Logos as messenger.[12] Further on Justin asserts that the Logos, who has exposed the lies of the Greeks and barbarians, finally became incarnate, and that he as Son of God taught justice and wisdom. Justin states this without, however, referring to the creative role of the Logos.[13] Finally, these and other still more explicit texts reveal that Justin understood Jesus Christ above all as a teacher and law-giver.[14] It has to be conceded that, as against Justin, the later apologists, Athenagoras and Tatian, were more interested in the Logos as creative.[15]

It should be remarked that the theory that Justin brought the Logos of St. John's prologue into relation with the Logos of Philo of Alexandria, cannot be maintained. First, Justin cannot be shown to be indebted to Philo of Alexandria, even though he pursues similar lines of thought. Secondly, there is no reference to St. John's prologue in Justin's writings: Theophilus is the first to cite it.[16] Yet, even with him, as with Justin, Proverbs 8:22f is much more important.[17] According to this passage the Son is called Logos before creation, has always been with God and was begotten by him, because God has created and fashioned all things through him. It is precisely this exegesis of that fundamental biblical passage that indicates on what grounds a relationship between the Logos and creation might be established: because it was vital to show that the Logos has always spoken to all men, Old Testament texts on pre-existence were referred to. It was then that the pre-existence of the Word or Wisdom was linked with creation. This entailed that when speaking of the accessibility to all men of God's revelation through the Logos, his part in creation was referred to, even more so as the audience being addressed had a burning interest in the explanation of the origin of all things.

2. The crucified Messiah is foretold by the Scriptures

In Justin's dialogue with Trypho the Jew it becomes apparent what form the dialogue with the Jews took around the middle of the second century.[18] According

---

[11] Justin, Apol I 46.
[12] Apol I 22.
[13] Apol I 5f.
[14] Cf. F. Normann, *Christos Didaskalos,* pp 107–24.
[15] Cf. G. May, *Schöpfung aus dem Nichts,* pp 139–42, pp 152–9.
[16] Theophilus, Autol I 22 with John 1:1–3.
[17] Cf. Justin Apol II 6; also M. Simonetti, 'Sull'interpretazione patristica di Proverbi, pp i 8.22', *Studi sull' Arianesimo,* Rome 1965, pp 9–87.
[18] Cf. J. Daniélou, *Gospel message and Hellenistic culture,* pp 199f, and J. Maier, *Jüdische Auseinandersetzung mit dem Christentum in der Antike,* Darmstadt 1982, esp. pp 132–5.

to this dialogue the Jewish-Christian controversy mainly revolved around three issues: the meaning of the Old Testament Law; Jesus, the Messiah foretold by Scripture; and the Church as the new people of God. In this comprehensive discussion the question about the crucified Messiah played a central role.

The issue of the crucified Christ was not at all new in Justin's time. It already formed the apostle's 'gospel' (I Cor 1:25–25; Gal 2:17–21). Luke already has this question answered by the risen Lord himself: the promised saviour had to 'suffer these things and to enter into his glory' (Luke 24:26, cf. 24:44–49 as well as already Mark 8:32f). From Justin's time this question, which was crucial right from the beginning, gained quite a new resonance. On the one hand the Christians' consciousness that 'not man, nor an angel, but God has saved us' (Isa 63:9),[19] became far more pronounced. Thus 2 Clement had already declared around 140: 'Brethren, we must think of Jesus Christ as of our God, as of the judge of the living and dead, and must not entertain a narrow vision of our salvation.'[20] How deeply the faith in a divine saviour was rooted in the Christian faith of that time, is testified beyond doubt by the invocation of Christ in the worship of the community.[21] On the other hand the basic dogma of Greek philosophy concerning the impassibility of God gained an even greater influence. This seemed to exclude, more than had been the case earlier, a suffering saviour who should be the divine saviour at the same time.[22]

Justin himself tried to solve the problem by means of the *testimonia*. He does the same with the other questions raised by his Jewish opponents. He refers to the words of the prophets (*logoi*) and the prophetic prefigurations (*typoi*), which prove unambiguously that the suffering of the Messiah corresponds exactly with the Scripture, which is inspired by the prophetic spirit.[23] In particular he refers to the words and events through which the cross had been foretold. In this way he finds types of the wood of the cross,[24] and refers to the outstretched arms of Moses praying[25] or to the bronze serpent raised upon a pole.[26] The thorough exegesis of Psalm 21 (22) is of particular bearing here.[27] It is in fact the first exegesis which consists of discussion at length of a scriptural text in a methodical and detailed way, in this instance a passage which was traditionally interpreted in messianic terms. It is followed by allusions to the

[19] Isa 63:9 is well used as testimonium by Irenaeus, Tertullian and Cyprian. Cf. *Biblia Patristica* I, Paris 1975, p 159, and II, Paris 1977, p 159.
[20] IIClem 1.1; also K. Wengst, *Schriften des Urchristentums* II, 228ff, with the references to IIClem 12.1–3 and 17.5.
[21] Cf. Justin, Apol II 13; Dial 64. Also E. von Severus, 'Gebet I', RAC 8, 1972, cols. 1134–258, esp. 1196–204, 1217ff (Origen) Cf. also his bibl.
[22] Cf. Justin, Apol I 13; Apol II 13. Also W. Pannenberg, 'The Appropriation of the Philosophical Concept of God as a Dogmatic Problem of Early Christian Theology', *Basic Questions in Theology*, vol. 1, London 1971, pp 119–83.
[23] Cf. Justin, Dial 90.2.
[24] Dial 86.
[25] Dial 90.4f.
[26] Dial 92.1–94.5.
[27] Dial 98.1–111.2.

paschal lamb, the red cord of Rahab of Jericho and to the narrow-mindedness of the Jews.[28]

In looking more closely at this 'scriptural evidence', the greater part of which had been employed before, and to the more or less detailed explanations which Justin adds, it becomes noticeable that Justin does not confine himself to showing the suffering of Jesus to be scriptural, but goes on to seek more or less expressly to deepen faith in the crucified Lord. In particular the continuous exegesis of the famous Passion-psalm necessarily led to a more realistic understanding of the cross and thus showed clearly that man's salvation is grounded exclusively in the cross.[29]

It is important, too, that Justin in explaining the prophecies presupposes the difference between the two appearances (parousiai).[30] By doing that he is not only able to emphasize that the passages on the lowliness of the Messiah have already been fulfilled, whereas the words concerning his glory will find fulfilment only at the consummation of the ages.[31] Using this differentiation he is also able to declare the incarnation, the first coming of the Messiah, to be the summit of the history of salvation as experienced so far, and therefore to integrate the largely anti-judaistic theme of Jesus' suffering into his salvation-historical theology of the Logos.[32] He combines the theme of the suffering Messiah in another way with the doctrine of Logos, which appeals more to the Greek mind. According to him the fulfilment of the Old Testament prophecies, which had been pronounced long before the advent of the Logos in the flesh, is possible only because the Logos himself has announced this through the prophets who spoke in the Holy Spirit.[33] In this way he provided a demonstration of the truth in a way valid in the terms of the Greek understanding of the world.

3. The triumph of the Redeemer over the powers of the world

Even more closely connected with the theology of Logos than the doctrine of the crucified Lord is that of the heavenly saviour who has gained victory over the powers of this evil world.[34] In the view of the apologists, and above all for Justin, the self-revealing Logos is also the divine power, God's *dynamis,* who has come to expel darkness from this world.

For a full understanding of this soteriology, which is particularly characteristic of the time of the apologists, two points are to be taken into consideration. On the one hand, in the second century life was felt to be subject to a sharp dualism. According to this view the visible, material world is somehow identified with evil. The divine, however, is considered to be entirely

---

[28] Dial 111.3–112.4.
[29] Cf. esp. Dial 103.8. See also Dial 100.1–5, with the distinction between Son of God and Son of man.
[30] Dial 111.1. Cf. Dial 40.4; 110.5.
[31] Cf. Dial 89.1: Trypho's objection.
[32] Cf. Dial 2.13.
[33] Cf. esp. Apol I 36; I 53.
[34] Cf. B. Studer, *Soteriologie*, pp 65–73.

transcendent, untouched by this earthly world. The Christians themselves, in spite of their sense of the unique creator of all things, tended to oppose God to the world, the flesh to spirit, heaven to 'this world' and thus show contempt for the social and cultural values of their environment.[35] On the other hand, at that time a highly developed demonology is encountered, which in some respects overlapped with this dualism, and in any case could only strengthen it.[36] The Christians themselves made use of this demonology in their search for the answer to two questions which were crucial for them: first, why the public opinion of Roman society rejected Christianity, and second, why there was idolatry. They also explained the persecutions of the Christians to be caused by the subversive action of wicked demons, whom they identified with the fallen angels, as Jewish tradition had done already.[37] In the same way, as had been done by the Jews before, they traced idolatry back to the rebellious demons, who by the arts of seduction, by persecution and by counterfeits of the Christian rites had intended to make men worship them as gods.[38]

In this at once dualistic and demonological context the Christians developed their understanding of Christ's battle against the demons. According to Justin, Jesus himself had to hold his own against the demons in his temptation[39] as well as in his suffering.[40] Even more than Jesus, the Church had to defend her existence and in particular her pure doctrine against the same demons, as in earlier times all the just, like Socrates, had already been forced to do.[41] In this context Justin emphasizes the invincible reign of Christ, as Ignatius and Polycarp had done before him. He recalls Christ's power in his suffering on the cross and his exorcisms, which the gospels recount, and he states that the same power is still manifest in the Church.[42] Other authors understand Christ's victory over the devil as having also included that over death.[43] On the other hand, this theology of victory, especially as represented by Justin, was not restricted just to Jesus' death, but rather comprised all his mysteries: the virgin birth, the temptation, the proclamation of the gospel, the passion as well as his work in the Church and finally his second coming. Everywhere the Logos revealed – and still reveals – his *dynamis*.[44]

This theology of victory must be seen to form the basis for the later theory of redemption.[45] Following on certain New Testament themes – such as the liberation from the demons, the precious blood or the 'ransom for many', but also

[35] Cf. R. Minnerath, *Les chrétiens et le monde*, pp 6ff.
[36] Cf. P. G. van der Nat, 'Geister, III. Apologeten u. lateinische Väter', RAC 9, 1976, cols. 715–61; G. Tavard, 'Dämonen, V. Kirchengeschichtlich', TRE 8, 1981, pp 286–91, and esp. H. Wey, *Die Funktionen der bösen Geister*.
[37] Cf. Justin, Apol I 5f; Athenagoras, Suppl 25.3f.
[38] Cf. Justin, Apol I 64.
[39] Dial 125.2ff.
[40] Apol I 63.10.
[41] Cf. Apol I 8; Dial 131.
[42] Apol I 6f; Dial 30.3 etc.
[43] Cf. Melito, HomPasch 54, Ps.Hippolytus, In S. Pascha 57; OdSal 42.11f.
[44] Cf. J. Daniélou, *Gospel message*, pp 162ff.
[45] Cf. B. Studer, *Soteriologie*, pp 70–3 with bibl.

the ignorance of the powers (I Cor 2:7f) – several soteriological themes were developed at that time, which were seriously affected by the antagonism of light and darkness, of heaven and earth and everywhere betray the presence of demons. These themes, which are to some extent intermingled, deal with the angels who failed to recognize the mystery of Jesus, the intentional deception of the powers, who otherwise would not have brought Jesus to the cross, and the just victory of Christ, who did not want to overcome the evil powers by his power but by justice.[46] These themes were further developed later on by Origen, and especially by Gregory of Nyssa as well as by Augustine, in a way that bowed too much to the popular opinion of that day and is no longer comprehensible to us. Nevertheless, in an assessment of these themes it must not be forgotten that the true Christian idea of Christ's victory over death and the devil and all evil powers was behind it all.[47]

II. TOWARDS A DEEPER PHILOSOPHICAL UNDERSTANDING OF THE LOGOS-THEOLOGY

1. The visible and second God

The theology of Logos which had as its characteristics the doctrine of the revealing Word, the justification of the Messiah's divine cross by means of Logos-inspired prophecy, as well as the concept of the triumph of the Logos over all evil, must not be understood as a mere soteriology. It is also meant as a testimony to the Logos himself. It presupposes the revealing, suffering and victorious Logos to be a divine being, yet not simply identical with the creator of all things, but rather a second God, visible and therefore having come into being. These further implications apparently commanded attention with Justin and even more with his followers. These apologists did not endeavour just to show the fact of the difference between God and his Word, between Father and Son, they also sought to explain more closely the nature of this difference.

In order to establish the distinction, the apologists leant on traditional testimonia, which in one way or another expressed the difference between Father and Son: Genesis 1:26; Psalm 109:1; Psalm 44:7–14; Proverbs 8:22ff. In particular, since Justin all appearances of God in the Old Testament had been ascribed to Christ as the angel of the Lord.[48] This line of argumentation was strongly supported by the differentiation between the persons, which was usual in

---

[46] Cf. Ignatius, Eph 19.1–3; Clement of Alex., Excerpta ex Theodoto 61.6f; ActThom 45.

[47] Cf. G. Aulén, *Christus Victor*, London, 1931, and the various studies by R. Schwager, esp. 'Der Gott des Alten Testamentes und der Gott des Gekreuzigten. Eine Untersuchung zur Erlösungslehre bei Markion und Irenäus', ZKTh 102, 1980, pp 289–313 (reprinted in *Der wunderbare Tausch*, Munich 1986, pp 7–31).

[48] Cf. Justin, Dial 54–65. Note the interpretation of Gen 18:1–16 with Abraham and the three men. Also J. Lebreton, *Histoire du dogme de la Trinité* II, pp 663–77; J. Barbel, *Christos Angelos*, pp 50-63, and L. Thunberg, 'Early Christian Interpretation of the three Angels in Gen 18', StudPatr 7 (TU 92), Berlin 1966, pp 560–70.

ancient textual exegesis.[49] It was in this manner that Genesis 1:26 ('Let us make man') and Proverbs 8:22ff (on Wisdom which has always been with God) in particular were interpreted.[50] The philosophical treatment of biblical texts proved to be even more important. From Middle Platonism was adopted the idea that the invisible God who has not come into being is to be distinguished from a second, visible God, who has come into being and is the mediator between the first God and the world.[51]

The apologists, however, did not confine themselves to the fact of the difference between Father and Son. They also sought to make it comprehensible. Following Proverbs 8:22ff they envisaged (with the exception of Athenagoras) the difference to be established through *generation*. The axiomatic Greek conception of the divine impassibility obliged them to explain this generation as something entirely spiritual. Accordingly, Justin speaks of a generation, which happens in the same way as the will proceeds from the intellect.[52] Theophilus of Antioch goes one step further. He compares the generation of the Son from the Father with the emergence of the outer word (*logos prophorikos*) from the inner word (*logos endiathetos*).[53] Similarly also Tatian[54] and to some degree Athenagoras.[55] In Justin himself this further distinction of two modes of existence of the Logos only appears in a rudimentary form.[56] In all this it is quite evident that the apologists in their attempts to elucidate the emergence – or, more precisely, the generation – of the Logos argue the whole time at the level of cosmology. According to them God generated the Word (or the Son) with a view to creation, in order to create and order all things through the Word. The main reason for this certainly questionable view came without doubt – and this is not always properly taken into account – from the traditional testimonia. These always spoke of the eternal Word or the eternal Wisdom in a cosmological context. The extended explanation of these passages, however, resulted in concepts, which had not been foreshadowed in the biblical wisdom literature.[57]

2. A theology of the incarnation

In spite of the importance of the concept of Logos the Apologists' and in particular Justin's theology must by no means be reduced to a Logos-theology. For them it was always a matter of Jesus Christ as the Logos who became incarnate in the last days. Thus for Justin the incarnation marked the clear high point of salvation history. Only the Christians, whose teacher was Jesus of

---

[49] Cf. C. Andresen, 'Zur Entstehung und Geschichte des trinitarischen Personenbegriffs', ZNW 52, 1961, pp 1–39.

[50] Justin, Apol I 36.

[51] Cf. Justin, Dial 127.1–4; 38.1; 62.4; Apol I 63; Theophilus, Autol II 22.

[52] Dial 128.4

[53] Theophilus, Autol II 22.

[54] Tatian, Graec 5.7.

[55] Athenagoras, Suppl 10.

[56] Justin, Apol II 6.2; Dial 62.4.

[57] Cf. A. Grillmeier, *Jesus Christus*, pp 227f (=*Christ in Christian Tradition*, pp 110f), and esp. G. Kretschmar, *Trinitätslehre*, pp 27–61.

Nazareth, took part in the fulness of divine truth, which was revealed by the Logos. Precisely in reference to this Justin introduced the distinction between the first and second advent of Jesus.[58] Thus he placed the incarnation, and in consequence, the cross at the centre of history. In this way he created a strong evangelical counterweight to his perhaps too philosophically orientated theology of revelation[59] – quite apart from the fact that according to him the power of the Logos which has appeared in Jesus did not only overcome error but also evil.

Neither Justin nor the other apologists are concerned, however, with the question as to how the unity of the divine and human in Christ is to be understood. Justin 'never explicitly states the relationship between the saving power of suffering (which he clearly accepted, cf. Dial 103,8) and the divine dignity of the Word, our teacher.'[60] It must nevertheless be remembered that in a (lost) treatise he defended the resurrection of the flesh, and that, according to him, the risen Lord is going to recompense all the just at his second coming.[61] Thus he already anticipates the later theme of *salus carnis,* which cannot be conceived without a very realistic understanding of the incarnation. A real incarnation is in fact presupposed in numerous texts about the suffering of Jesus. In this way the question about the one Christ who is God and man at the same time has already clearly emerged. The same is true of the comparison which Justin introduces between the incarnation and the eucharist. When he says: 'as through the Word of God, Jesus Christ, our saviour, became incarnate and was flesh and blood for our salvation, so through the word of prayer which is from him, the eucharist meal is constituted',[62] one finds in this comparison, surprising at such an early period, an important anticipation of the later Logos-sarx theology.[63]

III. THE DOCTRINE OF THE PROPHETIC SPIRIT AND THE MESSIANIC GIFT

Remarkably enough, the Holy Spirit, acknowledged in the baptismal faith, is granted only very little space in the apologists' authentic theological reflexion, which can be summed up in the key word of Logos-theology. Nevertheless, to ascribe mere binitarianism to Justin and the other apologists, would not be correct.[64]

---

[58] Cf. note 30.

[59] Cf. P. Stockmeier, 'Offenbarung', HDG I/1a, pp 41f.

[60] Cf. P. Smulders, 'Christologie', MySal III/1, p 406.

[61] Cf. Justin, Apol I 52, Dial 39.

[62] Apol I 66. Cf. Apol I 33.

[63] Cf. A. Grillmeier, *Jesus Christus,* p 203 (=*Christ in Christian Tradition,* 90f).

[64] Cf. J. P. Martín, *Espiritu Santo,* and M. Simonetti, 'Note di cristologia pneumatica', Augustinianum 12, 1972, pp 201–32, P. J. Rosato, 'Spirit Christology: ambiguity and promise', ThSt 38, 1977, pp 423–49; W. Rordorf, 'La Trinité dans les écrits de Justin Martyr', Augustinianum 20, 1980, pp 285–97 (liturgical formulae).

As regards Justin in particular, he clearly presupposes a trinitarian faith when he argues in defence of the Christians' religious persuasion against pagan objections of atheism[65] as well as when he describes the liturgy of the Christian community.[66] In these texts he defines the third witness of the baptismal invocation as the 'prophetic Spirit', which stands in third place, and he adds that any person who is enlightened is thereby also cleansed in his name. He maintains, too, that in the eucharist as well as on other ocasions God is offered praise in the name of (or: 'through') both the Son and the Spirit. The most important designation 'prophetic Spirit' is also found elsewhere. Justin ascribes to him the testimonia, the promises of which have been fulfilled in the life of Jesus and in the Church.[67]

Another theme does not occur as often, and has therefore been neglected by modern research.[68] Justin can also speak of the Holy Spirit as the gift of the Messiah, as the anointing with which Jesus has been anointed, in order to pass it on to Christians. This thought is encountered in connection with the contrast between John as Elijah, and Jesus, and above all in the exegesis of Isaiah 11.[69] In this second instance Justin answers the objection that Jesus could not be the Messiah as he had not received the gifts of the Holy Spirit. This objection is, for him, invalid, since Jesus received the Holy Spirit at his baptism in order to communicate him to all believers. This theme of the messianic gift is admittedly less trinitarian and more christological and soteriological in character.[70] Still, it reckons with the divine power of the Holy Spirit. It also anticipates the distinction between the divine and the human which is going to become so important in the Arian controversy.

What has been observed in Justin's pneumatology is also true to some extent of the other apologists. The clear liturgical formulae of Justin are, however, encountered in them only rarely. More than Justin they tend to regard the Pneuma from its cosmological and anthropological aspect.[71] This is in part connected with the fact that they address almost exclusively a pagan audience and therefore refer less to the vision of the history of salvation, grounded in the Old Testament. Still they too offer some interesting hints. So Tatian speaks of the Spirit of Christ who leads to new life.[72] Athenagoras refers to the prophetic Spirit who like a sunbeam comes out of the Father and returns to him. He also states with an almost Nicene precision that Father, Son and Spirit are one in power, whereas they are different in order.[73] Theophilus finally clearly distinguishes between Logos and Pneuma,

[65] Justin, Apol I 6f, 13.1–3; also F. Fascher, *Der Vorwurf der Gottlosigkeit in der Auseinandersetzung bei Juden, Griechen und Christen,* Festschrift O. Michel, Leiden 1963, pp 78–105.

[66] Justin, Apol I 61–7.

[67] Cf. Apol I 12.10; 31.1; Dial 32.8 etc.

[68] Cf. J. P. Martín, *Espiritu Santo,* pp 182–242.

[69] Justin, Dial 39.49; 87f. Also J. P. Martín, *Espiritu Santo,* pp 231–5.

[70] Cf. A. Grillmeier, *Jesus Christus* pp 70ff, and esp. J. P. Martín, 'Il rapporto', Augustinianum 20, 1980, pp 471–83.

[71] Cf. M. Simonetti, 'Note', Augustinianum 12, 1972, pp 217–26, and W. D. Hauschild, *Gottes Geist und der Mensch,* pp 197–206: on Tatian.

[72] Tatian, Graec 13.

[73] Athenagoras, Suppl. 10.2f. Also L. W. Barnard, 'God, the Logos, the Spirit and the Trinity in the theology of Athenagoras', StudTheol 44, 1970, pp 70–92.

the divine wisdom, even though he also ascribes to the former traits of the Wisdom of the Old Testament and of the Greeks. In his exegesis of the creation story, the first by a Christian author, he conceives of the first three days as an image of the Father, Word and Wisdom, and in this context employs for the first time the word TRIAS.[74]

From the preceding exposition it may be discerned how the Greek apologists of the second century in the new missionary situation that had been caused by the enormous spread of Christianity came not only to broaden the traditional proclamation in terms of terminology, but also to include the implicit philosophical problems, above all those regarding the relation between Father and Son. Their missionary interest moved them from the first to an all-encompassing theology of salvation history. In this they granted a central position to the Logos through whom God has addressed all men. Thus they emphasized more clearly his pre-existence, which was required for universal salvation. His saving function, however, was limited more or less to the revelation of God. In their view Jesus is classed primarily as a teacher, who reveals the divine will to humankind. Similarly the biblical argumentation which was undertaken to prove the pre-existence of the Logos resulted in a narrowing of scope. The correlation between Word and creation, which was implied by the Old Testament testimonia and supported by the philosophical ideas being employed in this context, narrowed the theological base of the doctrine of the Trinity in spite of all the interest in understanding the relationship between God and Logos as being that of generation. Openness towards the mystery of the cross, particularly in Justin, did not change the situation very much. Nor did it reestablish the Easter perspective of trinitarian faith. This cosmological narrowing of reflexion on God and the Logos partly explains the weak development of pneumatology. In such an understanding of the world the Holy Spirit did not really find a place. On the other hand the general acceptance of intermediate spiritual entities made it possible both to distinguish the Son and the Spirit from the angels and also to place them on the side of God. It was precisely this admittedly exaggerated interest in spiritual beings which also entailed a somewhat one-sided conception of the saving work of Christ as victory over the demons, which marks the beginning of a somewhat questionable theory of redemption. An evaluation which seeks to do justice to this defective soteriology and its theological background must take into account the fact that the theological reasoning of the apologists is no longer completely accessible. It must also take into consideration that the New Testament writings, the canon of which was not yet fixed, did not possess for them their later theological authority. The writings of Paul and John which are fundamental for later trinitarian as well as christological doctrine had not yet gained full acceptance in Christian communities of that time. Justin and the other apologists were therefore not able to arrive at the insights of later theologians.

---

[74] Theophilus, Autol II 10; 15; 18–22.

5. Irenaeus' Antignostic Doctrine of *Salus Carnis*

BIBLIOGRAPHY

A. Houssiau, *La christologie de s.Irénée*, Louvain 1955.

A. Benoît, *S. Irenée, Introduction à l'étude de sa théologie*, Paris 1960.

A. Orbe, *La teología del Espiritu Santo* (Estudios Valentianianos IV), Rome 1966.

A. Orbe, *Antropología de San Ireneo*, Madrid 1969.

L. Doutreleau and L. Regnault, 'Irénée', DSpir 7/2, 1971, cols. 1923–69 (with bibl.).

H. J. Jaschke, *Der Heilige Geist im Bekenntnis der Kirche. Eine Studie zur Pneumatologie des Irenäus von Lyon im Ausgang vom altchristlichen Glaubensbekenntnis*, Münster 1976 (with bibl.).

A. Orbe, *Cristología gnostica. Introdución as la soteriologia de los siglos II y III*, Madrid 1976.

K. Koschorke, *Die Polemik der Gnostiker gegen das kirchliche Christentum*, Leiden 1978.

R. Tremblay, *La manifestation et la vision de Dieu selon s.Irénée de Lyon*, Münster 1978.

R. Berthouzoz, *Liberté et grâce selon la théologie d'Irénée de Lyon*, Fribourg 1980.

R. Schwager, 'Der Gott des Alten Testaments und der Gott des Gekreuzigten. Eine Untersuchung zur Erlösungslehre bei Markion und Irenäus', ZKTh 102, 1980, 289–313, now collected in *Der wunderbare Tausch*, Munich 1986, pp 7–31.

C. Colpe, 'Gnostizismus', RAC 11, 1981, cols. 640–59.

See also:

Y. de Andia, *Homo vivens. Incorruptibilité et divinisation de l'homme chez Irénée de Lyon*, Paris 1986.

In the course of the second century an attitude of mind developed within the Christian communities which is today summed up in the concept of 'gnosticism'.[1] Even though the concept concerns schools and sects with quite different ideas they have yet so much in common that it is not unreasonable to speak of a religious movement. In fact it was acknowledged as the ideal in almost all gnostic groups to recollect one's own affinity to God in true gnosis, and thereby to free oneself from this world, and at the same time to attain salvation for oneself and the whole cosmos. The often cited fragment of Theodotus preserved by Clement of Alexandria expressed this clearly in just a few words: '. . . who we were, and what

---

[1] On this very complex problem esp. see the following studies: R. Haardt, *Die Gnosis. Wesen und Zeugnisse;* K. Koschorke, *Die Polemik der Gnostiker gegen das kirchliche Christentum;* C. Colpe, 'Gnostizismus', RAC 11, 1981, cols. 640–59, with bibl.

we have become, where we were, where we were placed, whither we hasten, from what we are redeemed, what birth is, what rebirth', 'that is what gnosis is about, which is necessary to make baptism complete . . .'.[2]

In this soteriological vision, in which man is brought into relationship with God and the world from the point of view of the theologians of the great Church three items are brought into question: the resurrection or the salvation of the whole man; the possibility of seeing by grace God the totally other; the inner freedom of the spiritual man. It is not so easy though to carve out these three points in question from the gnostic texts themselves. First the writings in question are preserved mostly only fragmentarily and indirectly through quotations in the writings of their opponents. Secondly the mythical and symbolic way of expression of the gnostics is not easy to understand, and besides, in the gnostic writings Jewish and hellenistic ideas are blended, so that the origin of each individual idea cannot be traced without difficulty. Finally the gnostics are not the only heretics opposed by the great church. Her polemics were directed also against others such as the Ebionites and the Montanists, so that it is often difficult to determine unambiguously their actual object of attack.[3]

The theology developed by the great church against heretical gnosticism becomes tangible first in the writings of Irenaeus of Lyons. He opposes Valentinian and Marcionite gnosis mainly in the work that he himself entitled 'Exposition and refutation of the false gnosis', which is cited today as *Adversus Haereses*.[4] This thoroughly polemical treatise is in essence a reworking of the vision of saving history developed by Justin with reference to Jewish and pagan objections. Formally what is new in this interpretation of saving history is that Irenaeus secures his position by the apostolic tradition without which in his view there is no true gnosis of the Bible. In concrete terms this means that he bases himself on the whole of Holy Scripture, including the New Testament writings, and particularly on Paul and John, and that he tests his exegesis with the *regula veritatis*.[5] From the point of view of content, what is new in Irenaeus' soteriology lies in his taking over the true gnostic concerns. For Irenaeus, because of the loving revelation in the Son and the communication of the Holy Spirit, saving history leads to knowledge of the invisible God by the whole man. According to him, too, salvation is achieved through gnosis, through a gnosis, however, in which, when it is perfected, the whole man is able to see God.[6]

---

[2] Clement of Alex., Excerpta 78.2. Other texts with C. Andresen, 'Erlösung', RAC 6, 1966, cols. 121f.

[3] Cf. N. Brox, *Offenbarung, Gnosis und gnostischer Mythos bei Irenäus von Lyon*, Salzburg 1966.

[4] Cf. Irenaeus, AHaer IV 41.4; V praef. and Eusebius, HE V 7.1; also the edition by A. Rousseau et. al. eds., *Irénée de Lyon, Contre les Hérésies*: SChr 100, 152f, 210f, 263f, 293f, Paris 1965–1982.

[5] Cf. AHaer III 2.1f; III 15.1; IV 35.4; V 20.2 etc; also A. Benoît, *S. Irénée*, with the compilations of the relevant texts.

[6] Cf. esp. R. Tremblay, *Manifestation et vision*.

I. THE INCARNATION AS THE FOUNDATION OF THE UNITY OF THE HISTORY OF SALVATION

Contrary to the dualistic tendencies of his gnostic opponents Irenaeus outlined a soteriology which is completely founded on unity.[7] The themes of the unity of God, the creator and invisible Father, the unity of Christ, true God and true man, as well as the unity of material nature and spiritual man feature among the most prominent.[8]

In this vision of unity the third issue is certainly the crucial point. It may be labelled the doctrine of *salus carnis*.[9] Irenaeus without doubt intends to expound the doctrine that the one God leads the one human race from creation through to perfection. This unity, however, he emphasizes with respect to the salvation of the whole man. In the same way the one Christ has become true man in order to save all men. He has truly suffered and has truly risen, and all this is said with a view to the *salus carnis*.

In fact for Irenaeus salvation consists in the fact that man achieves the state, which God has founded in him when he created him in his image and likeness. Through knowledge of God man will become similar to the immortal God and thus be enabled to behold the God who is over all, as he is.[10] In other words, man, who is created by the Word in the image of God and in the Spirit has received the capacity for a close likeness to God, reaches his perfection when he has become accustomed to bearing God, and has become a spiritual man, when in the knowledge of the Son he himself has become a son and is able to partake in God's immortality.[11]

The way to this perfection, which is to embrace the individual as well as the whole of mankind, necessarily leads through incarnation. In it God became very close to man, in it man could realize his true state, and his likeness to God was finally sealed.[12] This would have been so if Adam had not sinned. Even without original sin the likeness to God in which man is grounded would have become his final possession only by a complete union with the incarnate Word.[13] In view of the first man's sin the incarnation, however, has taken on an additional meaning. It has taken place to bring about restoration and salvation as well. In this context Irenaeus also speaks of the passion of Christ as the wiping away of human guilt, as reconciliation with the offended God, and as liberation from the captivity of the devil. Precisely in connection with this goal for the incarnation, as a result of sin, Irenaeus was encouraged to emphasize that only a mediator, who is God and man at the same time, is able to save mankind.[14]

---

[7] Cf. esp. the concluding passage AHaer V 36.3.

[8] Cf. AHaer I 10.1; I 22.1; IV praef. 4; IV 41.4.

[9] Cf. G. Joppich, *Salus carnis. Eine Untersuchung in der Theologie des hl. Irenäus von Lyon*, Münsterschwarzach 1965.

[10] Cf. AHaer IV 7.4; V 6.1; V 12.1.

[11] Cf. AHaer V 8.1; IV 20.5.

[12] Cf. AHaer III 20.3; III 16.6.

[13] Cf. AHaer V 12.2; V 5.1.

[14] AHaer V 14.3. Cf. AHaer III 18.7; V 13.3; V 21.1–3; also B. Studer, *Soteriologie,* pp 77f, with other texts, and A. Orbe, 'San Ireneo y la doctrina de la reconciliación', Greg 61, 1980, pp 5–50.

Because of this emphasis on the salvation of the whole man, including the bodily part, who because of sin is in need of redemption, Irenaeus demonstrates the incarnation of the divine Word to be inevitably necessary. But Irenaeus gives to the incarnation an even more central positic . in the history of salvation than Justin did. The central significance of the incarnation is confirmed through various themes that for Irenaeus mark the historical process of trial, through which alone man is able to attain his fundamental immortality. In fact, salvation does not mean a return to paradise, but rather growth from Adam's childlike immaturity to the maturity of being children of God. It is perfected in an ever-growing habituation of man to God, which has been started in Christ. In this sense Irenaeus speaks of the economy of salvation.[15] He conceives of this as a single, all-embracing pattern of salvation: creation, the world, man, salvation, the Old and New Testament. Discerning in this event different moments he yet relates all these to the incarnation, thus integrating them into a single whole.[16] The same is true of the theme of recapitulation (anakephalaiosis).[17] This ambiguous term Irenaeus employs to develop the idea of the economy of salvation. By this he understands that Christ has recompensed Adam's misdeed, that he has linked end with beginning, and, what is more, that he has united in himself the whole of the human race.[18] Thus Christ was able to become head of all things, the principle of unity in the Holy Spirit and source of all salvation.[19] Finally, Irenaeus does not merely presuppose that the history of salvation is accomplished and is being accomplished through a process of development – from creation to the history of Israel and the incarnation of Christ and from this through the period of the Church and the millennium to final perfection –, he understands this to entail, rather, a growth in man's spiritual freedom. A merely natural development, in his view, would be unworthy of God as well as of man. Only as free beings could men appreciate the bounty of grace.[20] Even in the misery of sin it was only as free creatures that they were able to realize that they were not immortal by nature.[21] Only in freedom could they learn to seek the good and reject evil.[22] It was in such a history of freedom that Christ could be more fully realized as the one, in whom the beginning was not only restored but surpassed by far, in whom grace had become really more abundant, greater and more universal.[23] With such an explanation of history Irenaeus was better able to explain the novelty of Christianity than had Justin. Whereas the gnostics, particularly Marcion, more or less sacrificed the history of the Old Testament, he was able to explain through

[15] Cf. AHaer III 24.1; III 16.6; III 12.12f, II 68; also A. Benoît, *S. Irénée,* pp 225ff, as well as J. P. Jossua, *Le salut,* pp 51–4, with a survey of the history of research on this topic.

[16] Cf. AHaer II 12.13.

[17] Cf. E. Scharl, *recapitulatio mundi,* Freiburg 1941, and esp. J. Daniélou, *Gospel message,* pp 166–70.

[18] Cf. AHaer III 18.1.7; IV 20.8; V 1.2; V 14.1; V 23.2.

[19] Cf. AHaer V 20.2, Demonstr 34.

[20] AHaer IV 37.6.

[21] AHaer V 3.1.

[22] AHaer IV 39.1, cf. IV 37.1.

[23] AHaer III 18.6f; IV 19.2, IV 31.1.

this history of salvation centred in Christ, why Christ became man at such a late point in time, and how the Christian faith in spite of all its stupendous novelty is rooted in a long-standing tradition.[24]

Even though it was interest in historical progress that led Irenaeus to take less seriously sin in paradise, and even though he has made considerable concessions to the Judaeo-Christian tradition in his conception of a millennium situated between the first and second resurrection, his historical theology of salvation nevertheless captivates in its unique all-embracing unity.[25] His starting point was the *salus carnis,* the immortality of the whole man. Setting out from this anthropological theme he discovered that God had to enter history as true man. It was only in the God-man that the likeness to the invisible God could be secured in a free history of humanity. Only so could he make plain against the religious assumptions of his time that man may expect salvation only from God and that he may also hope for this salvation for his entire being.

This consistently worked-out soteriology also exhibits clearly the premises of the christological question proper.[26] Precisely in the interest of safeguarding the *salus carnis* Christ's true humanity was to be presupposed, or, more precisely, his solidarity with the whole race of Adam. At the same time his true Godhead was required. In the course of this doctrine of salvation the question as to how the divine and the human are united in Christ could not in the long run be left unanswered. The question of the one Christ, true God and true man, became urgent in the horizon of Irenaeus' historical theology of salvation, all the more so as the second-century gnostics made an improper distinction between Jesus and the higher Christ.[27] Irenaeus himself did not yet raise this specific question, still less did he answer it in a comprehensive way. But he simply maintained against all gnostic attempts to sever the heavenly from the earthly that one and the same person is God and man, Word and flesh.[28] He, however, was not yet moved to provide a theological clarification of faith in the mystery of God's incarnation with regard to the unity of God and man. Still, he enriched theological terminology in this context. Thus he understands the virgin birth, which had been predicted by the prophet, as an allusion to the divine nature of Christ.[29] Similarly he contradicts gnostic dualism, stating that the only-begotten Word of God, who is always present in the human race, has been united and joined with his creature, according to the will of the Father, and thus has become flesh.[30] Above all, Irenaeus coined the term of unity, 'one and the same' (unus et idem/ipse),[31] which will gain dogmatic importance and be sanctioned by the fathers of Chalcedon in

---

[24] Cf. AHaer IV 9.1; also A. Orbe, *Antropología,* pp 502–15, and A. Houssiau, *Christologie,* pp 54–128: on the newness of the Lord's presence.

[25] On the problem of milleniarianism cf. J. Daniélou, *The Theology of Jewish Christianity,* pp 377–404, and W. Bauer, 'Chiliasmus', RAC 2, 1954, cols. 1073–8.

[26] Cf. A. Houssiau, *Christologie,* and A. Grillmeier, *Jesus Christus,* pp 212–19, with bibl. (=*Christ in Christian, Tradition* pp 98–104).

[27] Cf. AHaer I 9.1–3; also A. Orbe, *La Cristología gnostica.*

[28] Cf. AHaer III 4.2; III 9.3, also Clement of Alex., Excerpta 7.3f.

[29] AHaer III 21.4. The Latin translation, however, is not clear.

[30] AHaer III 16.6.

[31] AHaer I 9.2f; III 16.2f; III 16.8: heis kai autos; III 17.4.

the sense of *una persona, mia hypostasis* (DS 302). Even though Irenaeus did not advance very far in theological clarification of the christological question proper, he lets it be clearly understood that such a question can only be justified in a soteriological context.

'For this reason therefore the Word of God became man, and He who is the Son of God became the Son of man, that man, receiving the Word of God . . . might become son of God. For how could we otherwise have participated in incorruptibility and immortality, . . . unless first the Incorruptible and Immortal had become what we are?'[32] Thus the question of the bishop of Lyons which marks the beginning of the christology of the *admirabile commercium,* in which the soteriological import of the incarnation is to be summed up most appropriately.[33]

II. THE TRINITARIAN STRUCTURE OF THE HISTORY OF SALVATION

As has already be shown in the above exposition of Irenaeus' historical theology of salvation, this essentially involves salvation as accomplished by the Father through the Son in the Holy Spirit. This is not surprising if the central position in his doctrine of *salus carnis* of the incarnation as having been prophesied by the Spirit and fulfilled in the Church, is taken into consideration. In fact, the reader of the two writings of Irenaeus will not fail to notice how consistently he refers to the action of Father, Son and Spirit in the history of salvation.

1. Baptismal faith: the foundation of Irenaeus' whole theology

To reduce Irenaeus' theology to the scheme 'Father – Son – Spirit – Son – Father' would certainly be an over-simplification. Nevertheless, this scheme provides the key to the understanding of his theology. Whether he deals with the universal history of salvation or the individual Christian's experience of baptism, in all instances Irenaeus proceeds in accordance with a double trinitarian movement: a line of descent which leads from the Father through the Son to the Spirit which is imparted to us, and a line of ascent which leads back from the Spirit in us through the Son to the Father.[34]

This admittedly over-simplified scheme is to be found above all in the baptismal catechesis, which Irenaeus presents in the *Epideixis.*[35] The connection with baptism to which the text explicitly refers, must be given considerable

---

[32] AHaer III 19.1.

[33] Cf. AHaer V praef.; IV 4.1; IV 16.5; also P. Smulders, 'Christologie', MySal III/1, p 410.

[34] Cf. esp. AHaer IV 33.7; also J. Lebreton, *Histoire du dogme de la Trinité* II, pp 587ff, H. J. Jaschke, *Der Heilige Geist*, pp 330f, and A. Houssiau, 'Le baptème selon Irénée de Lyon', EThL 60, 1984, pp 45–59.

[35] Demonstr. 5ff. On the significance of the Epideixis (Demonstr) see A. Benoît, *S. Irénée*, pp 234–50, esp. pp 235ff.

emphasis. For it does not only reveal the kerygmatic value of the entire exposition, it also emphasizes that for Irenaeus the saving act of the Trinity is chiefly performed in baptism. The text itself may be summarized in the following way: Irenaeus confesses faith in the Father, the Son and the Holy Spirit, and in doing this clarifies the soteriological function of each of the three concerning creation, and in particular concerning man. For this reason he employs the scheme of Eph 4:16: The Father is above all – the Son is with all – the Spirit is in all. In the following passage he refers yet again to the *regula fidei,* with particular reference to the same three articles, dealing with the specific soteriological functions of Father, Son and Spirit. Finally he recalls that baptism through the Son in the Holy Spirit grants rebirth towards God. For those who bear the Spirit are led to the Son, and the Son presents them to the Father, who gives them immortality. Without the Spirit's aid the Son would not be recognized, nor the Father without the Son's aid. For the knowledge of the Father is the Son, and the knowledge of the Son takes place in the Spirit, who is given to us by the Son according to the Father's will.[36]

This trinitarian concept is encountered in a different form in a text of no less importance in the fourth book of *Adversus Haereses.*[37] According to this the Father, who himself cannot be recognized, out of love reveals himself through the Word. Creation, for its own part, was not set in motion by an angel but through the Word (Son) and through Wisdom (Spirit) (n.1). This is evident first in the testimonia concerning the Word, according to which the incarnation of the Word, the high-point of his activity, forms the revelation of the Father and the foundation of man's immortality (n.2). The testimonia concerning the Spirit-Wisdom, who was always with the Father, prove the same point (n.3). The prophecies too predict that the Word will be seen on earth and the Spirit will be outpoured, to lead men to the Father (n.4). The meaning of the prophecies is described in a general formula:

'*Potens est enim in omnibus Deus, visus quidem* Tunc *per spiritum* Prophetice, *visus autem per Filium* Adoptive, *videbitur autem et in regno caelorum* Paternaliter, *Spiritu quidem praeparante in Filium Dei, Filio autem adducente ad Patrem, Patre autem incorruptelam donante in vitam aeternam'*(n.5).

Finally two expositions of the prophets' visions follow (n.6–12).[38] Whereas in Epideixis 5–7 the saving act of Father, Son and Spirit is extended to the whole of the history of salvation, the present text seems to restrict the saving activity of each of the persons to a particular time: Old Testament – New Testament – kingdom of heaven. The explanation usually given is that Irenaeus has simply taken over this text. In any case, elsewhere he traces in every single epoch of the history of salvation the action of Father, Son and Spirit.[39]

---

[36] Cf. the parallel texts in SChr 62, p 42 note 6.

[37] AHaer IV 20: SChr 100, pp 627–74, with the commentary in SChr 100*.

[38] Esp. note the trinitarian formula in AHaer IV 20.6.

[39] Cf. H. J. Jaschke, *Der Heilige Geist,* p 199, with AHaer IV 38.3 and pp 239f, with AHaer IV 39.9 and Demonstr 5. Cf. also AHaer IV 33.7 (preserved also in Greek).

2. The 'two hands of the Creator'

Irenaeus, like his predecessors Justin and still more, Theophilus of Antioch, discusses God's saving activity especially in the context of creation. Leaving aside the fact that he identifies unambiguously the Word with the Son, and the Wisdom with the Spirit, he develops more comprehensively than the others the theme of the two creative energies of God. Moving within an antignostic context in which the identification of the God who creates the world with the God who reveals himself in love is vindicated, Irenaeus stresses that the creator did not need creatures for his creative activity. Instead he employed his *progenies,* i.e. the Son and the Spirit. These he calls God's hands, which as such are superior to all angels.[40] Another reason why Irenaeus adopts the theme of the two creative energies is to show that just as at the beginning, in creation, so in the entire history of salvation God is active together with the Son and the Spirit.[41] Finally he also refers to the two hands of God when expounding the concept of *salus carnis* which is based on the real incarnation.[42]

The theme of the 'two hands', to which Irenaeus returns on several occasions, yet always in the context of salvation history,[43] is obviously of biblical origin (cf. Job 10:8; Ps 118:73). In traditional exegesis it had already been used, particularly when dealing with man's creation (*plasmatio*).[44]

When speaking of the 'two hands' of God, he is not interested in the pre-existence of the Son and the Spirit as such. On the contrary, he opposes speculations about what happened before creation. Thus he does not care about the difference in the two states of the Word, which is found in Theophilus, to whom he is otherwise indebted. Nevertheless he emphatically holds fast to the eternal bond of the Son and the Spirit with God, when speaking of the two energies of God in creation and history. According to his doctrine Son and Spirit are at once with the Father, and differ from every creature. They are not angels or servants of God. This is clearly true also of the Spirit. In fact, whilst the Son is called *progenies*, the Spirit is called *figuratio* and thus presented as a product of God.[45]

Even though Irenaeus does not follow through his reflexion on the eternal origin of the Son and the Spirit, he still bears in mind their differences with respect to creation and history (*oikonomia*). Thus the Father is the one in whom all things consist and to whom all initiative is to be traced back. The Son functions as the example according to which the Father acts and at the same time as the power through which the Father performs everything, whereas the Spirit is to establish order and keep everything within it.[46] This way of handling the difference of activity of Father, Son

---

[40] AHaer IV 7.4 (with an antijudaistic ring).

[41] AHaer IV 20.1; cf. IV 20.6.

[42] AHaer V 1.3; cf. V 5.1.

[43] Cf. the compilation of the texts in J. Lebreton, *Histoire du dogme de la Trinité* II, p 579, and J. Mambrino, 'Les deux mains du Père dans l'oeuvre de S. Irénée', NRTh 79, 1957, pp 355–70.

[44] Cf. AHaer IV, praef. 4, with Gen 1:26f.

[45] Cf. AHaer IV 7.4. See SChr 100/1, pp 212–19, and A. Orbe, *La Teología del Espíritu Santo*, pp 462–71.

[46] Cf. H. J. Jaschke, *Der Heilige Geist*, p 188, with AHaer IV 20.1, and J. Lebreton, *Histoire du dogme de la Trinité* II, pp 584ff, with AHaer IV 38.1–3.

and Spirit will not be forgotten in later tradition. Origen[47] and Basil[48] in particular will remember it. It remains to be mentioned that Irenaeus has adopted the theme of the two creative energies according to traditional exegesis of Genesis in a chiefly soteriological context, and has brought it into connection with the exposition of the baptismal faith, primarily in his explanation of the first article.[49] Thus he not only gives to the theme a kerygmatic character but equally proves its ability to furnish a trinitarian doctrine.

3. The vision of God in the Son through the grace of the Holy Spirit

Without doubt, Irenaeus attempted in his antignostic polemic to vindicate as possible full knowledge of God through his Son. This fundamental issue determined, more than just the theme of the 'two hands', his whole reasoning on the joint saving activity of Father, Son and Spirit. This can be clearly proved, as Tremblay has convincingly shown, if Irenaeus' theology of history is considered under the two points of view of *manifestatio* and *visio*. For the sake of simplicity these two points of view are dealt with together in the following exposition.[50]

The Word first revealed its incarnation in the Old Covenant, in the visions, words and deeds of the patriarchs and prophets.[51] Thus the just of the Old Testament, inspired by the Holy Spirit, were capable of seeing the Son and with him the Father to some extent. They did not yet behold the Son's face but only the things that referred to the Son. Thus their vision of the Son was merely a foretaste, neither was their knowledge of God a perfect one. But this came to pass through the grace of the Holy Spirit.[52] Having been made man the Word made himself discernible in his earthly flesh, i.e. in his life of obedience, and thus in himself revealed the Father. It is a vision of his face. But this is reserved for the just. This vision is still not yet perfected as it was only a foretaste of the direct vision of the Father. This as yet imperfect vision is perpetuated in the Church, above all in the Eucharist. But this provisional vision in also realized in the Holy Spirit.[53] With the resurrection of the dead the millennium begins, the kingdom of the Son.[54] At this point the just of the Old Testament as well as the believers in the incarnation of Christ will behold the Son in his glorified humanity.[55] The Holy Spirit will make this vision possible when he raises the dead and makes the blessed advance to it. After a thousand years the kingdom of the Son will be transformed into the kingdom of the Father.[56] The second resurrection will take place. Then all the saints, together with the Son, to whom they have been assimilated by the grace of the Spirit, will enjoy a direct vision of the Father. The Father, inaccessible in

---

[47] Origen, PA I 3.5.
[48] Basil, Spir 16.38.
[49] Demonstr 5.
[50] Cf. besides A. Tremblay, *Manifestation et vision*, also P. Stockmeier, 'Offenbarung', HDG I/1a, pp 49ff: on the different phases of salvation history.
[51] Esp. cf. AHaer IV 20: on prophecy.
[52] Cf. AHaer IV 14.2; IV 7.1–3; Demonstr 5 and 7.
[53] Cf. AHaer III 16.3f.
[54] Cf. AHaer IV 14.4; IV 20.5; V 31.1ff.
[55] Cf. AHaer III 16.8.
[56] Cf. AHaer V 35.1f; V 32.1; V 36.2.

himself, will communicate himself in his love. Thus they will not only be children of God in the full sense but will be wholly like the invisible God.

It should have become clear how emphatically Irenaeus works out, in his soteriology of revelation and vision of God, not only that Son and Spirit, in all stages of the history of salvation, and in the fulfilment to come, act together with the Father, but also that the Father, who is beginning and end, is definitely granted the first position, and thus he envisages salvation as an integral union with the Father.[57]

The polemic against the gnostics, who questioned the resurrection of the flesh, led Irenaeus to develop a theology of the history of salvation in which the incarnation, the revelation of the Father and the beginning of immortality stand at the centre. The emphasis on the incarnation of the Son of God, the sole mediator of God and man, raised the question of the one Christ, true God and true man. Irenaeus gave a straightforward answer on this point: The Word and the man born by Mary are one and the same. However, he did not make any effort to give this answer further treatment. Thus, more than his christology, his soteriology prepared the way for later tradition, particularly for Athanasius and Gregory of Nyssa. Irenaeus' vision of the history of salvation is marked by a definite trinitarian structure. It does not only take into account the mediatorship of the Word, but also that of the Holy Spirit. Irenaeus, however, did not concern himself with elucidating the origin of the Son and of the Spirit. His trinitarianism is restricted throughout to the *oikonomia*. This did not prevent him from proving that the Son, the eternal Word, and the Spirit, the eternal Wisdom, together with the Father, who is superior to all, are utterly different from the whole of creation. He certainly has not reached the theological position of the Fathers of Nicea, but he has still anticipated their faith through his definite confession of the divinity of the Son and the Spirit.

The progress in Irenaeus' historical theology of salvation, which is an indubitable fact, can be explained on the following grounds: the antignostic polemic led him to describe more precisely the revelatory function the Word has together with the Spirit in the incarnation. Also, the need to hold to the *regula fidei,* and his own spiritual experience, too, moved him to place the baptismal faith in all its aspects in the limelight. Finally, he lived at a time, when antignostic polemic had caused the mainstream Church to establish the authority of the whole bible. Thus he established a christology 'from above' and a doctrine of the two paracletes, in accordance with John, and unambiguously upheld the *salus carnis* in accordance with the Apostle, quite apart from the fact that his defence of the unity of Old and New Testament necessarily contributed to the strengthening of the concept of the history of salvation.

[57] Cf. AHaer IV 6.4.

6. The Antimonarchian Conception of the History of Salvation in Tertullian, Hippolytus and Novatian

BIBLIOGRAPHY

K. Wölfl, *Das Heilswirken Gottes durch den Sohn nach Tertullian,* Rome 1960.
R. Braun, *Deus Christianorum. Recherches sur le vocabulaire de Tertullien,* Paris 1962 (²1976) (with bibl.).
L. Bertsch, *Die Botschaft von Christus und unserer Erlösung bei Hippolyt von Rom,* Trier 1966.
J. Moingt, *Théologie trinitaire de Tertullien,* 4 vols, Paris 1966–1969.
R. J. de Simone, *The treatise of Novatian the Roman presbyter on the Trinity,* Rome 1970.
C. Fredouille, *Tertullien et la conversion de la culture antique,* Paris 1972.
J. P. Mahé, *Tertullien. La chair du Christ* (SChr 216/7), Paris 1975.
V. Loi and M. Simonetti, eds., *Ricerche su Ippolito,* Rome 1977.
J. Daniélou, *The Origins of Latin Christianity* (*A History of Early Christian Doctrine before the Council of Nicea,* vol. 3), London 1977.

See also:
A. A. *Nuove ricerche su Ippolito,* Rome 1989.
M. Simonetti, 'Gli inizi della riflessione teologica in Occidente', *Storia della Teologia,* pp 249–71.

At the beginning of the third century the gnostic problem, which Irenaeus of Lyons was the first to oppose on the part of the mainstream Church, was still an active threat. This is clear chiefly from the various antignostic writings by Tertullian, as well as from the refutation of heresies by Hippolytus of Rome and also from Origen's theological work.

As far as Tertullian, the first Latin theologian, is concerned, he like Irenaeus was faced with the challenging question as to how the novelty of Christian faith could be defended against Jews and pagans, without compromising the basis of the gospel.[1] His adversaries, too, are to be found among the gnostics

---

[1] Cf. C. Fredouille, *Tertullien,* pp 235–300.

and Marcionites. Without doubt he is indebted either to the bishop of Lyons or the same traditions as him. Thus it is not surprising that his theology, too, is governed by the defence of *salus carnis*. He even dedicated treatises to this very issue.[2]

This is also true, essentially, of Hippolytus of Rome.[3] As is apparent especially from the exposition of the true faith at the end of his refutation of gnostic heresies, he also reinterpreted Justin's salvation-historical doctrine of Logos in terms of Irenaeus.[4] Also, according to Hippolytus, the Logos, having been generated before creation, is not only mediator of creation and revelation, but in his incarnation has also renewed mankind, which was created by a Creator-God.[5]

However, in about 200 a new theological problem was added to the previous ones.[6] The unity of Father, Son and Spirit was questioned at that time, more urgently than before. The apologists certainly had differentiated God from the Word and had also attempted to explain more closely the relationship of the first and the second God. But they had not yet really touched on the question of the eternal relationship of the two. Similarly Irenaeus had, in view of the baptismal faith and the New Testament writings, rendered Justin's vision of the history of salvation in a much more thoroughly trinitarian way, and thus had distinguished more explicitly the two powers of the Father, the Son and the Holy Spirit. But he had not solved the question of God's unity, and had even evaded it. Towards the end of the second century, however, this theme could no longer be avoided. Still, the problem was not all that new, as is apparent particularly from Irenaeus' comments, even if the polemic against the gnostics, who in their speculations dissolved the divine being into various entities, led to avoidance of the question or to the settling of it with a simplistic answer.

In fact, in the course of the second century a tendency of Jewish and anti-pagan inspiration emerged which emphasized God's unity. This tendency which was rooted in the polemic of the Alexandrine Jews and the apologists against polytheism, and which flared up in the course of the fight against second century gnosticism, developed especially in Asia Minor. Starting from there it reached Rome before 200, and later on North Africa. It was represented first by Noetus of Smyrna and Praxeas, later also by Sabellius. In Rome as well as in Carthage these 'monarchians', as they have been called since Tertullian, were given support by those who were suspicious of all learned theology.[7] They were also on the side of

---

[2] Cf. B. Studer, *Soteriologie*, pp 81f.

[3] Cf. A. Grillmeier, *Jesus Christus*, pp 231–40, with bibl. (=*Christ in Christian Tradition*, pp 113–17).

[4] Hippolytus, Refut X 32f.

[5] Cf. R. Seeberg, *Dogmengeschichte*, §14, 20, with a reference on the interrelation between Irenaeus and Hippolytus.

[6] For the following cf. the presentations of the so called monarchianism or patripassianism in histories of Church dogma, and esp. J. Daniélou, *Latin Christianity* and A. Grillmeier, *Jesus Christus* pp 241–5, with bibl. (=*Christ in Christian Tradition*, pp 118–21).

[7] Cf. Tertullian, Prax 3.1f.

those who fought Montanism, a charismatic movement, which had also come to the west from Asia Minor.[8] Against these monarchians the author of the treatise *Contra Noetum* (before 213), Tertullian and Hippolytus of Rome took their stand, later also Novatian. Thus they became opponents not only of the heretics (the gnostics) but also of the 'simplices'. As a result, during the first half of the third century in Rome and Carthage we encounter a theology of the history of salvation, which by and large still moves within the horizon of Irenaeus of Lyons's concern with *salus carnis*. However, it was driven by a new controversy within the Church, to understand the trinitarian *oikonomia* in time as a revelation of the trinitarian *dispositio* in eternity.

I. THE INCARNATION AS THE BASIS OF RESURRECTION IN TERTULLIAN

Tertullian, as is apparent from his antiheretical writings, like Irenaeus developed his theology from the *salus carnis*. This is indicated by one of his stunning aphorisms: *Caro salutis est cardo.*[9] He, as well, expounds a vision of the order of salvation in which the creation and perfection of man occupy first position. God, who had already planned all through the inner Word, uttered his Word in order to realize visibly his plan of creation.[10] Thus the Word in creation proved to be an organizing and aiding power.[11] Creation itself was aimed at man. God formed him with his hands: with the Word and the Spirit.[12] Thus man, though made of clay, was an image of Christ and with the breath of life through the Holy Spirit was granted likeness to God.[13]

So Tertullian's doctrine of salvation is essentially on a par with that of Irenaeus. Above all, he also views the creation of man from the perspective of the incarnation of the Word.[14] Thus the incarnation is necessary for the salvation of man himself, regardless of sin.[15] Still the differences between the two soteriologies are not to be ignored. First, Tertullian developed a far more complex doctrine of man as the image of God. This entails a less linear conception of the history of salvation. For him it culminates not so much in the *plenitudo Christi* as in the requital of judgement. Thus for him it is much less about man's reaching a mature perfection as about the recovery of that integrity which has been lost by sin.[16]

---

[8] Cf. H. Bacht, 'Montanism', LThK 7, 1972, 578ff; 'Montanisme', DSpir 10, 1980, cols. 1670–6, with bibl.

[9] Tertullian, Res 8.1.

[10] Hermog 45.1; Prax 6.3.

[11] Hermog 23.3, Prax 6.3.

[12] Hermog 45.1, cf. Res 5.6.

[13] Res 6.3, 9.1.

[14] Res 6.3f.

[15] Cf. K. Wölfl, *Tertullian* p 211, with Carn 10.1 and Marc II 27.1; and 231, with Anima 1.4 and Prax 24.5.

[16] Cf. B. Studer, *Soteriologie,* p 85, with bibl.

Secondly, and more important, Tertullian emphasizes far more the redemptive function of the incarnation. He puts more stress on the sin committed in paradise. God's plan of salvation, accordingly, acquires a new, additional significance.[17] Following this line he more exactly defines the consequences of Adam's sin: as the reason for God's wrath, as the beginning of all misery, as the reason for man's liability to death, and not least as the cause of the merciless fight with the devil.[18] Thus Tertullian brings out far more clearly the connection between the incarnation and the mystery of Easter. According to him in order to die Christ had to be really born. An angel or an heavenly being was not capable of saving us through death. Instead it had to be a real man from the human race.[19] This view in particular moved Tertullian to describe human birth in the most vivid colours. However, he accepted unquestioningly a sinless Jesus, which doctrine the earlier tradition had linked up with the virgin birth.[20] In the same way, it was only because he was true man that Christ could become the forerunner of our resurrection, by virtue of which he will change us some day into the incorruptibility of God.[21]

The realism concerning the incarnation, which in Tertullian as in Irenaeus is comprehensible from the *salus carnis,* was highly reinforced by his stronger sensitivity to the Pauline doctrine of man's sin and Jesus' saving death. This realism also moved him to define the incarnation itself in more philosophical terms.[22] On the one hand he negatively rejects any way of understanding the incarnation that would somehow question God's impassibility. When the Word of God became flesh and was made man, he did not thereby change into flesh.[23] The incarnation did not involve confusion of the divine substance of the Word and the flesh in a third entity. Otherwise the Word would cease to be God, and the flesh would no longer be true man. 'Out of the two Christ would be neither of them but a third thing, entirely different from them both.'[24] A confusion like that would contradict scripture, which calls Christ *filius dei* and *filius hominis.* This entails – and this is Tertullian's positive statement concerning the incarnation – that Christ consists of two substances which are fundamentally different in their characteristics, the divine and the human. 'We see a twofold mode of being, not confused, but unified in one person, God and man, Jesus (..). The properties of each substance thus remain intact, so that the Spirit worked in him, in his own way, portents, miracles and signs, and the flesh suffered in its own way ...

---

[17] CultFem I 8.2: on the role of the devil.

[18] Cf. K. Wölfl, *Tertullian,* pp 184–7 (texts).

[19] Carn 6.6f.

[20] Cf. Carn 4; 16; 23, Orat 7.1. Note the interpretation of Rom 8:3: similitudo carnis peccati in Carn 16.3f.

[21] Cf. Res 48.8 and 56.6.

[22] On this point see R. Cantalamessa, *Cristologia,* also A. Grillmeier, *Jesus Christus* pp 245–57, with bibl. (=*Christ in Christian Tradition,* pp 121–31).

[23] Cf. Prax 27.1.6; also R. Cantalamessa, 'Incarnazione e immutabilitá di Dio', RFilosNeoscolast 67 1975, pp 631–47, and J. P. Hallmann, 'The mutability of God: Tertullian to Lactantius', ThSt 42, 1981, pp 373–93.

[24] Prax 27.9.

hungry . . . thirsty . . . weeping . . . anxious to the point of death and finally it also died.'[25]

For a full understanding of this more technical conception of Christ's incarnation, which prefigures the Church's later official definition of the christological faith, the following aspects of differentiation have to be taken into account. First it must be remarked that the doctrine of the two substances is intended to define more precisely the issue of the double birth, the one from the divine Father, the other from a human mother.[26] Substance, accordingly, is intended to mean partaking in the substance of the origin, that will later be defined as *homoousios*.[27] It is noteworthy, too, that Tertullian does not simply distinguish two *substantiae* and attribute the suffering only to one, the *caro,* for he extends his christology of separation also to the distinction between the will of the Father and the will of Christ. According to him, the will of the Father, who intended the death of Christ on account of our sins, is to be distinguished from the will of Christ, who was wholly obedient to the Father. Without going further into the subjective side of the Saviour's passion, he develops this distinction above all in the exegesis of Psalm 21:2 in Matthew 27:46.[28] He does not, however, aim to establish two wills in Christ himself. Finally, the formula *una persona* is not so unambiguous as it seems at first sight. Tertullian has certainly acknowledged the unity of Christ. But it is not certain whether he wanted to express with the term *una persona* his unity as subject or whether he was not rather more simply intending to distinguish in this way the Son from the Father. In any case, his formulae of the *duae substantiae,* or the *duplex status in una persona* did not gain acceptance immediately in Latin theology, and Augustine, who is to use similar formulae, is almost certainly not directly indebted to Tertullian.[29]

Finally Tertullian's soteriology differs from that of Irenaeus by moving in an entirely novel direction. For the first time Latin language and Roman mentality come to the fore.[30] This is true not only of the above-mentioned technical distinction, of the interest in the will of Christ, but also of the way in which Tertullian speaks of *satisfactio* and *meritum* when tackling human repentance. For it is these very terms which are later employed to define Christ's work of salvation.[31] Already with him the forensic bias in theological reflection gains prevalence, in which man's justification by God is going to be traced back to the justice of the only just man, Christ.[32]

It remains to be said that Hippolytus of Rome, like Irenaeus and Tertullian, views creation and salvation as being closely interrelated. According

[25] Prax 27.10f.
[26] Cf. Carn 18.1f.
[27] Cf. B. Studer, 'Consubstantialis Patri – consubstantialis matri', REAug 18, 1972, pp 85–115.
[28] Cf. esp. Prax 29f.
[29] On Tertullian's teaching concerning the one person of Christ and the impact of this for further development see J. Moingt, *Tertullien,* pp 668–74, and A. Grillmeier, *Jesus Christus,* pp 250–5 (=*Christ in Christian Tradition,* pp 125–9).
[30] Cf. R. Braun, *Deus Christianorum,* and C. Fredouille, *Tertullien.*
[31] Cf. M. Brück, '"Genugtuung" bei Tertullian' VigChr 29, 1975, pp 276–90. See also G. Hallonsten, *Satisfactio bei Tertullian* (Studia Theologica Lundensia 39), Malmö 1984.
[32] Cf. esp. R. Braun, *Deus Christianorum,* pp 475–545.

to him, too, Christ has come to renew man who is created by the one creator according to his image.[33] That is why, also for him, the incarnation of the Word, through the Virgin and the Holy Spirit, forms the central core of the history of salvation. Like Tertullian he pays more attention to the mystery of Easter, particularly of the Passion, as the reconstitution of the true life, than does Irenaeus.[34]

II. ROOTING THE HISTORY OF SALVATION IN THE ETERNAL TRINITY

Even though Tertullian like Irenaeus has devised his unified order of creation and salvation with regard to the *salus carnis,* he goes still further than Irenaeus in several aspects. This concerns not so much the aforementioned differences in their conception of salvation, as the way in which Tertullian strives to trace the *sacramentum salutis* back to the period before creation. Whereas Irenaeus shies away from penetrating the inner core of the divine mystery, for Tertullian there already existed an *oikonomia* in God before there was one in creation, the Old Testament and finally in the incarnation.[35] The coming of Christ, which forms the central core of the history of salvation, was actually designed to reveal that original economy.[36] For a full understanding of this theological innovation it is necessary to take into consideration the whole antimonarchian movement, which is responsible for this progress in the *intellectus fidei,* rather than to limit our investigation to Tertullian.

1. The more conscious distinction between Father and Son

Right at the beginning of his treatise *Adversus Praxean* Tertullian makes it clear just how urgent it was in his time to improve the salvation-historical vision of Justin and Irenaeus. According to him the issue was that of fighting monarchian tendencies and refuting the objections of the *simplices* against the *oikonomia.*[37] Thus it was vital for him to work out more clearly the teaching, traditional since Justin, on the difference between Father and Son. For this reason he took over and extended the traditional testimonia Genesis 19:24, Genesis 1:26; Psalm 109.[38] What is more, he elaborated the grammatical exegesis of these proof-texts. In this he indicated the use of the plural or distinguished the *personae.*[39] In the same way

---

[33] Hippolytus, Refut X 34.5: GCS 26, p 263: interpretation of Gen 1:26f.

[34] Cf. A. Grillmeier, *Jesus Christus,* pp 237–40, and esp. V. Loi, 'L'omelia "In s.Pascha" di Ippolito di Roma', Augustinianum 17, 1977, pp 461–84.

[35] Cf. Prax 2.1.

[36] Cf. Prax 31.2.

[37] Cf. Prax 3.1.

[38] Prax 11–14.

[39] Prax 7.11f; also C. Andresen, 'Zur Entstehung und Geschichte des trinitarischen Person-begriffes', ZNW 52, 1961, pp 1–39, esp. pp 18–25.

he recalled the traditional metaphors of sun and ray, root and shoot, etc.[40] Finally, he also referred to baptismal faith and the *regula fidei*.[41]

By expounding the distinction between Father and Son in the context of the *oikonomia,* of creation, history of Israel and incarnation, Tertullian gives a better account of it, in that he shows it to rest essentially on the *dispositio* of the divine substance itself. Reinterpreting the baptismal faith in a more philosophical way, he in fact distinguishes the *nomen generale* from the *nomina specialia*. In this context he introduces a contrast between *substantia – status – potestas,* expressions with a more general significance, and the special expressions *forma – gradus – species* as well as *persona*.[42] Thus he envisages the distinction between Father and Son not only from the point of view of the saving deed but also from that of their true being. Admittedly, he still relates the Son's divine birth to creation. But he not only emphasizes more strongly than has been done before the *ante constitutionem mundi,*[43] he also vigorously speaks of God as having always constituted his *sermo* in his *ratio*.[44]

Similar reasoning can already be found before Tertullian in the treatise *Contra Noetum*.[45] In this writing the anonymous author first combats with traditional testimonia the identification of God with the suffering Christ (nn. 1–7). In a second part he upholds the thesis that God is one as far as power (*dynamis*) is concerned, whereas he is threefold in his revelation (*epideixis*) according to the *oikonomia*. Even though he employs trinitarian formulae (nn. 9–14) when presenting scriptural evidence for his thesis, his intention is primarily to show that God wanted to reveal himself through the Word in creation, history and, above all, in the incarnation, in which the Word has entirely become the Son.(cf. nn. 10,15).[46]

After Tertullian, Hippolytus of Rome, too, took over the distinction between the inner and the self-revealing Word. Viewing the origin of the inner Word in close connection with the history of salvation, he decisively distinguishes it from the creatures. According to him the Word has been generated out of the Father's *ousia*.[47] For that reason, however, he had to defend himself against the charge of ditheism. He counters with the accusation of patripassianism and brings this doctrine, to which, according to him, Pope Callistus I also adheres, into connection with Sabellius' concept of the one person (*prosopon*).[48] Later still, about the middle of the third century, Novatian sought to take a mediating stand.[49]

---

[40] Prax 8.5ff.
[41] Prax 26, Bapt 13.
[42] Prax 2.4.
[43] Prax 5.1.
[44] Prax 5f.
[45] Cf. R. Butterworth, *Hippolytus of Rome, C.Noetum.* Text introduced, edited and translated, London 1977, and A. Grillmeier, *Jesus Christus,* pp 231–7 (=*Christ in Christian Tradition,* pp 113–17), where he also discusses the still open question of authorship.
[46] Cf. also Hippolytus, De Christo et Antichristo 4.
[47] Hippolytus, Refut X 33.
[48] Refut IX 12.
[49] Cf. R. J. de Simone, *Novatian,* and A. Grillmeier, *Jesus Christus,* pp 257f (with bibl.) (=*Christ in Christian Tradition,* pp 131ff).

In his *De Trinitate* he not only defended the true manhood and true Godhead of Christ (cc. 9–25), but also by means of the traditional *testimonia* accounted for the difference between Father and Son (cc. 26f). In this context, besides the christological expression of *utramque substantiam in unam nativitatis christi foederasse concordiam,* he also coined the trinitarian formulae of *concordiae unitas cum personarum tamen distinctione* and *per substantiae communionem ad patrem revolvitur.*[50]

2. From binitarian to trinitarian reflexion

Even in 200 pneumatology is still at a very early stage of development. As before the Holy Spirit is named in the *regula fidei* and the baptismal catechesis and is invoked in the liturgy together with the Son as mediator of divine grace.[51] He is regarded, too, as guaranteeing the unity of Old and New Testament.[52] The theologians, however, who already reflect in a more elaborate manner on the relationship of the Logos to the Father, are very little concerned to go on to define the Spirit's position within the divine sphere. Still, they do not fail to create the presuppositions for a thoroughgoing doctrine of the Trinity.

The treatise *Contra Noetum* accordingly speaks of a threefold *epideixis* (n. 8). It also expounds the baptismal faith by pointing to the gift of the Spirit (n. 9). What is more, in expounding John 1:1–3 it adds to the two *prosopa* (roles/parts) the third *oikonomia,* the grace of the Holy Spirit (n. 14). If it can be assumed that the author of this writing is the same as that of the interpretation of the Song of Songs, which is attributed to Hippolytus, his exposition in *Contra Noetum* finds valuable amplification in this piece of Old Testament exegesis. In this the Holy Spirit appears not only as the prophetic spirit but also as the power and aroma of Christ.[53]

After his conversion to Montanism Tertullian shows interest in prophecy, i.e. in the revelations of the Spirit, thanks to which the *disciplina,* though not the *regula fidei,* is given further development.[54] This was all the more decisive, as he, at the same time as the Montanists, turned against the antitrinitarian theology of the Monarchians. Tertullian, nevertheless, had already in his catholic period spoken a great deal of the Holy Spirit, in the tradition of Irenaeus, as working in the Church and sanctifying the believer.[55] As, however, is clear from *Adversus Praxean,* as a Montanist he highly elaborated his pneumatological thought. More than Irenaeus and Theophilus had ever done before, he transformed binitarian reflection into trinitarian reflection. This is the case in his references to the testimonia,[56] as well as when he employs metaphors: sun, ray, point of light;

---

[50] Novatian, Trin 67, cf. 140; 151; 192.

[51] Cf. J. Moingt, *Tertullien* I, pp 75–86.

[52] Cf. Tertullian, Marc V 8.12; Prax 11.7–10; also J. E. L. Van der Geest, *Le Christ et l'Ancien Testament,* Nijmegen 1972, pp 233–8.

[53] Cf. P. Meloni, *Ippolito e il Cantico dei Cantici: Ricerche su Ippolito,* pp 97–120.

[54] Cf. Monogam 2.1–4, VirgVel 1.4f; also C. Fredouille, *Tertullien,* pp 290–7, esp. pp 294f.

[55] Praescript 13.5; 28.1; Bapt 6.1f; 19.2.

[56] Cf. Prax 11.7–10.

spring, river, canal etc.[57] What is more, he applies the *nomina specialia* to the Spirit: *portio – derivatio – forma – gradus – persona.*[58] In this context there is no doubt that the Spirit also belongs to that *dispositio,* which according to Tertullian, existed already *ante constitutionem mundi.* Still, Tertullian does view the Spirit mainly within the context of the history of salvation, together with creation and sanctification. This is true particularly for his formula *a patre per filium.*[59] More than with the Son, the question of its eternal origin is left open with the Spirit.

Hippolytus of Rome does not touch on the issue of the Spirit in his refutation of heresies. The *Traditio Apostolica* attributed to him, however, contains a remarkable testimony to the faith in the work of the Holy Spirit through the liturgy, and in the Spirit's indwelling in the baptized and the ministers of the Church.[60] Novatian's christologically orientated expositions, too, do not entirely lack pneumatology. One chapter of *De Trinitate* (29) can actually be regarded as a hymn of the Spirit's work in the Church. Even though it is more the salvation-historical vision which is developed here, it must not be overlooked that Novatian places the Holy Spirit in the same line as the Father and the Son and underlines at the same time his personal status.

3. The attempt to explain the unity of the three persons

In their polemic against the Unitarians, who spoke of the one unique Lord and in this way also accounted for the presence of God in Christ (*compassio Patris*), the author of *Contra Noetum,* Tertullian, Hippolytus and Novatian felt the urge to defend the distinction between the Father and the Son. For soteriological reasons they extended this reflection also to the Holy Spirit. Even though they went so far as to be accused of ditheism or tritheism, they could not call in question the monotheism of the Bible and contemporary philosophy, the less so as they had to defend against the Marcionites the unity of the order of creation and salvation.

The contemporary theological situation first demanded an exegesis of the relevant texts, particularly John 10:30 ('My Father and I are one') and 14:8 ('show us the Father'), which strongly emphasize the unity of Father and Son. It was also necessary to form an appropriate counter-balance to the *testimonia,* traditional since Justin, in favour of the distinction. Thus discussion of the contentious question was first exegetical in character, even though the rhetorical and philosophical presuppositions of the time played a considerable part, too.

The author of *Contra Noetum* contrasts the threefold *epideixis* and *oikonomia* (nn. 10–14) with the unity of the divine power, which comes from the Father alone (n. 11), and the unity of divine will in the government of the world. How far these reflections, however, move within the framework of *oikonomia,*

---

[57] Prax 8.7.
[58] Cf. Prax 2.4; 11.10; 30.5.
[59] Prax 4.1.
[60] Cf. TradApost 3; 6–8; 21 (ed. Botte).

becomes especially clear from the fact that he does not like identifying the Word with the eternal Son.

Tertullian is even more concerned to vindicate the unity of the three divine guarantors of our salvation. Thus he explains the political term of monarchy in the sense of the Son's partaking in the power of the prince (*potestas principis*).[61] In the same way he prefers those metaphors that express derivation (*derivatio*) and division (*divisio*): spring, river, canal.[62] What is more, he introduces a dynamic concept of *substantia,* which enables him to understand the Father as *tota substantia,* and the Son and Spirit, on the other hand, as *derivatio totius et portio.*[63] All these considerations, which for him are merely preliminary thoughts (*praestructiones*), are confirmed by scriptural proof, i.e. by testimonia which show that the divine distinctions do not involve actual separation, as well as by refuting opposing scriptural proofs.[64] So Tertullian succeeds in giving a technical formulation to the fact that the *dispositio divina* reaches back even to the period before creation, and that there is in God an eternal origin (*census*) with three grades (*gradus*).[65] For him Son and Spirit are, accordingly, 'partakers' (*consortes*) of the single divine substance of the Father,[66] which is *una substantia in tribus cohaerentibus.*[67] They can be separated as persons but not in substance.[68] Even these more philosophically formulated expositions remain too strongly connected with the history of salvation, and do not draw out the deeper reason for the personal distinction of Father, Son and Spirit. Still, they make an enormous step forwards towards later Church dogma, which is to define the trinitarian and christological mystery in similar terminology.

Hippolytus of Rome is less definite than Tertullian. At least, he points out the unity of Father and Son. He also states that the Son is derived from the Father's essence and thus from God, whereas the cosmos has been created *ex nihilo.*[69] Following the line of Tertullian Novatian, too, acknowledges the unity of Father and Son, the *communio substantiae*[70] He is on the way, too, to an understanding of the eternal *generatio* of the Son, which is independent of creation.[71]

It was in a more intra-ecclesiastical controversy that the antimonarchian theologians gave the salvation-historical theology of Justin and Irenaeus a more dogmatic, ecclesiastically binding character. More open to contemporary rhetoric and philosophy, they developed a technical terminology which was to be adopted by later official Church dogma. As far as the content is concerned, it is to their

[61] Prax 3.2f.
[62] Prax 8.6f.
[63] Prax 9.2.
[64] Prax 11–17 (testimonia) and 18–26 (refutations). For the literary construction of Prax see R. D. Sider, *Ancient Rhetoric and the Art of Tertullian,* Oxford 1971.
[65] Prax 2.4.
[66] Prax 3.5.
[67] Prax 12.7.
[68] Prax 12.6.
[69] Refut 33.
[70] Trin 192. See H. Weyer, *Novatianus, De Trinitate* (Darmstadt 1962), pp 204f.
[71] Trin 94; 184; 190.

credit that they laid the foundation for the distinction between the *oikonomia* and the eternal *dispositio,* the salvation-historical and the metaphysical ways of looking at the mystery of Father, Son and Spirit. This entails that three *agentes,* differing from each other, come together in a unity of will and action, and that the three are different from the world. For the development of Church doctrine above all the refutation of patripassianism was decisive. Thus these theologians were capable of clearly distinguishing not only Father and Son, but also divine and human substance in Christ. Their endeavours, however, succeeded only partly in an unambiguous vindication of the divine unity. Their reflections are also too much bound to the *oikonomia* to be capable of excluding a certain subordinatianism. Finally, they have lost – in spite of all their emphasizing the Easter mystery in soteriology – the Easter vision of the Trinity as opposed to one that sets out from creation.

7. Origen's Christian Gnosis

On the research on Origen see

H. Crouzel, *Bibliographie critique d'Origène*, Steenbrugge 1971.
L. Lies, 'Zum Stand heutiger Origenesforschung', ZKTh 102, 1980, pp 61–75.
U. Berner, *Origenes*, Darmstadt 1981.
H. Crouzel, *Bibliographie critique d'Origène*, Suppl. 1, Steenbrugge 1982.

BIBLIOGRAPHY

M. Harl, *Origène et la fonction révélatrice du Verbe incarné*, Paris 1958.
P. Nemeshegyi, *La paternité de Dieu chez Origène*, Paris 1960.
H. Crouzel, *Origène et la connaisance mystique*, Bruges 1961 (See also the numerous other studies by the same author, esp. Greg 57, 1976, pp 109–25, and Augustinianum 20, 1980, pp 97–107).
G. Gruber, *Zoe. Wesen, Stufen und Mitteilung des wahren Lebens bei Origenes*, Munich 1962.
R. Gögler, *Zur Theologie des biblischen Wortes bei Origenes*, Düsseldorf 1963.
M. Eichinger, *Die Verklärung Christi bei Origenes. Die Bedeutung des Menschen Jesus in seiner Christologie*, Vienna 1969.
J. Rius-Camps, 'Communicabilidad de la naturaleza de Dios según Origenes', OCP 34, 1968, pp 5–37; 36, 1970, pp 201–47; 38, 1972, pp 430–53, 40, 1974, pp 344–63.
J. Rius-Camps, *El dinamismo trinitario en la divinización de los seres racionales según Origenes*, Rome 1970.
H. J. Vogt, *Das Kirchenverständnis des Origenes*, Cologne 1974.
P. Nautin, *Origène*, Paris 1977.
B. Studer, 'Soteriologie der Kirchenväter', HDG III/2a, Freiburg 1978, pp 85–95 (with bibl.).
L. F. Ladaría, *El Espíritu en Clemente Alejandrino*, Madrid 1980.
See also:
J. W. Trigg, *Origen: The Bible and Philosophy in the Third-Century Church*, Atlanta, 1983, and London, 1985.
G. Q. Reijners, *Das Wort vom Kreuz. Kreuzes- und Erlösungssymbolik bei Origenes*, Cologne 1983.
B. Neuschäfer, *Origenes als Philologe*, Basle 1987.
H. Crouzel, *Origen*, Edinburgh, 1989.

The theological work of Origen, the great Alexandrine teacher, overlaps with the entire first half of the third century.[1] During this period the intellectual situation remained on the whole the same as that at the turn of the century. Like Irenaeus and Tertullian, and also Clement of Alexandria, Origen was opposed to the

---

[1] For Origen's biography see P. Nautin, *Origène*.

gnostic movement. Like the author of *Contra Noetum,* Tertullian and Hippolytus he had to argue with the unitarianism of certain ecclesiastical groups. So, too, he had to deal with heretics as well as with the 'simple' who were averse to any kind of speculation. In other words, he was faced with the task of defending an ecclesiastical Logos Christology as well as a true Christian gnosis.[2]

Origen's encounter with these two theological movements, which both reach far back into the second century, took place in a new intellectual climate, on which the cosmopolitan culture of Alexandria had a considerable effect. On the one hand he was influenced by the ancient problem of the one and the many, just like Neoplatonist philosophy, which was developing there at the same time.[3] On the other hand, the ideas of Alexandrine hermeneutics, which had been already decisive for Philo and certain gnostics, impinged on his strongly biblically orientated theological work.[4] The aim of his theology, which was scientific in the proper sense, did not, however, prevent Origen from putting all his efforts at the service of the intellectual quest of the Christians, and all this in full accordance with the *regula fidei.*[5] With good reason he is, therefore, regarded today both as *vir spiritualis* and as *vir ecclesiasticus.*[6]

Origen developed a theology characterized by two features. On the one hand, it is distinguished by its interest in intellectual inquiry. For Origen distinguishes between the certain *data* of the Christian faith and the chance of raising new questions, which the Bible itself has left open.[7] It is precisely by this way of searching inquiry (*gymnasia*) that he sought to lead his disciples and his readers through the understanding of reality and of the mysteries of Scripture to union with the Logos, the image of God.[8] On the other hand, Origen is concerned so to rethink the *data* of the *regula fidei* in the context of the knowledge of God and the soul as well as that of God and the world, that they yield the structures of a Christian conception of the world. In his search for a theological synthesis his first aim was to present a systematic exposition of the first principles (*archai*) – Trinity, rational beings, the world. This he did in his famous work *De Principiis,* in two series of treatises and a summary.[9] He did not fail here to correct

[2] Typical of his position which attacks on both sides is the Commentary on St. John on the one hand, in which Origen opposes ecclesiastical exegesis to Heracleon's gnostic interpretation of the Bible, and the Dialogue with Heraclides on the other hand, in which he takes his stand against a simplistic orthodoxy. See also N. Brox, 'Der einfache Glaube und die Theologie', Kairos NF 14, 1972, pp 161–87, and A. Le Boulluec, 'La place de la polémique antignostique dans le Peri Archon', Origeniana I, Bari 1975, pp 47–61.

[3] Cf. Origen, Peri Archon (=PA) I 6.2; II 1.1, with the annotations in the edition of H. Görgemanns and H. Karpp, pp 217ff; 285ff.

[4] Cf. PA IV 1–3 (a biblical hermeneutic). Also R. Gögler, *Zur Theologie des Wortes bei Origenes*; B. Neuschäfer, *Origenes als Philologe.*

[5] Cf. PA I praef., with R. C. Baud, 'Les "règles" de la théologie d'Origène', RchSR 55, 1967, pp 161–208.

[6] Cf. W. Völker, *Das Vollkommenheitsideal des Origenes,* Tübingen 1931, and H. Crouzel, *Origène et la connaissance mystique.*

[7] Cf. PA I, praef. 4–10, also H. Crouzel, *La connaissance mystique,* pp 400–9.

[8] Cf. PA I, praef. 3: wisdom as the aim of theological research; PA III 6.8: the eternal gospel, goal of all knowledge.

[9] On the intention and the structure of PA cf. esp. M. Harl, G. Dorival and A. Le Boulluec, *Origène, Traité des Principes,* Paris 1976.

philosophical views which were opposed to the Christian faith and thus to develop a doctrine, compatible with faith, on creation, on human freedom, on resurrection, and especially on the Holy Spirit.[10]

This new, inquiring and systematic theology is rightly called Christian gnosis. It is gnosis not only because it follows up the problems of the gnostics of the second century but also and primarily because it takes up again the true concerns of those first Christian theologians: above all the search for the knowledge that would provide a foundation for the salvation of mankind and the world.[11] It is, however, a Christian gnosis. It not only takes seriously the *regula fidei* but also sets itself in a salvation-historical perspective, as Justin and Irenaeus had done before, in spite of all its interest in the development of the Many from the One and in the return of the Many to the same One. This concern for ecclesiastical teaching and for the historical vision of the Bible is especially evident when Origen expounds the link between baptism and the Trinity,[12] when he goes into the question of the purpose of liturgical prayer,[13] follows up the Jewish exegesis of the Bible,[14] replaces the scheme of God-*nous*-soul with that of God-Logos-Pneuma,[15] and, finally, when he, with all his predilection for allegory, does not forget the historical link between the Old and the New Testament.[16]

For an adequate evaluation of this philosophical, gnostic reinterpretation of the baptismal faith two points need to be considered. First, it has to be realized that the more systematic expositions of Father, Son and Spirit, as well as of the incarnation of the Word, are to be found for the most part in the disputed work *De Principiis,* which is to a large extent hypothetical in character. It must also be realized that this writing is an early work, to be supplemented by the expositions of the much more mature commentary on John as well as with the strongly anti-pagan work, *Contra Celsum.* Secondly, it must be noted that the theological magnum opus *De Principiis* is to a large extent extant only in a Latin version, which was only completed after the council of Nicea and thus reflects the reservations of anti-Arian theology about the position of Origen.[17] This later interpretation of this doctrine must, therefore, be taken into account. That is why the text of *De Principiis,* has, as far as possible, to be compared with the extant Greek writings.[18] In this comparison it has to be remembered that in modern research on Origen, conclusions are very often biased, and therefore range from the opinion that Origen is more a Neoplatonist philosopher than a Christian, to the view that almost the whole of Nicene orthodoxy is already present in his work.

[10] Cf. PA I 3.1f; II 10.1; Cels IV 14; VI 64.

[11] Cf. J. Daniélou, *Gospel message,* pp 445–500, with Clement of Alex., Stromat VI and VII, and Origen PA II 11.6 and HomNum 17.4.

[12] Cf. PA I 3.2, Colo VI 33 (17); HomJer 2.3.

[13] Cf. DialHeracl 4.17–5.7; Orat 15.1f.

[14] Cf. PA I 3.4: on Isa 6:3; Cels VI 18ff.

[15] Cf. esp. PA I 3.1 and PA I, praef. 2 and 4.

[16] Cf. PA I 3.1, also PA I, praef.4; II.7.

[17] Cf. B. Studer, 'Zur Frage der dogmatischen Terminologie in der lateinischen Übersetzung von Origenes' De Principiis', *Epektasis, Mélanges patristiques offerts au Cardinal Daniélou,* Paris 1972, pp 403–14, also the relevant annotations in the edition of H. Görgemanns and H. Karpp.

[18] Besides Celsus and Colo note HomJer, CoMt 10–17 and Orat.

I. ORIGEN'S SYSTEMATIC ANSWER TO THE QUESTIONS OF HIS TIME

As a Christian gnostic Origen sought to provide a valid and comprehensive answer to the burning questions of his time within the framework of the *regula fidei*. For this reason he first developed a Logos-Christology, which was to develop further the historical theology of salvation of Irenaeus and Justin according to the new theological and spiritual concerns.[19]

1. The mediatorship of the Logos

The Logos-christology, which Justin intended to employ in answer to the problems of his time, and which essentially stood behind the historical conceptions of Irenaeus and Tertullian, acquired still sharper contours with Origen. The great Alexandrine had to wrestle with the basic problem of Greek philosophy, that of the relation of the One to the Many.[20] According to the middle Platonic solution of this problem, which he himself adopts, the transition from the One to the Many necessitates a mediator, who belongs to both spheres. This role of the mediator is appropriated to the Logos. For Origen, accordingly, the Son, as image of the Father, is Wisdom and Word. In relation to the Father he is Wisdom, whose knowledge he is.[21] In relation to the world he is Word, the communication of what he beholds in the Father.[22]

The external function of the Logos for Origen is twofold: it refers to creation and to the history of salvation. In creation the Logos is the link between God and world. Through him the world has been created. As the world soul he established its order.[23] Thus he establishes salvation, which consists in the conservation of the world. Even his incarnation served salvation in this sense of conservation.[24] In the history of salvation the Logos is behind all human events.[25] In the Old Testament he exercises the work of prophetic insight: mediated through chosen men and through his own appearances.[26] In the fulness of time he was made man, to rid men of demons, to re-establish the Law and to provide the example of a virtuous man.[27] His mediatorship lasts on in the Church and in all Christians as individuals: in their prayer, knowledge and love.[28] His mediatorship is even extended to the angels and powers.[29] Thus the Logos gradually unifies all with himself, without violating the freedom of

---

[19] Cf. B. Studer, *Soteriologie*, pp 88–92, and A. Grillmeier, *Jesus Christus*, pp 266–80, with bibl. (=*Christ in Christian Tradition*, pp 138–48).

[20] Cf. PA I 6.2; II 1.1.

[21] PA I 2.2.

[22] PA I 2.3.

[23] PA II 1.3; I 2.9; I 3.5f.

[24] Cf. PA II 6.3.

[25] Cf. PA II 6.1.

[26] Cf. PA I, praef 1; CoIo VI 4.17.

[27] PA III 5.6; III 3.2.

[28] PA I 3.8, cf. Cels VI 68; 79; HomLc 15.1.4.

[29] PA IV 4.5; IV 3.13 (left out by Rufinus); HomLev 1; Cels VII 17.

individual beings.[30] When he has perfected this, he himself, as the head of the Church will subordinate himself to the Father, and God will be all in all.[31] This will mean the fulfilment of salvation, which is realized in the lasting presence (*parousia*) of the Logos in creation and history.[32]

2. *The mystery of the Logos*

The mediatorship of the Logos in creation and history means the revelation of God: saving communication of truth, an introduction to the ascent to the eternal vision of God. This conception of Logos-Teacher or Logos-Light is certainly found already in Justin and Irenaeus.[33] It essentially goes back to the apocalyptic understanding of the mystery of Jesus (cf. Matt 11:25ff; 13:11; I Cor 2:17; Rom 16:25). Origen, however, clearly sees salvation as established even more in the revelation of the Logos.[34]

On one side, the Alexandrine attempts to define more precisely the activity of revelation. For him the Logos is already wholly revelation thanks to his position as mediator. He is present everywhere as the divine light. For that reason all things that have been created through him, as well as all events that have been effected through him in history, are reflections of his light: mysteries that at one and the same time veil and reveal him. This can be explained by the absolute transcendence of God. The Father is entirely invisible. If in spite of this he reveals himself out of his goodness, he does it by means of the Word. The reason for this is that man's openness to God has been disturbed by sin. Because man is alienated in this world, he is in need of the Word's accommodation. He, accordingly, assimilates himself to man. He stoops down, he appears in history, becomes scripture, and finally man.[35]

On the other side, Origen enquires as to how revelation becomes real as man's salvation. As an answer he qualifies the aforementioned openness of man to God with his doctrine of the image of the Logos. He develops a comprehensive doctrine of religious knowledge and works out his biblical hermeneutics in which he includes the various disciplines of ancient education. According to him the Logos has created man in his own image. He continually governs all religious knowledge. He himself stands behind all intellectual knowledge and thus created the requirements for the gnosis which should help man to attain salvation for himself and the world.[36]

3. *The incarnation as the greatest mystery of the Logos*

If the Logos reveals the invisible God everywhere – in creation and in history – by his

[30] Cf. PA III 5.6–8.
[31] Cf. PA I 6.1f; III 5.6.
[32] Cf. PAI 2.10.
[33] Cf. pp 45f; 63ff above.
[34] Cf. M. Harl, *Origène,* also P. Stockmeier, 'Offenbarung', HDG I/1a, pp 62–5.
[35] Cf. PA I 2.8; Cels VII 17. Also H. U. von Balthasar, 'Le mysterion d'Origène', RchSR 26, 1936, pp 513–62; 27, 1937, pp 38–64.
[36] Cf. H. Crouzel, *Connaissance mystique,* and H. de Lubac, *Histoire et Esprit. L'intelligence de l'Écriture d'après Origèn,* Paris 1950.

presence full of light, he does it in the highest way by means of his incarnation through Mary. Here the accommodation to mankind is fulfilled, without which the divine Word and in him God himself would not be recognized.[37] According to Origen the ascent to gnosis is made possible only through the manifold nature of the Logos. The Word has to accommodate himself to the spiritual needs of each individual. He becomes for them respectively Son, Wisdom, life, redemption, physician, the Only-Begotten, beginning. These titles not only transcribe the fulness of the Logos, but constitute the ladder, as it were, on which the soul ascends to the Word, which itself is the image of God.[38] Because among these *epinoiai* that of the Word is the most distinguished title of Christ, and as this title has been fully revealed only in the incarnation, this latter proves to be the beginning of the soul's mystical ascent, a beginning which is to be surpassed one day, but which is nevertheless absolutely necessary.[39] In other words: the incarnation is basic to salvation in this gnosis, for the sake of which God has created man and all things and leads all beings to perfection through his edifying providence.[40] The central significance of the incarnation of the Word is also evident in that Origen compares the structure of Holy Scriptures with it, when he speaks of the word and the flesh of the Bible, and understands the reading of it as a continual search for Christ.[41]

This doctrine of the incarnation as the greatest mystery of the Logos holds special weight for Origen in his conception of Jesus' human soul.[42] According to Origen the incarnation could not possibly have happened without a human soul. The spiritual Logos could never have been united directly with a body.[43] This primarily philosophical conception, even though it is supported by scriptural testimony, establishes the soul in the centre of Origen's christology.[44] As this soul was always attached to the Word, it did not fall from God like the other spiritual beings. Thus it always remains attached to the Logos like iron penetrated by fire.[45] In this way Origen not only sought to explain the deep union of the divine and human in Christ, but also made a decisive soteriological statement. On the one hand he makes out the soul of Jesus to be the model for any union with the Word,[46] on the other he anticipates the later principle: *quod non assumptum – non sanatum.*[47] His theory, however, is burdened by the doctrine of pre-existence of souls.[48]

---

[37] Cf. PA I 2.4, Cels VI 68.

[38] Cf. A. Grillmeier, *Jesus Christus*, pp 270–4, with bibl. (=*Christ in Christian Tradition*, pp 141–5). Among the texts cited there see esp.CoIo I 19f.109–24; I 24.151–7; I 28.191–200.

[39] Cf. PA I 2.8.

[40] Cf. PA III 5.8. Also M. Harl, *Origène*, pp 228–42.

[41] Cf. CoMt frag.: MG 17, 289AB; Cels VI 77; Philocalia XV 19: MG 14, 1313B. Also P. Stockmeier, 'Offenbarung', HDG I/1a, p 64f.

[42] Cf. A. Grillmeier, *Jesus Christus*, pp 276–80 (=*Christ in Christian Tradition*, pp 145–8).

[43] PA II 6.3.

[44] Esp. cf. PA II 6.3–7; IV 4.4.

[45] Cf. PA II 6.3; CoIo I 32 (36); XX 19 (17); Cels V 39.

[46] Cf. PA II 6.7; I 3.8.

[47] Cf. DialHeracl 7; CoMt XII 29; CoIo XXXII 18.225; Cels IV 19. Also P. Smulders, in MySal III/1, p 419.

[48] Cf. PA II 6.3. Also A. Grillmeier, *Jesus Christus*, pp 276ff (=*Christ in Christian Tradition*, pp 146ff).

II. SUPPLEMENTS NECESSITATED BY THE 'REGULA FIDEI'

The systematic structure of Origen's theology of the Logos is obviously directed by his interest in the philosophical question of the relation of the One to the Many. But it cannot be overlooked that it is basically a matter for him of a traditional, though newly thought-out vision of the history of salvation. For he has placed the historically understood incarnation at the very heart of his doctrine of the revealing mediatorship of the Logos. To how great an extent he has been faithful to the preaching of the Church, in spite of all his philosophical presuppositions, the following exposition should make clearer still.

1. The position of the Holy Spirit

The Logos-centred soteriology of Origen obviously follows the system which distinguishes between God, Logos and world. From that point of view Origen's position could be regarded as binitarian. However, he does not content himself with a mere theology of the Logos.[49] Fully indebted to the rule of faith, he transcends the platonic scheme of *hen – logos – psyche*, in that he fits the Holy Spirit into his doctrine of salvation. He even stresses that the philosophers were not capable of recognizing the existence of the Holy Spirit, as he is only accessible through Holy Scripture.[50] Still, it has to be noticed that Origen refers to the Spirit in the context of individual soteriology rather than of ecclesiology.[51] Nevertheless, he goes beyond the view of the apologists and places himself in the perspective of Irenaeus, for whom there is no *oikonomia* without the Spirit, and even in that of Tertullian, who includes the Holy Spirit in the *dispositio divina*.

Following Irenaeus Origen understands the trinitarian *oikonomia* as: God the Father, the creator and beginning of all things – the Logos, principle of the rationality of all spiritual beings – the Holy Spirit present in all saints.[52] According to this scheme the Holy Spirit is not lower in dignity than Father and Son. Entirely on the same side of the divide as Father and Son, and different from all creatures, he is distinguished in his mode of activity, in that he sanctifies the just. To him also belong the inspiration of the Bible and its spiritual understanding.[53] Like Tertullian Origen traces back the Spirit's saving work to his existence in the divine, perfectly holy life. The Holy Spirit, too, is a divine hypostasis.[54] He does not, however, go into detail over the origin of the Spirit and leaves open the question as to how this differs from the generation of the Son.[55] It should be emphasized that Origen, too, links up the sanctifying power of the Spirit with

---

[49] Cf. G. Kretschmar, *Der Heilige Geist in der Geschichte,* p 114.
[50] PA I 3.1.
[51] Cf. H. J. Vogt, *Das Kirchenverständnis des Origenes,* pp 330–6.
[52] PA I 3.5f.
[53] PA IV 2.1f; II 11.7.
[54] Cf. PA I 1.3; I 3.4, CoIo II 10.75.
[55] Cf. PA I, praef. 4; II 2.1; CoIo II 10.75f.

baptism and counts him in the adorable Trinity.[56] His work being limited to sanctification, this does not imply that he is lesser in power but that man in his freedom is able to some degree to open himself up to him.[57] Like the other divine hypostases, he is unchangeable.[58]

2. The unity of the three hypostases

Considering that in baptism, the beginning of Christian life, the whole adorable Trinity is invoked, Origen expressly teaches that Father, Son and Spirit form the divine Trinity and thus are distinct from each other and, taken as a whole, from all creatures.[59] The term *trias,* however, does not often occur,[60] but what it denotes is always present. The same goes for the difference from creation.[61]

The distinction between the hypostases does not only refer to their part in salvation history. Son and Spirit are not only powers of the Father, they are hypostases, *pragmata,* like the Father.[62] In spite of his rejection of all modalistic oversimplifications, Origen like the other antimonarchians is concerned for a full preservation of biblical monotheism. He does full justice to this aspect.[63] In also acknowledging that the Trinity is recognized more perfectly owing to the incarnation and the pouring out of the Spirit, he proves his sense of the unique Godhead, that in the New Testament is revealed as Trinity.[64]

The endeavours to render monotheism beyond all doubt at first concern the relation of Father and Son.[65] Origen speaks here of a unity of will and action and in this context employs the comparison with marriage and also with the union of Word and soul.[66] Similarly he regards the Word as the image of the Father or as the revelation of divine glory.[67] Above all, he takes up the theme of the eternal, wholly spiritual generation. The Son proceeds, just as the will proceeds out of the mind.[68] This is why he is spiritual like the Father, why he is of the same *ousia.*[69] Thus Origen also accepts the idea of the *homoousion,* even though he does not employ the term *homoousios.*[70]

While the theme of the unity of all the persons is not prominent, it is by no means neglected. Origen sees the unity of all the three hypostases as stemming

---

[56] PA I 3.2.5; CoIo VI 33.166.

[57] Cf. PA I 3.5ff.

[58] Cf. PA I 3.4.7; I 5.5.

[59] Cf. PA I 3.2, II 4.3.

[60] Cf. CoIo X 39.70, VI 33.166. In the Latin translation of PA this term can not always be established as authentic. See B. Studer, *Zur Frage der dogmatischen Terminologie,* pp 404f.

[61] Cf. PA II 2.2; IV 3.15.

[62] Cf. CoIo II 10.75. Also CoIo 10.21; Cels VIII 12.

[63] Cf. DialHeracl 4.

[64] Cf. PA I 3.7.

[65] Cf. DialHeracl; CoIo II 2.16.

[66] Cf. Cels VIII 12; CoIo XIII 36.228–235; PA IV 4.4; DialHeracl 2f.

[67] PA I 2.6; IV 1.

[68] PA I 2.6; IV 4.1; CoIo XIII 36.234. On the eternal generation see PA I 2.4; HomJer 9.4.

[69] Cf. CoRom 7.13.

[70] Cf. R. P. C. Hanson, 'Did Origen apply the word homoousios to the Son?', *Epektasis. Mélanges patristiques offerts au Cardinal Daniélou,* Paris 1942, pp 293–304 (reprinted in idem, *Studies in Christian Antiquity,* Edinburgh 1985, pp 53–70).

chiefly from the fact that the Father is *arche,* fulness and source of divine life, whereas Son and Spirit possess it only through partaking in it, in a derived way. In this sense the Father alone is *ho theos,* God as such.[71]

In this view of the divine unity Origen does not succeed entirely in ruling out subordinationism. He, accordingly, accepts grades within God.[72] This assumption is confirmed in his exegesis of Isaiah 6[73] and in the conception of the Logos as the image of God, i.e. as the visible and circumscribed God.[74] In this respect Origen's opinion that the eucharistic prayer is to be directed to the Father is not relevant here; for this opinion is perfectly compatible with the tradition of the Church's liturgy.[75]

3. The doctrine of Jesus' death and resurrection

Origen's Logos-theology clearly presents itself as a soteriological theory. For in it the Logos leads the world, which has been created through him, to full salvation. This is above all due to his incarnation, through which he has most fully accommodated himself to men and thus perfected all earlier theophanies. To this extent Origen's Logos-centred soteriology fits in with the salvation-historical perspective of the Christian faith, and thus differs from all gnosticism. This soteriological doctrine which includes the kenosis, contains, however, further supplements to the *regula fidei,* which considerably deepen its salvation-historical character.

In fact, Origen does not pass over the traditional themes of the victory and sacrificial death of Jesus. According to him the mediatorship of the Logos necessarily entails a kenosis, a renunciation of divine dignity, which has finally reached its apogee in the death of Jesus.[76] In that the Word in death took on himself the sin of the world, and bore all our weaknesses, he has humbled himself to the utmost. Through death the kenosis of the Word has reached its culminating point. It is precisely here that the great turning-point occurs, the resurrection which Christ is to bring to perfection on his great day for the whole Church.[77]

At the same time the death of Christ is the sacrifice for all.[78] Because Christ as the true high priest, who outshone all other priests, sacrificed himself by dying, and thus was related to God in love as no one else has ever been, he surpassed all pagan heroes and Christian martyrs in sacrificial self-surrender.[79] Secondly, this sacrificial death was also a victory over the demons. In his power Jesus was able to gain victory over death, and, being himself entirely without sin, he was able

---

[71] Cf. PA I 2.13; I 3.8; CoIo II 2.8; II 10.72; XIII 25.151. The son as second God: Cels V 39.

[72] Cf. CoIo XIII 25.151 and II 10.72, with the annotations in SChr 120, p 252. Also PA I 2.13; I 3.5; Cels V 37; CoIo I 19.115.

[73] Cf. PA I 3.4.

[74] Cf. J. Daniélou, *Gospel message,* pp 375–86, esp. pp 380f, with CoIo I 39.291f.

[75] Cf. Orat 15.1f. Also P. Nautin, *Origène,* p 116.

[76] CoIo VI 57.293; VI 5.29, V 20.119.

[77] CoIo X 35.229.

[78] CoIo VI 53–58; XXVIII 19.165.

[79] Cf. Cels I 31; VII 55.

fundamentally to overcome sin.[80] To this context of Christ's victory also belongs the theory of redemption, which Origen has developed more than his predecessors.[81]

Even if the resurrection of Christ assumes a much smaller place in the theology of Origen, texts referring to it are not to be overlooked.[82] In these not only is the resurrection of Jesus explained as a spiritualization of Jesus' human nature, but he distinguishes three steps in the process of the resurrection: the descent into the underworld to set the just free, the appearances to the disciples to lead them into the fulness of truth, and the ascension as the glorification of the whole of humanity.[83] To this Origen adds the resurrection as the beginning of that mediatorship which the glorified Christ exercises in the Church by his *parousia* and his subjection of all things.[84]

Finally, in line with the kenosis of the Word lies Origen's doctrine of Jesus as the sole teacher.[85] As with the preceding tradition, Origen, too, refers to the logia of the Master. He points even more to the example of Jesus. For him Jesus' manhood forms the model of our ascent to the Father.[86] He also speaks of the following of Jesus as consisting in being crucified with Jesus, of the imitation of his humility and the exercise of his virtues.[87]

The greatness of Origen's theology certainly consists not only in the fact that he reinterpreted the data of the baptismal faith in the context of a vision of the history of salvation, which he himself developed and interpreted afresh, but also that this reinterpretation was carried out with the scientific means of his time. In his work, which aimed at both theological research and spiritual concerns, in his *exercitatio mentis,* Origen arrived at noteworthy conclusions: he succeeded in transforming the accepted Logos-christology into a system which in spite of all its deficiencies (pre-existence of souls, *apokatastasis*) is distinguished by a remarkable consistency. He is able – in opposition to all modalism – to work out clearly the real distinctions between Father, Son and Spirit, as well as the difference between divine and human ousia in Christ, without calling in question the unity of the Trinity and the union of the divine and human in Christ. He had to leave unanswered, however, a number of questions: concerning the origin of the Holy Spirit, the difference between creation and generation, the equality in essence of Father, Son and Spirit, the origin of the soul of Jesus.

The lack of certainty and clarity on the abovementioned points ultimately resulted from the fact that Origen placed his interpretations of the baptismal faith so much at the service of his scientific explanation of the world. The cosmological perspective involved two problems in particular. First, Origen, although clearly distinguishing the Trinity from creatures, understood the eternal generation of the

---

[80] Cels VII 17.

[81] Cf. pp 50f. above and R. Seeberg, *Dogmengeschichte* I, p 526f.

[82] Cf. B. Studer, 'La résurrection de Jésus d'après le "Peri Archon" d'Origène', Augustinianum 18, 1978, pp 279–309, now *Dominus Salvator*, pp 213–50.

[83] CoIo X 37.245.

[84] Cf. HomLev VII 2; SerMt 70; Cels II 65; CoRom VII 3ff.

[85] Cf. F. Normann, *Christos Didaskalos,* and M. Harl, *Origène,* pp 243–68.

[86] Cf. CoMt XII 29. Also M. Harl, *Origène,* pp 279–85, 342.

[87] PA II 6.3; IV 4.4. Also M. Harl, *Origène,* pp 117f.

Son too much as a presupposition for an eternal creation. Secondly, he was not able to avoid the tendency to debase the reality of incarnation and to regard it merely as the means for man's spiritualization. Still, he not only advocated a Logos-mysticism, but also a Jesus-mysticism. As will be shown more precisely later on, this Logos-theology was of enormous influence for later theology. The following themes are particularly worthy of note: the foundation of the later trinitarian formula *mia ousia – treis hypostaseis;* the first steps towards the christological doctrine of the perichoresis of the two natures in Christ; the doctrine of the history of salvation as summed up in the mystery of the Logos; the doctrine of the Holy Spirit as the source of Christian freedom.

8. The Approach to Nicea

BIBLIOGRAPHY

W. Marcus, *Der Subordinatianismus,* Munich 1963.
F. Ricken, 'Nikaia als Krisis des altchristlichen Platonismus', TheolPhil 44, 1969, pp 321–41.
W. A. Bienert, *Dionysius von Alexandrien. Zur Frage des Origenismus im 3. Jahrhundert,* Berlin 1978.
A. M. Ritter, 'Arianismus, 3. Vorgeschichte' TRE 3, 1978, pp 694–8.
B. Studer, *Soteriologie der Kirchenväter,* pp 96–115.
A. Grillmeier, *Jesus der Christus im Glauben der Kirche* pp 283–99 (=*Christ in Christian Tradition,* pp 153–66).
F. Ricken, 'Zur Rezeption der platonischen Ontologie bei Eusebios von Kaisareia, Areios und Athanasios', TheolPhil 53, 1978, pp 321–52.
R. Lorenz, *Arius judaizans? Untersuchungen zur dogmengeschichtlichen Einordnung des Arius,* Göttingen 1979.
H. Dörrie, 'Die andere Theologie. Wie stellten die frühchristlichen Theologen des 2.–4. Jahrhunderts ihren Lesern die griechische Weisheit (=den Platonismus) dar?', TheolPhil 56, 1981, pp 1–46.
L. Abramowski, 'Dionys von Rom (+268) und Dionys von Alexandrien (+264/5) in den arianischen Streitigkeiten des 4.Jahrhunderts', ZKG 93, 1982, pp 240–72.
See also:
R. D. Williams, *Arius, Heresy and Tradition,* London 1987, pp 117–74.
M. Simonetti, 'L'Oriente dopo Origene', *Storia della Teologia,* pp 233–47.

With his Logos-theology, in which he endeavoured to give a valid Christian answer to the philosophical and religious concerns of his time, Origen exerted an enormous influence on posterity. Since, however, this reinterpretation of the traditional baptismal faith, which was centred on the Logos as mediator between God and the world, involved some risks for orthodoxy, a theological crisis could not be avoided in the long run. This crisis, which was to lead to the council of Nicea, was above all characterized by the antagonism between unitarian and trinitarian tendencies. These two options which take a different stand concerning the baptismal faith by and large coincide with a simplistic theology, which is averse to speculation, and a more scientific one, that is to say, with an anti-Origenist and an Origenist theology. In more recent research these two viewpoints are also labelled as Asiatic and Alexandrine theology respectively.[1] However,

---

[1] Esp. cf. M. Simonetti, 'Teologia alessandrina e teologia asiatica al concilio di Nicaea', Augustinianum 13, 1973, pp 363–98, and R. Cantalamessa, 'L'omelia "In S.Pascha"'.

these geographical terms could give occasion for misunderstanding. For in Asia Minor, and especially in Antioch, adherents of Origen are to be found. Therefore it would seem better to characterize these two theological tendencies as unitarian and trinitarian. The first school of thought may be regarded as a theology marked by the influence of the Jewish-Christian, Palestinian tradition, whereas the second may be considered as being of Hellenistic origin. For the rest, owing to the lack of documentation, it is not easy to get a precise idea of the theological trends which immediately preceded the council of Nicea.[2] Thus it is useful to recall the various motifs which in the first three centuries determined the development of trinitarian and christological doctrine and were in this way decisive for the period immediately preceding Nicea. In this way one can not only arrive at a better understanding of the second half of the third century, but also draw up a general picture of the beginnings of Christian theology.

I. THE SEARCH FOR A BALANCED DISTINCTION OF THE HYPOSTASES

Like the author of *C.Noetum,* Tertullian and Hippolytus of Rome, Origen surely performed a decisive service in the development of trinitarian dogma when he took his stand against modalistic tendencies among certain groups in the Church. The significance of this opposition to so-called patripassianism is still more evident from the following two considerations:

First, the problem of the distinction between Father and Son was tied up with the basis of trinitarian faith itself. For it refers back to the Easter experience in which the Trinity was essentially revealed. Thus this distinction was less about the relation of God with his creative Word in accordance with certain Old Testament testimonia, than about the relationship between the self-giving love of God and the self-giving obedience of Christ, as Paul and John both suggest. The stand against patripassianism was also related to the problem of the suffering and yet divine saviour, which was the crucial point of the apologetic endeavours. Finally, the Easter experience, which the post-apostolic Christians enacted in baptism, the eucharist and in the annual and weekly celebration of Easter, was also involved.

Secondly, the discussions about patripassianism could not be evaded if the invocation and worship of Christ was to be reconciled with the requirements of biblical and philosophical monotheism. This was particularly true of those groups that adhered less to the terminology of the baptismal faith and had a tendency to call Christ Father.[3]

The clear abrogation by Origen and the other antimonarchian theologians of patripassianism, which was largely approved of by those groups in the Church

[2] Cf. A. Grillmeier, *Jesus Christus,* pp 283–99, with bibl. (=*Christ in Christian Tradition,* pp 153–66).

[3] Cf. R. Cantalamessa, 'Il Cristo-Padre negli scritti del II-III secolo', RSLR 3, 1967, pp 1–27, and V. Grossi, 'Il titolo cristologico "Padre" nell' antichità cristiana', Augustinianum 16, 1976, pp 237–69.

which were less open to scientific theology, must be judged, particularly in the light of its prehistory, to have had a vast impact.[4] The difference between Father and Son thus became dogma, but this entailed two significant problems. First, the terminology, which was employed in this context by Origen and his adherents, lacked clarification. Too often, instead of speaking of three hypostases they spoke of three realities (*pragmata*) or three beings (*ousiai*) and thus appeared to regard Father, Son and Spirit as three entities entirely distinct from each other. Secondly, it was difficult to reconcile the unity of Father, Son and Spirit with the conception of God the Father as the sole principle, without improperly subordinating Son and Spirit to the Father. All the more so as in contemporary philosophy the One, the Spirit (*nous*) and the soul were understood as related hypostases which were nevertheless different in degree.[5]

Just how significant this twofold problem of a common terminology and of equalizing the position of Father, Son and Spirit was felt to be in the second half of the third century, is evident from an incident which involved Dionysius of Alexandria and Dionysius of Rome about 260.[6] As is apparent from a letter from the latter to the former (DS 112–115), and above all from later testimonies by Athanasius[7] and Basil,[8] certain groups accused the bishop of Alexandria of separating Father and Son, of denying the eternity of the Son, of speaking of the Father apart from the Son, of rejecting the *homoousios* and of describing the Son as a creature.[9] It was not too difficult for Dionysius to defend himself against these accusations. Still, Basil thinks Dionysius has carried his opposition against Sabellius too far.[10] At any rate, the fear of a Sabellian interpretation of the *homoousios* must have been the reason why he rejected this expression and, when urged by Rome, used it only with qualification.[11]

Like Dionysius the other bishops and teachers of Alexandria, such as Theognostus, Pierius and Peter the martyr, stood for the Origenist doctrine of the three hypostases and thus for the distinction between Father, Son and Spirit, even though not to the same extent.[12] The same is true of Lucian of Antioch, the teacher of Arius.[13] The extent to which their positions were determinative for the council of Nicea and the following discussions, must now be investigated more closely.

---

[4] Esp. cf. the statement of Pope Calixtus I against Sabellius in Hippolytus, Refut IX 12. See also the fairly trinitarian confession in the letter of Cornelius to Cyprian: ep 49.2: CSEL 3/1, 611.

[5] Cf. Plotinus' teaching on the three hypostases. Also H. Dörrie, 'Die andere Theologie', TheolPhil 56, 1981, pp 1–46, esp. p 30, also W. Ullmann, 'Die Beziehungen von Trinitätslehre und Christologie im 6. Buch von Origenes' Johanneskommentar', *Origeniana Secunda*, Bari 1980, pp 165–76.

[6] Cf. A. Grillmeier, *Jesus Christus*, pp 284–290 (=*Christ in Christian Tradition*, pp 153–9), also W. A. Bienert, *Dionysius*.

[7] Athanasius, De sententia Dionysii.

[8] Basil, ep. 9.

[9] Cf. L. W. Barnard's summary, 'The antecedents of Arius', VigChr 24, 1970, p 177, in A. Grillmeier, *Jesus Christus*, p 285 (=*Christ in Christian Tradition*, pp 156f).

[10] Basil, ep. 9.2.

[11] The question may be raised as to whether this third century debate on the homoousios is not a mere fiction of Athanasius designed for his argument with the homoiousians. Cf. L. Abramowski, 'Arianische Streitigkeiten im 4.Jh.', ZKG 93, 1982, pp 240–72.

[12] Cf. W. A. Bienert, *Dionysius*, pp 222f and R. Lorenz, *Arius judaizans?*, esp. pp 32f, 94–100.

[13] Cf. R. Lorenz, *Arius judaizans?*, pp 181–203.

II. THE BEGINNINGS OF THE LOGOS-SARX CHRISTOLOGY

The Logos-theology, founded by Justin and the other apologists and perfected by Origen, is certainly a scientific answer in the proper sense to the basic concerns of the Christians of the second and third centuries. With the doctrine of the omnipresent Logos a valid answer was found to the question of the possibility of salvation open to all men, Jews and pagans alike. At the same time this theology was able to give a deeper foundation to the unity of the history of Israel and that of the messianic community, already presupposed by Jesus and the apostles and to present the Christian faith, according to the aspirations of Christian intellectuals, as the true philosophy. Above all the Logos-theology allowed them to describe more definitely the nature of Christ as being at the same time divine and human. On the one hand, it expressed more clearly than Jewish Christian categories (Torah, angel, Spirit etc.) were able to do the pre-existence of Christ before all creation. On the other, it was capable of giving a better account of Johannine theology (which had become the canon within the canon, and according to which the pre-existent word of God had become flesh). It enabled them to emphasize that it was not a man, not an angel, but the Son of God himself who had redeemed mankind.[14]

Yet, a christology modelled on Logos-theology is by no means problem-free. First, it hardly refers to the Holy Spirit at all. In fact, the baptism of Jesus ranges low in importance. It does not matter to this theology that, when Jesus was baptized in the river Jordan, he was filled with the Holy Spirit in order to pass on this Spirit to all those who were to be baptized. It is by its appropriation by the Logos that the flesh is entirely filled with the divine life.[15] Still more serious is the difficulty that the Logos-theology necessarily had to face if the Logos-sarx pattern of St. John's prologue is understood entirely according to Greek premises, and the Logos, accordingly, is thus seen more or less openly as the principle of life of the man Jesus.[16]

This danger for Logos-theology surfaced for the first time in about 260.[17] At that time in Antioch two opposing christological tendencies clashed, which coincided with the abovementioned theological movements. On the one hand there was the unitarian, so-called Asiatic theology. As it intended to ascribe to God alone the whole work of salvation, it did not regard Christ as the Logos, i.e. the mediator between God and world, but rather as the firstborn among many brethren, as the one who has opened the way to God for men. This unitarian and at the same time adoptionist theology was represented above all by Paul of Samosata, who became bishop of Antioch in 260. According to him Jesus was inspired by the Logos, linked with him in a union (*synapheia*) of grace. The Word

---

[14] Cf IIClem 1.1f; Justin, Dial 26.1–14; Tertullian, Marc IV 22.11; also chapter 4 note 19 above.

[15] Cf. Dionysius of Alex., frag.: ed. Feltoe, pp 242f, cited in A. Grillmeier, *Jesus Christus*, p 295 (=*Christ in Christian Tradition*, pp 163f).

[16] Cf. R. Lorenz, *Arius judaizans?*, pp 211–15.

[17] Cf. A. Grillmeier, *Christ in Christian Tradition*, pp 164ff.

itself, like the Holy Spirit, he understood as a mere energy of the one God. Consequently he was condemned by a synod of Antioch (268/69).[18]

This synod was dominated by Origenist bishops who defended the other theological tendency. Their christological persuasion, however, is known only from a letter of bishop Hymenaeus of Jerusalem, which has come down to us only in fragmentary form, and the authenticity of which is not universally acknowledged, as well as from records of the council which are also extant only in fragments.[19] According to these the pre-existent Son of God was so united with man that Christ in his ousia is one and the same. His unity, therefore, may be compared with that of body and soul. That is why human attributes – birth, hunger and thirst, suffering – can be ascribed to the Word itself. Even the unity of Word and flesh can be understood in the same way as the relation of inner and outer man.[20] This practically excludes the human soul and thus human freedom. Contrary to Origen's ideas Jesus' human consciousness and his obedience to the Word are denied.[21]

So already in the third century the Christological drawbacks of the Logos-theology came to light, and they were to be overcome only about 400, in the course of the controversy between Antiochene and Alexandrine christology.[22] As, however, the christology of Cyprian of Carthage (+258) shows, even at that time a christology of pre-existence could be upheld, which did not call in question the human in Christ.[23]

In fact, around the middle of the third century, the African martyr-bishop developed a christology, which clearly acknowledges the divine in Christ without forgetting that the man Jesus was our master and teacher.[24] Also the numerous allusions to the coming judge and to the presence of Christ in the Church do not detract from the human in Christ.[25] On the contrary, when dealing with these two basic themes he expresses the fact that the glory of Christ is rooted in his historical act of salvation.[26] This is especially apparent in Cyprian's eucharistic teaching. According to this Christians in the eucharist really receive the body and blood of Christ, because in it the remembrance of Christ's Passion is celebrated, and the priest acts as the representative of Christ.[27]

[18] Cf. Eusebius, HE VII 29f; also M. Richard, 'Malchion et Paul de Samosate. Le témoignage d'Eusèbe de Césarée', EThL 35, 1959, pp 325–38 (=OpMin 2, Turnhout 1977, n. 25).

[19] Cf. A. Grillmeier, *Jesus Christus*, p 297 note 43 (for bibl.) (=*Christ in Christian Tradition*, pp 165 note 43).

[20] Cf. H. de Riedmatten, *Les actes de procès de Paul de Samosate*, Fribourg 1952, p 147: frag. p. 22ff. On the criticism of these texts see A. Grillmeier, *Jesus Christus*, pp 297f (=*Christ in Christian, Tradition* p 165). Even though these texts may turn out to be false or reworked in the sense of Apollinarianism, it can nevertheless be maintained that by 300 Jesus' inner life was hardly taken into account. Cf. R. Lorenz, *Arius judaizans?*, pp 211–22.

[21] Cf. Origen, PA II 6.3.

[22] Cf. chapter 15 below.

[23] Cf. B. Studer, *Soteriologie*, pp 96–106, and T. Kaczmarek, '"Sacramentum Christi" nell'insegnamento di s. Cipriano', Rome 1983.

[24] Cf. Cyprian, Orat 2; 8; 11; 29; ep. 58.1f.

[25] Esp. cf. Patient 6–9: on the example of Jesus.

[26] Cf. Patient 23f. on the twofold adventus; Orat 34: on Jesus' suffering; OpEl 1: on Christ's saving work.

[27] Cf. ep. 63, esp. 63.14 and 17.

The same applies even more to the christology of Lactantius.[28] Starting from his typical Roman premises this Latin rhetor emphasizes that only the God-man could mediate between God and man.[29] For Lactantius Christ is primarily teacher of justice (*magister iustitiae*), leader to virtue (*dux virtutis*) and victor over death (*victor mortis*). All this, however, he could only be because he is God and man together. Only as God was he able authoritatively to proclaim justice, and only as man was he able to serve mankind as the example of justice, i.e. of virtue which holds out till death.[30] A mere man, on the other hand, would not have been capable of leading the weak flesh to immortality. God made man, on the other hand, could lead the way for weak flesh and thus liberate it from death that ruled over the flesh. He was able to help the flesh to that perfect virtue which is to be crowned with immortality.[31] It could be argued that the soteriological teaching of Lactantius, as well as that of Cyprian, elucidates too little the union of the divine and human. The soteriological significance of this union, however, is clearly expressed by the statement that only Christ as God *and* man could be the source of eternal *salus*.[32]

III. THE CRISIS OF THE COSMOLOGICAL LOGOS-THEOLOGY

Even though the Logos-theology – at least in Justin – had not at first been designed to give an explanation of the relation between God and world, but rather confined itself to giving an answer to the question of universal salvation, it gradually came to be dominated by the cosmological perspective.[33] This can be easily understood if the following three facts are considered. First, the Old Testament testimonia, through which the pre-existence of the saviour of all mankind was to be proved, were by and large connected with the issue of creation. So, above all, Proverbs 8:22ff and Genesis 1:1–3.[34] Further, the New Testament basis for the Logos-theology is also cosmological in character. Even though St. John's prologue, Colossians 1:3–23 and Hebrews 1:1–3 were not immediately used as testimonia in the second century, they nevertheless show how much the Christian tradition was inclined to regard Christ as Word and Wisdom not only in the sense of a mediator of divine revelation, but also in the sense of the beginning of creation.[35] This was – and this is the third fact – suggested by the cosmological

---

[28] Cf. B. Studer, *Soteriologie*, pp 106–15.

[29] Cf. Lactantius, Instit IV 25: main soteriological passage.

[30] Cf. Instit IV 11.14; IV 24.18f. Also Instit IV 10.1, IV 11.7; IV 12.15.

[31] Cf. Instit IV 25.6ff.

[32] Cf. Instit IV 12.6f: Jesus signifying salvator.

[33] In this respect Athenagoras and Theophilus go beyond Justin. Cf. above pp. 5Qff.

[34] On the Christian exegesis of these texts cf. M. Simonetti, *Studi sull'Arianesimo*, pp 9–87, and P. Vignaux, ed., *In Principio. Interprétations des premiers versets de la Genèse*, Paris 1973.

[35] Theophilus, Autol II 22, is the first to clearly refer to St. John's prologue. On the cosmological background of these Old Testament texts see A. Grillmeier, *Jesus Christus*, pp 96–132 (=*Christ in Christian Tradition*, pp 23–32).

climate of the first two Christian centuries. Apart from the fact that the correlation between the history of salvation and creation is constitutive of the Old Testament itself as Genesis 1–11, Isaiah and Baruch show, Jewish as well as Greek circles were at that time already very interested in cosmology. This is proved first of all by Philo of Alexandria's commentaries on Genesis as well as by the Gnostic speculations, particularly those in which the basic philosophical question of the relation of the One to the Many was determinative.[36]

This extremely close link between christology and cosmology, which gradually became constitutive of Logos-theology from Justin onwards, could not remain unchallenged in the long run. It is very unlikely, though, that at that time there was a consciousness of the extent to which the *per quem omnia facta sunt* had become preponderant over against faith in Christ, who was obedient to death, and therefore in the resurrection acknowledged as Son of God. Even the theological difficulties of the Logos-theology, connected though they were with their philosophical counterpart, were hardly sensed. The hellenistic conceptions of the Logos as the second and visible God were scarcely criticized. The conflict, however, between the Biblically based doctrine of *creatio ex nihilo* and those opinions which saw the generation of the Logos as connected with God's will to create the world could not remain hidden.

In fact, during the second century it was clearly and expressly worked out that God has created the whole world out of nothing.[37] In this context it was already maintained that the Logos has neither emerged from nothing, nor from the material world, but out of God's *ousia,* a statement to which Theophilus of Antioch already comes very close, and which is fully confirmed by Origen.[38] Origen also makes an unambiguous distinction between incorporeal Trinity and corporeal creation,[39] but does not pursue this very consistently. He distinguishes the generation of the Son which takes place within the adorable and incorporeal Trinity, in a wholly spiritual sphere, from the creation of the non-divine world in a way that is not entirely free from misunderstanding: what hindered him was his conceptions of eternal creation.[40]

This development of the Christian doctrine of *creatio ex nihilo* proved to be all the more unfortunate for the Logos-theology, for at that time certain philosophers began to discuss the problem of eternal creation.[41] Atticus (2nd century) had already rejected the Aristotelian thesis of the eternity of the world.[42] The common Platonist tradition still held to it in the second and third centuries. However, the mere fact that the conception of the eternity of the world was no longer universally upheld in philosophical circles encouraged Christian authors in their criticism of it.

[36] Cf. P. Heinisch, *Der Einfluß Philos auf die älteste christliche Exegese,* Münster 1908.

[37] Cf. G. May, *Schöpfung aus dem Nichts.*

[38] Cf. Theophilus, Autol II 22; Origen PA I 2.2; I 2.6.

[39] Cf. PA II 2.2, IV 3.15.

[40] Cf. PA I 2.10 (not in Rufinus – cf. H. Görgemanns and H. Karpp, p 145 note 33); PA I 4.3f.

[41] Cf. H. Dörrie, 'Die andere Theologie', TheolPhil 56, 1981, pp 1–46.

[42] Atticus, in Eusebius, PraepEv XV 6; also H. Dörrie, art. cit. pp 34f; *Logos-Religion oder Nous-Theologie. Die hauptsächlichen Aspekte des kaiserzeitlichen Platonismus:* Festschrift C. de Vogel, Assen 1975, pp 115–36.

Together with the changes on the cosmological horizon, which round about 300 was apparently more and more determined by the Christian teaching of *creatio ex nihilo,* the presuppositions for a new understanding of the mediatorship of the Logos were created. The Logos could no longer simply be placed between God and the world as Origen under the influence of middle Platonic philosophy had done.[43] On the contrary, a decision had to be made as to whether the Logos through whom all things are made should be assigned to the divine sphere of the creator or to the created world. In other words: the Logos-theology, as developed on the basis of wisdom-literature and middle Platonic philosophy by the apologists and above all by Origen, experienced a crisis. Arius, as will be shown more precisely later on, is to assign the Logos clearly to creation, this contention being based on the traditional exegesis of Proverbs 8:22 and reinforced by a rigid use of the middle Platonic conception of a second God. The council of Nicea and Nicene theology, on the other hand, will defend faith in Christ, the only-begotten Son of the creator, and thus begin expressly to differentiate the economic from the immanent Trinity.[44]

In a survey of the whole development of Christian theology during the first three centuries and especially of the theological movements before the turn of the third century, the results of these first endeavours to understand the mystery of Christ, and the questions which still remained open, may be described as follows.

The baptismal faith, which derives from the apostolic tradition, is made more precise in that the Son and the Spirit are not only clearly distinguished from the Father but also clearly united with him so far as their being and activity are concerned. As far as the Son is concerned, he is acknowledged as the Logos, which is spiritually generated before all time, and thus is the principle of creation and revelation.[45] The divinity of the Spirit, however, which is characterised primarily as the principle of prophecy and as messianic gift, is given less emphasis.[46] Finally, the unity of the Son and the Spirit with the Father is understood from their common activity, which originates in the Father and leads back through the Son in the Holy Spirit to the Father.[47]

This whole process of clarifying the baptismal faith happened first of all as the result of a salvation-historical perspective, even though attention begins to be directed to the divine, eternal being of Father, Son and Spirit. This is also apparent in the various ways in which the saving work of Christ is described, and it is presupposed throughout that he was able only as God and man to be mediator between his Father and his brethren. Among the various soteriological functions, those of revelation (Word and teacher)[48] and that of the victory over the devil and

---

[43] Cf. Origen, PA I 2.2ff, I 4.5; I 7.1 etc.

[44] Cf. the various studies by F. Ricken, esp. 'Nikaia als Krisis des altchristlichen Platonismus' TheolPhil 44, 1969, pp 321–41, and W. Marcus, *Der Subordinatianismus.*

[45] This is true of the apologists, Irenaeus, Tertullian and Origen.

[46] So esp. Justin, cf. chapter 4, note 67, and Origen, PA I 3.1–8.

[47] Cf. Irenaeus, Demonstr 5ff, and Origen, PA I 3.1.7f.

[48] This theme is connected with Greek intellectualism, but also with Jewish-Christian apocalyptic thought and even with the biblical conception of the word of God, which makes itself known in the law and in the prophets.

the demons are given particular attention.[49] Regarding this it is particularly clear that Christ must be God and man in order to be the saviour of all men by word and example, and by power and participation in human weakness.

Even though the one, and at the same time threefold, work, that is confessed in the baptismal faith, is chiefly seen in its salvation-historical context, its ontological foundations begin to gain attention. However, a clear and express distinction between the economic and the immanent Trinity has not yet been reached. Although the apocalyptic opposition of the two aeons, as well as the hellenistic conception which restricts the power of deification to divine beings, pointed the way to that distinction, the divine plurality remained too bound up with history. The generation of the Son is still seen more or less as the prerequisite of creation.[50] The procession of the Spirit, in so far as it is taken into consideration at all, is defined more closely only with regard to sanctification as acting *per filium.*[51]

The understanding of the incarnation of Christ corresponds to this. As the difference between economic and immanent trinity is presupposed rather than made explicit, so also here person and work are hardly distinguished. Still, such a difference is distinctly anticipated in the teaching about the christological titles (*epinoiai*).[52] A predilection here for the divine titles is, however, not to be misunderstood.[53] In such a context it is no surprise that in the elucidation of the person of Christ the scheme of Logos-sarx could arise, in which the pre-existence and the subjective unity of Christ could easily be safeguarded, while what is human in Christ, above all the human soul of Jesus, was neglected or even denied.

The extent to which the baptismal faith was clarified in the first three centuries – without solving all the questions at stake – is shown by the position that trinitarian and christological terminology had reached by about 300. As far as the Trinity is concerned, a formula is needed which would express divine unity and plurality together. Origen and his adherents may speak of three hypostases.[54] But, quite apart from the vagueness of this term, it did not remain unchallenged. The unity of God is felt to be endangered when this term is applied to Father, Son and Spirit.[55] Also the term *trias,* in Latin *trinitas,* which has already become conventional, only refers to the plurality, not to the unity. In this respect the antithesis of Tertullian: *tres cohaerentes – una substantia* proves to be more complete.[56] But even this formula lacks precision, quite apart from the fact that Tertullian did not apply the term *substantia* to the Son and the Spirit in the same

---

[49] Cf. chapter 3.

[50] Cf. Theophilus, Autol I 22; Tertullian, Prax 5f; Origen, PA I 2.2; Novatian, Trin 84; 184; 190.

[51] Esp. cf. Origen, PA I 3.7.

[52] Cf. A. Grillmeier, *Jesus Christus,* p 270 (=*Christ in Christian Tradition,* p 141): the names of Jesus signifying his essence and function, with the reference to Origen, CoIo I 20.

[53] First of all the title of 'Son' in the sense of baptismal faith and that of 'Logos' with its philosophical implications gained acceptance.

[54] Cf. Origen, CoIo II 10.75. Also M. Simonetti, *La crisi ariana,* esp. pp 11f, 16f, 30, 60f.

[55] Cf. the Sabellian reaction, which is also partly shared by the hierarchy. Also A. Grillmeier, *Jesus Christus,* pp 283–7 (=*Christ in Christian Tradition,* pp 153–7).

[56] Cf. Tertullian, Prax 25.1. In this text, however, the distinction between the tres cohaerentes (=tres personae) and una substantia has not yet arrived at the short formula. Cf. Prax 2.4; 12.6f; 26.9.

way as he did to the Father (*summa-portio*).[57] What is more, it cannot be excluded from consideration – as the incident with the two Dionysii bears witness – that already in the third century difficulty was felt of describing the same thing in Greek and Latin terms. The same is more or less true of christology. The Greeks, too, have not found a formula which could define distinction and unity together.[58] Even here Tertullian seems at first sight to have made more progress with his formula *duplex status – una persona*.[59] But, apart from the fact that the *una persona* cannot be fully understood in a christological sense, Tertullian does not clearly indicate on what the unity of the two substances is based. In effect, he merely juxtaposes them. So the state of theological terminology confirms that the endeavours towards a faithful understanding of baptismal faith have attained substantial results in the first three centuries, although this cannot be regarded as a comprehensive clarification of all the relevant questions.

[57] Cf. Tertullian, Prax 9.2f, also Prax 3.5.
[58] So it is characteristic of Origen and his followers to employ ousia, hypostasis and physis in more or less the same sense. See R. Seeberg, *Dogmengeschichte* I, pp 511 and 518f.
[59] Cf. Tertullian, Prax 27.11.

PART TWO
The Nicene Turning Point

BIBLIOGRAPHY

A. Spindeler, *Cur Verbum caro factum? Das Motiv der Menschwerdung und das Verhältnis der Erlösung zur Menschwerdung in den christologischen Glaubenskämpfen des 4. und 5. Jahrhunderts*, Paderborn 1938.

M. Simonetti, *Studi sull'arianesimo*, Rome 1965.

R. Lorenz, *Das 4. bis 6. Jahrhundert (Westen)* (=Die Kirche in ihrer Geschichte I/C.1), Göttingen 1970.

H. Jedin and J. Dolan, eds., *History of the Church*, vol. 2: *The Imperial Church from Constantine to the Early Middle Ages*, London 1981.

M. Simonetti, *La crisi ariana nell'IV secolo*, Rome 1975.

F. Dinsen, 'Homousios. Die Geschichte des Begriffs bis zum Konzil von Konstantinopel', thesis: Kiel 1976.

C. Pietri, *Roma Christiana*, Rome 1976 (with bibl.).

A. de Halleux, 'La réception du symbole oecuménique, de Nicée à Chalcédoine', EThL 61, 1985, pp 5–47 (cf. RThLouv 15, 1984, pp 275–96).

See also:

R. P. C. Hanson, *The Search for the Christian Doctrine of God. The Arian Controversy 318–381*, Edinburgh 1988.

Th. Böhm, *Die Christologie des Arius* (Studien zur Theologie und Geschichte 7), St. Ottilien 1991 (with bibl.).

B. Studer, 'La situazione ecclesiale', *Storia della Teologia*, pp 307–20.

9. Nicea – Starting Point for a New Theology

BIBLIOGRAPHY

E. Boularand, *L'hérésie d'Arius et la 'foi' de Nicée*, Paris 1972.

F. Dinsen, 'Homousios. Die Geschichte des Begriffs bis zum Konzil von Konstantinopel (381)' thesis, Kiel 1976.

A. de Halleux, 'Dieu le Père tout-puissant', RThLouv 8, 1977, pp 401–22.

G. C. Stead, *Divine Substance*, Oxford 1977.

A. M. Ritter, 'Arianismus', TRE 3, 1978, pp 692–719. (The bibl. presents a useful summary of recent research.)

R. Lorenz, *Arius judaizans? Untersuchungen zur dogmengeschichtlichen Einordnung des Arius*, Göttingen 1979.

F. Ricken, 'Platonische Ontologie als Interpretament des christlichen Kerygmas im Umkreis von Nikaia', thesis, Innsbruck 1979/80 (cf. ZKTh 102, 1980, pp 503f, and esp. TheolPhil 44, 1969, pp 321–41; 53, 1978, pp 321–52).

Y. Congar, 'Le monothéisme politique et le Dieu-Trinité', NRTh 103, 1981, pp 3–17.

R. C. Gregg and D. E. Groh, *Early Arianism. A View of Salvation*, Philadelphia 1981 (cf. AThR 59, 1977, 260–75).

R. Lorenz, 'Eustathius von Antiochien', TRE 10, 1982, pp 543–6.

D. S. Wallace-Hadrill, 'Eusebius von Caesarea', TRE 10, 1982, pp 537–543.

R. Lorenz, 'Die Christusseele im arianischen Streit', ZKG 94, 1943, pp 1–51.

See also manuals of the history of dogma and of the Church, and esp. studies on Constantine the Great, such as H. Kraft, *Konstantin der Große*, Darmstadt 1974.

See also:

D. S. Wallace-Hadrill, *Eusebius of Caesarea*, London 1960.

N. H. Baynes, *Constantine the Great and the Christian Church*, London [2]1972, with a preface by H. Chadwick.

R. D. Williams, *Arians, Heresy and Tradition*, London 1987.

O. Skarsaune, 'A Neglected Detail in the Creed of Nicea (325)', VigChr 41, 1987, pp 34–54. (This study confirms the views defended in the following chapter.)

G. Feige, *Die Lehre Markells von Ankyra in der Darstellung seiner Gegner* (Erfurter Theologische Studien 58), Leipzig 1991.

G. Feige, *Markell von Ankyra und das Konzil von Nizäa (325): Denkender Glaube in Geschichte und Gegenwart* (Erfurter Theologische Studien 63), Leipzig 1992, pp 277–96 (important for the historical valuation of Nicea).

The council of Nicea may with good reason be regarded as signalling a new era of Church history. In fact, it marks the beginning of a close co-operation between the Churches of early Christianity and the Roman empire, which was to bring about unforeseeable consequences for all fields of ecclesiastical life.[1] As far as the more outward aspect is concerned, a structure was fashioned at that time which resembled a good deal that of the civil organization of the empire, out of which the five great patriarchates were to emerge. As regards the more inward aspect, liturgy, preaching, theology and Christian spirituality were all refashioned and moulded by an increasing openness towards the political and cultural outlook of the Constantinian era. This openness included laying the foundations of Christian orthodoxy which was orientated towards *salus publica*, and which was to form the basis of all Christian confessions from the end of the fourth century onwards.

The orthodox faith, settled at Nicea for the first time for the whole of Christianity, at first only had reference to the divinity of Christ. However, this definition subsequently proved decisive for faith in the true divinity of the Holy Spirit, and in consequence also pointed the way towards a formulation of faith in the one Lord Jesus Christ, true God and true man. Even soteriology, the doctrine of the work of Christ, was not left untouched by the Nicene faith. Furthermore, Nicene orthodoxy made a deep impact on the worship of the Church and in Christian spirituality. So it is not too much to regard Nicea as the starting point of a new theology and to label as the Nicene era the fourth century in particular, in which the faith of Nicea gradually became the common confession to all Christians. Similar reasons justify the decision to use the heading 'Nicene Turning Point' for the second part of this introduction to the faith of the early Church.

I. THE SOLUTION OF THE ORIGENIST CRISIS

1. Historical survey

About 320 a theological dispute arose in Alexandria, initiated by Arius, a presbyter of the Church there, which therefore has come to be known in the history of dogma as the Arian controversy. But apart from the fact that the dispute between Arius and his bishop Alexander became quickly widespread, it would be more appropriate to speak of a crisis in Origen's Logos-Theology, or simply of the Origenist crisis of the beginning of the fourth century.

In fact, at the time of Nicea there were two opposing theological strands, represented, to oversimplify somewhat, by the followers and opponents of Origen. The Origenist tendency, which goes back to the third-century Alexandrine theologians, but was also influenced by Lucian of Antioch, Arius' teacher, was represented by three groups: by Arius and his friends, by the supporters of Eusebius of Caesarea and by the moderate Origenists under Alexander of Alexandria. Common to them was the acceptance of the Origenist doctrine of the hypostases as well as a strongly cosmologically orientated theology of the Logos. The anti-Origenist tendency, which, however, only

---

[1] Cf. A. M. Ritter, 'Das Konzil von Nizäa und sein Dogma', C. Andresen, ed., *Dogmengeschichte* I, pp 166ff.

emerges only after the council, was led by Eustathius of Antioch and Marcellus of Ancyra and supported by the Western bishops. Following in the footsteps of a monarchian theology they thought in terms of one hypostasis and thus rejected the Origenist approach to Trinitarian doctrine. The effect this second movement had during the sessions of the Nicene Synod itself, is difficult to trace from the rather poor and and even biased reports that are still accessible.

The crisis broke out within Origenist theology itself. In developing further Origen's theology of Logos, Arius placed the Logos on the side of creation, thus blurring the difference between the eternal generation of the Son and the creation of all things. Alexander, on the other hand, in opposition to him upheld Christ's eternal divinity. For his purpose he required the help, in terms of ecclesiastical policy, of the anti-Origenists. Therefore he allied himself with them, while at the same time standing in the tradition of the great Alexandrine teacher. So there are two grounds for referring to an Origenist crisis: first, because Origen's conception of the Logos-mediator was disputed among his own adherents; secondly, because this intra-Origenist debate aroused the opposition of the monarchian-orientated theology against the Origenist doctrine of three hypostases, or at the very least exarcerbated it.

This twofold Origenist crisis, however, was not actually solved at the synod of Nicea, which was convoked and presided over by Constantine. First, in Antioch shortly before the council a preliminary decision was reached. The bishops who gathered there in 324/25 already confessed the 'only-begotten Son', 'begotten of the Father', and saw in him the 'image of the paternal hypostasis itself'.[2] Secondly, the decision which was made by the fathers under the presidency of Constantine at Nicea in 325 was to be accepted by all the churches of the empire only after a complicated process of reception, which disturbed Christians, particularly in the east, for decades.

2. The Nicene dogma: Jesus Christ, Son of God and Creator

When the first imperial synod interfered in the doctrinal debate which had broken out in Alexandria, in order to restore peace among the bishops, it took its stand essentially in opposition to Arius. Their creed (DS 125) and the attached anathemas (DS 126), were obviously polemically orientated, only later did they take on the sense of a positive formulation of the norm of faith; at any rate the testimony of Athanasius points in this direction.[3] Therefore it is necessary to consider, even if briefly, how and why Arius developed the Origenist teaching about the Logos, thus provoking the reaction of his bishop who was concerned about the co-eternity of the Son.

By the turn of the century a new theological attitude to the concept of *creatio ex nihilo* had emerged in the apologetics directed against the pagans, probably also under the influence of philosophical discussion. This made it urgent

---

[2] Cf. EpSynod: Opitz no. 18.11; also L. Abramowski, 'Die Synode von Antiochien (324/25) und ihr Symbol', ZKG 86, 1975, pp 356–67.

[3] Cf. H. J. Sieben, *Konzilsidee*, p 513.

to give an unambiguous answer to the question still left open in Origen's cosmology, governed as it was by the problem of the One and the Many: that is, whether the Logos was to be placed on the side of creation or of the Creator. Arius himself decided for the first option. According to him the pre-existent Logos cannot be equal to the Father, who alone is uncreated; thus he cannot possibly have come out of the being of the Father. He was rather created out of nothing like all creatures. However, he is the first creature; he was created before time, while the other creatures came into being through him in time. In short, he is only a secondary God, not without beginning like the Father.[4]

In justifying his conception of the creatureliness of the Son, Arius sought to remain entirely on the ground of Holy Scripture. Apart from referring to Jesus' baptismal commission (Matt 28:19f), he primarily based his argument on Proverbs 8:22ff, according to which the divine wisdom was created by God before all creation. He also understood the theophanies of the Logos in the Old Testament to prove that he has come into being. He was also able to back his reference to scripture by the traditional exegesis of the relevant texts. Decisive, however, was the philosophical, and (perhaps even more) the soteriological background of his theology. Accordingly, the Logos, although the principle of all things, as primary duality, could never possibly partake fully in the primary monad which is the Godhead – quite apart from the fact that any kind of generating is to be excluded from the wholly unchangeable God. On the other hand, the central idea of Arius' preaching – that the Logos has become flesh in order to be the model of all God's children and the example of enduring obedience – in principle made it impossible to grant him equal status with the unchangeable God.[5]

The council of Nicea, however, in its creed, which was shaped like a baptismal symbol, countered the Arian thesis that the Logos was a creature with faith in Christ who stands wholly on the side of the creator. Accordingly, the one Lord Jesus Christ is the Son of God. This basic assumption can be expressed more precisely, in biblical and at the same time philosophical terms, by saying that as the 'only begotten' he is generated *out* of the Father, that is to say, out of the Father's essence (*ousia*), and is thus true God. He was generated, not created. Therefore, according to his essence he is equal to the Father (*homoousios*), and all things in heaven and earth have come into being through him (DS 125). As is further explained antithetically in the following anathemas, it must not be held of the Son that he has begun to exist at a certain point of time, neither that he comes out of nothing, nor out of another being (*hypostasis* or *ousia*), nor that he has been created, is changeable or mutable (DS 126).

[4] Cf. esp. Arius, ep. ad Eusebium: Opitz no. 1.2; creed: Opitz no. 6.2f; Thalia, in Athanasius, Synod 15.3: Opitz II/1, pp 242ff. For the philosophical background see E. P. Meijering, 'ÉN POTE HOTI OUK ÉN HO HUIOS. A Discussion on Time and Eternity', VigChr 28, 1974, pp 161–9 (reprinted in: id., *God Being History*, Amsterdam – Oxford – New York, 1975, pp 81–8), as well as F. Ricken, 'Platonische Ontologie als Interpretament des christlichen Kerygmas im Umkreis von Nikaia', thesis, Innsbruck 1979/80 (cf. ZKTh 102, 1980, pp 503f), and R. Lorenz, 'Die Christusseele', ZKG 94, 1983, pp 46ff.

[5] Cf. ep. Alexandri: Opitz, no. 14.11–14.

If the letter of Eusebius to his community in Caesarea, which has come down to us through Athanasius, is reliable, the members of the council of Nicea found the generation of the Son and his having no beginning especially difficult to understand.[6] This confirms that in spite of their granting priority to the Father they were concerned to distinguish the true sonship of Christ clearly from all creatureliness, and at the same time from any sonship of God by grace. Anyhow, the way in which the defenders of the Nicene faith then came to argue, first of all Athanasius, but also Hilary and Basil, is highly significant. They not only took care to emphasize the incomprehensibility of the eternal generation of the Son. They also sought to distinguish it from adoption in particular by means of their distinction between the 'only-begotten' and the 'first-begotten'.[7] They also stressed the soteriological argument, according to which one and the same has created us out of nothing and redeemed us from sin, and only the true God is able to divinize man.[8] Finally they were fond of indicating that Christ is to be worshipped only if he is truly God like the Father, and that in particular baptism in his name can only occur if this requirement is satisfied.[9]

3. The formulation of the Nicene faith

In the Nicene Creed the doctrine of the only Son of God is more closely defined by means of two expressions of a philosophical, or rather, technical kind: 'out of the Father's ousia' and 'homoousios with the Father'(DS 125). The anathemas, in addition, contain the formula which states that the Son is neither derived out of another hypostasis, nor out of a different ousia (from that of the Father) (DS 126).

Even though the expression homoousios is closely connected with that of 'out of the ousia of the Father' in a historical as well as a material respect, it still became highly significant in its own right. When from about 350 Athanasius increasingly came to identify the language of the Nicene Creed itself with the norm of the orthodox faith,[10] an intense discussion on the dogmatic value of the homoousios flared up, which was not settled until the reconciliation of the strict Nicenes and the so-called homoiousians in the year 362.[11] On the other hand the homoousios is the focal point of attention of modern research on the Nicene faith. Even today historians of Church dogma do not agree on its origin and meaning.[12]

---

[6] Cf. ep. Eusebii, Opitz no. 22.7.16; also Athanasius, Decret 19: Opitz II/1, pp 15f.

[7] Cf. Athanasius, CAr II 21: MG 26, 189C; II 61f: MG 26, 277; Basil CEunom II 23: MG 29, 624A; Basil(?) IV 3: MG 29, 701Bff; Gregory of Nyssa CEunom 4: MG 45, 363C, 639D; Diodore, ExplPs 109, CPG II, 3818; Eutherius, 5th cent., CPG III, 6147; Confut 18: ed. Tetz pp 34ff; also the Serdican formula: Hahn §157, and Athanasius, Vita Antonii 69.3; MG 26, 941 AB, Tom Antioch 7: MG 26, 804A–805A. For the whole issue cf. A. Grillmeier, Jesus Christus, pp 102–21, esp. 114 note 336 and 119 note 358 (=Christ in Christian Tradition, pp 20–6).

[8] Cf. Athanasius, Incarn 40.5 with Isa 63:9; CAr II 69f; III 63; Basil, Spir 28.69.

[9] Cf. Athanasius, Incarn 49.6; CAr I.34; Basil Spir 10.24; 29.75; Didymus (?), Trin I 34: MG 39, 437A.

[10] Cf. H. J. Sieben, Konzilsidee, pp 40–52.

[11] Cf. Athanasius, TomAntioch. MG 26, 796–809.

[12] A. M. Ritter, 'Nizäa', C. Andresen, Dogmengeschichte I, pp 169ff. For a survey of the research see id., TRE 3, 1978, p 706. G. C. Stead, Divine Substance, pp 250f, and esp. F. Dinsen, 'Homoousios. Die Geschichte des Begriffs bis zum Konzil von Konstantinopel', thesis, Kiel 1976.

Still the most plausible explanation is that the *homoousios* was inserted into the creed, which greatly resembled a baptismal symbol though it was in fact the text of a synod, because Arius himself had rejected it in order to exclude the generation of the Son, which in his view was unworthy of God.[13] Ambrose already understood it in this way.[14]

Two points, however, are certain. First, the fathers of the council felt obliged to secure the biblical language of the baptismal faith by means of technical expressions, primarily by means of *homoousios*. At any rate, Athanasius later on stressed that the biblical means of expression were insufficient.[15] His explanation was confirmed by the restless search for ever-new formulae of faith, which lasted from the death of Constantine (337) till 360, without arriving at a decisive result.[16] No less clear than this formal point is the content of the formula '*homoousios* with the Father'. On the one hand, the synod intended to express by means of this expression not the uniqueness of the divine substance but rather Christ's true divinity. As a parallel to the formula 'out of the Father's *ousia*', which is indebted to the Alexandrine tradition,[17] and in contradiction to the condemned formula 'out of another being' (DS 126), the *homoousios* cannot be understood as meaning 'one in essence' but only as meaning 'equal in essence'. This is also in line with the statements of Alexander, who speaks of the perfect likeness of the Son,[18] and, moreover, refers to the theology of the image, which is basic to the Nicene doctrine.[19] Nor is this affected by the fact that soon after the Council the unitarian party of Marcellus of Ancyra and the Origenist theologians under the leadership of Eusebius of Caesarea were in fierce combat;[20] for this combat certainly revolved around the question of one or three hypostases, and not around the *homoousios*.[21] In this context it is very instructive to note that the most unitarian creed, that of the 'western' synod of Serdica (342/43), expresses most uncompromisingly the uniqueness of the hypostasis, whereas it does not mention either the *homoousios* or 'out of the Father's *ousia*'.[22] Even the *Expositio fidei*, which is difficult to date, the sole concern of which is to counter the Sabellian *monoousios* with the Nicene *homoousios*, not only speaks of the 'Father's image, worthy of the same honour', but also of the Son as having a perfect likeness to the

[13] Cf. F. Ricken, 'Nikaia als Krisis des altchristlichen Platonismus', TheolPhil 44, 1969, pp 321–41.

[14] Ambrose, Fid III 15.125, with an allusion to Eusebius of Nicomedia.

[15] Athanasius, Decret 19: Opitz II/1, pp 15f, also F. Ricken, art. cit.: TheolPhil 44, 1969, pp 333f, as well as M. Simonetti, *La crisi ariana*, pp 88–95.

[16] Cf. J. Daniélou and H. Marrou, *The Christian Centuries*, I, pp 255ff.

[17] Cf. R. Lorenz, *Arius judaizans?*, pp 72–5, with Origen, CoIo frag. 9, and Theognostos, frag.2 = Athanasius, Decret 25.2: Opitz II/1, pp 20f, and p 208, with Eusebius Caes., DemEv V 1.20; cf. also Eccl.Theol II 14.

[18] Alexander, ep. ad episcopos: Opitz no. 4b,13; ep. ad Alex. Thess.: Opitz no. 14,38.47.52.

[19] Cf. besides Alexander, ep. ad Alex.Thess.: Opitz, no. 14.47, the confession of Lucian of Antioch: Hahn §154; the EpSynod of Antioch: Opitz, no. 18.10, as well as Eusebius Caes., DemEv IV 3.

[20] Cf. esp. Eusebius Caes., EcclTheol, CPG II, 3478.

[21] The homoousios occurs neither in the undoubtedly genuine fragments of Eusthatius of Antioch, nor in Marcellus of Ancyra. Cf. M. Simonetti, *La crisi ariana*, p 148, as well as F. Dinsen, 'Homoousios', pp 73 and 76; also L. Abramowski, 'Dionys von Rom (+268) and Dionys von Alexandrien (+264/65) in den arianischen Streitigkeiten des 4.Jahrhunderts', ZKG 93, 1982, pp 240–72.

[22] Serdican formula in Hahn §157.

Father.[23] On the other hand, *homoousios* expresses the full equality of the Son with the Father as based on the eternal generation. Precisely for this reason, Arius and Eusebius of Nicomedia had already rejected the *homoousios* before the council,[24] and during the synod itself it was a bone of contention.[25] The interrelation between equality of nature and natural origin is confirmed as being fundamental by the synonymous use of *homophyes* and *homogenes*, concepts which are encountered in Eusebius and above all in Athanasius' defence of the *homoousios*.[26]

To sum up, according to the Nicene faith Christ is true God because he is the true Son of God. To put it more technically: He is the *monogenes*, because his *ousia* is derived from the Father; and as he is begotten out of the Father and not created, his *ousia* is equal to that of the Father. In consequence, he is co-eternal with the Father, and as the Son, who is born out of the Father (*per naturam*, not *per voluntatem*), so partakes of the nature of the Father that he himself is also creator.

II. THE CONSEQUENCES FOR FURTHER TRINITARIAN DISCUSSION

Without doubt the Nicene faith became in the course of the fourth century the basis of the Christian life. It became the standard of ecclesiastical orthodoxy, and was recognized as such by the government. It served as the norm of preaching and exegesis, shaped the liturgy and the whole of spirituality. Yet it was long time before it was universally and finally received. Moving within the confines of the baptismal faith the Nicene synod had not yet answered the decisive questions. Still, by means of its condemnation of Arius and its positive formulation of the faith, it had opened the way for the solution of questions that were still open.

1. The question of the divine generation

Even though Arius did not simply refuse point blank to call Christ Son of the Father, he nevertheless fundamentally excluded from God a *generatio per naturam*.[27] At this point he seemed to follow Origen and Eusebius, who, however, had only spoken out against a too material understanding of this generation.[28] The council of Nicea, however, emphasized the true sonship of Christ. It presented the one Lord Jesus Christ as the *monogenes*, as the true and only Son, explained his

---

[23] ExposFid, CPG II, 2804: MG 26, 201A.
[24] Cf. Arius, ep. ad Alexandrum: Opitz no. 6.5f; Eusebius Nicomed.: Opitz no. 8.3–5.
[25] Cf. Eusebius Caes., ep. de synodo: Opitz no. 22.9f.
[26] For Eusebius cf. G. C. Stead, *Divine Substance*, pp 221f; Athanasius, De sententia Dionysii, CPG II, 2121.
[27] Cf. G. C. Stead, 'The Thalia of Arius and the Testimony of Athanasius', JThSt NS 29, 1978, pp 20–52, esp. p 32.
[28] Cf. R. Lorenz, *Arius judaizans?*, pp 72–6, 203f.

Sonship as being 'out of the Father's *ousia*', and employed the concept of *homoousios*. In proceeding thus it was, however, unable to remove the reservations which had been expressed before and during the negotiations of the synod. On the contrary, it remained a matter of urgency for a long time to defend the divine sonship against all misunderstandings. Thus Athanasius, Hilary and other Nicenes, and even Eusebius, strove hard to meet complaints against divine generation as being somehow animal, unworthy of God, and to spiritualize the concept of *homoousios*, in so far as they had themselves accepted it.[29] For that reason they developed further the theology of the image, which went back mainly to Origen, and which had already been granted a prominent position in the creed of Antioch (324/25).[30] A spiritually understood concept of image was not only able to safeguard the perfect likeness between the Father and the Son, but also to distinguish clearly the Son as the sole image of the Father from those who are themselves the image of God only according to this image (*kat'eikona*).[31]

2. *A fundamental decision in favour of the divinity of the Holy Spirit*

Remarkably enough in the original version of the Nicene symbol the third article is limited to the words: 'and in the Holy Spirit'(DS 125). Indeed, during the synod of 325 the issue of faith in the Holy Spirit was not discussed. Arius himself made mention of him only incidentally.[32] Debates on the Holy Spirit would not start before about 360, when the so-called Tropici and some of the Homoiousians expressly denied his divinity. By the succinct remark 'We also believe in the Holy Spirit', the question was, however, already settled. Like Jesus' command to baptize (Matt 28:19f), the baptismal instruction of the Didache, the baptismal questions and creeds, this remark grants to the Spirit an equal status with the Father and the Son, and makes him an object of faith. Yet, the same formula is also part of the confession of Eusebius, connected with an allusion to the command of baptism, which even occurs in the creeds of Lucian, Arius and Asterius.[33]

With the reception of the *Nicaenum* the third article was, however, understood in the sense of the second. In fact, Athanasius and Basil in the debates with the so-called pneumatomachians argued entirely in line with the Nicene doctrine of the true God, who is to be distinguished from all creatures. As far as Athanasius is concerned, for him the soteriological principle of deification is valid for the Holy Spirit no less than it is for the Son. He even bases the true Godhead of the Son on the fact that he is able to communicate the Holy Spirit for the purpose of man's sanctification.[34] Basil, on the other hand, avoids calling the Holy

---

[29] Cf. M. Simonetti, *La crisi ariana*, pp 271ff; P. Galtier, *S. Hilaire de Poitiers*, Paris 1960, pp 88–95.

[30] Cf. H. Crouzel, *Théologie de l'image de Dieu chez Origène*, Paris 1956; R. Bernard, *L'image de Dieu d'après s.Athanase*, Paris 1952; also Lucian's confession: Hahn §154.

[31] Cf. Origen, PA I 2.6; Athanasius CAr III 10: MG 26 341C–344A; also H. Crouzel, 'Bild', TRE 6, 1980, pp 499–502.

[32] Cf. R. Lorenz, *Arius judaizans?*, p 166: on the exegesis of Isa 6:3.

[33] Cf. R.Lorenz, *Arius judaizans?*, p 190.

[34] Athanasius, Serap IV 20.

Spirit God. He does not even state his identity in essence with the Father, perhaps because the *homoousios* was too much linked with the idea of generation. However, in keeping with Nicea he from the first emphasizes that the Holy Spirit is no creature, not a serving spirit, but Lord of all spirits and creatures.[34a]

3. The search for a more appropriate terminology

An agreement based on the mere claim to power by the emperor, which had been achieved during the first imperial council, was not in itself to be expected to bring about a final solution of the Origenist crisis. Indeed, the discussions went on, focusing on a crucial point. It proved to be all the more necessary to express unambiguously the uniqueness of God, in the sense of 'Hear, O Israel, the Lord our God is one Lord' (Deut 6:4). An agreement on this point was particularly difficult, since Christ, according to his divinity, was unmistakeably given equal status with the Father. This is shown by the debate about the terminology of the common faith.

Following monarchian theology Marcellus of Ancyra defended a modalistic-sounding doctrine of the Trinity, which hardly went beyond an economic conception. Thus for him a doctrine of three really distinct hypostases was out of the question.[35] His western friends took a less extreme stand. Yet, even they with their tradition of the *una substantia* were little inclined to accept three hypostases. The creed of Serdica (342/43) is the most eloquent expression of their difficulty.[36] In a fragment which possibly dates back to the same time Eustathius of Antioch juxtaposes the one nature (*physis*) with the three persons (*prosopa*), and in doing this already indicated where any further development was to lead.[37] Since about 350, Athanasius, moved by faithfulness to the authentic wording of the *Nicaenum*, endeavoured to establish the *homoousios*.[38] For the three hypostases, however, he cared little. The author of the aforementioned *Expositio fidei* did reject the Sabellian *monoousios*, yet he could not sympathize with the three hypostases.[39] Following Origenist theology, the bishops in Basil of Ancyra's circle, accepted two or three hypostases, which resemble each other in every respect. Fearing a too unitarian interpretation of the Nicene faith, they, however, preferred the *homoiousios* as against the Athanasian *homoousios* and therefore figure in the history of dogma as homoiousians.[40]

This wide range of opinions among bishops and theologians, who all felt themselves to be unanimous in their rejection of radical Arianism and in their

---

[34a] Basil, Spir 16.38; cf P. Luislampe, *Spiritus vivificans*, pp 49ff.

[35] Cf. Marcellus of Ancyra, frag 66: GCS 14, 197, 23ff, and ep. ad Liberium p 11f; also M. Simonetti, *La crisi ariana*, pp 68, 148f.

[36] Serdican formula in Hahn §157.

[37] Cf. Eustathius of Antioch., frag 84, CPG II, 3387; for the authenticity and the dating (344/5) of the fragments cf. R. Lorenz, 'Die Eustathius von Antiochien zugeschriebene Schrift gegen Photin', ZNW 71, 1980, pp 109–28; cf. also frag. 87.25f and De engastriomytho 24, and Athanasius, TomAntioch 6: MG 26, 801C.

[38] Cf. Athanasius, Decret 20: Opitz II/1, pp 211.17; also H. J. Sieben, *Konzilsidee*, pp 34–40.

[39] ExposFid: MG 26, 201A.

[40] Cf. M. Simonetti, *La crisi ariana*, pp 259–66.

faith in the true Godhead of Christ, was made possible because the council of Nicea did not define more precisely either the 'out of the Father's *ousia*' or the '*homoousios* to the Father', and also because it placed side by side in one of its anathemas the concepts of *hypostasis* and *ousia* without further explanation. Still, the fathers of the council by means of their choice of terminology, vague though it was, had made a fundamental decision. What remained, was to find a precise expression which unlike the obviously unsatisfactory *homoousios* safeguarded the essential unity of Father, Son and Spirit no less than their full equality.

III. THE NICENE ATTEMPT AT THE CHRISTOLOGICAL QUESTION

Although the representatives of the Christian churches, with the Roman emperor presiding, had accepted a common creed, in order to safeguard not only their unity of faith but also peace in the whole empire, it still took a long time, as has been shown, before it was really received. The prolonged debates, held first in the east, and then increasingly in the west, at first sight concerned the true Godhead of the Son. From about 360 they also included the true Godhead of the Spirit. Somehow they always entailed a correct understanding as to why and how Christ was made man. Even though these christological and soteriological points of view retreated for a certain time into the background, sooner or later they were bound to come fully to light.[41] So by 360 the strict Nicenes around Athanasius and the homoiousians finally came closer to each other. The *Tomus ad Antiochenos* of 362, the main testimony to this reconciliation, already contains clear references to the christological question.[42] As concerns this controversy about the mystery of Christ which by then had been opened up, the Nicene faith proved no less capable of leading the way than it had in the settlement of the Trinitarian crisis.

1. The Christology of distinction and the question of the one Christ

In the East as well as in the West a christology of distinction had emerged during the third century. Origen had clearly distinguished between the divine and the human in Christ,[43] and through his teaching on the union of the Logos with the human soul had prepared the way for the comparison of the union of divinity and humanity with the union of soul and body.[44] Tertullian had pointed in the same direction with his distinction between two *substantiae* and *status*.[45] This already

---

[41] For the christological background of the Arian controversy see A. Grillmeier, *Jesus Christus*, pp 382–5 (=*Christ in Christian Tradition*, pp 245–8), and R. Lorenz, *Arius judaizans?*, pp 211–24; cf. ZKG 94, 1983, pp 1–51. Even now the dating of the christological controversy proper has still not been exactly established.

[42] Cf. Athanasius, TomAntioch 7: MG 26, 804A-805A, also A. Grillmeier, *Jesus Christus*, pp 472–7 (=*Christ in Christian Tradition*, pp 318–26).

[43] Cf. Origen, Colo I 28.191–200, Cels VII 16.

[44] Origen, PA II 6.3.

[45] Cf. Tertullian, Prax 27.11f.

strongly philosophically-tinged christology of distinction was, however, given a further powerful impetus by the decisions of Nicea.

The Nicene theologians were very concerned to distinguish clearly between the divine and human in Christ, in order to be able to counter the objections which their opponents had against Christ's divinity in view of his weakness and suffering. This so-called *regula canonica* for the exegesis of the christological texts in scripture, already adumbrated in Origen, was employed by Athanasius, Eustathius and Marcellus in particular.[46] The treatise *De incarnatione et contra Arianos*, which is attributed by some to the last mentioned, is particularly remarkable in that it extends the distinction between the divine and human to volition.[47] However, the more this rule of distinction was employed in christological exegesis and the more a rational justification was sought for it, so much the more urgent became the question about the unity of Christ. In fact, soon after the council objections were raised by some against this christology of distinction. They accused their opponents of speaking of two Christs or two sons. It is, however, not possible to discover precisely, when and by whom this objection was first raised.[48]

The question about the one and the same Christ was, however, prejudiced by that christology which is characterized, in a somewhat simplified manner, as Logos-sarx-christology. Already in the third century it was brought forward by Malchion against Paul of Samosata. About 300 this notion, which appears at first sight to be biblical (cf. John 1:14), but is actually much closer to hellenism, was widespread. Whereas Origen was very concerned to underline the role of the human soul of Jesus, his pupils, above all, Eusebius of Caesarea, by and large neglected it. The unorthodox opinion of the Alexandrine master on the pre-existence of souls may be to blame here. When in consequence Arius and his friends more or less expressly rejected the idea of the soul, even their opponents, including Athanasius, did not for a long time attach importance to the fact.[49] Eustathius alone is an exception here.[50] Only much later, especially from 362 onwards, would this error become clearly manifest as such.[51] It is understandable considering the long period during which the Logos-sarx scheme was accepted as a matter of course, that the question of the one Christ was not asked at all or, if it was, merely on the level of the logical unity of subject.

Still, the Nicene faith was to some extent able to express the unity of Christ, by making, with regard to the one Lord Jesus Christ, statements referring to the divine and the human. In any event, in the fifth century both Nestorius and

---

[46] Cf. Origen, CoIo XIX 2.6; Cels III. 28; Athanasius, CAr III, pp 26–58; Marcellus, SermFid 7, CPG II, 2803; frag. 27; 57; 60; Eutherius, frag 47.

[47] Ps.Athanasius, IncarnArian 21: MG 26, 1021; also M. Tetz, 'Zur Theologie des Markell von Ankyra, III', ZKG 83, 1972, p 170.

[48] Cf. M. Tetz, 'Zur Theologie des Markell von Ankyra, II', ZGK 79, 1968, pp 34ff, as well as R. Lorenz, *Arius judaizans?*, pp 215–19: 'Die zwei Christusse'.

[49] Cf. A. Grillmeier, *Jesus Christus*, p 375, and R. Lorenz, *Arius judaizans?*, pp 211–22.

[50] Cf. Eustathius, frag. 15; 41, and also R. Lorenz, 'Eustathius von Antiochien', TRE 10, 1982, pp 543–6, no. 3.3.

[51] Cf. Athanasius, TomAntioch 7: MG 26, 804B.

Cyril of Alexandria, each in his own way, appealed to the terminology of the *Nicaenum.* In the view of the followers of Cyril the fathers of Nicea themselves had already anticipated the *unus ex Trinitate passus est;* a contention which itself was to have repercussions for Trinitarian theology.

2. The search for a formulation of Christology

Even though the impact of the formula 'consubstantial with the Father', which the council of Nicea had inserted in its creed, and which the Nicene theologians around Athanasius in the fifties sought to get universally established, should not be overestimated, their endeavours in this respect were still of far-reaching significance, not only for Trinitarian doctrine but also for christology. For the discussions on the *homoousios* and its dogmatic significance did lead various theologians of the fourth century to give a more detailed theological account of the human generation of Christ.

The antithesis of Son of God and Son of Man had certainly already been of considerable significance in the pre-Nicene theology. In the context of the reception of the Nicene faith, however, an increasingly clearer differentiation between the two births gained acceptance.[52] The fact that post-Nicene theology included an increasingly sharp antithesis between the Son out of (*ek*) God and the Son out of (*ek*) Mary, caused it more and more to distinguish, particularly in the second half of the fourth century, between two births, two natures, two consubstantialities.[53] Thus the question became ever more urgent as to how the one who has been born twice, still can be one Son, one subject or person.[54]

This fundamental question of christology proper was set rolling by post-Nicene theology not only on the material level of the equally 'inexpressible births'(cf. Isa 53:8, LXX), but also on the terminological level. The attempt to express the divine sonship not only in biblical terms as *monogenes,* but also in technical terms as being 'out of the Father's *ousia*', and especially with the related term *homoousios,* was to be a breakthrough for christology. Indeed, Apollinaris after 360 in explaining the incarnation of the Logos, was to introduce the double *homoousios,* denoting equality in essence with the Father and with us.[55] In the process of clarifying this christological formula, which the council of Chalcedon was to sanction, though in a somewhat different sense, it was the debate on the trinitarian *homoousios* in particular that prepared the ground.

The same is true of the other technical terms, *hypostasis, physis, prosopon,* which either at Nicea itself or afterwards were put up for discussion and gradually became part of christology. With reference to this whole process of reception it may even be reasonably maintained, that the Apollinarian and later on the Nestorian controversy were by and large concerned with clarifying

---

[52] Cf. Athanasius, CAr I 28f; Decret 11f; 21, and Hilary, Trin VI 21–32; also note 29.

[53] Cf. B. Studer, 'Consubstantialis Patri – consubstantialis matri', REAug 18, 1972, pp 87–115.

[54] Cf. the explanations of the anithesis 'Son of God' – 'Son of Man', and esp. of the antithesis 'only begotten' – 'first begotten' in A. Grillmeier, *Jesus Christus,* pp 56f, 110–12.

[55] Cf. Apollinaris, De unione 8: ed. Lietzmann, p 188.9–18, frag. 161; 163: ed. Lietzmann, pp 254f; also B. Studer, art. cit.: REAug 18, 1972, pp 98f.

how terminology taken over from trinitarian doctrine was to be adapted to christology. The development that Nicea had initiated by introducing into the common creed a terminology which went beyond biblical language had to be brought to a comprehensive conclusion for trinitarian as well as for christological doctrine.

How complicated the course of this whole linguistic ruling was, is very clear from the fact that dogmatic accord had to be fixed in two (or even more) languages. So the meaning of *homoousios* does not coincide with that of its Latin translation *unius substantiae* (or *essentiae*). It was even more difficult to take *hypostasis* or even *prosopon* as equivalent to *persona*. A sense of language was required here and, what is more, tolerance, which all did not possess in the same measure, as the examples of Gregory of Nazianzus and Jerome show.[56]

3. The distinction between 'theologia' and 'oikonomia'

In the perspective of the Nicene faith in Jesus Christ, the true and eternal Son of God, it became possible to view the relationship between Father and Son in purely theological terms, without considering his mediatorship in creation and salvation. This had not been so in pre-Nicene theology.[57] For this latter had closely linked the generation of the Son with God's saving activity. It is characteristic of the primitive creeds that the title of Father refers to creation, not to the Son.[58] No less revealing is Origen's and even more Eusebius' understanding of *soter* as primarily the Logos, who sustains and governs the world.[59] It was this cosmological perspective in particular which prevented any clear distinction between the eternal Trinity and its activity in the history of salvation. In the light of the doctrine of *creatio ex nihilo*, however, the communication of the divine essence to the Son was distinguished from creation through him, and further the procession of the Spirit distinguished from his work of perfection. Thus the Trinity in its own essence no longer appeared to be dependent on its outward revelation. So Gregory of Nyssa was able to divide his main work, the Great Catechetical Sermon, into a 'theological' and an 'economic' part. In the first part he dealt with the Trinity in itself and in the second with the incarnation and the sacraments.[60] His way of structuring was to become the accepted thing.[61] In the process of time the theological and the economic, however, were too sharply distinguished. Owing to the principle *omnia opera ad extra communia sunt*, which was designed to defend the essential equality of Father, Son and Spirit against the subordinationist conceptions of the Arians, it became increasingly

[56] Cf. Gregory of Naz., or. 21.33f; Jerome, ep. 15 (to Damasus, in 375), also B. Studer, 'Der Person-Begriff in der frühen kirchenamtlichen Trinitätslehre', TheolPhil 57, 1982, pp 168f.

[57] Cf. W. Marcus, *Der Subordinatianismus,* and B. Studer, *Soteriologie,* pp 118f.

[58] Cf. A. de Halleux, 'Dieu le Père tout-puissant': RThLouv 8, 1977, pp 401–22, esp. pp 405–8.

[59] Cf. Eusebius, DemEv V 3f; EcclTheol I 9; also F. Ricken, 'Die Logoslehre des Eusebius von Caesarea und der Mittelplatonismus', TheolPhil 42, 1967, pp 341–58, esp. p 351, as well as B. Studer, 'A propos des traductions d'Origène par Jérôme et Rufin', VetChr 5, 1968, pp 137–55; esp. pp 146ff.

[60] Cf. J. Barbel, *Gregor von Nyssa, Die große katechetische Rede,* pp 23–9.

[61] Cf. A. Grillmeier, 'Vom Symbolum zur Summa', *Mit ihm und in ihm,* pp 585–636, esp. pp 618ff.

difficult for theologians to safeguard adequately the inner coherence of *theologia* and *oikonomia*.[62] It would not be easy for them to explain why only the Son has become man and why only the Holy Spirit is poured out into the hearts of believers.

The Nicene distinction between *theologia* and *oikonomia* had other consequences, too. For the defence of the second article of the *Nicaenum* required that the existence of Christ, in so far as he is out of the Father's essence, be connected with his creative activity, and his life out of Mary, on the other hand, with his saving activity. As this article was practically the only one debated at the council itself, there developed the tendency of discussing the distinction between theology and economy only in the field of christology, i.e. to restrict the statements on God and the history of salvation to the antithesis 'God, eternal Creator – God-man, Saviour'. This christological simplification is characteristic in particular of the Nicene theology of the West. Thus the Latin theologians and the Roman liturgy identify *Deus* and *Dominus* and speak of Christ as *Dominus et Salvator, conditor et redemptor, formator et reformator, creator et recreator*.[63] Along these lines the depiction of Christ as Pantokrator was developed. Yet, this brand of christocentrism is also found in the east, particularly with Athanasius. He also reduces the mystery of Christ to a rather abstract, bifocal vision, and speaks of God and man: namely of the God who has become man in order that men may become God.[64] The monastic movement also has a similar tendency, as will be seen more clearly in the examples of Evagrius and Maximus the Confessor.

The fact that the council of Nicea, as against Arius, did place Christ entirely on the side of the creator, enabled it to define faith in the true Godhead of the Lord Jesus Christ, and thus created the basis for the orthodoxy of the imperial Church. Its dogma has remained to the present day the basis of any Christian creed. In so far as it granted equal status to Father and Son, Nicea also stood at the beginning of a theological development which in the course of the fourth and the fifth centuries was to include the doctrine of the Holy Spirit – as much God as the Father and the Son – and that of the one Lord Jesus Christ – true God and true man. This entailed a dogmatic terminology, towards which the Nicene creed and its anathemas pointed the way. Moreover, the decision of the first ecumenical council, which concerned the very heart of Christian faith, had repercussions on the prayer, thought and feeling of the whole of the imperial Church, even of the whole of later Christianity. It really marked a turning point. The significance of this statement has, however, yet to be verified and substantiated, first of all in this second part, but to a large extent also in the third, concluding part.

---

[62] Cf. e.g. Basil, ep. 189.7; Ambrose Fid I 2.13; IV 6.68; also A. Schindler, *Trinitätslehre*, pp 126f.
[63] Cf. B. Studer, art.cit.: VetChr 5, 1968, pp 149ff.
[64] Cf. Athanasius, CAr I 37ff; III 32.

10. The Nicene Theology of Athanasius and Hilary

BIBLIOGRAPHY

P. Galtier, *S. Hilaire de Poitiers*, Paris 1960.

A. Fierro, *Sobre la gloria en San Hilario*, Rome 1964.

J. Roldanus, *Le Christ et l'homme dans la théologie d'Athanase d'Alexandrie*, Leiden 1968.

C. Kannengießer, 'Hilaire de Poitiers', DSpir 7, 1968, cols. 466–99 (with bibl.).

A. Laminski, *Der Heilige Geist als Geist Christi und Geist der Gläubigen*, Leipzig 1969.

J. Doignon, *Hilaire de Poitiers avant l'exile*, Paris 1971.

J. M. McDermott, 'Hilary of Poitiers: the infinite nature of God', VigChr 27, 1973, pp 172–202.

H. Saake, *Pneumatologica. Untersuchungen zum Geistverständnis im Johannese-vangelium, bei Origenes und Athanasios von Alexandreia;* Frankfurt 1973 (cf. PWK Suppl 14, 1974, pp 387–412).

M. Tetz, 'Markellianer und Athanasios von Alexandrien', ZNW 64, 1973, pp 75–121.

C. Kannengießer, ed., *Politique et théologie chez Athanase d'Alexandrie*, Paris 1974.

E. P. Meijering, *Orthodoxy and Platonism in Athanasius: Synthesis or Antithesis*, Leiden 1974.

L. F. Ladaría, *El Espiritu Santo en San Hilario de Poitiers*, Madrid 1977.

H. C. Brennecke, *Hilarius von Poitiers und die Bischofsopposition gegen Konstantius II. Untersuchungen zur 3. Phase des arianischen Streites (337–61)*, Berlin 1984.

L. Longobardo, 'Il linguaggio teologico di Ilario di Poitiers', Asprenas 29, 1982, pp 257–91; 381–405.

See also:

L. Ladaría, *San Hilario de Poitiers, La Trinidad* (Biblioteca de Autores Cristianos 481), Madrid 1986 (with bibl.).

L. Ladaría, *La Cristología de Hilario de Poitiers* (Analecta Gregoriana), Rome 1989.

A. Pettersen, *Athanasius and the Human Body*, Bristol 1990.

The agreement of the council of Nicea, as imposed by imperial authority, did not just bring a theological development to a conclusion, it was also to form a starting point for new debates between the intellectual movements which at that time existed within the churches of the Roman empire. These debates, however, still operated for quite a long period more at the level of ecclesiastical politics. Only about 350 did they begin to take on a stronger theological character. This was first caused by a growing tension in the relationship between the single churches and bishops, which stemmed from the autocratic rule of Constantius and the consequent political predominance of the anti-Nicene bishops. No less serious were the radical offshoots of Arian theology, which commenced with the appearance of the strict Arians Aetius and Eunomius.

In these debates of the fifties and sixties of the 4th century two theologians above all were prominent, Athanasius of Alexandria (+373) and Hilary of Poitiers (+367). Even though they differed in some respects and belonged to two different ecclesiastical spheres, they resembled each other in proving to be unwearying fighters for Nicene orthodoxy in the field of ecclesiastical politics as well as at the level of theology and historiography. Holding fundamentally to the decisions of Nicea, they nevertheless adapted themselves to their opponents, especially in respect of terminology, thus improving the chances for the re-establishment of ecclesiastical peace. Both bishops were not only concerned for the defence of the true baptismal faith but also and indeed more about the question of *cur Deus homo*. Precisely by means of their doctrine of God they sought to reach a deeper understanding of the meaning of the incarnation. Thus it can be shown in a particularly illuminating way from their theology the extent to which in patristic theology trinitarian and incarnational doctrine were interrelated.

I. THE DEIFYING INCARNATION ACCORDING TO ATHANASIUS

1. The revision of Irenaeus' soteriology

Even though Athanasius has entered church history as the advocate of the Nicene dogma of Christ's true divinity, he is, nevertheless, better understood as a theologian of God's incarnation. The question of the meaning of salvation through the Son of God is in fact predominant not only in his treatise *De incarnatione* but is basic to the whole of his theological work, most of which involves polemics against the Arians, as also to his spiritual writings. Like Irenaeus he is concerned with assimilation to the immortal, which man is able to reach through knowledge of the Son.

No doubt Athanasius in his thoroughly soteriological theology takes over from tradition a whole range of themes: the death of Jesus as ransom, the atonement for many, the victory of the cross, the triumph over the devil, the preparation of the way to heaven, the *pax christiana,* in which both the divine monarchy as well as monotheism is established, etc.[1] Still, this variety of traditional themes can be disregarded, and his soteriology summed up in the simple antithesis: incarnation – deification.[2] The deification of man, for the sake

[1] Cf. the catechesis on the death and resurrection of Christ in Athanasius, Incarn 25.1–27.3; also C. Andresen, 'Erlösung', RAC 6, 1966, cols. 190ff, and M. Tetz, 'Athanasius v. Alex.', TRE 4, 1979, pp 333–49.

[2] Cf. Athanasius, CAr I 38; II 70; ep. ad Adelph. 4; also esp. J. Roldanus, *Le Christ et l'homme dans la théologie d'Athanase d'Alexandrie.*

of which the Word has become flesh, on the one hand included the victory over death, the restoration of incorruptibility, and on the other, the recovery of knowledge of God, the restoration of God's image or the status of sonship.[3]

This doctrine of the deifying incarnation is to be understood in the context of a salvation-historical vision, in which the loss of immediate knowledge of God and of incorruptibility are seen to be the consequences of Adam's sin. Accordingly man could return to God only on the condition that thanks to the incarnation of the Logos he could encounter him directly and through the presence of the Logos in a human body immortality could in principle be again secured. Thus the original state of man was established despite all difficulties. His situation had improved to such an extent that he could be indeed regarded as a new creation. In the future mankind as such was never again able to lose its privileges with which it had been endowed at creation. For in the Word made man it had for all time been given a part in the divine life. In this respect Athanasius goes beyond Irenaeus. He views the process of becoming like God not just as the end of a long process, but as essentially a new creation, which would not have happened without sin. He also emphasizes, more than Irenaeus, faith as the beginning of union with the Word and thus of the process of becoming like the immortal God.[4]

2. The development of pneumatology

The deification of man, which is established in the incarnation of the Logos, is realized in the Holy Spirit. This conception is already adumbrated in his earlier writings. However, it only becomes fully developed in 359, in his writings on the divinity of the Holy Spirit. In these writings the Holy Spirit is depicted as the Word's gift to mankind. Already before his incarnation the Logos had communicated his Spirit to the saints of the Old Testament. Since then, however, he sanctifies all men with him, and precisely through this proves that he himself and the Spirit are true God.[5]

Thanks to this communication of the Spirit of Christ men partake in the Logos, which makes them new creatures. For as Word Christ gives the gifts of the Father, and as man he receives these gifts for mankind.[6] Thus through the Spirit the Word is united with the immortal God.[7] This fundamental theme is connected with the traditional view that Jesus, in his baptism for us, has received the unction of the Spirit and in the resurrection has passed it on,[8] and similarly with it the idea of the Spirit as the seal with which Christ strengthens man for the combat with the demons and prepares them for life eternal.[9] For the whole of

---

[3] Cf. Incarn 9.1–4; 10.1; 16.5; 19.1; 54.1–3, and CAr II 69.
[4] Cf. Incarn 15.1–7; 4.4; 20.1, and CAr II 14; II 65f; II 75; Serap I 9; also J. Roldanus, op. cit., p 360.
[5] Cf. CAr I 48; II 18; Serap I 27; I 31; also A. Laminski, *Der Heilige Geist als Geist Christi und Geist der Gläubigen*, pp 155–65.
[6] CAr I 45; I 48; I 50; III 25.
[7] Serap III 6. Cf. CAr II 59.
[8] CAr I 47; ExposPs 132.2.
[9] CAr I 47–50; III 23; Serap I 23ff.

Athanasius' ecclesiology is founded on the idea that the body of Christ, as communion with God and with the brethren in Christ, is constituted by the communication of the Holy Spirit through the glorified Lord.[10]

Thus Athanasius, in line with Irenaeus and Origen, integrated the activity of the Holy Spirit into his theology of *cur deus homo*. This he did chiefly in defending, against the so-called Tropici, the divinity of the Holy Spirit.

3. The christological foundations of Athanasius' soteriology

The soteriology of deification rests essentially on two christological presuppositions: on faith in the true divinity of the Word, and on faith in his true incarnation. In order to be able to save mankind Christ had to be consubstantial with the Father as well as with man.[11]

Athanasius did not yet expressly formulate the double consubstantiality; for this he would have needed a more developed doctrine of the two births and the two natures and at the same time a less reserved attitude to the term *homoousios*.[12] Still, in reality he presupposed the double consubstantiality. This is obvious as far as the divine consubstantiality is concerned,[13] but there is no doubt as regards the human consubstantiality.[14] This does not, however, mean for him that Christ possessed a human nature like ours in all respects, including even a soul,[15] he rather understands this to express full solidarity with the whole family of man, which reaches back to Adam.

The fact that Christ is entirely on the side of God (*consubstantialis Patri*) and has entered into solidarity with all men (*consubstantialis nobis*) is, according to Athanasius, vital for the restoration of the knowledge of God as well as for the restoration of immortality.[16] Only the Word of God incarnate can bring man, who is alienated in the sensual world, back home to the spiritual realm.[17] And it was only through God's presence in the flesh that the abolition of death could be finally guaranteed.[18]

For the most part Athanasius had no difficulties in safeguarding the unity of Christ in this soteriology, which implied the distinction between the divine and the human.[19] For him the Word is of course the subject of all soteriological statements.[20] The Logos primarily appears as the one who has made flesh his own

---

[10] CAr III 23ff; cf. I 37.

[11] Cf. B. Studer, *Soteriologie*, pp 129f.

[12] Cf. M. Simonetti, *La crisi ariana*, pp 273ff.

[13] Cf. esp. Athanasius, De sententia Dinoysii; also L. Abramowski, 'Arianische Streitigkeiten des 4. Jh.', ZGK 93, 1982, pp 240–77.

[14] Cf. Athanasius, Sentent 10, and CAr II 61; 69; 75.

[15] Cf. A. Grillmeier, *Jesus Christus*, pp 460–3, with bibl. (=*Christ in Christian Tradition*, pp 308–10).

[16] Cf. esp. Incarn 54.1ff and CAr III 33; 53.

[17] Incarn 11.1–16.1 and CAr II 81.

[18] Incarn 9.1f; 20.4ff; 29.1 and CAr II 69.

[19] Cf. A. Grillmeier, *Jesus Christus*, pp 463–72 (=*Christ in Christian Tradition*, pp 310–18).

[20] Cf. CAr III 57, and Incarn 16.4; CAr III 26.

and uses it as a tool.[21] However, Athanasius does not try to clarify this unity any further. For within his Logos-sarx scheme it was too obvious to him that it had to be subjected to further discussion.

II. THE GLORIFYING INCARNATION ACCORDING TO HILARY

Hilary of Poitiers did not arrive on the scene until the Arian controversy had already reached its political and theological peak. Even though he is indebted to the Latin tradition, especially in his commentary on Matthew which was written before he was exiled, his theology is in many respects like that of Athanasius.[22] He moves, too, in the soteriological tracks of Irenaeus. He is also indebted to Origen,[23] at least in his later works, particularly in his commentary on the Psalms. And, above all, he is an advocate of the Nicene faith.[24] So it is not surprising that the incarnation is also very significant for him, even though it is developed in a different manner.[25]

1. A theology of glory

Even though it may seem somewhat one-sided, it is nevertheless appropriate to view Hilary's theology in the perspective of *gloria,* glory.[26] His vision of saving history is to a large degree marked by the biblical theme of the glory of God. God is in fact represented here as the source of the glory in which the Son partakes from eternity (the Spirit is hardly mentioned in this context).[27] Thus the fulness of God is constituted by his glory, prior to any outward revelation.[28] It is in the same perspective of glory that he sees the destination of man. Out of *humilitas, infirmitas, corruptio, corpus mortis,* he is to reach the glory through which alone he comes to possess the eternal life and immortality of God.[29] Even though Hilary in his expositions of the goal of man avoids representing the body as something evil, he nevertheless follows a strongly spiritualizing tendency, particularly in the

---

[21] Cf. Incarn 44.3f; CAr III 35.

[22] For Hilary's theology before his exile cf. esp. J. Doignon, *Hilaire de Poitiers avant l'exil,* and P. C. Burns, *The Christology in Hilary of Poitiers' commentary on Matthew,* Rome 1981.

[23] Cf. the already somewhat one-sided evaluation by Jerome, VirIll2 100, and epp 61.2; 112.20 among others; also M. J. Rondeau, *Les commentaires patristiques du psautier,* pp 147ff.

[24] Already Augustine counts Hilary among the catholicae doctores ecclesiae. Cf. CIul I 3,9 (with the whole context), and Trin VI 10.11. Also ML 9.13; Cf. also Sulpicius Severus, Chron II 45.7, according to which Hilary freed Gaul from heresy. It is also noteworthy that Jerome, VirIll 100, refers to Hilary's main work De Trinitate under the title Contra Arianos.

[25] This is true esp. of Trin VIII–XII; Cf. Trin IX 3 with a clear confession of Christ, true God and true man.

[26] Cf. B. Studer, *Soteriologie,* pp 130–5, and esp. A. Fierro, *Sobre la gloria.*

[27] Cf. Trin II 8; III 13; VIII 46f; IX 54; XI 5; Hymnus 'Ante saecula qui manes': CSEL 65, 210, pp 25–9.

[28] Cf. Trin IX 54: Jesus Christ in the gloria of the Father; Trin XI 17: on the Father of claritas.

[29] Cf. e.g. Trin III 7; TractPs 118.4.1; 145.2; More texts in A. Fierro, *Sobre la gloria,* pp 52–69.

writings which were influenced by Origen.[30] Being formed out of the earth man can become the image of God in the full sense only when his *forma servilis* is transformed for eternal life.[31]

This translation to eternal glory is possible only because Christ, who from eternity is the Son begotten in the glory of God, renounced his glory and became man, in order to return to the glory of God.[32] One day the whole of mankind will partake in the glory of God, when Christ will subject everything to the Father.[33]

Hilary, however, is not content simply to emphasize the role of the incarnation in glorification. Rather he sees the *assumptio carnis,* as he likes to define the incarnation, in a thoroughgoing ecclesiological perspective.[34] Having been made man Christ has united all men with him *per naturam* so that they are equally included in him. This *communio naturae* demands that men in the Church accept Christ in faith and in the sacraments.[35] Thus the Church is realized as *corpus gloriosum Christi* and there is accomplished what was begun in the incarnation and will be perfected in eternal life.[36]

Hilary is also concerned to describe eternal life more precisely. In doing this he takes over the Pauline themes of transformation according to the image of God, of replenishment with the divine fulness and of spiritualization.[37] Above all he defines eternal life as the exclusion of *corruptio* and possession of the *gloria Dei.*[38] This does not mean that he is merely thinking in terms of new life. Like the anti-gnostic authors he thinks rather of a *reformatio,* of a perfection of original creation, or more specifically, of the perfection of the body, which is required for the full life of the soul, for the vision of the glory of God.[39]

This soteriological doctrine, the central core of which is the *assumptio carnis* as *exaltatio gloriosa totius Christi,* is basically a continuation of Irenaeus' and Tertullian's doctrine of *salus carnis,* but it is simpler and clearer: simpler, because Hilary, in accordance with the Nicene faith, restricts his exposition to the essential features of the true faith, and because, influenced by the development of Pauline and Johannine exegesis as well as by the Origenist tradition, he has made *gloria* his key word;[40] but also clearer, because throughout he identifies Christ's saving act with his renunciation of glory, through which he has gained the glorification of the whole of mankind which he has assumed[41] and because on the

---

[30] Cf. esp. TractPs 119.19, with a negative evaluation of the bodiliness, but also already CoMt 14.18; 31.2, with a strong antithesis between earthly existence and the life in glory.

[31] Cf. TractPs 118.20.9f, and TractPs 118.3.3; Trin XI 49.

[32] Cf. Trin IX 6; 54f; TractPs 138.19.

[33] Cf. Trin XI 40–49: on I Cor 15:27f; TractPs 126.17: on the eternal heritage, TractPs 147.2: depiction of the heavenly Jerusalem.

[34] Cf. CoMt 19.5; Trin II 24f; TractPs 51.16f; 54.9.

[35] Cf. TractPs 51.16; 91.9; Trin VIII 16.

[36] Cf. TractPs 15.17; Myst 1.5; also A. Fierro, *Sobre la gloria,* pp 184–97.

[37] Cf. TractPs 50.2; Trin IX 8.

[38] Cf. TractPs 118.3.3; 67.37.

[39] Cf. TractPs 143.7; 2.41; Trin XI 49.

[40] Cf. A. Grillmeier, *Jesus Christus,* pp 580f (=*Christ in Christian Tradition,* p 395), and A. Fierro, *Sobre la gloria,* pp 335ff: on the reception of Origen and the significance for Hilary of I Cor 15:42ff, Phil 3:21, John 17.

[41] Cf. Trin X 7.

other hand, he traces *salus carnis* back to the glorification which occurs through participation in the immortality of the eternal and ever living God.[42]

2. The incarnation as the foundation of glorification

Hilary's teaching on the glorification of man, which he develops mainly in reference to Paul (Phil 2:11; 3:21) and John (17:5 and 17:21), is simply presented as a very dynamic, historical vision of divine salvation.[43] This is particularly apparent in the text in which Hilary discerns three stages in the existence of Christ, each of which commences with a birth: Christ as the Son begotten in glory from eternity – Christ born of Mary as God and man – Christ having become fully God through the resurrection.[44] The historical character of Hilary's soteriology also appears in the basic theme of *profectus*.[45] This states that God was made man through the incarnation, whereas man, in his exaltation, becomes God. However, the incarnation does not mean a loss on God's side, rather a gain, for it signifies man's ascent to God (*profectus ad Deum*).[46]

In this historical view of salvation the incarnation, which forms its central core, is of course given a very dynamic character. For Hilary it is nothing other than the revelation of the triune God, in particular of sonship in God and thus of our divine sonship.[47] The extent to which the incarnation forms the central point in Hilary's theology of salvation history is evident not only from his exegesis of St. Matthew's gospel and of the Psalms, which is entirely christologically orientated,[48] but also from the way he bases his defence of Jesus' divinity on the incarnation, in the last five volumes of his anti-Arian work *De Trinitate*.[49]

Behind this historical Christ-centred vision stands a more metaphysically orientated perspective.[50] Hilary intends to take seriously Christ as the great mystery of God's revelation in the flesh at every layer of his being. For that reason he develops a christology which can be labelled 'christology of distinction'.[51] This is not surprising if it is taken into account that in his polemics against the Arians he largely follows Latin theology, which with respect to Christ had spoken

---

[42] Cf. Trin XI 39f.

[43] Cf. esp. Trin XI 21–28: on I Cor 15:21–8.

[44] Cf. esp. Trin IX 6; further TractPs 138.9.23; Trin XI 40ff; also A. Grillmeier, *Jesus Christus*, p 581 (=*Christ in Christian Tradition*, p 396).

[45] Cf. A. Fierro, *Sobre la gloria*, pp 205–8.

[46] TractPs 2.27: 'quia natura carnis post resurrectionem glorificata ad profectum eius quam antea habuerat claritatis provehebatur.' Cf. Trin III 16; VIII 15; TractPs 55.12.

[47] Cf. A. Grillmeier, *Jesus Christus*, p 580 (=*Christ in Christian Tradition*, p 395). On the one hand Hilary emphasizes the unitas naturae of the Son with the Father; cf. Synod 76 and Trin V 37. On the other hand he points to the communio naturae of God with man, as based on the incarnation; cf. Trin XI 16.

[48] For the exegesis of Hilary see, besides J. Doignon, *S. Hilaire de Poitiers avant l'exil*, also N. Gastaldi, *Hilario de Poitiers, Esegeta de Salterio*, Paris 1969.

[49] Trin VIII–XII; also P. Galtier, *S. Hilaire*, pp 108–58.

[50] In his more metaphysical view Hilary reduces the three nativitates of Trin IX 6 to two nativitates, two genera, or two naturae. Cf. Trin IX 5; 7.

[51] Cf. the useful summary in J. N. D. Kelly, *Early Christian Doctrines*, pp 334f.

of two *substantiae* or *status*.[52] The strong tendency of clearly distinguishing the divine and the human in Christ became even more intensified, since at one and the same time he had to face not only the Arian opposition but also Photinus, the bishop of Sirmium. Whereas the Arians raised objections against Jesus' true divinity from his weakness and suffering mentioned by the gospels, Photinus, on the other hand, seeks to take all this as evidence for the mere humanity of Jesus.[53] Hence Hilary was obliged, against both heretical tendencies, to draw out even more sharply the difference between the human and divine with the help of the so-called *regula canonica*. And, in the context of this Arian question, the two *nativitates* and the two *naturae* are especially relevant.[54]

The sharper distinction between the two natures in Christ resulted in a considerable deepening of both the doctrine of the true divinity and the doctrine of the true humanity, compared with earlier Latin tradition. As far as the true Godhead is concerned he follows Nicea in stating that the Son is perfectly equal to the Father. *Plenitudo in utroque divinitatis perfecta est. Non enim diminutio Patris est Filius nec Filius imperfectus a Patre est.*[55] This equality is not brought into question by the incarnation of the Son. Being true Son of God from eternity, Christ does not cease to be God when he is made man.[56] Hilary certainly speaks in no uncertain terms of the incarnation as kenosis or *evacuatio*. This consists in renouncing the *forma dei* and in assuming the *forma servi*. Still, the Son does not cease to abide in the divine nature; for in the kenosis the only thing he has deliberately relinquished is the outward manifestation of his unity of being with the Father, i.e. his *splendor gloriae*. In the miracles, however, he is proved to be God, even though through the *forma servi*.[57] What happened was merely a *demutatio habitus,* a change in behaviour, not in nature.[58] As regards the true humanity Hilary's stand is, however, less decisive. He certainly goes further than the Arians and even than Athanasius in that right from the start he takes the human soul of Jesus into consideration. In analysing Jesus' grief at the tomb of Lazarus he expressly states that the soul of Jesus mourned.[59] But, according to Hilary, Jesus took on suffering and weakness only with regard to us. For not only was the Logos essentially incapable of suffering, but so too were the body and soul of Christ, as they were entirely caught up in the Logos; thus a miracle was needed to render them capable of suffering for our sake. Thus Hilary upheld against the Arians a theology of glorification, with which he sought to remove any occasion for referring to the humiliating weakness of the human existence of Christ.[60]

[52] For the sources of Hilary, esp. concerning his relationship to Tertullian, cf. J. Doignon, *S. Hilaire,* pp 169–225, esp. pp 210f, with CoMt 5.1.

[53] For the anti-Photinian polemic of Hilary see esp. Trin X 20f, but also Trin I 16.

[54] Cf. Trin IX 14: 'Haec igitur demonstranda a me paucis fuerunt, ut utriusque naturae personam tractari in Domino Iesu Chrsto meminissemus.' Also Trin IX 49; 51; TractPs 2.33; 54.2; 68.25.

[55] Trin III 23: comments on John 10:30; also Trin III 4.

[56] Cf. Trin IX 16: 'non amiserat quod erat.' Also Trin IX 3.6; X 16.

[57] Cf. Trin IX 14.51; XII 6.

[58] Trin IX 38; cf. IX 14.51; X 22.

[59] Cf. Trin X 24.55, and also TractPs 53.12: on the freely accepted suffering; CoMt 33.5; Trin X 12.37f.

[60] CoMt 31.4–7; Trin X 23.48; also A. Grillmeier, *Jesus Christus,* pp 584f (=*Christ in Christian Tradition,* pp 396f).

Although Hilary in the fight against the Arians took the distinction of the two natures even further than the earlier Latin tradition had done, he nevertheless took just as seriously the unity of Christ. He does not speak like Tertullian of *una persona*, but he nevertheless emphasizes the real union of the two natures. *Utrumque unus existens, dum ipse ex unitis naturis naturae utriusque res eadem est.*[61] In this sense he also speaks of *admixtio.*[62] In full accordance with his theology of glorification he underlines that the initiative belongs to Christ as true God. For it is the Son of God, who takes on the flesh, and mingles ours with his,[63] who raises up and glorifies the *caro.*[64] It remains to add that the union of the divine with the human is also presupposed when he states that the glorification of man is exclusively founded on his inclusion in the humanity of Jesus. Christ has not only taken on flesh, but with it the whole of humanity.[65]

Thus Hilary was led by his opponents to extend his defence of the true Godhead to the true incarnation of the Son of God. This then enabled him to elucidate more clearly why Christ in his abasement and in his exaltation has become the revealer of that glory through which he has always been the Son of the Father.

3. An undeveloped pneumatology

Any reader of *De Trinitate* will note how little Hilary has to say about the Holy Spirit. If the emphasis which he places on the distinction between the divine and human in Christ by means of the antithesis *spiritus-caro* is also taken into consideration, one could be tempted to speak of a Spirit-Christology and thus of binitarianism.[66]

In the context of his very dynamic vision of the mystery of Christ, Hilary indeed likes to designate the divine by *spiritus* and the human by *caro.*[67] *Caro* here denotes, and without any moralistic overtones, humanity, whereas *spiritus* refers to the divinity of Jesus, which was predicted by the prophets, and which can be acknowledged through Jesus' humanity 'in the Spirit'.[68] Thus for Hilary the body of Jesus is at the service of his spirit,[69] and the sin against the Spirit (Matt 12:31) involves calling into question of Christ's divinity.[70]

The scheme *spiritus sanctus = donum divinitatis Christi*, which Hilary consistently pursues in his commentary on Matthew, must not, however, lead to the assumption that he conflates 'divinity of Christ' and 'Holy Spirit' in the sense

---

[61] Trin IX 3; cf. also the emphasis on the unity of subject in Trin X 22, as well as in Trin X 18f; 60ff.

[62] Trin II 24, with the notion of admixtio; cf. Trin IX 7.51, according to which the divine nature works in the human.

[63] Cf. Trin IX 51; II 26; Tract 68.25; 58.2.

[64] Cf. TractPs 68.25, Trin IX 41; IX 11.

[65] Cf. note 34.

[66] Cf. A. Grillmeier, *Jesus Christus*, pp 581ff, who relies on L. F. Ladaría, *El Espiritu en San Hilario de Poitiers*, Madrid 1977.

[67] Cf. CoMt 4.1.14; 16.9; 27.8; 31.2f, as well as Trin IX 14: 'ut manens Spiritus Christus idem Christum homo esset.'

[68] Cf. esp. CoMt 17.3; 22.1, as well as 24.11; 25.1.

[69] Cf. CoMt 2.5.

[70] CoMt 12.17f; Cf. 12.15; 31.5.

of binitarianism. First, for Hilary the idea that God means Spirit is obviously fundamental. Secondly in the later commentary on the Psalms a different attitude is found from that contained in his exegesis of Matthew;[71] Nor, above all, should the relevant texts in *De Trinitate* be overlooked. In the second book, in which he sets out from Jesus' command to baptize (Matt 28:19f), he expressly formulates *nec deesse quidquam consummationi tantae reperietur, intra quam sit in Patre et Filio et Spiritu sancto, infinitas in aeterno, species in imagine, usus in munere.*[72] Here he makes it plain that there is a Holy Spirit, who is different from the Father and the Son,[73] and that we, incapable of comprehending in our weakness either the Father, or the Son, are in need of the gift of the Holy Spirit, in order to understand the difficult doctrine of the incarnation of God.[74] For that reason he announces in the prologue that in order to present the whole of faith he is going to deal with the Holy Spirit, too.[75] He fulfils his promise, however, only by a short appendix, which he adds to the last book.[76] Still, here he emphasizes in Nicene terms that the Holy Spirit is no creature and that the only thing that could be said about him is that he belongs to God.[77]

Thus Hilary clearly confesses the Trinity of the baptismal faith. If, however, he does not go into the doctrine of the Holy Spirit, this is apparently because at the time of the writing of *De Trinitate* (356–360) it was not yet an urgent matter for him, even though he was already aware of difficulties in this respect.[78]

Even though Athanasius as well as Hilary are to be regarded as the great defenders of Nicene faith, their theology proves to a very large extent to be an answer to the question *cur Deus homo*. In fact, both of them, each in his way, place the incarnation of God at the centre of their thought. The debate with the contemporary heresies, above all with the views of the Arians, led them to deepen in various ways the soteriology which they had adopted from Irenaeus, Tertullian and Origen. Athanasius here succeeds in elucidating more clearly the reason why there can be no salvation, i.e. no full knowledge of God in immortality, without the incarnation of the true God, and also without the mission of the Spirit of Christ. Hilary, on his own part, certainly influenced by the Nicene faith, developed his doctrine of the glorifying incarnation of God, according to which there is no partaking in the divine glory without kenosis and without the exaltation of the eternal Son of God.

In all this both Athanasius and Hilary were more successful in establishing the true godhead of Christ than in expounding his true humanity. Even though Hilary from the very beginning clearly recognizes the human soul of Jesus, he,

---

[71] Cf. A. Grillmeier, *Jesus Christus,* p 582.

[72] Trin II 1.

[73] Cf. Trin II 29ff, esp. 31, where *Spiritus-deus* and *Spiritus-donum* are distinguished.

[74] Cf. Trin II 33; IV 17.

[75] Cf. Trin I 21; for the dating of the prologue see J. Doignon, *S. Hilaire.* p 82f. According to this Trin I 1–19 had perhaps already been drafted before the exile, while Trin I 20–36 in any case was only added later.

[76] Trin XII 55f.

[77] Trin XII 55.

[78] Cf. M. Simonetti, *La crisi ariana,* p 310, and also Hilary, Synod 53–6.

nevertheless, like Athanasius, tends to overemphasize the influence of the divinity on the humanity. Thus he too acknowledges the impact of the Arian controversy. Like Athanasius, he has no difficulty in confessing, in spite of all the distinctions involved, the union of the two natures of Christ. Admittedly, he, like Athanasius, was not able to comprehend and formulate in formal terms the essential basis of this unity.

It remains to say that an exposition of their theology of the saving incarnation of the Son of God, which was worked out in the light of Nicea, still does not comprise all that Athanasius and Hilary have to tell us about the mystery of the Trinity, revealed in Christ. The following discussion of the spirituality of the imperial Church will put their contribution to the liturgical and spiritual life of the Church of the fourth century in an even clearer light.

11. The Spirituality of the Imperial Church

BIBLIOGRAPHY

E. Peterson, *Theologische Traktate*, Munich 1951.

J. Kollwitz, 'Christus II. Basileus', and 'III. Christus-Bild', RAC 2, 1954, cols. 1257–62; 3, 1957, 1–24.

W. Dürig, *Pietas liturgica*, Regensburg 1958.

A. A., *Théologie de la vie monastique*, Paris 1961.

A. Guillaumont, *Les 'Kephalaia Gnostica' de l'Évagre le Pontique et l'histoire de l'origènisme chez les Grecs et les Syriens*, Paris 1962, cf. TRE 10, 1982, pp 565–70 (with bibl.).

P. Beskow, *Rex gloriae. The Kingship of Christ in the Early Church*, Uppsala 1962.

J. A. Jungmann, *The Place of Christ in Liturgical Prayer*, London ²1989.

H. U. Instinsky, *Die alte Kirche und das Heil des Staates*, Munich 1963.

E. Dassmann, *Die Frömmigkeit des Kirchenvaters Ambrosius von Mailand*, Münster 1965, cf. TRE 2, 1978, pp 362–86 (with bibl.).

R. Farina, *L'impero e l'imperatore cristiano in Eusebio di Cesarea. La prima teologia politica del cristianesimo*, Zürich 1966.

E. Sauser, *Frühchristliche Kunst. Sinnbild und Glaubensaussage*, Innsbruck 1966 (with bibl.).

F. Szabó, *Le Christ créateur chez s. Ambroise*, Rome 1968.

W. Hagemann, *Wort als Begegnung mit Christus. Die christozentrische Schriftauslegung des Kirchenvaters Hieronymus*, Trier 1972.

G. Toscani, *Teologia della Chiesa in sant'Ambrogio*, Milan 1974 (with bibl.).

U. Süssenbach, *Christuskult und kaiserliche Baupolitik bei Konstantin dem Großen*, Bonn 1977.

M. J. Rondeau, *Les commentaires patristiques du psautier (IIIᵉ-Vᵉ siècles), I. Les travaux des Pères grecs et latins sur le psautier. Recherches et bilan*, Rome 1982.

See also:

J. Driscoll, *The 'Ad Monachos' of Evagrius Ponticus* (StudAnselm 104), Rome 1992 (with bibl.).

To get an idea of how the early Christians thought and felt about Jesus, how they let him influence them and how they in consequence lived their baptismal faith, it is not sufficient to take into consideration the ecclesiastical proclamation of the faith and the theology based on it. Rather, attention must be given to the area of life which is defined as Christian spirituality or Christian piety. Consideration must also be given to the Christian ideals which moved the believers of earlier times and to the attitude with which they faced the problems of human life. This is of course true also for the period which began with the council of Nicea and which can be called the era of the imperial Church.

The spirituality of that time is marked by a very pronounced christocentrism. This orientation towards Christ, above all evident in the title 'Lord and Saviour' (*Kyrios soter – Dominus salvator*), is without doubt rooted in the Nicene faith. The debate about the true divinity of Christ made Christ, and him as king of glory, the centre of the life of faith, far more than had been the case before. This development was also decisively furthered by the growing monasticism of the time. The monastic movement, which preserved the old ideals of the spirituality of baptism and martyrdom for a new age, sought its fulfilment not only in imitation of Jesus as the one who was obedient to the end, but also, and above all, in union with the deifying God-man. Finally, the forms of expression of this new Christ-centred spirituality are to be explained to a large extent by the changed political and social position of the Church, which also determined in many respects the struggle over the Nicene faith and the rise of monasticism. In fact, at that time, the image of Christ assumed, to a degree unknown before, political and military traits. The Christ of the imperial Church was no longer the Christ of the martyrs' Church; he was rather a *Christus Imperator,* the *Rex gloriae.*

I. CHRISTUS – IMPERATOR

The new situation, which had been caused by the victorious resistance of Christianity to its pagan persecutors and by Constantine's conversion to the Church in the first decades of the fourth century, did not of course remain unnoticed by the contemporary Christian historians. This is especially the case with Eusebius, the bishop of Caesarea in Palestine, who is renowned for being the first historian of the Church. For he was the first to develop a theology of history, which may properly be called political theology.[1]

This theology of history did not, however, appear all at once. Eusebius rather worked it out gradually as he was exposed to the greatness of the Roman Empire and became the friend of the first Christian emperor.[2] In its final stages (certainly after 324), the Logos is represented as the original image, the emperor its copy. As the saviour subordinates the higher empire to the Father, so the emperor, the friend of God, prepares his subjects for the empire of the Son. The Word fights invisible adversaries, whereas the emperor fights the visible enemies of truth, the pagans and the heretics. The Word sows the truth of salvation in the believers' hearts, the emperor, on the other hand, proclaims to the world the laws

---

[1] R. Farina, *L'impero e l'imperatore cristiano in Eusebio di Cesarea,* p 258; cf. also J.-M. Sansterre, 'Eusèbe de Césarée et la naissance de la théologie "césaropapiste"', Byzantion 42, 1972, pp 131–95. 532–94; D. S. Wallace-Hadrill, 'Eusebius von Caesarea', TRE 10, 1982, pp 537–43 (bibl.).

[2] Cf. A. Grillmeier, *Jesus Christus,* pp 388–94 (=*Christ in Christian Tradition,* pp 250–6), with bibl. note about the development of Eusebius' conceptions of historical theology.

of *pietas* and *justitia.* The Word opens the gates of heaven, whereas the emperor leads the multitudes into the basilicas so that all who are governed by him may find salvation.[3] Thus the whole universe appears to be *logikos,* being sustained in welfare by the Word and by its image on earth, the emperor. As the emperor is the copy of the image, his duty is to imitate the Word's example in all respects. Through this *mimesis* he should participate in the power of the Word. In this imitation he succeeds all the more easily, since he, as God's friend, is continually inspired by the spirit of God.[4]

In the light of this political theology, or rather, soteriology, it becomes comprehensible why from that time on Christ has been regarded as *imperator,* as lord of the world.[5] In fact, in the new ideological climate of the emerging imperial church a kind of exchange between christological and imperial titles was soon effected. On the one hand there were transferred to Christ titles, which typically had an imperial meaning, such as *rex universitatis, pambasileus,* while biblical names for Christ, such as *kyrios, soter, rex gentium, creator,* were reinterpreted in an imperial sense. On the other hand, the emperor was given titles, which embrace a christological meaning, such as servant of God, shepherd, peacemaker, physician of souls, father.[6] In this context the title of *Dominus salvator* is especially worthy of note. Even though it goes back to the New Testament, in the fourth century it gained particular significance. As regards content it reproduces the Nicene antithesis of *creator* and *redemptor.* Its success and political ring, however, cannot be understood without the imperial background, for in a similar way Constantine and his sons let themselves be called *conservator dominus noster.*[7]

This 'imperial' christology also constitutes the framework for the reception by the imperial Church of the Roman concept of *salus.* The Christians probably took over this 'salutology' right from the beginning. In spite of all their rejection of pagan idolatry, they still prayed, as did the Jews before them, for the safety of the emperor and thus for the welfare of the state.[8] The imperial Church, however, does not only pray for the now Christian emperor,[9] it is convinced that the emperor, if he fears God and defends the true faith, attains from heaven welfare for himself and the empire.[10] Christian authors like Ambrose do not hesitate to turn this salutology to account as christology. They speak of *salus aeterna, salus generis humani* and suchlike, and thus indicate that the Christian believer expects from Christ *salus vera,* just as the citizen hopes for

---

[3] Eusebius Caes., De laudibus Constantini 2.2ff: GCS, Euseb. I, p 199.

[4] Cf. R. Farina, *L'impero,* pp 123–7, with other texts from De laudibus Constantini.

[5] Cf. E. Peterson, *Theologische Traktate,* Munich 1951, pp 149–64: Christus als Imperator, as well as J. Kollwitz, 'Christus Basileus', RAC 2, 1954, cols. 1257–67, and J. Kollwitz, 'Christusbild', RAC 3, 1957, cols. 1–24.

[6] Cf. R. Farina, *L'impero,* pp 195–200, with Eusebius, PraepEv XII 44.1f, and E. Sauser, *Frühchristliche Kunst,* pp 410f.

[7] Cf. B. Studer, 'A propos des traductions d'Origène par Jérôme et Rufin', VetChr 5, 1968, pp 137–55, and B. Studer, *Soteriologie,* pp 122f.

[8] Cf. I Clem 60.4; Tertullian, Apol 30; also K. Baus, HKG I, pp 358f.

[9] Cf. the edict by Galerius and Lactantius, Instit VII 21.17; also C. Andresen, 'Erlösung', RAC 6, 1966, cols. 181ff, and N. Brox, 'Soteria und Salus', EvTh 33, 1973, pp 253–79, esp. pp 273ff, 277.

[10] Cf. Ambrose, Fid II 16, pp 136–43.

his welfare from the emperor.[11] In a similar way the Fathers and, in consequence, the liturgy, speak of the *adventus salvatoris* or *apparitio salvatoris,* thus evoking associations with the advent of an emperor or a commander into a city.[12]

The impact of this politically inspired theology, finally, is evident from the manner in which, in liturgical and synodal gatherings, the ancient acclamation is taken over.[13] A good example is the *Te Deum,* where such acclamations are woven together with biblical formulae.[14] The extent to which ecclesiastical thought and feeling, and thus also a Christ-centred spirituality, have been shaped by the political ideology of the fourth century,[15] is confirmed by the rise and the form of certain feasts (Christmas, Epiphany, the Ascension of Christ),[16] by the fact that churches are formed on the model of, and named after, imperial basilicas,[17] as well as by the imperial depiction of Christ in the apses of churches.[18]

II. CHRISTUS – REX GLORIAE

The re-interpretation of the biblical title *Rex gloriae,* 'lord of glory', is to be seen in the same political perspective as gained its most striking expression in the theology of Eusebius.[19] For Eusebius the perseverance of the church over against her persecutors and the subsequent liberation under Constantine are to be equated with the victory of Christ himself.[20] This victory will be consolidated in the christianized empire under the emperor, the image and representative, and will be perfected some day when Christ subjects all to the Father.[21] For Eusebius Christ does not only prove to be the true emperor, but also to be the triumphant lord of the whole world.[22]

[11] Cf. C. Andresen, 'Erlösung', RAC 6, 1966, cols. 163–80, and esp. H. U. Instinsky, *Die alte Kirche und das Heil des Staates,* Munich 1963.

[12] Cf. e.g. Ambrose, HomLc 10.39, on Luke 21:27; Augustine, Quaest 83.58.3; Leo, Tract 63.2, with salus ventura, 63.4; also C. Andresen, 'Erlösung', RAC 6, 1966, cols. 182f, 185.

[13] Cf. T. Klauser, 'Akklamation', RAC 1, 1950, cols. 227–31; C. Andresen, 'Erlösung', RAC 6, 1966, cols. 182f, 185.

[14] Cf. E. Kähler, *Studien zum Te Deum und zur Geschichte des 24.Psalmes in der alten Kirche,* Göttingen 1958.

[15] Cf. the relevant articles in LThK and TRE; also W. Dürig, *Pietas liturgica,* pp 196–207: 'Pietas als Terminus der liturgischen Heilands- und Rettertheologie'.

[16] Cf. E. Sauser, *Frühchristliche Kunst,* pp 456–511, and U. Süssenbach, *Christuskult und kaiserliche Baupolitik bei Konstantin.*

[17] Cf. E. Sauser, *Frühchristliche Kunst,* pp 456–511, and C. Ihm, *Die Programme der christlichen Apsismalerei vom 4.Jh. bis zur Mitte des 8.Jh.,* Wiesbaden 1960.

[18] Cf. E. Peterson, *Theologische Traktate,* pp 54–147: 'Der Monotheismus als politisches Problem', also A. Schindler, ed., *Monotheismus as politisches Problem? Erik Peterson und die Kritik der politischen Theologie,* Gütersloh 1978, and E. Peterson, *Il monoteismo come problema politico,* Brescia 1983.

[19] Cf. P. Beskow, *Rex gloriae.*

[20] Cf. among others Lactantius, MortPers 1, introduction, Instit VII 27, and Eusebius Caes., HE I 1.2; VIII 16.1f; X 9.6–9; X 10.1–5.

[21] Cf. Eusebius Caes., De laudibus Constantini 1.6: GCS, Euseb. I, pp 198f.

[22] Cf. Eusebius Caes., HE X 4.15f (taken from the speech held at the consecration of the church of Tyre). Other texts in P. Beskow, *Rex gloriae,* pp 261–8.

It is true that this triumphalist christology is rooted in the bible: in the monarchy of the Old Testament, above all in the psalms, in the apocalyptic setting of the Easter message, which presented Christ as *Kyrios* (I Cor 2:8). The Church of the martyrs also never lost a feeling for the *Rex gloriae*.[23] Nevertheless, we have to recognize in this Christian triumphalism a particular feature of the preaching and spirituality of imperial christianity, which was overwhelmed by the impact of the triumph of the Christian faith, and thus more open than earlier generations to the ideas of *pax romana,* the pacification of the world by the Romans, and of *salus generis humani,* the welfare of all men, secured by the Romans.[24] It is not to be excluded that the theme of the subjection of all things (I Cor 15:45ff), which was of such great interest in the polemics against the Arians and against Marcellus of Ancyra, had particular relevance in the Churches' new situation.[25] At any rate, it is not difficult to trace the Roman language of triumph in the sermons of the fourth and fifth century. Ambrose, Augustine and Leo are fond of using such language to describe the way of the cross or the ascension of Christ.[26]

This triumphalist christology of the fourth century is further confirmed by the veneration of the cross of Christ which arose at that time.[27] Indeed, the depiction of the cross, as we find it in the Constantinian churches, appears to be a novelty which cannot simply be reduced to the sign of the cross of earlier tradition.[28] For the political significance of the symbol of the cross differs from the originally apotropaic use of the sign of the cross and also from its eschatological meaning. There is the link between the *crux invicta* and the *labarum* of the Roman legions and other imperial insignia. This is reinforced by the victorious cross of the legend of Constantine's victory at the Milvian bridge ('With this sign you shall conquer').[29] Hence the *theologia gloriae,* which stands behind the Constantinian *crux invicta,* must be understood in the same way as the transformation of the *labarum* into the monogram of Christ (or into a cross). Even later the cross will retain this triumphal, eminently political sense, as the so-called Imperial Cross bears witness.[30]

[23] Cf. P. Beskow, *Rex gloriae,* pp 173–86, with the Acta Scilitanorum, AD 180, pp 5f, 17; Acta Apollonii, AD 183/85, p 8f; Hippolytus, Antichr 6; Cyprian, ep. 10.4; also L. Koep, 'Kaisertum und Christusbekenntnis im Widerspruch', JbAC 4, 1961, pp 58–76.

[24] Cf. R. Farina, *L'impero,* pp 131–65, with Eusebius Caes., PraepEv I 4.2–5; DemEv VII 2.19–23; HE X 1.1, and C. Andresen, 'Erlösung', RAC 6, 1966, cols. 163–80.

[25] Cf. P. Beskow, *Rex gloriae,* pp 231–236, and E. Schendel, *Herrschaft und Unterwerfung Christi. 1.Kor 15,24–27 in Exegese und Theologie der Väter bis zum Ausgang des 4. Jh.,* Tübingen 1971, esp. pp 111–43.

[26] Cf. Ambrose, Fid IV 1.1–2.26; HomLc 10.107–112; Gregory of Nyssa, In Christi Ascensionem: MG 46, 693A-D; Augustine, TractIo 36.4; serm. 263.1; Leo, Tract 69.4; 74.1; also B. Studer, 'Die anti-arianische Auslegung von Ps 23,7–10 in De Fide IV 1–2', Y. Duval, ed., *Ambroise de Milan,* Paris 1974, pp 245–66, esp. pp 260–3.

[27] Cf. H. Jedin and J. Dolan, eds., *History of the Church,* vol II, pp 319–21, and esp. P. Stockmeier, *Theologie und Kult des Kreuzes bei Johannes Chrysostomus. Ein Beitrag zum Verständnis der Kreuzverehrung im 4.Jh.,* Leiden 1967.

[28] Cf. C. Andresen, 'Erlösung', RAC 6, 1966, cols. 178ff, and H. Rahner, *Symbole der Kirche,* Salzburg 1964, pp 361–431: Antenna crucis.

[29] Cf. Lactantius, MortPers 44.5, and Eusebius Caes., Vita Constantini I 27–32; also H. Jedin and J. Dolan, eds., *History of the Church,* vol. 1, pp 410ff.

[30] Cf. C. Andresen, *Die Kirchen der alten Christenheit,* pp 330f, who sides with E. Dinkler, *Signum crucis,* Tübingen 1969.

Constantine the Great has in yet another way advanced triumphalist christology. Not only must the appearance of the *crux invicta,* the *tropaion soterion* be attributed to him, but also the beginning of the veneration of the relics of the cross.[31] According to a tradition to which already Ambrose testifies,[32] the mother of the emperor is said to have rediscovered the true cross. At any rate, Constantine caused to be erected not only the basilica of the Resurrection in Jerusalem, but also the martyrion for the relics of the cross; both churches were consecrated in 335.[33] In consequence, we encounter in the Holy City the veneration of the cross, to which Cyril of Jerusalem[34] and the account of the pilgrim Egeria bear witness.[35] The chapel of the cross with its relics became the main object of pilgrimages to the Holy Land, which are established in the fourth century.[36] Thus the veneration of the cross, which commenced at that time, confirms the extent to which the imperial Church has seen in Christ the triumphant king, the true Lord of the earth.[37]

III. CHRISTUS – OMNIA

Without doubt the 'imperial' and the 'triumphalist' christology of the fourth century expresses in a very special way how markedly Christ-centred the spirituality of the Christians of the imperial Church has become. It is not so easy, however, to ascertain the extent to which this christocentrism is to be traced back to the new political situation of the Church and the extent to which other factors, above all the struggle for the Nicene faith, were of influence. It can, however, be taken for granted that this christocentrism is to be found in the whole of ecclesiastical life, and thus by no means bears only political features. A glance at contemporary christological exegesis, at the christocentrism of Eastern monasticism, as well as at Ambrose's spirituality of Christ, makes this clear.

As regards christological exegesis, it should suffice to point to the development of the exegesis of the psalms.[38] For the psalms are known to have

---

[31] Cf. D. Schaefers, 'Kreuz IX: Geschichte der Kreuzreliquien', LThK 6, 1961, 614f, and esp. G. Frolow, *La relique de la vraie croix. Recherches sur le développement d'un culte,* Paris 1961, and P. Stockmeier, *Theologie und Kult des Kreuzes* pp 194–202, and F. Thélamon, *Paiens et chrétiens au IVe siècle. L'apport de l'Histoire ecclésiastique de Rufin d'Aquilée,* Paris 1982, esp. pp 344ff: the discovery of the cross.

[32] Ambrose, ObitTheodos 43–8; Cf. Cyril of Jerus., ep. ad Constantium 3–6 (CPG II, 3587), who in order to confirm the authenticity of the relics of the cross reports a vision of the cross, and Rufinus, HE X 7f: ML 21, 475f.

[33] Cf. P. Maraval, *Égérie, Journal de voyage,* SChr 296, Paris 1982, pp 60–6, with sources and a bibliographical note.

[34] Cf. besides ep. ad Constantium 3–6, Cyril of Jerus., Catech 4.10, 10.19; 13.4; 17.10.

[35] Egeria, Itin 36.5–37.3.

[36] Cf. B. Kötting, *Peregrinatio religiosa,* Münster 1950; B. Kötting, 'Wallfahrt', LThK 10, 1965, 942–6, and H. Dorner, *Pilgerfahrt ins Heilige Land. Die ältesten Berichte christlicher Palästinapilger* (4th-7th cent.), Stuttgart 1979.

[37] This also implies a new understanding of the Christus praesens in Ecclesia.

[38] Cf. B. Fischer, *Die Psalmenfrömmigkeit der Märtyrerkirche,* Freiburg 1949; A. Rose, *Psaumes et prière chrétienne,* Bruges 1965, and esp. M. J. Rondeau, *Les commentaires patristiques du psautier.*

taken a prominent place right from the beginning in the christological collections of *testimonia*. After the New Testament writings, the best witness for this is Justin, who in his commentary on the 21st psalm supplies one of the first examples of a continuous scriptural commentary.[39] Origen and Eusebius further extended the exegesis of the psalms, and this fully in line with their hermeneutics, according to which the whole bible contains the Logos.[40] Athanasius goes beyond them in that he has left us a special treatise on the use of the psalms, the *Epistula ad Marcellinum*.[41] There he states that the psalms are like a mirror, in which we can not only recognize human life but also the image of Christ.[42] Latin exegesis, as it is first of all represented by Jerome and Augustine, even envisages in the psalms a prayer to Christ. Thus it transfers to the prayer of the psalms a form of prayer which in early Christian spirituality had already long before been developed alongside liturgical prayer, which was directed exclusively to the Father.[43] In Augustine this christological exegesis will finally reach its most perfect expression. Following the Donatist Tyconius he distinguishes in the psalms between *vox Christi capitis, vox Christi corporis* and *vox totius Christi*.[44] Hence the exegesis of the psalms in the fourth century (with the exception of that of the Antiochene exegetes) gives an idea of the extent to which the spirituality of that time has become christocentric.[45]

Another form of christocentrism from that time we encounter in the spiritual teaching of the eastern monks.[46] For when after the end of the persecution monasticism first began to spread from Egypt to all churches of the empire, it took over, together with the ancient Christian ideals of faithfulness to baptism, full self-surrender in martyrdom, and virginity consecrated to God, the christocentrism that was inherent in all this. Under the influence of the Arian controversy and the corresponding christological exegesis, as well as of the Christ-centred spirituality of the imperial Church, attachment to Christ had grown still more radical with the monks of the fourth century.[47]

The first testimony to this is presented us by Athanasius in his *Vita Antonii*, in that, in this first biography of a monk, he represents the famous hermit as an

---

[39] Justin, Dial 98.1–105.6.

[40] Cf. M. J. Rondeau, *Les commentaires patristiques du psautier*, pp 44–77 (collection of texts).

[41] Athanasius, Ad Marcellinum, CPG II, 2097; cf. M. J. Rondeau, *Les commentaires patristiques du psautier*, pp 79f, and H. J. Sieben, 'Athanasius über den Psalter', TheolPhil 48, 1973, pp 157–73.

[42] Athanasius, Ad Marcellinum 12ff: MG 27, 24B-25C.

[43] Cf. A. Grillmeier, *Jesus Christus*, p 592, bibl. note (=*Christ in Christian Tradition*, p 403).

[44] Cf. M. Pontet, *L'exégèse de s. Augustin prédicateur*, Paris n.d., pp 387–418, and H. U. von Balthasar, *Aurelius Augustinus, Über die Psalmen*, Einsiedeln 1983 (a selection from the commentaries on the psalms in German translation).

[45] It is worth considering in this context how e.g. Ps 94:1 (Vg) and Isa 43:10 are employed in relation to New Testament texts. A fine example of this method is found with the 5th cent. author Faustus of Riez, De Spiritu Sancto 1.1: CSEL 21, 106; cf. similarly, Hilary, TractPs 126.10f; Ambrose, Expl Ps 48.1–5; ExposPs 118.19.5–11. For the Antiochene exegesis of the psalms, on the other hand, Theodore of Mopsuestia is typical. He expounds only Pss 2, 8, 44, 109 in the messianic sense. On this issue see M. Simonetti, *Profilo storico dell'esegesi patristica*, Rome 1981, who refers to R. Devreesse, *Essai sur Théodore de Mopsueste*, Città del Vaticano 1948, pp 73ff.

[46] Cf. B. Studer, *Soteriologie*, pp 153f, and esp. U. Ranke-Heinemann, *Das frühe Mönchtum. Seine Motive nach den Selbstzeugnissen*, Essen 1964.

[47] Cf. H. Jedin and J. Dolan, eds., *History of the Church*, vol. 2, pp 339ff.

imitator of Christ and at the same time a defender of true faith in Christ.[48] This christocentrism finds an even more original expression with Evagrius, a famous representative of the Origenist monks.[49] According to him it is fitting that Christ in particular should lead rational beings back to the original contemplation of the Godhead. For various beings intervene in this ascent in their different ways: the demons try to draw back higher beings to their level, whereas the angels strive to lead other beings to the angelic life. In this struggle the main role falls to Christ. He is a spiritual being like the others, however he has remained faithful to the Word. Through him the second creation has been initiated for the salvation of all, and through him all will be liberated some day and brought back to the unity of all, i.e. to the equality of all in the contemplation of the Word.[50] Even though in this doctrine of the spiritual life certain elements are to be found which according to the later norm of faith cannot be regarded as orthodox, such as the pre-existence of souls, or the universal restoration,[51] the great ideal must be acknowledged, according to which the monk must through knowledge unite himself with Christ, and thus attain to contemplation of the eternal Word.[52] At any rate, this christocentrism of Evagrius exerted an immeasurable influence on eastern as well as western monasticism. In the east the monks, especially those under his influence, are going to side with monophysitism, which promises divinization.[53] In the west his influence will reach, by means of John Cassian and the *Regula Magistri,* as far as the Rule of St. Benedict, and thus to almost the whole of Western monasticism.[54]

A christocentrism, no less pronounced, though of a different kind, is found in Ambrose of Milan (+397). This saint, who changed from being a statesman to being the spiritual head of the western imperial city, not only to a large extent shaped ecclesiastical life in Italy of that time, overcame Arianism in so far as it remained in the West, promoted the quest of western theology for parity with eastern theology, surpassing Hilary in this respect, but, and what is more, became the teacher of spiritual life for the Western Church.[55]

His teaching on perfection is clearly centred around the ideal of *Christus omnia.*[56] Ambrose certainly in his treatises *De fide* and *De Spiritu Sancto* made

[48] Cf. L. Bouyer, *La vie de s. Antoine. Essai sur la spiritualité du monachisme primitif,* St.Wandrille 1950, and C. Mohrmann et al., *Vita di Antonio,* Verona 1974.

[49] Cf. A. Guillaumont, *'Kephalaia Gnostica',* esp. pp 151–6; A. Guillaumont, 'Evagrius', TRE 10, 1982, pp 565–70, with bibl.

[50] Cf. Evagrius, CentGnost, S¹, II 75f (fall); III 26 (creation of the corporeal world through Christ); II 6 (return to gnosis); VI 86 (the angelic help); IV 18 (knowledge through Christ), IV 8f; III 72 (perfection through Christ).

[51] Cf. A. Guillaumont, *'Kephalaia Gnostica',* esp. pp 156–70, and A. Grillmeier, *Jesus Christus,* pp 561–8 (=*Christ in Christian Tradition,* pp 377–84).

[52] Cf. Evagrius, CentGnost III 72; IV 8.

[53] Cf. A. Guillaumont, *'Kephalaia Gnostica',* pp 128–33; TRE 10, 1982, pp 568f; A. Adam, *Dogmengeschichte* I, pp 347–51.

[54] Cf. S. Marsili, *Giovanni Cassiano ed Evagrio Pontico,* Rome 1936; for the christocentrism esp. of the Regula monasteriorum see the ed. of C. Butler, Freiburg ²1927, and A. Borias, 'Le Christ dans la règle de s.Benôit', RBén 82, 1972, pp 109–39.

[55] Cf. E. Dassmann, *Frömmigkeit;* E. Dassmann, 'Ambrosius von Mailand', TRE 2, 1978, pp 362–86, with bibl.

[56] Cf. besides E. Dassmann, *Frömmigkeit,* pp 116–34; 211–14, K. Baus, 'Das Nachwirken des Origenes in der Christusfrömmigkeit des hl. Ambrosius', RQ 49, 1954, pp 21–55.

himself a determined defender of Nicene trinitarian dogma, and elsewhere has much to say about the Trinity.[57] His later writings in particular are orientated towards trinitarian doctrine; proof of this is his theme of the knowledge of the Father through the Son.[58] Nevertheless, with Ambrose Christ is always in the foreground. He even devoted a treatise especially to the incarnation.[59]

This christocentrism appears first of all in the extensive identification of *Deus* and *Dominus,* but also in the use of the formula *Dominus salvator.*[60] These phenomena can also easily be found elsewhere after 380.[61] Further there is the characteristic fact that Ambrose directs prayer far more often directly to Christ.[62] Finally, christocentric notions proper are worthy of note. They will later, with Augustine, become dominant: *Christus via – Christus patria* and *per Christum hominem ad Christum Deum.*[63]

This christocentric reduction is certainly for the most part caused by the anti-Arian orientation of Ambrose's theology.[64] However, account must be taken of the influence of Neoplatonism, which is now found in the ecclesiastical community of Milan.[65] Against this background it is easier to understand what Ambrose means when presenting Christ as the light, which mediates to us knowledge of the Father,[66] just as it can be better appreciated why he is able to reduce the illuminating function of Christ so easily to the relationship: *Christus – lux – anima.*[67]

Despite all his dogmatic and philosophical interests, Ambrose's christocentrism never becomes abstract. It proves rather to be very personal and existential. For the bishop of Milan *Christus omnia* means always *Christus pro nobis,* or, still more, *Christus pro me.*[68] It is true, the christology of all the Fathers must be understood as soteriology. Even Nicene theology with all its interest in the doctrine of God, never neglected the *qui propter nos homines* (DS 125): a theology, fully orientated to the incarnation of the Son of God, such as that of Athanasius or Hilary, makes this clear. However, there are but a few Christian authors who have emphasized to this extent the *pro nobis.* To Ambrose Latin theology owes the *felix culpa,* i.e. the *mirabiliter condidisti, sed mirabilius*

[57] Cf. L. Hermann, 'Ambrosius von Mailand als Trinitätstheologe', ZKG 69, 1958, pp 197–218, with bibl.; G. Toscani, *Ambrogio,* pp 247–86.

[58] Cf. E. Dassmann, *Frömmigkeit,* pp 123, 211–14, with Fid V 12.150; ExplPs 38.24; HomLc 2.93f.

[59] Cf. besides G. Toscani, *Ambrogio,* pp 286–332, A.-L. Fenger, *Aspekte der Soteriologie und Ekklesiologie bei Ambrosius von Mailand,* Frankfurt/Bern 1981, with bibl.

[60] Cf. for Christ as *Dominus* and *Deus* e.g. Ambrose, InterpellDav III 11.28–31, for Dominus salvator or salutaris Fid II 1.16; ExplPs 45.11, 16; HomLc 2.1; 4.57, for creator-redemptor Fid III 2.7f; HomLc 4.58, and for principium et finis Exam I 4.15–5.19; Sacr V 1.1.

[61] Cf. B. Studer, 'A propos des Traductions d'Origène par Jérôme et Rufin', VetChr 5, 1968, pp 137–55, esp. pp 138, 152f.

[62] Cf. E. Dassmann, *Frömmigkeit,* p 213, with a reference to K. Baus, art.cit.: RQ 49, 1954, p 46.

[63] Cf. Ambrose, HomLc 2.46f; 9.2; ep. 4 (40). 4; InterpellDav III 4.17; ExposPs 118.22.7 (per Christum ad Patrem).

[64] Cf. esp. F. Szabó, *Le Christ créateur.*

[65] Cf. G. Madec, *S. Ambroise et la philosophie,* Paris 1974.

[66] Cf. Exam II 5.19; Spir I 14.140–3.

[67] Cf. ExposPs 118.21.24.

[68] Cf. de virginitate 16.99; epp 4.4; 24 (82), 13; InterpellDav III 11.28–31; cf. also the notion of 'Christ omnipresent': HomLc 2.13.

reformasti.[69] And not without reason the *Exultet* was later attributed to him.[70] Above all he manifested to posterity in an outstanding way, how personally, even affectionately, the *pro nobis* must be understood.[71]

This thoroughly personal Christ-spirituality has probably found its deepest expression in what Ambrose, said on the *doctor humilitatis,* a theme which may be regarded as the most precious heritage which he bequeathed to his most famous convert, Augustine. According to this, it is the humility of Christ that led him to become man, and it is this humility of Christ that we most need to imitate.[72]

Thus Ambrose's christocentrism clearly confirms almost everything that can be said of the spirituality of the fourth century. It is in every respect about a personal relation to Christ, the incarnate saviour. With all the emphasis on the presence of Christ within the Church and in the individual soul Christians of that time never forget that the saving presence of Christ is based on his saving acts in history, above all in his death and resurrection; this is why they worship on Sundays, perform baptism and every year observe the memory of the mysteries of Jesus.[73]

A quotation from Jerome may confirm how much Ambrose reproduces the ideal of spirituality of the end of the fourth century: *Christus omnia, ut, qui omnia propter Christum dimiserit, unum inveniat pro omnibus et possit libere proclamare: pars mea Dominus* (Ps 72:26).[74]

In the spirituality of the imperial Church Christ above all features as God, as the almighty ruler of the universe. This is certainly connected with the Arian controversy, which resulted in granting to Christ equal status with the Father in all respects, even with regard to omnipotence, immortality and invisibility.[75] The influence of political theology must, however, also be reckoned with, for Constantine the Great has made Christ his imperial God, his lord and saviour.[76]

This noticeable emphasis on the divinity of Christ appears on closer investigation to constitute a pronounced christocentrism. This observation is not greatly affected by the fact that theology in the first half of the fourth century had to defend the equality of the Son with the Father, and in the second half the divinity of the Holy Spirit, thus clearly expressing the doctrine of the eternal Trinity in contemporary language. It must however be taken into account that the baptismal faith, which in the liturgy is ever anew reflected on and, above all,

[69] Cf. ExplPs 39.20; 37.58; HomLc 2.41; Iac I 6.21; also F. Szabó, *Le Christ créateur,* pp 84ff.

[70] Cf. L. Kunz and H. Lausberg, 'Exultet iam angelica turba', LThK 3, 1959, 1318f, with bibl.; A. Chupungco, 'Exultet', EEC 1, 1992, pp 313f.

[71] Cf. Ambrose, ExposPs 118.8.7; 118.12.37; De bono mortis 6.26; HomLc 2.41; ExposPs 118.20.19; ep. 36(2), 18–22.

[72] Cf. ExposPs 118.20.3, 18.20; 118.14.46; ApolDav I 81; Fid III 7.52: principium humilitatis Christi.

[73] Cf. B. Studer, *Soteriologie,* pp 145ff.

[74] Jerome, ep. 66.8.

[75] Cf. Ambrose, Fid II 4.34–37; III 2.11ff; III 3.21f; V 2.36; also B. Studer, *Die antiarianische Auslegung von Ps 23, 7–10 . . . ,* pp 249–55; F. Szabó, *Le Christ créateur,* pp 31–5.

[76] Cf. Constantius, ep. 5: CSEL 26, 210.4f; ep. ad Alexandrum et Arium; Eusebius, Vita Constantini II 64: GCS, Euseb. I, 67.

experienced afresh, has always kept alive the mystery of the triune God in the consciousness of the believer.[77]

The orientation towards Christ as God in the spirituality of the imperial Church must not however be overrated. Also the differences between east and west must be heeded, as will be shown more thoroughly in the following discussion. It is true that Christ's manhood retreats still further in the life of faith. His inner life arises no particularly active interest. This is understandable when we take into consideration that for a long time the soul of Jesus had been widely neglected for theological and philosophical reasons.[78] For all that it is not to be forgotten that it is precisely in the era of Nicene dogma that pilgrimages to the Holy sites of Palestine and the veneration of the cross begin. The Jesus-spirituality of such as Ambrose, Jerome, and others, which was inherited from Origen, must not be overlooked. When the Christ-spirituality of the fourth century bears on the humanity and also the physical and spiritual weakness of Jesus, it does so, however, with a predilection for a triumphalistic perspective. This sense of the glorification of Jesus, of his suffering and death, like the preference for his royal and sovereign dignity, must be understood in relation to the new situation of the liberated and victorious Church.

---

[77] Cf. esp. the mystagogic catecheses by Cyril of Jerus. and by Ambrose of Milan; also B. Studer, *Soteriologie*, pp 148ff.

[78] Cf. A. Grillmeier, *Jesus Christus*, pp 495ff (=*Christ in Christian Tradition*, pp 341ff). It should be noted that the Church fathers had very little interest in developing a general human psychology.

12. The Formulation of Trinitarian Faith by the Cappadocians

BIBLIOGRAPHY

K. Holl, *Amphilochius von Ikonium in seinem Verhältnis zu den großen Kappadoziern*, Tübingen 1904.

H. Dörries, *De Spiritu Sancto. Der Beitrag des Basilius zum Abschluß des trinitarischen Dogmas*, Göttingen 1956.

E. Mühlenberg, *Die Unendlichkeit Gottes bei Gregor von Nyssa. Gregors Kritik am Gottesbegriff der klassischen Metaphysik*, Göttingen 1966.

W.-D. Hauschild, 'Die Pneumatomachen. Eine Untersuchung zur Dogmengeschichte des 4.Jahrhunderts', thesis, Hamburg 1967.

B. Pruche, *S. Basile, Sur le S. Esprit* (=SChr 17 bis), Paris 1968 (cf. RchSR 52, 1964, pp 204–32).

J. Barbel, *Gregor von Nyssa, Die große katechetische Rede*, Stuttgart 1971.

R. Hübner, *Die Einheit des Leibes Christi bei Gregor von Nyssa. Untersuchungen zum Ursprung der 'physischen' Erlösungslehre*, Leiden 1974.

M. Tetz, 'Über nikänische Orthodoxie. Der sog. Tomus ad Antiochenos des Athanasius von Alexandrien', ZNW 66, 1975, pp 194–222.

P. J. Fedwick, *The Church and the Charisma of Leadership in Basil of Caesarea*, Toronto 1979, with bibl.

P. Luislampe, *Spiritus vivificans. Grundzüge einer Theologie des Heiligen Geistes nach Basilius von Caesarea*, Münster 1981.

A. Meredith, 'The Pneumatology of the Cappadocian Fathers and the Creed of Constantinople', IrTheolQu 48, 1981, pp 196–211.

W.-D. Hauschild, 'Eustathius von Sebaste', TRE 10, 1982, pp 547–50.

A. M. Ritter, 'Eunomius', TRE 10, 1982, pp 525–8.

R. Schwager, Der wunderbare Tausch. Zur 'physischen' Erlösungslehre Gregors von Nyssa: ZKTh 104, 1982, pp 1–24, now collected in *Der wunderbare Tausch*, Munich 1986, pp 77–100.

P. J. Fedwick, ed., *Basil of Caesarea*, Toronto 1981.

M. Simonetti, *'Genesi e sviluppo della dottrina trinitaria di Basilio di Cesarea'*, Atti di Messina, dic. 1979, Messina 1983, pp 169–97.

See also:

K. Koschorke, *Spuren der alten Liebe. Studien zum Kirchenbegriff des Basilius von Caesarea* (Paradosis 32), Freiburg 1991 (with bibl.).

R. Pochet, *Basile le Grand et son univers d'amis d'après sa correspondance* (Studia Ephemeridis 'Augustinianum' 36), Rome 1992 (with bibl.).

I. HISTORICAL ORIENTATION

Under the decisive influence of the emperor Constantine the Great the first ecumenical council had in its condemnation of Arius in fact compromised the whole Origenist school. Hence a strong reaction from this side could not fail to emerge. At the latest after the death of Constantine, who had approved the Nicene decisions, the adherents of Origenist theology had to put up a fight. A criticism of the faith of Nicea was inevitable, the more so as it had left undiscussed some decisive questions. Thus it did not define how the divine unity was to be understood; neither did it explain any further, in what sense the eternal generation is the cause of both the distinction between as well as the equality of Father and Son; finally the Nicene creed does not even speak of the joint activity of Father, Son and Spirit, scarcely mentioning the latter. On the level of terminology more clarity was required, too, for the keyword *homoousios* had not been closely defined. This posed a problem, the more so as Marcellus of Ancyra's interpretation of the Nicene faith was regarded as Sabellian, and met with passionate rejection on the part of any defender of the Origenist doctrine of the three hypostases.

None of these questions found a final solution before 360. The time was not yet ripe. Neither had a reconciliation been achieved between the strict Nicenes, who unwaveringly adhered to the *homoousios* and, moreover, accepted only one hypostasis, and the so-called Semiarians,[1] who in opposition to the radical Arians stood for the *homoiousios,* and who in opposition to the Sabellians emphasized the doctrine of the three hypostases. Nor had the question of the divinity of the Holy Spirit been expressly raised. Certainly there had been preliminary decisions. So on the unitarian front Marcellus of Ancyra had already been ousted.[2] On the other hand Cyril of Jerusalem had not only distanced himself from the Arians, but had included in his theology, which was kerygmatic in character rather than dogmatic, even the divine activity of the Holy Spirit (since 348).[3] But it was not until 360 that the two above-mentioned prerequisites for a comprehensive consensus in the faith had been met.

In fact, the two moderate wings had met together at the synod of Alexandria (362), as the *Tomus ad Antiochenos,* drafted by Athanasius, above all bears witness.[4] This rapprochement had been made possible on three grounds. Since 356 Aetius and Eunomius had propagated a more radical Arianism. They

---

[1] For the term 'Semiarians' cf. Epiphanius, Haer 73.1 and Augustine, Haer 52; also M. Simonetti, *La crisi ariana,* p 240, who, however, prefers to the old expression 'Semiarians' the term of 'Homoiousians'; and esp. J. Gummerus, *Die homoeusianische Partei bis zum Tode des Konstantius,* Leipzig 1899.

[2] Cf. A. Grillmeier, *Jesus Christus,* p 439 (=*Christ in Christian Tradition,* pp 295f); G. Feige, *Die Lehre Markells,* pp 135–216.

[3] E. Yarnold, 'Cyrillus von Jerusalem', TRE 8, 1981, pp 261–6; and A. Bonato, *La dottrina trinitaria di Cirillo di Gerusalemme,* Rome 1983.

[4] Athanasius, TomAntioch: MG 26, 796–809; also M. Simonetti, *La crisi ariana,* pp 358–70, and esp. M. Tetz, 'Über nikänische Orthodoxie. Der sog. Tomus ad Antiochenos des Athanasius von Alexandrien', ZNW 66, 1975, pp 194–222, and L. Abramowski, 'Trinitarische und christologische Hypostasenformeln', TheolPhil 54, 1979, pp 38–49.

stated Father and Son to be absolutely unequal, and regarded the Holy Spirit as having been created by the Son.[5] By their intransigency they not only strengthened the resistance of the Nicenes, but also provoked the Homoiousians under the leadership of Basil of Ancyra. Moreover in 361, Constantius, who had helped radical Arianism to triumph, died. His successor Julian, on the contrary, proved to be tolerant of the Anti-Arians, even of Athanasius himself. What is more, by then doctrinal positions had converged. The Homoiousians, while emphasizing the distinction between the hypostases, dismissed the Arian doctrine and accepted the *homoiousios kata panta.* The Nicenes, under the leadership of Athanasius, dissociated themselves from the strict Unitarians and also tolerated the *homoiousios.* The reconciliation itself, which had thus been made possible, was especially evident in the fact that the Eustathians were conceded the expression *mia ousia,* while the Meletians were allowed the formula of the three hypostases.[6]

The *Tomus ad Antiochenos* also speaks of the Holy Spirit.[7] This issue had already been raised before the time of the synod of Alexandria. Since 359 Athanasius had argued against the so-called tropici in his four letters to Serapion.[8] At the same time certain Homoiousians, probably in Constantinople,[9] denied the divinity of the Holy Spirit. Thus not only on the formal level, by allowing different terminology, but also as far as content is concerned, by means of the debate about the divinity of the Holy Spirit, the trinitarian question proper had been set rolling.

II. THE DOGMATIC FORMULA
MIA OUSIA – TREIS HYPOSTASEIS

Before going into the history of the most important trinitarian formula, it is necessary to take account of the limited significance of the history of such formulae. The dogmatic formulae must not be considered as being at the very centre of the historical development of the Christian doctrine. This is especially true of the time before 400, when dogmatic freedom was much greater than in later times. From that point of view, a partition of fourth-century dogmatic history into two parts, determined by the two formulae *homoousios* and *mia ousia-treis hypostaseis,* must appear to be very problematic. It is more in keeping with the real issues if the first phase is characterized by the phrase 'Christ is Son, not creature', while the second phase is characterized by the twin statements: 'Father and Son are different' (against the Sabellians) and 'Father and Son are one' (against the Arians).[10]

---

[5] Cf. M. Simonetti, *La crisi ariana,* pp 253–9: on the Anomoeans, also L. Abramowski, 'Eunomius', RAC 6, 1966, cols. 936–47, and A. M. Ritter, Eunomius: TRE 10, 1982, pp 525–8, with bibl.

[6] Cf. Athanasius, TomAntioch 5: MG 26, 801; also M. Simonetti, *La crisi ariana,* pp 367f. Cf. also Basil, ep. 361, CPG II, 2900: authentic.

[7] Athanasius, TomAntioch 5f: MG 26, 801.

[8] Athanasius, epp ad Serapionem: MG 26, 529–676; also A. Laminski, *Der Heilige Geist,* pp 32–5.

[9] Cf. M. Simonetti, *La crisi ariana* pp 364ff.

[10] This is evident chiefly from the writings or passages which represent the *via media* between Arians and Sabellians. Cf. e.g. Gregory of Nyssa, Adv. Arium et Sabellium de patre et filio (CPG II, 3141); CatMagn 1.3; Basil, ep. 210.5; hom. 24; Spir 30.77; Gregory of Naz., or. 2.37; 31.9; Ambrose, Spir III 16.117; EpSynod of Constantinople: COecD, p 28, ll. 27–38.

One should not overlook the fact that dogmatic formulae possess less significance in ordinary preaching and came to the fore above all in apologetic writings, or in expositions addressed to intellectuals.

1. The prehistory of the Formula

In the course of the post-Nicene discussion it became ever clearer that the *homoousios* of Nicea was inadequate. It was too ambiguous to command general agreement. It could be interpreted in a Sabellian sense, thus becoming unacceptable to the adherents of Origen's three hypostases.[11] A formula was required which at the same time expressed unity and distinction. The need for a such a twin-formula at last became urgent when the synod of Alexandria of 362 accepted the formula of the three hypostases as well as the formula of one hypostasis or one ousia.[12]

Already before that time the Homoiousians in their manifesto of 359 had spoken of three hypostases, and one deity or origin. But they still used *hypostasis* and *ousia* synonymously.[13] In the same period Marius Victorinus bears witness that certain Greeks spoke of three hypostases out of one ousia.[14] Although it can no longer be determined whether he supposed these Greeks to be Christian theologians like Didymus, or pagan Neoplatonists, the fact that the *ek ousias* had replaced the *mia ousia* is worthy of note. Above all this formula betrays another way of thinking. The Cappadocians, who were to represent the formula *mia ousia – treis hypostaseis,* presupposed the Trinity and searched for the unity, while here the hypostases proceed from the one *ousia,* thereby possessing being in a diminished degree, something the Cappadocians were to reject. Finally, at the synod of Alexandria no decision in favour of the twin-formula had yet been reached. Rather, as has already been indicated, the Meletians were allowed to speak of three hypostases while the Eustathians were allowed to use the formula of one *ousia.*[15]

2. The contribution of Basil of Caesarea

Basil of Caesarea, who was close to the Homoiousians, did not yet use the twin-formula itself. But he is the first to distinguish clearly between *hypostasis* and *ousia.* He worked out this distinction in his polemic against Eunomius, who had identified the one *ousia* with unbegottenness (*agennesia*). In contrast Basil contended that unbegottenness should be regarded as *idion* and therefore as *hypostasis,* rather than as *koinon* or *ousia.*[16] In the later pneumatological

[11] Cf. the Serdican Formula: Hahn §157; also M. Simonetti, *La crisi ariana,* pp 183ff. Also Basil, epp 125.1; 210.5 and ep. 38.1 (actually by Gregory of Nyssa).

[12] Athanasius, TomAntioch 5: MG 26, 800.

[13] Cf. Epiphanius, Haer 73.12–22, and Athanasius, ep. ad Afros 4, etc., where *ousia* and *hypostasis* are used synonymously; also A. M. Ritter, *Das Konzil von Konstantinopel,* p 284f, and M. Simonetti, *La crisi ariana,* p 276, note 77.

[14] Marius Victorinus, AdvAr II 4 and III 4; cf. M. Simonetti, *La crisi ariana,* pp 513f, and esp. A. M. Ritter, *Das Konzil von Konstantinopel,* p 285, note 2.

[15] Athanasius, TomAntioch 5: MG 26, 800f.

[16] Basil, CEunom I.9; II. 28; ep. 125.1.

controversy (373/76) he was still more precise, as his *De Spiritu Sancto* and the letters 214 and 236 prove.[17] He identified, in line with Stoicism, the *ousia* as what it had in common (*koinon*) with the substratum (*hypokeimenon*), which is qualified by quality (*poion*), i.e. by the *hypostasis*.[18] Doing this he explained the three hypostases in terms of paternity, sonship and sanctification and defined the hypostasis as *tropos tes hyparxeos*, as the way in which *ousia* is received.[20] Finally he took begetting to be the way in which the Son receives being, while he was not prepared to comment on the individuality of the origin of the Holy Spirit.[21]

In his endeavour to distinguish what is proper to Father, Son and Spirit from what is common to them all, Basil is clearly influenced by the philosophy of his time. His eclectic procedure, however, is not to be underestimated. On closer inspection his endeavours can be understood as a way of explaining the mystery of the Trinity in a way that corresponded to the logic of his time, in which, as with the Stoics, a distinction was drawn between the common and the individual.[23] The possibility must not be excluded, however, that Basil in his trinitarian terminology was also influenced by Apollinaris of Laodicea.[24]

3. The working out of the double formula by the other Cappadocians

Besides Basil, Gregory of Nazianzus is the first to be considered, as he is distinguished by his ability to give a clear expression to theological thoughts. He defined the *idion* as, respectively, unbegottenness, generation and procession,[25] while the *homoousios* was applied to all three hypostases as if to three individuals.[26] Moreover, he identified *prosopon* with the term *hypostasis*, thus placing a stronger emphasis on the unity.[27] Finally he coined quite useful formulae which at the same time express unity as well as trinity.[28]

It is the merit of Gregory of Nyssa, the greatest Christian philosopher among the Eastern Church fathers, to have reinforced in his *Contra Eunomium* and in letter 38 (numbered with Basil's letters), the distinction between *ousia* and *hypostasis*.[29] In the letter mentioned, which was ascribed to his brother until very

[17] Cf. esp. Spir 18.47, and Spir 16.38; 17.41; 18.44f and epp 214.4; 236.6.

[18] Cf. P. Luislampe, *Spiritus vivificans* p 175, who for the Stoic background refers to R. Hübner, 'Gregor von Nyssa als Verfasser der sog. Ep. 38 des Basilius', C. Kannengießer, ed., *Epektasis. Mélanges patristiques offerts au Cardinal Daniélou*, Paris 1972, p 480.

[19] Epp 214.4; 236.6.

[20] Spir 18.46; hom. 24.3f; also K. Holl, *Amphilochus von Ikonium*, pp 240–6, esp. p 241.

[21] Spir 18.46; hom 24.3f.

[22] Cf. R. Hübner, art.cit. p 482f, with bibl.

[23] Cf. besides R. Hübner, art. cit. pp 476–481, esp. L. I. Scipioni, *Richerche sulla Cristologia del 'Libro di Eraclide' di Nestorio*, pp 98–106, and H. Dörries, *De Spiritu Sancto*.

[24] Cf. epp 361–4, CPG II, 2900; also M. Simonetti, *La crisi ariana*, p 512: summary of Apollinaris' teaching.

[25] Gregory of Naz., or. 25.16; 26.19; 29.2; 31.29; also J. Barbel, *Gregor von Nazianz, Die fünf theologischen Reden*, Düsseldorf 1963, p 221, note 3.

[26] Cf. or. 31.10.

[27] Cf. or. 39.11.

[28] Cf. or. 25.17; 28.31; 31.9; 33.16; 38.11f.

[29] Cf. Gregory of Nyssa, CEunom II (Refut), 205: MG 45, 260C, AdvApol 8: MG 45, 1239A; ep.89: MG 46, 1089C; CatMagn 1.1; also besides R. Hübner, art.cit., P. J. Fedwick, 'A Commentary of Gregory of Nyssa or the 38th letter of Basil of Caesarea', OCP 44, 1978, pp 31–51.

recently, he explains, in an Aristotelian sense, *koinon* as genus, and *idion* as individual. The question as to how the individuality of the hypostasis is related to the ousia, does not interest him.[30] Moreover his explanation entailed the danger of tritheism; in consequence he had to defend himself against such accusations.[31] Still, he succeeded, with his twin-formula *mia ousia – treis hypostaseis*[32] and his interpretation of the hypostases in terms of *agennesia – monogenes – dia tou hyiou*, to point the way forward for the Church's doctrine of the Trinity.[33]

Amphilochus is worthy of note, too. He took over in a synodal letter not only Basil's doctrine of the Holy Spirit, but also the distinction between *physis* and *hypostasis*.[34] Moreover, he emphasizes the single divine *arche* while retaining the three hypostases.[35]

4. The significance of the terminological contribution of the Cappadocians

A complete picture of the extent to which the formula *mia ousia – treis hypostaseis* proved significant for the history of dogma cannot be gained without also taking into consideration the council of Constantinople (381), which officially recognized this formula.[36] For the present the following may be stated: The formula, which certainly stems from the Cappadocian group, represents a theological position which in essentials corresponds to that of Nicea and Athanasius, insofar as it is about unity of equality rather than of number. In this sense the Cappadocians cannot be accused of Neo-Nicenism, as has happened until very recently.[37] For the Cappadocians approach the problem of the relation of Father, Son and Spirit from a different perspective. While the council of Nicea dealt with the difference between the terms begotten and created – which point of view reappears in Basil's discussion of the divinity of the Holy Spirit –, the essentially trinitarian discussion of the Cappadocians deals with the question as to how the three can be one. To this question the twin-formula *mia ousia – treis hypostaseis* presents a more satisfactory answer than the Nicene *homoousios*. For it expressly amplifies the Origenist tradition of the three hypostases with the unitarian tendency of Athanasius and his Western friends, and, further, gives it a clearer philosophical expression. With regard to this new formulation of the

---

[30] Gregory of Nyssa, ep. 38 (numbered with Basil's): MG 32, 323–40, also R. Hübner, art. cit; pp 484ff.

[31] Cf. Ad Ablabium quod non sint tres dei (CPG II, 3139), and ep. 38.4 (Basil's): MG 32, 329B-333A.

[32] Cf. CatMagn 1, Ablab: MG 45, 117A, 120B, 124D, 133Df; CEunom II (Refut), 12f: MG 45, 472CD; cf. also Apollinaris, Fides 14; 19; 25; 33: ed. Lietzmann pp 172.3f; 173.23f; 176.9f; 180.14, and also E. Mühlenberg, *Apollinaris von Laodicea*, Göttingen 1969, pp 234f, and Didymus (?), Trin II: MG 39, 760B (Neoplatonist doctrine; hypostases).

[33] CEunom I 278ff: MG 45, 336BD; also B. Schultze, 'Die Pneumatologie des Symbols von Konstantinopel als abschließende Formulierung der griechischen Theologie', OCP 47, 1981, pp 5–54, esp. pp 46–52.

[34] Amphilochius, ep. synod.: MG 39, 96C: In the context Matt 28:19 is explained in an anti-Arian as well as in an anti-Sabellian sense; also H. Dörries, *de Spiritu Sancto*, pp 171ff.

[35] Amphilochius, ep. synod.: MG 39, 97C.

[36] Ep. synod.: COecD, p 28, ll. 21–7.

[37] Cf. K. Beyschlag, *Dogmengeschichte*, pp 262–70, esp. 268, note 176, with certain qualifications.

problem and the broader sweep of the answers, we should not speak of a Neo-Nicenism in the sense of a revised understanding of the *homoousios* (specific rather than numeric), but rather of a reinterpretation of Nicene faith in the sense of an express acknowledgement of the unity in the Trinity of the baptismal faith. However, even the twin-formula is not completely satisfactory, as will soon appear.

III. THE SEARCH FOR A FURTHER EXPLANATION OF THE DIVINE UNITY

The Cappadocian twin-formula evidently reflects endeavours to show in terms of contemporary logic that the unity of Father, Son and Spirit must be sought on a different level from their threeness. Seen from a dogmatic viewpoint it brings about that *via media* between Arianism and Sabellianism, which the synod of Alexandria confessed and the Cappadocians also made their own.[38]

Elegant though this formula seems to be, its insertion into the confession of the Church had its problematic aspects. The Cappadocians themselves did not overlook the risks involved in the distinction between *ousia* and *hypostasis,* yet they were accused of tritheism. Any attempt to exclude Sabellianism while condemning Arianism made it necessary to expound the divine unity, which had always been part of the Judaeo-Christian heritage.

Even before the Cappadocians, Athanasius had supplemented the formula *ek tes ousias* for the generation with the formula *en patri,*[39] and had also spoken of the unity of *ousia.*[40] Even though he understood the unity within the context of full equality, he had given to understand by the theme of the mutual penetration of Father and Son, how seriously he took the problem of the unity. As concerns the Cappadocians themselves, their position is found primarily in writings especially devoted to this question: in homily 29 of Basil, in *Quod non sint tres dii* by the Nyssene and in the 31st sermon of Gregory of Nazianzus. In these and other writings the following reflexions are to be found:

1. The divine unity is an ineffable mystery

The paradox of speaking at one and the same time of Unity and Trinity in God did not remain unnoticed by the Cappadocians.[41] This difficulty is sensed in the almost contradictory statements with which Gregory of Nazianzus explains that the three hypostases are to be distinguished without separation, indeed to be united in distinction; for the divinity is one in the three, and the three are one being, in which the divinity exists.[42] Gregory of Nyssa for his part points to the

---

[38] Cf. note 10.

[39] Athanasius, Serap I 14; I 21.

[40] Athanasius, CAr I 18; III 3f; Decret 23.24; cf. Ps.Athanasius, CAr IV 1.

[41] Cf. already Basil, CEunom I 13ff.

[42] Gregory of Naz., or. 39.11.

peculiarity of the divine nature, which transcends all differences of essence, so that the divine ousia is much more really one than any universal.[43]

2. *The divine unity is founded on the* arche, *the Father*

According to Basil there are not three original hypostases. Rather the Father is the only original, the sole *arche*.[44] Thus he alone 'in principle' possesses the divinity. The Son and the Spirit, however, are God only in a 'derived' fashion, insofar as they stem from the Father. All the same, Basil also emphasizes, too, the togetherness, the *synousia,* of three completely spiritual entities.[45]

The notion of the Father as the sole *arche* establishing the divine unity is not without difficulties. First, divinity seems to be prior to the Father; secondly, the difference between the origin of the Son and of the Spirit remains unclarified, so that the two appear to be like two brothers. The first difficulty is solved by the Cappadocians by identifying the Godhead and the Father.[46] Moreover, they emphasize that each person is 'one'.[47] As far as the second difficulty is concerned, Basil leaves it to the realm of mystery.[48] Gregory of Nazianzus, however, distinguishes in a somewhat formalistic manner between generation and procession.[49]

The Nyssene speaks besides of the Spirit, who proceeds through the Son, and introduces thereby a formula which is to assume a great significance later on.[50] So his position resembles that of Eunomius, with the difference however that he does not regard the Holy Spirit as a creature.[51] Behind this there stands a tradition which ultimately goes back to Origen and which even Marcellus had represented in his way.[52]

3. Schesis *as the explanation of the divine unity*

In line with Origenist teaching on the *epinoiai* Basil distinguishes two kinds of terms: those that denote the thing in itself, and those that denote it in relation to something else, such as son, friend etc. In the second sense the Son of God is no different from the created sons. He is different, however, with respect to the *ousia,* which in his case is divine and in that of the human sons mortal.[53] Proceeding

[43] Gregory of Nyssa, Ablab: MG 45, 133A-136A; also E. Mühlenberg, *Gregor von Nyssa,* pp 133f.

[44] Cf. esp. Basil, Spir 16.38, and Spir 16.37; ep. 210.5; hom 24.1.3; also Gregory of Naz., or. 20.7; 29.2; 31.14, and Gregory of Nyssa, Ablab: MG 45, 133A-C; AdvMaced 13: MG 45, 1317A.

[45] Basil, hom. 24.4: MG 31, 609AB.

[46] Basil, CEunom I 20, Gregory of Naz., or. 42.14; Gregory of Nyssa, ComNot: MG 45, 177A; cf. Apollinaris, ep. 362 (numbered with Basil's).

[47] Basil, Spir 18.44; Gregory of Naz., or. 31.15; Gregory of Nyssa, CEunom I 313: MG 45, 348CD.

[48] Basil, Spir 18.46, cf. CEunom II 32; 34; hom. 24.6.

[49] Gregory of Naz., or. 25.16; 31.8.

[50] Gregory of Nyssa, CEunom I 280; 378: MG 45, 336D; 369A; Ablab: MG 45, 133C; AdvMaced 6: MG 45, 1308B.

[51] Cf. K. Holl, *Amphilochus von Ikonium,* p 242, with a reference to Gregory of Nyssa, CEunom I 216: MG 45, 316C.

[52] Cf. Origen, PA I 3.5; Colo II 10 (6), and also Epiphanius, Ancoratus 70f; for Marcellus cf. M. Tetz, 'Zur Theologie des Markell von Ankyra', ZKG 75, 1964, p 269.

[53] Cf. Basil, CEunom II 9f, and CEunom I 20; II.22; also M. Simonetti, *La crisi ariana,* pp 463f.

from this, the Nyssene points out that the Son is not distinguished from the Father in terms of *ousia* or *physis,* but only in terms of *schesis* (relationship).[54] He also speaks of a natural *schesis,* of a relation between Father and Spirit which has always existed.[55] Gregory of Nazianzus, on his part, states that the name of Father does not denote *ousia* or *energeia,* but rather *schesis.*[56] Amphilochus finally points out that the names of Father, Son and Spirit do not refer to *ousia* as such, but to the *tropos tes hyparxeos,* the mode of being, thus indicating a kind of relationship.[57] While the Cappadocians suggest that there is in God no absolute, but only a relative distinction, they have prepared the way for the later teaching of the *relationes subsistentes.*

4. The unique saving activity of Father, Son and Spirit

In line with earlier tradition, in particular that of Origen and Athanasius, the Cappadocians finally secured the unity of the three hypostases, by referring to a single saving activity of Father, Son and Spirit. In particular they speak of a common will and of a single *energeia* of the three divine persons.[59] It should indeed be noted that Basil and Gregory take care to emphasize the various ways in which the one divine activity is accomplished through the three hypostases. So for Basil the Father is the original, the Son the creative and the Spirit the perfecting cause.[60] On similar lines Gregory of Nyssa explains that the divine activity emanates from the Father, progresses through the Son, and is perfected in the Holy Spirit.[61]

IV. THE UNFOLDING OF PNEUMATOLOGY

Behind the search for a formula capable of expressing both the unity and the threeness of Father, Son and Spirit, as well as behind the endeavours to explain the divine unity, there stood continually the question of the Holy Spirit. Without this question there could be no proper trinitarian theology; hence the trinitarian discussions only commenced after 360.[62] Still, it must not be overlooked that the

---

[54] Cf. Gregory of Nyssa, CEunom II (Refut) 16: MG 45, 473B; also M. Simonetti, *La crisi ariana,* pp 464–8.

[55] Gregory of Nyssa, Ablab: MG 45, 133C; ep 38.7 (Basil's); Cf. Eusebius Caes., EcclTheo I 10: MG 24, 841C.

[56] Gregory of Naz., or. 29.16.

[57] Amphilochius, frag 15: MG 39, 112B-D; cf. K. Holl, *Amphilochius von Iconium,* pp 243ff.

[58] Cf. Origen, CoIo XIII 36,228–235, and Athanasius, CAr III 6; Serap I 28–31; also R. Seeberg, *Dogmengeschichte* I, p 511 and II, pp 67f.

[59] Basil, CEunom I 23; II 21; Spir 8.21; 16.37, and Gregory of Nyssa, ep. 189.7f (Basil's); ep. 5.

[60] Basil, Spir 16.38f; 26.64; epp 210.3; 236.6; Gregory of Nyssa, AdvMaced 13: MG 45, 1317AB; Ablab: MG 45, 128BC.

[61] Gregory of Nyssa, Ablab: MG 45, 125C.

[62] Cf. the texts which expressly emphasize the later date of the pneumatological controversy, trying to explain this fact either from the relative obscurity of the Bible or from the silence of Nicea on this point: Basil, ep. 125.3; Gregory of Naz., ep. 58: MG 37, 113–17; or. 31.21, 26; Amphilochius, ep. synod.: MG 39, 96.

controversy about the distinction between *ousia* and *hypostasis* goes back further; that, at any rate, endeavours to safeguard the unity of God while preserving the faith in the divinity of Christ had led the way chronologically by quite a bit.[63] The debate about the Holy Spirit did not bring about the solution of the other problems, but it urged them on.

In other words, the dynamic inherent in the faith of Nicea necessarily resulted in an unfolding of the faith in the Holy Spirit and thus of the whole of the baptismal faith. Rejecting the same Nicene faith, on the other hand, almost necessarily involved expressly placing the Holy Spirit on the side of the creatures, as can be seen in Eunomius and some of the Homoiousians.[64] Once the question of the Holy Spirit was raised, the whole trinitarian question became much more urgent.

1. Athanasius

As has already been mentioned, around 359 the so-called Tropici moved Athanasius, the most zealous defender of the Nicene faith, to defend with equal energy the divinity of the Holy Spirit.[65] Athanasius accordingly dealt with the relation of God and Spirit on analogy with that of God and Son. Yet he never called the Holy Spirit God, but he unambiguously placed him on the side of God, above all spiritual beings.[66]

To prove this the Bishop of Alexandria first of all appealed to the deifying power of the Holy Spirit.[67] He saw in this a proof, too, of the divinity of the Son. For according to him only the true Son of God is able to communicate to man the divine Spirit. However he neglected to discuss the nature of the Spirit's origin.[68] On the other hand, he emphatically invoked the baptismal faith. If the Holy Spirit were merely a creature, Christ would not in the baptism unite man through him with himself and with the Father.[69] It may be remarked that Athanasius, apparently with regard to these new debates, which seemed to postpone ecclesiastical peace yet further, behaved in a more accommodating way towards the non-Nicenes at the synod of Alexandria.[70]

2. Basil of Caesarea

Even though much credit is due to Athanasius for the unfolding of pneumatology, his younger episcopal colleague, Basil of Caesarea, can claim before the bar of history to have been the most prominent theologian of the Holy Spirit in the

---

[63] Cf. Cyril of Jerus., cat 16.24, and the texts of Athanasius in note 58.

[64] Cf. Athanasius, TomAntioch 3: MG 26, 800; CAr III 15; Gregory of Naz., or. 29.2; 31.5; Eunomius, Apol 25–28; Ps.Athanasius, DialCMaced, CPG II (2285); Socrates, HE II 45; also M. Simonetti, *La crisi ariana*, pp 480–7.

[65] Cf. A. Laminski, *Der Heilige Geist*, esp. pp 30–5.

[66] Athanasius, Serap I 12; 25; 28; ep. ad Max. 5; also H. J. Sieben, *Die Konzilsidee*, p 56.

[67] Serap I 23f; CAr III 24.

[68] CAr II 18; cf. Serap I 19ff.

[69] Serap I 29; IV 7; CAr II 41f.

[70] TomAntioch 3: MG 26, 797, 800; also M. Laminski, *Der Heilige Geist*, p 120f.

Eastern Church.[71] This honorary title is confirmed by the fact that the second ecumenical council in its remaking of the Nicene creed essentially restates St.Basil's teaching on the Holy Spirit.[72]

Basil himself exhibits his pneumatology chiefly in his treatise *De Spiritu Sancto,* written 374/5. To reach an understanding of this writing, it is imperative to take into consideration its prehistory as well as other testimonies, while reckoning with the difficulty of dating these other writings.[73]

Even before the pneumatological controversy Basil had dealt with the question of the Holy Spirit in the third book of his *Contra Eunomium* (362/3 or 365). In this writing he placed the Holy Spirit clearly on the side of the creator, as Athanasius had done in his *Tomus ad Antiochenos.*[74] He accordingly called him Lord and Holy One.[75] He also recalled the biblical names which are attributed to the Holy Spirit, underlined the experience of baptism and did not forget to emphasize the ineffable mystery of the Spirit.[76] In the letter *De fide,* which he wrote soon afterwards and which was later included in the *Asceticon,* he spoke of the Spirit as being unique and referred to Jesus' command to baptize and to liturgical doxologies.[77]

Shortly before the outbreak of the pneumatological controversy, in 372/3 Basil sent two letters to Tarsus in which he stated as necessary for the *communio fidei* the acceptance of the *Nicaenum* and the confession that the Holy Spirit is no creature.[78] In other, more private, letters of that time he more precisely stated his teaching by more positive terms: the Spirit is closely related to the Father, he possesses eternity, glory, lordship and deity and, moreover, is the principle of knowledge and sanctification.[79] While the Son is called *homoousios,* the Spirit receives the same honour as Father and Son.[80] He is not outside the divine *ousia.* Therefore he is no creature, but rather is able to liberate, to vivify and to sanctify. Because of the command to baptize, the doxology is also to be directed to him.[81] Basil refers in all these texts to the words of the doxology 'together with the Spirit', without expressly defending them. However, he had by then already caused such doxologies to be sung in his churches.[82]

---

[71] Cf. P. Luislampe, *Spiritus vivificans,* esp., pp 162–88.

[72] Cf. R. Staats, Die basilianische Verherrlichung des Heiligen Geistes auf dem Konzil von Konstantinopel (381): KerDog 25, 1979, pp 232–53; A. de Halleux, 'La profession de l'Esprit-Saint dans le Symbole de Constantinople', RThLouv 10, 1979, pp 5–39: critical of the contention that personal influence on the drafting of the 3rd article of the NC can be traced; A. Meredith, 'The pneumatology of the Cappadocian Fathers and the Creed of Constantinople', IrTheolQu 48, 1981, pp 196–211.

[73] Cf. W.-D. Hauschild, 'Basilius von Caesarea', TRE 5, 1979, pp 301–13, and P. J. Fedwick, *Church and Charisma,* pp 133–55.

[74] Basil, CEunom III 2.7: MG 29, 660A, 669AB; Cf. Athanasius, TomAntioch 3: MG 26, 800, and Apollinaris, ep. 364 (in Basil's letters).

[75] Basil, CEunom III 2.6: MG 29, 660C, 668C.

[76] CEunom III 7: MG 29, 670C.

[77] De Fide (CPG II, 2859): MG 31, 464–74; also P. Luislampe, *Spiritus vivificans,* p 30.

[78] Epp 113f.

[79] Ep. 105.

[80] Ep. 90; 372.

[81] Ep. 159; 373.

[82] Cf. Basil, Spir 1.3, and also B. Pruche, *Basile de Césarée,* SChr 17bis, pp 41–4.

In 373 Basil drafted a document that was also signed by Eustathius of Sebaste, who had once been his friend but was now his opponent and was soon to be the leader of the Pneumatomachians. This official document concerning the *communio fidei* determined the acceptance of the following points concerning the doctrine of the Holy Spirit: the Holy Spirit is no creature; He is not derived from God like the creatures; thus he is no servant spirit. To put it positively, he is holy by nature, inseparable from the divine nature. This fully tallies with the logic of the baptismal command. The *homotimia* however is not expressly mentioned.[83] Despite his initial approval, it caused Eustathius to break with Basil. Thus the pneumatological controversy began. Basil himself at first kept silent. Only when criticism raised against his doxologies no longer allowed further restraint, did he officially take his stand (September 374). He worked for a year on his work, entitled *De Spiritu Sancto*. Having completed it, he sent it to his friend Amphilochius in 375, who expressed his approval of it in a synodal letter.[84]

This writing is not homogenous.[85] Chapters 2–8 differ strongly from chapters 10–29, while chapter 9 stands apart and chapters 1 and 30 constitute the introduction and epilogue, respectively. The first part comments on the question of the controversial doxologies, and thus on the *homotimia* of Father, Son and Spirit. The second part is perhaps made up out of the discussions which Basil had held with Eustathius two years before. At any rate, chapters 10ff range much more widely than the issue of the doxologies and go into the whole set of problem which had been raised by the Pneumatomachians.[86] The main thesis stated by this treatise is: there is a correlation between unity of worship and unity of nature. This thesis is substantiated from different points of view: the words of the doxology 'together with the Spirit' are not unbiblical and can be justified positively from tradition. The unity of the Spirit with Father and Son is also established by the baptismal liturgy. Thus it would be unjust to deny to the Spirit the same faith and the same adoration. The second, certainly more conclusive argumentation is finally confirmed with biblical texts, which speak of the manifold activity of the Holy Spirit in creation, in the sanctification of angels and men, in the life of Jesus, in the building-up of the Church and in perfection.[87]

This extremely impressive doctrine was reinforced in further writings, homilies[88] as well as letters.[89] Basil expounded there in a thorough way the significance of the praise of God and also refuted the reproach of tritheism.

For a full evaluation of Basil's teaching on the Holy Spirit it may be useful to distinguish between content and method. As regards the content, progress can be traced from an initial negative stand to a more and more positive one. While Basil

---

[83] Ep. 125.3.

[84] Cf. B. Pruche, *Basile de Césarée*, SChr 17bis, pp 41–57.

[85] Cf. B. Pruche, *Basile de Césarée*, SChr 17bis, pp 111–36.

[86] Cf. B. Pruche, 'Autour du Traité sur le Saint-Esprit de s. Basile de Césarée', RchSR 52, 1964, pp 204–32.

[87] Cf. esp. Basil, Spir 16, and also P. Luislampe, *Spiritus vivificans*, pp 49–161: 'Das Wirken des Heiligen Geistes in der Heilsgeschichte'.

[88] Basil, hom 24; 15; 29.

[89] Cf. esp. ep. 263 (addressed AD 377 to the Western bishops).

at first chiefly pointed out that the Spirit is no creature, with the passage of time he more and more emphasized his natural communion with God, and that he is worthy of adoration. As regards his method, it is worth noting the degree of significance that is attributed to the baptismal experience. Starting from this Basil was obviously moved to recall the coherences (*akoloutheia*) in the command to baptize.[90] Moreover, the authority of the Nicene creed had to increase for him according as he equated the position of the Spirit with that of the Son.[91] In this context he took over from a creed attributed to Gregory Thaumaturgus the double antithesis 'Godhead – creation' and 'lordship – service'.[92] Finally, the need to establish the words of the doxology 'together with' as being in line with tradition, moved him to develop the concept of unwritten tradition as well as the argument from the Fathers.[93]

In this context Basil distinguishes between *kerygma* and *dogma*, between what the Church publicly declares in councils, and what is taught in the baptismal instruction.[94] With regard to this distinction Basil's so-called *oikonomia*, i.e. his reservations in openly proclaiming the Holy Spirit as God and as *homoousios*, can be better understood. It was probably the fear of encouraging once more the suffering and misery which the debate concerning the *homoousios* had inflicted upon the Church, that caused him to avoid applying this title to the Holy Spirit.[95] He obviously went through a certain development here. Having overcome hesitation, in *De Spirito Sancto* he made clear and plain statements about the divinity of the Holy Spirit: He is worshipped as God, and is therefore to be recognized as being one with the Father and the Son. Even though Basil, as regards the question of the Holy Spirit, more and more overcame his former reserve, yet he was always concerned respectfully to safeguard the mystery of the Spirit, particularly as far as his origin is concerned.[96]

3. The other Cappadocians and Didymus of Alexandria

In contrast to Basil Gregory of Nazianzus did not refrain from calling the Spirit God and *homoousios*.[97] As has been said before, he attempted to state at least formally the difference in origin of the Son and the Holy Spirit with the notions of generation and procession, respectively.[98] If, with regard to deification, he emphasized the divinity of the Spirit more than his friend Basil, this can be explained by the influence of Origen.[99]

[90] Cf. esp. Spir 10.25f; 14.31; 15.35; 29.75, ep. 125.3; also P. Luislampe, *Spiritus vivificans*, pp 122–7.
[91] Cf. epp 9.3; 114; 125.1; 140.2, also P. J. Fedwick, *Church and Charisma*, pp 69 note 145 and 94.
[92] Cf. Gregory Thaumaturgus (?), Expos Fid IV 2, cited in Gregory of Nyssa, Vita Gregorii Thaum.: MG 46, 912D-913A; also K. Holl, *Amphilochus von Iconium*, pp 117ff, with references to Basil, ep. 204.6; CEunom III 4, and Basil, ep. 159.2; Spir 16.38. For the modern criticism of the Cappadocians'appeal to the miracle worker cf. P. J. Fedwick, *Church and Leadership*, p 3, note 10.
[93] Basil, Spir 29.
[94] Spir 27.66, with note 4 in SChr 17bis, pp 478f.
[95] Epp 51.1; 90.2. Also P. Bruche, *S. Basile de Césarée*, SChr 17bis, pp 79–11, note on older books; and P. Luislampe, *Spiritus vivificans*, pp 187f.
[96] Spir 18.46; Cf. Basil, HomPs 32.4, and Gregory of Naz., or. 41.6.
[97] Cf. Gregory of Naz., or. 31.10 (dated 379).
[98] Gregory of Naz., or. 23.11; 25.16; 29.2; 31.7f; 39.12.
[99] Cf. K. Holl, *Amphilochus von Iconium*, pp 163f.

Gregory of Nyssa definitely applied the *homoousios* to the Spirit. Clearly for him this concept was less strictly connected with its traditional relation to the notion of generation, than it was for Basil.[100] On the other hand, with his concept of the Son's mediatorship (*mesiteia*) in the procession of the Holy Spirit, he not only surpassed Basil but also Gregory of Nazianzus.[101] The significance of his 'through the Son' can, however, be fully evaluated only in the context of the council of Constantinople.

From Didymus of Alexandria, too, a treatise *De Spiritu Sancto* has come down to us, but only in Jerome's Latin translation.[102] Basil's teaching appears to be further deepened in this work. The significance of the treatise, however, lies more in the fact that it was widely distributed in the West. Augustine, too, could have known it, either through Ambrose, or directly through the Latin translation.[103]

The teaching of the Cappadocians on the Trinity and in particular on the Holy Spirit, as presented here, may well appear to be very abstract. And in a way that is true. Indeed, its negative character cannot fail to be noticed; it rather excludes than affirms. This concerns chiefly the trinitarian formula *mia ousia – treis hypostaseis*. However, it must be recalled that all dogmatic statements remain essentially negative. They do not intend to penetrate the mystery itself; they rather determine the framework within which the mystery, as proclaimed in the apostolic tradition, may be safeguarded. It is just this character of mystery, that Basil and his friends again and again bring out. In defining this merely limiting framework they made significant progress. They worked out and propagated a formula, which at the same time defines the oneness and the threeness of Father, Son and Spirit. They laid the foundation for the later doctrine of the trinitarian relations. Gregory of Nazianzus and Gregory of Nyssa did not avoid even the question of the Spirit's origin, but already contributed substantial elements to its solution.

It is true that the Cappadocians were not particularly concerned with deepening the doctrine of the immanent Trinity starting from the premise of the baptismal faith.[105] Their main interest was rather directed to the economic doctrine of the Trinity; and under their influence this would always remain the case in Eastern theology. The preceding exposition has not, however, touched upon the fundamental question, as to how the Cappadocians developed their conceptions of the Trinity, and in particular, of the Holy Spirit in the context of their teaching of the Church and of Christian perfection. In particular the way in which Basil's idea of the Church as *koinonia* is interrelated with his pneumatology has been neglected.[106] Neither has his teaching about the spiritual

---

[100] Gregory of Nyssa, AdvMaced 22: MG 45, 1329AB.

[101] Cf. note 50.

[102] Didymus, Spir (CPG II, 2544); Cf. also Apollinaris, Fides 8: ed. Lietzmann p 170.

[103] Cf. B. Altaner, 'Augustinus und Didymus der Blinde', *Kleine Patristische Schriften*, Berlin 1967, pp 97–301.

[104] Cf. A. de Halleux, 'La profession de l'Esprit-Saint', RThLouv 10, 1979, p 39.

[105] Cf. R. Seeberg, *Dogmengeschichte* II, p 128.

[106] Cf. P. J. Fedwick, *Church and Charisma*, pp 23–32, and K. Duchatelez, 'La "Koinonia" chez s.Basile le Grand', Communio 6, 1973, pp 161–80.

father been discussed in this present context.[107] However, two important points of view, more soteriological in character, should have become clear. First, it should have become apparent that Basil's trinitarian teaching is rooted in the baptismal experience of his communities. With him the baptismal faith, which from the very beginning proved decisive for the development of trinitarian doctrine, was established in a unique way. On the other hand, the impressive way in which Basil ever and again called on the doxologies, surely gives one a better grasp of the other root of the trinitarian faith, that of the liturgy. It should have become quite clear that in the final analysis the mystery of Father, Son and Spirit reveals itself only in worship.

[107] Cf. P. J. Fedwick, *Church and Charisma,* pp 77–110, and P. Luislampe, *Spiritus vivificans,* pp 23–7.

13. The General Reception of the Nicene Faith in about 380

BIBLIOGRAPHY

E. Beck, 'Ephraem Syrus', RAC 5, 1962, cols. 520–31, with bibl.

A. M. Ritter, *Das Konzil von Konstantinopel und sein Symbol*, Göttingen 1965.

G. L. Dossetti, *Il simbolo di Nicea e di Constantinopoli. Edizione critica*, Bologna 1967.

R. Murray, *Symbols of Church and Kingdom. A Study in Early Syriac Tradition*, London 1975.

W. Cramer, *Der Geist Gottes und des Menschen in frühsyrischer Theologie*, Münster 1979.

A. de Halleux, 'La profession de l'Esprit Saint dans le symbole de Constantinople', RThLouv 10, 1979, pp 5–39.

R. Gryson, *Scolies ariennes sur le concile d'Aquilée* = SChr 267, Paris 1980.

E. Beck, *Ephräms Trinitätslehre im Bild von Sonne/Feuer, Licht/Wärme* = CSChO, Subsidia 62, Louvain 1981.

See also manuals on the history of Church and doctrine, as well as studies published at the centenary of the council of Constantinople 1981.

See also:

S. P. Brock, *The Holy Spirit in the Syrian Baptismal Tradition*, Poona-Kerala 1977; id., *The Luminous Eye, The Spiritual World Vision of St Ephrem*, Rome-Kerala 1985.

A. de Halleux, 'Le IIe concile oecuménique. Une évaluation dogmatique et ecclésiologique', CrSt 3, 1982, pp 297–327.

A. de Halleux, '"Hypostase" et "Personne" dans la formation du dogme trinitaire (ca. 375–381)', RHE 79, 1984, pp 313–69, 625–70.

B. Studer, 'Der geschichtliche Hintergrund des Ersten Buches Contra Eunomium Gregors von Nyssa', in L. F. Mateo-Seco and J. L. Bastero, eds., *El Contra Eunomium . . .* , Pamplona 1988, pp 139–71 (now B. Studer, *Dominus Salvator*, pp 463–98).

In the sixties and seventies of the fourth century it was Athanasius and in particular the Cappadocians in the East of the Roman empire who had striven for ecclesiastical peace founded on the one faith. Their untiring political and theological endeavours were finally sanctioned in 381 by the synod of Constantinople, which has entered history as the second ecumenical council. The dogmatic decisions of this synod, which was attended almost exclusively by Eastern bishops, marked for the churches of the Eastern empire the completion of the development of trinitarian doctrine. The baptismal faith was further developed in these churches only in so far as the Monophysite Christians at first, and then also the Byzantine Christians, were to accept the dogma *'unus ex trinitate passus est'* and at the same time to exclude any tritheism.

At the same time the Latin Church also accepted the Nicene faith, as it was handed down to her by the bishops, the synods and the theologians of the East. She was ready to do so, as she had been prepared for this by her own trinitarian traditions, which went back to Tertullian. Yet the development of trinitarian doctrine was not yet finished for her. She was rather to complete the trinitarian dogma with the *filioque* and the definitions concerning the inner-trinitarian relationships.

An account of this general reception of the Nicene faith must not, however, be restricted to the churches of the Roman empire. Rather there are other churches to be taken into account, namely those churches which were already at that time situated more or less outside the frontiers of the Roman empire; this is especially true of the theology of the Syriac theologians.

These introductory remarks are intended to show that for an account of the history of the trinitarian dogma it is not enough to survey the so-called *Nicaeno-Constantinopolitanum,* or even perhaps as well the acts of the synod of Constantinople. Rather the whole ecclesiastical tradition must be contemplated, as it was represented towards the end of the fourth century. This is the only way of understanding the extent to which the faith of Nicea was accepted by all Christian churches at that time as the normative interpretation of the original baptismal faith.

I. THE INTERPRETATION OF THE NICENE FAITH BY THE COUNCIL OF CONSTANTINOPLE (381)

1. Occasion and course of the council

It is impossible here to go into the quite complex issue of the sources and the history of the council of Constantinople. Only the following facts may be recalled.[1]

The summoning of the synod in 381 was part of the endeavour of the political authorities to base the unity of the empire on the one Christian faith, as it had been defined at Nicea. This corresponded with the intention of many parts of the Church, which desired a united interpretation of the Nicene faith and in particular a clarification of the doctrine of the divinity of the Holy Spirit.[2] Yet it was not the essential issues of faith that stood in the foreground, but rather the need to settle the contentious affairs of ecclesiastical policy: the filling of the bishop's throne of Constantinople, the ending the Antiochene schism and a dividing up of ecclesiastical jurisdiction according to the political frontiers. Questions of faith

---

[1] Cf. A. M. Ritter, *Das Konzil von Konstantinopel;* M. Simonetti, *La crisi ariana,* pp 527–42; J. N. D. Kelly, *Early Christian Creeds,* London ³1972, pp 296–367; and esp. the studies published on the centenary of the council in 1981: in IrTheolQu 48/3–4, 1981, and in K. Lehmann and W. Pannenberg, eds., *Glaubensbekenntnis und Kirchengemeinschaft. Das Modell des Konzils von Konstantinopel,* Freiburg – Göttingen 1982, with a joint declaration of the study-groups of protestant and catholic theologians, pp 120–5.

[2] Cf. Ep. synod.: COecD p 25, l. 14–26, l. 36.

themselves could not however be excluded. To establish ecclesiastical unity it was vital to win over to the Nicene faith the so-called Macedonians who with their views questioned the divinity of the Holy Spirit and at the same time again solemnly to anathematize all heresies which had already been condemned.

2. The Niceno-Constantinopolitan Creed (DS 150)

As for the reconciliation with the Macedonians, which was desired by the emperor, first of all the Nicene creed was completed. For this task the first two articles of a version of the Nicene creed (N),[3] which was already in circulation, were adopted, while the third article on the Holy Spirit was newly revised. At first sight it appears to be moderate in its views, as it does not expressly call the Holy Spirit God thus clearly making concessions to the Macedonians. Gregory of Nazianzus, who took over the presidency of the council after the death of Meletius, did not favour the formulation as it was too vague in his eyes.[4] Yet fundamentally the formulation of the third article allowed no doubt. At any rate Gregory of Nyssa, Amphilochius and others consented to it.[5]

In fact the third article, in the spirit of Nicea, places the Holy Spirit quite unambiguously on the side of the creative deity. This is indicated by the expression *ton kyrion*. This is in line with the Cappadocians, in that the Spirit is no serving but a ruling spirit, thus belonging to the divine sphere. If *kyriotes* or *despoteia* were attributed to him with *douleia* excluded, his *theiotes* was acknowledged, and he was placed outside the *ktisis*.[6] The expression *zoopoion* may appear less strong, but it must be realized that the imparting of life includes sanctification and deification, which take place above all in baptism, in fact the whole of the creative work of the Holy Spirit.[7] The *ek tou Patros exporeuomenon* has an essentially anti-Macedonian ring. For it says that the Spirit too comes out of the Father's hypostasis, and must not be conceived as the creation of the Son. The Father is source and principle of divinity both in the case of the Son and in the case of the Spirit.[8] The most definite formula is without doubt *syn Patri kai Hyio symproskynoumenon kai syndoxazomenon*. In the view of Basil and the other Cappadocians this entails the avoided *homoousios*. Only because the Spirit is united with the Father and the Son and lives with them in *koinonia tes physeos*, does he possess *homotimia* with them.[9] The assertion of the Spirit as prophetic,

---

[3] Cf. G. L. Dossetti, *Il simbolo di Nicea e di Constantinopoli. Edizione critica*, Bologna 1967; B. M. Weischer, 'Die ursprünglich nikänische Form des ersten Glaubenssymbols im Ankyratos des Epiphanios von Salamis', TheolPhil 53, 1978, pp 407–14: NC is interpolated in Epiphanius.

[4] Cf. Gregory of Naz., Carmen hist. 1703–9; also A. M. Ritter, *Das Konzil von Konstantinopel*, pp 258–63.

[5] Cf. A. de Halleux, 'La profession de l'Esprit-Saint dans le Symbole de Constantinople', RThLouv 10, 1979, pp 5–39.

[6] Cf. Basil, Spir 20.51; ep. 159.2; Gregory of Naz., or. 41.6, and the creed ascribed to Gregory the Wonderworker: Hahn §185.

[7] Cf. Basil, Spir 9.22.

[8] Cf. Gregory of Naz., or. 31.8; Didymus (?), Trin II 5.7.

[9] Cf. Basil, Spir 6.15; 27.68 ep. 159.2; Gregory of Naz., or. 41.9; Gregory of Nyssa, ep. 24; also A. M. Ritter, *Das Konzil von Konstantinopel*, pp 302f.

taken over from earliest tradition, not only indicates that the unity of the two Testaments can only be recognized in the Spirit,[10] but also emphasizes the personal character of the *Pneuma,* which is otherwise less emphasized in the Greek text,[11] and at the same time places him in the most intimate relationship with Father[12] and Son.[13]

3. The Tome of Constantinople[14]

Intending to exclude all heresies that imperilled ecclesiastical unity, the Fathers of the council drafted the so-called tome, a kind of dogmatic treatise, towards the end of the synod. It is not, however, known in the original, which is lost, but only thanks to the *epistula synodica,* which was sent to the bishops of the West one year later (382).[15]

According to this authentic account of the council's decisions the Nicene faith is to be conceived as the original faith corresponding to the command to baptize. According to this the one deity, power and ousia of Father, Son and Spirit, and their divine dignity, must be accepted in three complete hypostases or personae. Thus the hypostases and their properties must not be confused, as Sabellius had done; neither must it be maintained with the Arians, Eunomians and Pneumatomachians that the ousia or divinity could be separated, or that the eternal Trinity, equal in essence, could be joined with a created nature.

In this definition, which reflects the theology of the Cappadocians, the synod has more clearly than in the creed (C), decided on beforehand, dissociated itself from the Pneumatomachians. They now expressly treat them as being on a par with the Arians. At the same time it confesses more decidedly than in the creed the divinity and consubstantiality of the Holy Spirit. It does not only speak of the consubstantial and eternal Trinity, but also employs the formula of one ousia in three hypostases.

On the other hand, the tome of Constantinople, summarized in the *epistula synodica,* shows more clearly than the symbol itself, how far the theology of the Cappadocians, which had been adopted, has outgrown Athanasius' trinitarian doctrine and even the decisions of Alexandria (362). It is true, Athanasius had openly taught the divinity of the Spirit and his inseparable unity with the Father and the Son; however, he had not yet integrated his pneumatology into such a comprehensive trinitarian doctrine.[16]

---

[10] Cf. Cyril of Jerus., Cat 16.3f, also already in the 2nd cent. Justin, Apol I 6 and 13.

[11] Cf. Basil, Spir 16.40: The Holy Spirit in the soul.

[12] Cf. Basil, Spir 16.37: Through the work of the Holy Spirit the presence of God in the prophets is realized. Cf. also Basil, Spir 16.41, and Cyril of Jerus., Cat 6.6; 16.24.

[13] Cf. Basil, Spir 16.39: the Holy Spirit in the prophets, in Jesus and in the Church.

[14] Cf. A. M. Ritter, *Das Konzil von Konstantinopel,* pp 239–53; M. Simonetti, *La crisi ariana,* p 527.

[15] COecD, pp 25–30 = Theodoret, HE V 9 (Greek) (CPG IV, 8602), and Cassiodorus, HistTrip IX 14 (Latin).

[16] Cf. A. M. Ritter, *Das Konzil von Konstantinopel,* p 307.

4. The significance of the Niceno-Constantinopolitan faith

The council of Constantinople did not intend at all to create a new formula of faith; its intention was rather to confirm the faith of Nicea, while adjusting it to the new situation. In this sense it is correctly referred to as the Niceno-Constantinopolitanian creed (NC). This creed is, however, not to be separated from the first canon and the tome of the synod summarized in the *epistula synodica*. Only if all the documents are taken into consideration, can one speak of the faith of Constantinople in the full sense, i.e. of the Nicene faith as it had been understood afresh in 381, at the end of the Arian controversy.

It is moreover necessary to address the question, as to the sense in which the council of Constantinople is to be conceived as ecumenical.[17] When it was being held it was not in fact, properly speaking, ecumenical. Even though it was summoned by the emperor, it represented only part of the imperial Church. At first only the churches of Asia Minor, of western Syria and of Palestine were represented. Later bishops from Egypt arrived as well as a number of bishops from Illyricum as representatives from the West. The great Latin Churches, however, stayed away from the synod. In other words: the council was heavily dominated by the theological tradition as represented by Meletius of Antioch and the Cappadocians, bishops with whom the other churches only lived in communion with some degree of reservation. Nevertheless, the synod of 381 can be regarded as an ecumenical council. For it was later recognized as such by all the churches of the Roman Empire, and even by the greater part of the other churches, by 550 at the latest. To this general reception the council of Chalcedon decisively contributed in that it not only appealed to the Fathers of Nicea, but also to the 150 Fathers of Constantinople (DS 300).[18]

The council of Constantinople may be regarded ecumenical in yet another sense. Leaving aside the question as to what authority can be ascribed to it and its creed, the interpretation of the Nicene faith, as it was presented in Constantinople, was shared by practically all the churches which at that time existed in the empire. This is chiefly indicated by the imperial decrees of that time which testify to the common faith of the whole empire.[19] The extent to which this is true also of the Latin churches and the churches of Syria, should become clear later in greater detail.

Finally the limitations of the faith of Constantinople, which has become the basis of the Byzantine church, and to which also the other churches have essentially agreed, should not be concealed. First, the distinction between *ousia* and *hypostasis* was not expounded any further; what is more, the question of the difference between the generation of the Son and the procession of the Spirit was

---

[17] Cf. R. Slenzka, 'Das ökumenische Konzil von Konstantinopel und seine ökumenische Geltung heute', Una Sancta 36, 1981, pp 198–209; also note 1.

[18] Cf. J. N. D. Kelly, *Early Christian Creeds*, London ³1972, pp 296–301.

[19] Cf. esp. the edict *Cunctos populos* by Theodosius I, of 28th Feb. 380, CodTheod 16.1.2, Mirbt 310, and the law on heretics of the same emperor, of 25th July 383, CodTheod 16.5.11; also A. M. Ritter, *Das Konzil von Konstantinopel*, pp 28–33, 221–8, esp. p 225, with Gregory of Naz., Carmen hist. XI 1282–9.

left open. Indeed the answer to it was even prejudged in the creed by the use of the formula of the procession from the Father.[20] These two regrettable omissions are quite understandable in view of the level of theology at that time. However, they were to provide an occasion for further debates, which even divided the Church. This is especially true of the first omission, for it had fatal consequences for the development of christology, as will be shown below.

II. THE ACCEPTANCE OF THE NICENE FAITH BY THE WESTERN CHURCHES

The situation of the Western churches about 380 presents a quite complicated picture.[21] First, its position over against the East was one of conflict. So Damasus favoured Paulinus of Antioch, who was supported by the Egyptians, as against Meletius, who was a friend of Basil. Moreover, Ambrose of Milan, who had led the opposition to the western Arians, did not agree in every respect with Damasus, bishop of Rome. Finally, the political situation was not easy. After the death of Valens (379) and of Gratian (380) Theodosius had become sole emperor. Though a Westerner and, chiefly for political reasons, also interested in the preeminence of the Roman church, when he failed to assert himself there, his main interest was with the church of Constantinople. This is evident from his summoning and holding the synod of 381. In view of the impossibility of taking into account all these different historical circumstances, first Damasus and then Ambrose will be given more detailed consideration.

1. The main outlines of Damasus' position

The extent to which the Nicene faith was accepted in the West around 380 can be learned chiefly from documents which are ascribed to Damasus, bishop of Rome (366–384). These documents consist of a number of letters, which have come down to us, only in fragments, however (cf. DS 144–7). Still more important is the so called *Tomus Damasi* (DS 152–80). In this doctrinal treatise, which according to the most recent research was already being drafted around 377/78 and not in 382,[22] the worst heresies are condemned in twenty-four anathemas: Sabellius, the Arians and Eunomians, but also Photinus and the Apollinarians.

These documents are significant, first because they reflect the interpretation of the Nicene faith as it had been established in the Latin church under the influence of Hilary of Poitiers (+367), Eusebius of Vercelli (+ ca. 371), and also by Athanasius who had more than once been to the West.[23] No less

---

[20] Cf. B. Schultze, 'Die Pneumatologie des Symbols von Konstantinopel als abschließende Formulierung der griechischen Theologie', OCP 47, 1981, pp 5–54.

[21] Cf. esp. C. Pietri, *Roma Christiana*.

[22] Cf. A. M. Ritter, *Das Konzil von Konstantinopel*, pp 248ff, note 3, and esp. C. Pietri, *Roma Christiana*, pp 873–80.

[23] Cf. C. Pietri, *Roma Christiana*, pp 797–803, 814ff, 832–9.

significant is the fact that the doctrine presented in them had been approved by the East too: by Meletius of Antioch, at a synod of 379 by the eastern emperor Theodosius in the aforementioned decree of the three emperors (Mirbt 310), as well as in the *epistula synodica* of Constantinople (382), which has already been cited several times.[24] In this context the testimony of Theodore of Mopsuestia, who states that the west had preceded the east in formulating the doctrine of the divinity of the Holy Spirit, is of some interest.[25]

The main doctrinal points in this Roman document are as follows: The Nicene faith, according to Latin tradition, concentrates on the unique generation of the Son and the full equality of Father and Son (*aequales,* no *gradus*).[26] Thus the old formula of *una substantia – tres personae* under Eastern influence has taken on a new meaning.[27] The Nicene faith, which had already been defended by Hilary, has not taken a finished form on two counts. First, under the influence of Athanasius and of Eusebius of Vercelli the teaching on the Holy Spirit is expressly clarified.[28] On the other hand, at least in the *Tomus Damasi,* the Sabellianism of Marcellus of Ancyra, who had always found good friends in the west, is expressly condemned.[29] Thus not only has the unity (*una substantia = ousia*) been confirmed, but also the Trinity expressed more clearly than before (*tres tamen personae*).[27]

Two points may be added. First, the doctrine of the Trinity also became significant for the Latin liturgy. For it was to address its prayers not only to Christ but also to the whole Trinity, although never to the Spirit alone.[30] Secondly, it is worthy of note that the *Tomus Damasi* excluded, along with trinitarian, christological errors: Photinus' conception of Christ as a mere man, and the Apollinarians' denial of the human soul in Christ.[31]

2. The main lines of Ambrose's trinitarian theology

For reasons which concerned ecclesiastical policy, Ambrose, bishop of Milan (+397), the most important city in the West at that time, was not able to assent without any qualifications to the council of Constantinople.[32] As he, however, depended on the same traditions which had led to the dogmatic decisions of 381, namely on Athanasius, Didymus and also on Basil, he came to confess practically the same Nicene faith.[33] This is evident from his fight against western

[24] Cf. C. Pietri, *Roma Christiana,* pp 844–53; also note 19.
[25] Theodor of Mops., HomCat 9.1.
[26] DS 144, 147, 163f.
[27] DS 144, cf. 173.
[28] DS 145, 168ff, 174f.
[29] DS 154, cf. 160.
[30] Cf. A. Adam, *Dogmengeschichte* I, p 250, and esp. J. A. Jungmann, *The Place of Christ in Liturgical Prayer,* London ²1989, pp 122f.
[31] DS 157–160, cf. 146.
[32] Cf. for Ambrose in general E. Dassmann, 'Ambrosius von Mailand', TRE 2, 1978, pp 362–86. For Ambrose's opinion on the synod of 381 in particular cf. H. von Campenhausen, *Ambrosius von Mailand als Kirchenpolitiker,* Berlin 1929, pp 141ff, 153ff.
[33] For Ambrose's sources cf. E. Dassmann, 'Ambrose', TRE 2, 1978, pp 373ff, and esp. the notes in the critical edition of O. Faller, CSEL 78 and 79.

Arianism,[34] which is reflected in the acts of the synods over which he presided.[35] The same is still more clearly manifest in his strictly theological works: *De fide ad Gratianum* (378–80), *De Spiritu Sancto* (381) and *De incarnatione* (381/2).[36] On the whole these writings merely reflect his preaching, as they include complete texts from his sermons.[37] Finally, his letters, in which Ambrose declares his position on controversial questions, must be borne in mind.[38] From these various writings the following points of doctrine are to be gathered:[39]

As for the doctrine of the Son, Ambrose strictly kept to the faith of Nicea. This is explained by the fact that his theological opponents represented a fairly radical Arianism.[40] Yet he exceeded Nicea in so far as he worked out more definitely certain divine attributes of the Son like *omnipotens* and *immortalis.*[41]

Like his contemporaries Basil and Didymus Ambrose wrote his own treatise on the Holy Spirit.[42] In this he takes over from the Greek authors the main argument according to which the Holy Spirit cannot be different in essence from the Father and the Son, as he deifies human beings.[43] In this context Rufinus too is to be mentioned. In his exposition of the baptismal creed he fuses the conceptions of Cyril of Jerusalem with Western tradition. According to this tradition the Spirit is distinct from the Father and the Son only in terms of person, and belongs, moreover, to the Son.[44]

As is to be expected of someone writing towards the end of the Arian controversy, Ambrose uses quite precise Trinitarian formulae. Thus in *De fide: Est quaedam indistincta distinctae inconprehensibilis et inenarrabilis substantia trinitatis.*[45]

Finally, the tension between the trinitarian and the christological spirituality of Ambrose should be recalled.[46] Certainly, he must for the most part be understood as a prominent witness to that christocentrism which had developed in

[34] Cf. R. Lorenz, *Das vierte bis sechste Jahrhundert,* pp 38ff, and esp. M. Simonetti, *La crisi ariana,* pp 435–54.

[35] Cf. Gesta Concilii Aquileiensis: CSEL 82, pp 315–68, and Ambrose, epp 9–12; also M. Simonetti, *La crisi ariana* 542–8, and esp. G. Cuscito, 'Aquileia, II. Council', EEC 1, 1992, pp 64–5. Cf. also the second part of the Tomus Damasi, ed. Turner I, pp 288–93, which is said to go back to a synod of Sirmium, 375–8. On that issue R. Lorenz, *Das vierte bis sechste Jahrhundert,* p 32f, and M. Simonetti, *La crisi ariana,* pp 438–41.

[36] Cf. the summarizing remarks in M. Simonetti, *La crisi ariana,* pp 524f, and esp. the studies by L. Hermann and G. Toscani, as cited in chapter 11, note 57.

[37] Cf. esp. Ambrose, Fid IV 1f: perhaps a sermon on the ascension, based on Ps 23:7–10; and ExplSymb.

[38] Cf. Ambrose, epp 9–12; 20; 21 (37); 14 (45).

[39] Cf. G. Toscani, *Chiesa,* pp 247–86.

[40] Cf. M. Simonetti, *La crisi ariana,* pp 544f.

[41] Cf. M. Simonetti, *La crisi ariana,* pp 545f, and chapter 11, note 75.

[42] Cf. G. Toscani, *Chiesa,* pp 54f, with a note on older books; B. Pruche, *Basile de Césarée:* SChr 17bis, pp 220–5.

[43] Ambrose, Spir I 6.80.

[44] Cf. Rufinus, ExposSymb 33 and 46; also B. Studer, *Soteriologie,* pp 150–3.

[45] Ambrose, Fid IV 8.91; cf. ExplSymb 3 and 5.

[46] Cf. chapter 11 above.

the West subsequent to Nicea. Yet his *Christus omnia* did not prevent him from bearing in mind that the Christian believer, together with the Son, is united with the Father in the Holy Spirit. Precisely in this way he exerted a lasting influence on the Western Church.[47]

III. THE ACCEPTANCE OF THE NICENE FAITH BY THE EASTERN CHURCHES

In the oriental churches which during the fourth and fifth centuries developed outside the imperial church, under the influence of the neighbouring great bishoprics, the Nicene faith had in the course of time also become established.[48] This was the case in Ethiopia, where the influence of Athanasius of Alexandria had asserted itself,[49] also in Arabia under the influence of Jerusalem and the Persian Church; (Southern Arabia, however, constitutes an exception, as an Arianizing brand of Christianity had been introduced there), and moreover in Armenia, which stood under the influence of Caesarea in Cappadocia.

Among the great bishoprics of churches independent of the imperial church, the Persian or east Syrian church is of particular interest, as it was situated in a region which stood in fierce opposition to the Roman empire. Also in this church, which had grown in spite of long-lasting persecutions above all in the fourth century, a theology is encountered, in which the Nicene faith is firmly established.[50]

The first prominent theologian of the Syriac theology of the fourth century is Aphraates (+after 345).[51] He represents an archaic kind of theology, hardly touched by Greek culture. He was opposed to Jewish groups; the anti-Arian discussion was of no significance for him. His theological position is, however, important for an understanding of the greatest Syriac theologian, St. Ephrem.[52]

Ephrem (+373), who enters church history chiefly as a poet, was hardly influenced by contemporary Greek theology,[53] yet depended on earlier Greek theology. His teaching shows a clearly anti-Arian position, and is very close to Athanasius and the Cappadocians. He represents an unambiguous doctrine of the

---

[47] Cf. E. Dassmann, 'Ambrosius', TRE 2, 1978, pp 379–83.

[48] Cf. the general introduction by J. Daniélou and H. Marrou, *The Christian Centuries*, I, pp 281–9.

[49] Cf. F. Heyer, 'Äthiopien', TRE 1, 1977, pp 572–596, esp. pp 575f; O. Rainieri, 'Ethiopia-Ethiopic', EEC 1, 1992, pp 289–91.

[50] Cf. J. Daniélou and H. Marrou, *The Christian Centuries*, I, pp 282f.

[51] Cf. G. G. Blum, 'Afrahat', TRE 1, 1977, pp 628–32, with bibl.; P. Bruns, *Das Christusbild Aphrahats des Perischen Weisen (Hereditas)*, Bonn 1990; R. Lavenant, 'Aphraates', EEC 1, 1992, p 54.

[52] Cf. besides G. G. Blum, 'Afrahat', TRE 1, 1977, pp 628–32, R. Murray, *Symbols of Church and Kingdom. A Study in Early Syriac Tradition*, Cambridge 1975; W. Cramer, *Der Geist Gottes und des Menschen in der frühsyrischen Theologie*, Münster 1979, pp 59–85; A. Grillmeier, *Jesus Christus*, pp 446–51, with bibl. (=*Christ in Christian Tradition*, pp 214–18).

[53] Cf. R. Murray, 'Epraem Syrus', TRE 9, 1982, pp 755–62, with bibl.

divinity of the Son, who is begotten from the Father and not created. Concerning the divinity of the Spirit he is less explicit.[54]

When about 400 the external situation of the Persian church settled down, it increasingly came into contact with the 'western' bishops, i.e. with Antioch and Constantinople. With the changed situation bishop Maruta of Maiperquat (+before 420) renewed the Persian church. The synod summoned at Seleucia-Ctesiphon in 410 acknowledged the decisions of Nicea, concerning dogma as well as discipline.[55] Towards the end of the fifth century the Church of Persia certainly became Nestorian, yet Nicene orthodoxy was not called in question by this.

The reception by the eastern Syriac church of the Nicene faith is all the more remarkable as it took place beyond the Roman borders in an only partially hellenized context still bearing strongly semitic features. Precisely for this reason, the relevant documents, in which the Greek texts were rendered in Syriac, show particularly clearly how little the gospel had been 'hellenized'.

The trinitarian doctrine of the Greek Fathers of the fourth century, as it had been established at the council of Constantinople (381) and at the same time essentially accepted by the churches of the Western empire as well as by the Eastern churches outside the empire, thus represents authentic trinitarian dogma. According to this, Father, Son and Spirit are three really distinct hypostases, or persons, and nevertheless one deity. The Son is consubstantial with the Father, insofar as he is begotten by him. The Spirit, on the other hand, is consubstantial with the Father, insofar as he proceeds from him through the Son. All three are one to the extent that their whole saving activity is the act of one unique God.[56] This dogma is the basis of any Christian theology, but has also remained the foundation of the liturgy of any Christian church. Hence a future reunification of Christians must in any event rest on this one faith.[57]

Although the dogma had been formulated, not all questions were answered. The question remained open as to how the second hypostasis was united with the man Jesus, i.e. the christological question. The difference beween the first and second procession remained unexplained, too.[58] With regard to this Augustine was to propose his own solution. The problems of the trinitarian dogma are for the main part intrinsic to the dogma itself.[59] Moreover, it has to be translated from Cappadocian into modern terminology. Above all the correlation not clarified by the Cappadocians between the immanent Trinity and the Trinity as it is present in salvation history certainly needs to be further clarified. For such

[54] Cf. A. Adam, *Dogmengeschichte* I, pp 252f, and esp. E. Beck, *Ephräms Trinitätslehre im Bild von Sonne/Feuer, Licht/Wärme* (=CSChO Subsidia 62), Louvain 1981, p 29, note 29 containing a reference to his earlier studies in StudAnselm 21 and 33.

[55] Cf. A. Adam, *Dogmengeschichte* I, pp 253f, with a reference to the Synodicon Orientale: ed. J. B. Chabot, Paris 1902, pp 22, 262f, and G. L. Dossetti, *Il simbolo di Nicea e di Constantinopoli*, pp 38–41, 120f.

[56] Cf. Ep. synod. of 382: COecD, p 28.

[57] Cf. R. Slenzka, art. cit. in note 17.

[58] Basil evaded this problem, cf. Spir 18.46, while Gregory of Naz., or. 31.8, with his distinction between generation and procession gave it only a very formal answer.

[59] Cf. the texts in which the Fathers recall the ineffable mystery of the Trinity, e.g. Athanasius, Serap I 20; Cyril of Jerus., Cat 16.24; Basil, Spir 9.22; Gregory of Naz., or. 31.8; Gregory of Nyssa, ep. 24.

a modern reception of the trinitarian dogma, which is chiefly indebted to the Greek fathers, Athanasius and the Cappadocians, the different mentalities and linguistic possibilities of that time certainly need to be taken into account.[60] In a modern rendering of the trinitarian dogma of the early Church it must no less be borne in mind, how much it was worked out in view of man's salvation in Jesus Christ.[61]

---

[60] Cf. A. Adam, *Dogmengeschichte* I, pp 92–105: linguistic prerequisites for the dogmatic reflection of the Church, with bibl.; G. L. Prestige, *God in Patristic Thought,* London 1936.

[61] Cf. L. Scheffczyk, My Sal II, pp 183–7: sociological aspects of the doctrine of the Trinity.

14. The Revelation of the Love of the Humble God According to Augustine

For the bibliography on Augustine in general, see:

C. Andresen, *Bibliographia Augustiniana*, Darmstadt ²1973, and the bibliographies in REAug and in other periodicals on Augustine. Also the bibliographies in the modern editions of Augustine, like Bibliothèque Augustinienne, Paris, and Nuova Biblioteca Agostiniana, Rome, and in the articles of *Augustinus-Lexikon*, edited by C. Mayer, Basle/Stuttgart 1986ff (see especially 'Christus').

BIBLIOGRAPHY

E. Portalié, 'Augustin', DThC 1 1909, cols. 2268–472 (still useful).
M. Schmaus, *Die psychologische Trinitätslehre des heiligen Augustinus*, Münster 1927, ²1967 (with bibl.).
J. Riviére, *Le dogme de la rédemption chez s. Augustin*, Paris 1930.
T. van Bavel, *Recherches sur la christologie de s. Augustine*, Fribourg 1954.
J.-L. Maier, *Les missions divines selon s. Augustin*, Fribourg 1960.
A. Schindler, *Wort und Analogie in Augustins Trinitätslehre*, Tübingen 1965.
O. du Roy, *L'intelligence de la foi en la Trinité selon s. Augustin*, Paris 1966.
K. H. Lütcke, *'Auctoritas' bei Augustin*, Stuttgart 1968.
R. A. Markus, *Saeculum. History and Society in the Theology of St. Augustine*, London 1970.
O. Brabant, *Le Christ, centre et source morale chez s. Augustin*, Gembloux 1971.
J. Verhess, 'Heiliger Geist und Inkarnation in der Theologie des heiligen Augustinus von Hippo', REAug 22, 1976, pp 234–53.
W. Geerlings, *Christus Exemplum. Studien zur Christologie und Christusverkündigung Augustins*, Mainz 1978.
B. Studer, 'Soteriologie der Kirchenväter', HDG III/2a, Freiburg 1978, pp 156–74 (with bibl.), now *Dominus Salvator*, pp 269–325.
A. Schindler, 'Augustin', TRE 4, 1979, pp 646–98.
B. Studer, 'Le Christ, notre justice selon s. Augustin', RchAug 15, 1980, pp 99–143 (with bibl.), now *Dominus Salvator*, pp 369–400.
B. Studer, 'Augustin et la foi de Nicée', RchAug 19, 1984, pp 133–54 (with bibl.).

See also:

J. Burnaby, *Amor Dei*, London 1938.
G. Bonner, *St. Augustine of Hippo. Life and Controversies*, London 1963; id., *God's Decree and Man's Destiny*, London 1987.
E. TeSelle, *Augustine the Theologian*, London 1970.

H. Chadwick, *Augustine,* Oxford 1986.

G. Madec, *La patrie et la voie. Le Christ dans la vie et dans la pensée de Saint Augustin* (Jésus et Jésus-Christ 36), Paris 1989.

B. Studer, *Gratia Christi – gratia Dei bei Augustinus von Hippo* (Studia Ephemeridis "Augustinianum"), Rome 1993 (with bibl.).

By the end of the fourth century all the churches of the Roman empire had accepted the Nicene faith according to the later interpretation of Athanasius and the Cappadocians. Thus the Arian controversy, except for less significant debates with Illyrian and Germanic Arians, had come to an end. When Augustine arrived on the theological scene about 390, he therefore encountered an already well-established trinitarian doctrine, which even the political authorities had declared to be the religious foundation of the empire's unity. He himself quite consciously joined the preceding tradition, as he expressly testifies in his great work *De Trinitate* when he says that he had perused all the relevant writings accessible to him.[1] Yet the anti-Arian tradition, for all its acknowledgement of the divinity of the Son and the Holy Spirit and precise trinitarian formulae, had not clarified all relevant problems. The questions of the character of the Spirit's procession, of the mutual relationship of the persons, and of their relation to the one divine being, were still open. Augustine took due account of this, as his speech *de fide et symbolo* shows, which he gave as a young priest in 393 before the African bishops.[2]

With regard to christology Augustine found himself in a different situation. It is true that discussions on the God-man had already been in train for some time. Augustine himself several times referred to these debates, which Apollinaris of Laodicea above all had sparked off.[3] Moreover, he had to counter the christological errors which had been ascribed to Leporius, a Gallican priest.[4] But the controversy about the one Christ, true God and true man, only got fully under way towards the end of his life. He himself hardly took notice of this controversy, neither was he able to take part in the council of Ephesus (431), to which he had been invited.

Insofar as Augustine, with respect to trinitarian doctrine, was able to assent to the clear-cut dogma that resulted from the fight of the catholic Church against the Arians, it is certainly right to expound his theology in the context of the aftermath of Nicea. On the other hand, it would not be unreasonable to present his theological thought in the context of Chalcedon. For in his christology he contributed decisively to the doctrinal decisions of this christological council, even if not directly, but through the mediation of Leo the Great. At any rate it is evident that Augustine's trinitarian teaching and his christology are closely interrelated.

---

[1] Augustine, Trin I 4.7; also BAug 15, pp 666ff. For the Greek sources cf. esp. the studies by B. Altaner in *Kleine Patristische Schriften,* Berlin 1967.

[2] FidSymb 9.19; Cf. BAug 15, pp 8f.

[3] Cf. among others, serm. 214.6 (AD 391); Div Qu 83.80 (AD 395); Conf VII 19.25; Haer 55.

[4] Cf. A. Grillmeier, *Jesus Christus,* pp 661–5 (=*Christ in Christian Tradition,* pp 464–7).

This close interrelation already marked his return to the faith of his childhood, as he himself recounts in his *Confessions*.[5] At that time the struggle for a true understanding of God was preeminent.[6] In this he was given valuable help here by Neoplatonism, as represented in the circle of Ambrose of Milan, even though he missed Christ in the Platonic philosophers. They pointed him towards the *patria,* but were not, however, able to show him the *via* that led there, because they were ashamed of the cross. Only Paul and John revealed to him how sinful man, through Christ in the Holy Spirit, can really belong to God.[7]

There emerges no less clearly the correlation between the Trinity and the incarnation in Augustine's own theological reflection. He had attempted, from personal interest, as he openly confesses in *De Trinitate,* to penetrate more deeply the mystery of the most holy Trinity; he was not stirred to do so by polemics, by other people's enquiries, or by pastoral concerns.[8] It was precisely here, in the endeavours urged upon him from within, that he could not renounce the mystery of Christ. In fact, two of his most profound expositions of the saving work of the God-man constitute part of that work, which contemplates the mystery of God.[9]

Finally, the numerous, more or less popular sermons show that for Augustine the mystery of the Trinity can only be disclosed by the *sacramentum Christi*. In the addresses and sermons of the bishop of Hippo there is no doubt that Christ, the Lord and Saviour, takes the central place. This is especially true of his *opus amplissimum,* the 'Enarrationes in Psalmos'. In this work everything revolves around Christ: around the head and the body, around the *totus Christus,* around Christ in us and in the Church.[10] Yet this all-embracing mystery of Christ is finally based on the presence of the Holy Spirit, in whom alone the believer can rejoice in belonging to Christ, and consists in nothing else than a growing union with the eternal Word of the Father.[11]

It is above all in Augustine that the mysteries of the Trinity and of God's saving incarnation are most clearly experienced as being inwardly interrelated. He brings home in a quite unique way the fact that the eternal love of God is only revealed in his humility in history.[12] Moreover, it is notable how systematically he developed a similar terminology for both these mysteries of the faith, thus paving the way for Western theology.

---

[5] Cf. Conf VII, with the commentary in BAug 13 and 14.
[6] Cf. Conf I 18.25; VII 1.1f; also BAug 13, pp 12–15: a dialogue with God.
[7] Cf. esp. Conf. VII 9.13–15; VII 18.24–19.25; VII 21.27; also BAug 13, pp 693–8.
[8] Cf. A. Schindler, *Trinitätslehre,* pp 1–11.
[9] Trin IV 1.3–20.30; XIII 10.13–19.24.
[10] Cf. e.g. EnPs 90.2.1; 148.8.
[11] Cf. EnPs 45.8; 86.1; 118.4.2.
[12] Cf. W. Mallard, 'The Incarnation in Augustine's Conversion', RchAug 15, 1980, pp 80–98, with the early texts CAcad III 19.42; Ord II 5.16; II 9.27; cf. further CatRud 4.7f; Trin IV 2.4; VIII 5.7–7.11.

I. THE MOST IMPORTANT WRITINGS ON THE TRINITY AND ON CHRIST

This is not the place to give an introduction to the whole of Augustine's theological work. It may be useful, however, to indicate briefly the character of those works in which the mystery of the Trinity and the saving incarnation of the Word of God are the main theme.

In the first place the theological magnum opus *De Trinitate* must be considered.[13] It is a thoroughly personal work, in which Augustine summed up his most profound thoughts. He had difficulties, however, in finishing it; it took him about twenty years. He himself called it an *opus laboriosum.*[14]

It is generally accepted nowadays that *De Trinitate* is made up of two main parts: a more dogmatic (books 1–8) and a more speculative part (books 9–15).The first part contains an exposition of the content (1–4), as well as a discussion of the formulation of the trinitarian faith (5–7/8). The second part, however, is devoted to a quest for a deeper understanding of the mystery of Father, Son and Spirit by means of an analysis of the inner life of man, who is the image of the trinitarian reality of the one God.[15] Both main parts also contain thorough and comprehensive expositions of the mystery of Christ. In the fourth book, which raises the question of the theophanies, Augustine sees the incarnation as the summit of God's appearances, and speaks of Jesus' death and resurrection as *sacramentum et exemplum* for the inner and the outer man, i.e. of their meaning for salvation.[16] In the twelfth and thirteenth book, in which he strives for an understanding of religious cognition, he presents Christ as *scientia* and *sapientia,* showing that man can attain the beatific vision of the eternal Word of God only through faith in the incarnation and the cross.[17]

Less speculative, but no less dogmatically significant, is the *Enchiridion de fide spe et caritate.*[18] It is a late work (423), in which the mature Augustine, by following the creed, brings to perfect clarity his theological thought. In particular chapters 10.33 and 28.108 are worthy of note, as in them he expresses his favourite thoughts on salvation.

Alongside these two theological masterpieces, the *Confessions* (ca. 400) must be mentioned. In this Augustine gives thanks to God the Father for the grace

[13] For the origin and character of Trin cf. besides A. Schindler, *Trinitätslehre,* pp 1–11, M. Schmaus, *Die psychologische Trinitätslehre des Heiligen Augustinus,* Münster 1927, [2]1966, and BAug 15 and 16. Other important texts on the Trinity: Agon 13; serm. 52 (AD 412/13), as well as the anti-Arian texts proper: cf. A. Schindler, op.cit., p 426.

[14] Ep. 174 (AD 416). For the chronology and the duration of the drafting of Trin cf. A. Schindler, *Trinitätslehre,* pp 6–9.

[15] Augustine himself more than once refers to the structure of his work. Cf. Trin I 2.4 and esp. XV 3.5. See also Trin VIII, where Augustine explains his theological method, cf. B. Studer, 'Una ricerca di sintesi del pensiero biblico', *Storia della Teologia,* pp 496f.

[16] Trin IV 3.5f; also B. Studer, '"Sacramentum et exemplum" chez s. Augustin', RchAug 10, 1975, pp 87–141, now *Dominus Salvator,* pp 141–212.

[17] Augustine, Trin XIII 19.24–20.26; also G. Madec, 'Christus scientia et sapientia nostra. Le principe de cohérence de la doctrine augustinienne', RchAug 10, 1975, pp 77–85.

[18] Cf. the German-Latin edition by J. Barbel, Düsseldorf 1960 and the English translation by E. Evans: id., *Saint Augustine's Enchiridion,* London 1953.

of Christ, with the help of which he was enabled to return to God from the misery of sin.[19] In particular he shows that it is only possible through the Lord's cross to ascend to God.[20] The most magnificent apologetic work of Christian antiquity, the twenty-two books of *De Civitate,* is also worth mentioning.[21] In this theology of history, on which Augustine had worked for many a long year to elucidate the meaning of the *tempora christiana,* Christ, his incarnation and his presence in history are the central themes. No other work points to Christ's mediatorship in more eloquent words.[22] The special presence of Christ in the sacramental life of the Church is worked out most thoroughly in the anti-Donatist works.[23] The anti-Pelagian writings, on the other hand, summarize yet more clearly how the grace of the one mediator continually works in the believer's heart.[24] It is chiefly the sermons, and above all the expositions of the Psalms, that speak in a vivid and popular way of the justice of the crucified and risen Lord, without which no one can stand before God.[25] Finally, Augustine worked out with clarity of thought his conception of the mystery of the Word's incarnation reaching back into the eternity of God in a number of letters, e.g. in the letter to the pagan Volusianus,[26] in his letter-treatise *De gratia Novi Testamenti,*[27] in his letter on the presence of God[28] and also in a letter on the meaning of the festival of Easter.[29]

II. THE MAIN LINES OF AUGUSTINE'S DOCTRINE OF THE TRINITY

1. Knowledge of the all-transcending God

In *De Trinitate,* the most complete expression of his trinitarian thought, Augustine attempted to find God for his own sake and that of others.[30] Thus he speaks of an *exercitatio mentis,*[31] of a spiritual striving for purity of heart, without which God cannot be beheld. Ever greater openness towards God is to be achieved by inner

---

[19] Cf. Conf I 1.1; Retract II 6, where Augustine epitomizes this work as praise for the just and merciful God; also BAug 13, pp 9–12, 26–36.

[20] Conf VII 18.24; VII 21.27.

[21] Cf. Augustine, *The City of God,* English translation by H. Bettenson, Harmondsworth 1972. See also B. Studer, 'Zum Aufbau von Augustins De Civitate Dei', *Mélanges T. J. van Bavel* (Leuven 1990), pp 937–51.

[22] Cf. esp. Civ IX 15–17; X 6; X 29.1; XI 2.

[23] Cf. esp. CEpParm III 4.8–8.16; also BAug 28, pp 86–94 with other texts.

[24] Cf. esp. NatGrat 40.47; serm. 169.10.12; PeccMerit I 15.19; PerfHom 20.43; also B. Studer, art.cit.: RchAug 10, 1975, pp 133–9.

[25] Cf. EnPs 93.19; 90.2.1; 100.6, TractIo 84.1f; TractEpIo 1.8f; serm. 157.3; also B. Studer, 'Le Christ, notre justice, selon s. Augustin', RchAug 15, 1980, pp 99–143, esp. pp 128–39.

[26] Ep. 137 (dated 411/12).

[27] Ep. 140 (dated 411/12).

[28] Ep. 187 (dated 417).

[29] Ep. 555 (dated c.400); also A. Roth, *Pascha und Hinübergang durch Glaube, Hoffnung und Liebe,* Festschrift C. Mohrmann, Utrecht 1973, pp 96–107.

[30] Trin XV 6.10.

[31] Trin XIII 20.26; XV 1.1; XV 6.10; XV 35; also BAug 16, pp 612ff, and A. Schindler, *Trinitätslehre,* p 226.

effort, which is necessary if the likeness of the soul's religious life to the triune God is to be more deeply grasped. As regards form, Augustine came to the conclusion that man is most truly the image of God when he thinks of God (*memoria Dei*), knows him (*intelligentia Dei*) and loves him (*amor in Deum*).[32] He was quite aware, nevertheless, that only those who believe in the incarnation of the Word and in particular in his deepest humiliation on the cross will attain the heights of the knowledge of God and therefore finally be united with God in the vision of the Word.[33] It is precisely beholding in faith the sufferings of the Lord that guarantees, according to Augustine, the certainty and confidence that the highest knowledge of the eternal Word will not be denied him. The same Word, for the knowledge of which man strives, in his loving humility has condescended to man to such an extent that man is able to ascend to him. He is *scientia* and *sapientia*.[34]

It is evident that in such a climate of religious inwardness the whole study of the trinitarian doctrine in the bible and tradition is marked by a sincere respect for the mystery. It is no less evident that even the most sublime and, apparently, merely philosophical speculations are always rooted in the gospel, in the *narratio de amore Christi*.[35]

2. The orthodox exposition of Holy Scripture

In the more dogmatic first part of *De Trinitate* exegesis takes a prominent place. Augustine accordingly makes clear from the very beginning that he intends in his expositions to rest on the *auctoritas scripturarum*.[36] Yet in the later books too references to the Bible are not at all lacking.[37] When he refers to the scripture he of course does it in line with the understanding of the orthodox commentators, the *catholici tractatores*.[38]

In seeking to comment on the trinitarian and christological texts of Holy Scripture in an orthodox manner, Augustine follows the so-called *regula catholica,* according to which the divine and human statements are to be distinguished in order to exclude the notion of the Son's inferiority to the Father, which the Arians had maintained.[39] It is notable that he refers the passage *'Pater maior me est'* (John 14:28) not exclusively to the incarnation, to the *secundum hominem,* in which state the Son is less than the Father, but also to the eternal generation, whereby the Son comes after the Father.[40]

---

[32] Trin XIV 12.15; XIV 14.18; also BAug 16, pp 635ff, and A. Schindler, *Trinitätslehre,* pp 212ff.

[33] Trin XIII 20.25; XIV 2.3.

[34] Trin XII and XIII. Cf. esp. XIII 19.24–20.26.

[35] Cf. the closing passage of the work: Trin XV 27.49–28.51, where Augustine again recalls the regula fidei, and concludes the whole with a prayer. Also CatRud 5.8: the NT is nothing but a narrative concerning Christ and an exhortation to love.

[36] Trin I 2.4; cf. K.H.Lütcke, *Auctoritas,* pp 128–36.

[37] This is true esp. of the issue of the inner-trinitarian procession of the Holy Spirit: Trin XV 26.45–27.48.

[38] Trin I 4.7; cf. BAug 15, pp 566ff, and K. H. Lütcke, *Auctoritas,* pp 136–46.

[39] Trin I 7.14; II 1.2; also BAug 15, p 577.

[40] Trin II 1.2, and already DivQu 69.1; also BAug 15, p 574f.

From earlier tradition Augustine takes over the so-called prosopic exegesis, which not only considers the grammatical position of a person in a statement but also seeks to evaluate the significance of a person through its function. Also in *De Trinitate,* although perhaps less markedly than in the *Enarrationes in Psalmos* or in other writings, the use of *persona* more or less recalls the exegetical meaning of the word, except perhaps in dogmatic formulae which are taken over from tradition.[41] Augustine, moreover, explains the relationship between the persons by means of the Aristotelian category of *relatio.* So he attempts by means of the principle *'relative quaeque persona ad alteram dicitur'*[42] to refute the Arian interpretation of the relevant texts.[43]

In particular Augustine applies his theological exegesis to the problem of the missions (*missiones*) of the Son and the Holy Spirit.[44] The Arians had concluded from relevant biblical passages that the Son and the Spirit were inferior to the Father, who had sent them. To counter this viewpoint Augustine develops the concept of *missio,* which essentially consists of an *apparitio,* i.e. a new way of being recognized.[45] Even in those theophanies which can be clearly ascribed to the Son or the Holy Spirit, their divine substance has never been visible; what is seen is merely something created, something that originated in the creative activity of the whole Trinity, even though it was the sign of the presence of only one Person.[46] Therefore one cannot, from the fact that the Son and the Spirit have been sent to this world, in order to be present and known there in a new way, conclude their inequality with the Father. With regard to their substance they are just as invisible as the Father.[47] From these considerations it is also evident that the theophanies of the Old Testament are not simply to be ascribed to the Logos as the visible God, as pre-Nicene exegesis and, in its wake, the Arians had done.[48] Because Father, Son and Holy Spirit are *aequaliter invisibiles* in respect of their substance, and yet can make themselves visible by means of creaturely forms of manifestation, the theophanies can fundamentally be attributed to any individual person, or to the Trinity as a whole. It is only the context of the narration that allows the attribution of the theophanies to one person or another.[49] In this context in particular the incarnation, which only happens to the Son, proves to be the highest of all theophanies. At the very moment when Mary conceived him by the Holy Spirit, the Word fashioned the man Jesus in such a way as to form a single person with himself. This made him not only the most lucid but also the lasting sign of his presence as revealing God's love.[50]

---

[41] Cf. Trin II 17.28; II 6.11; II 13.23; II 18.35; III 10.20; III 11.26 etc.; also B. Studer, 'Der Personbegriff in der frühen kirchenamtlichen Trinitätslehre', TheolPhil 57, 1982, pp 161–77, esp. pp 170–7.

[42] Civ XI 10.1.

[43] Cf. Trin V, esp. V 4.5; also BAug 15, p 584, and A. Schindler, *Trinitätslehre,* pp 147–62.

[44] Cf. J.-L. Maier, *Les missions divines,* and B. Studer, *Zur Theophanie-Exegese Augustins.*

[45] Cf. Trin XV 3.5, with the summary of books II-IV.

[46] Trin IV 21.30–2.

[47] Trin II 10.19–12.22; also BAug 15, p 578f.

[48] Cf. B. Studer, *Theophanie-Exegese,* pp 53–98, and G. Aeby, *Le missions divines de s. Justin à Origène,* Fribourg 1958.

[49] Cf. Trin III 10.21; II 17.32; also J.-L. Maier, *Les missions divines,* pp 107–10.

[50] Cf. Trin IV 20.28; IV 21.31; VIII 5.7; XIII 17.22.

3. Deepening the trinitarian faith

While Augustine took great pains to give a dogmatically unambiguous account of the Church's faith in Father, Son and Spirit, his main interest was without doubt directed to the *intellectus fidei,* the deeper understanding of the one catholic faith.

A further deepening of the orthodox faith consists for him primarily in explaining the *aequalitas personarum.*[51] Thus in the first four books of *De Trinitate* he attempts, especially as regards visibility, to show all three Persons to be equal.[52] Also the three following books (5–7), which are devoted to an exact formulation of the trinitarian dogma, revolve around this same problem: in the divine reality all is the same, except what is asserted in relative terms (5); a collection of the biblical proofs of the equality (6); the divine attributes assigned equally to all three persons (7).[53] The same is still more true of the second main part; for Augustine there strives after the most perfect image of the equality of the three Persons who are one God.[54]

In this search for an explanation of the *aequalitas personarum* Augustine obviously does not neglect the issue of divine unity. When he asks himself what the three persons really are, and in what sense they are equal, he wants to understand how their entire equality reveals their unity.[55] It is certainly striking how often he uses the terms *Deus – Trinitas, Unitas – Trinitas, Deus Trinitatis,* etc.[56] This should be no cause for surprise; for it is certainly due to his philosophical presupposition whereby the *essentia suprema* or the *summum bonum* constitute the central concept.[57] He has also been stirred by that anti-Arian tradition which was particularly concerned with the *una voluntas divina* and the unity of the saving activity of Father, Son and Spirit (*opera ad extra communia*).[58] In spite of all this an attentive reader of Augustine's main trinitarian texts cannot fail to notice that his line of thought progresses from Father, Son and Spirit to the one God.[59] Precisely because for him the three persons are entirely equal, and thus inseparable in being as well as in action, they are one single God. Thus Augustine represents a mode of explaining the trinitarian faith which is closer to the eastern tradition than it at first sight appears.[60]

The explanation of the *aequalitas personarum* in the one God is also served by the so-called doctrine of the psychological trinity, which has already been alluded to, developed by Augustine in the second part of *De Trinitate.*[61] Convinced that God has created man in his image (Gen 1:27), he ascends by the

---

[51] Cf. Trin VIII 1.1f; also B. Studer, 'Augustin et la foi de Nicée', RchAug 19, 1984, p 143.

[52] Cf. Trin XV 3.5: summary of Trin I-IV; Trin III 2.3; IV 21.32.

[53] Cf. Trin XV 3.5: summary of Trin V-VII; Trin VI 1.1; VI 5.7 etc.

[54] Cf. Trin XV 3.5: summary of Trin IX and XI; Trin IX 4.4; IX 12.18; XI 4.7; XV 14.23–16.25.

[55] Trin I 4.7.

[56] Cf. BAug 15, pp 20 and 570, with the cited texts.

[57] Cf. Trin V 2.3; VIII 3.4; XV 5.7.

[58] Cf. Trin I 5.8; also BAug 15, pp 573f, and A. Schindler, *Trinitätslehre,* p 126, and passim.

[59] Trin I 4.7; VII 3.5f. See especially Solil I 1.2–6; CatRud 24.47, and also the fact that Augustine uses in the *Confessions* the word *Deus* for the Father, e.g. VIII 1.2; IX 4.9; XI 9.11; XIII 4.5.

[60] Cf. B. Studer, 'Augustin et la foi de Nicée', RchAug 19, 1984, pp 149f, 154, where other writings are also taken into account.

[61] Trin VIII–XV; also M. Schmaus, *Die psychologische Trinitätslehre,* esp. pp 196–224.

trinity of *memoria – visio interna – voluntas* (the level of the senses) to the trinity *memoria – notitia – amor* (the intellectual level) and finally to the highest analogy *memoria Dei – intelligentia Dei – amor in Deum.*[61a] He is aware here that even the most perfect image in the human soul never fully matches the reality of the divine Trinity. In the last book he therefore underlines the differences which in spite of all similarity stand between the original and the copy. While man *owns* intellect and love, the whole divine Trinity *is* God.[62] Yet this does not disturb Augustine, on the contrary, according to him, the clear realization of the incomprehensibility of God is itself always a source of happiness.[63] He is also the first to admit that he does not even really know what the human soul is.[64]

In his struggle to fathom the mystery of the Trinity as far as is possible for man, Augustine could not pass over the problem of the difference between the two processions. Already as a young priest he had become aware of this question left open by tradition.[65] He was all the more bound to occupy himself with this problem, as he had anyway a lively interest in the Holy Spirit.[66] Because the biblical doctrine of the Holy Spirit as the gift of the risen Lord had always been dear to him, and because, moreover, he has regarded the Holy Spirit as *communio Patris et Filii,*[67] he could not help also reflecting on the difference between the origin of the Son and that of the Holy Spirit.[68] In doing this he chiefly went back to the psychological analogies. According to him, the procession of the Son is indeed comparable to that of *intelligentia* from *mens* or *memoria,* while the procession of the Spirit is like that of *voluntas* which necessarily proceeds from *intelligentia.*[69] Although this analogy certainly impressed him, it did not constitute the fundamental reason for the distinction. For this is founded rather on the *regula fidei.* In his exposition of the New Testament texts, according to which not only the Father but also the Son gives the Holy Spirit, Augustine in fact concludes that those who do not understand the psychological metaphor, should rely on scripture and keep to the *regula fidei.*[70] It is not insight, which in this life never finally penetrates, but the *auctoritas fidei* which is decisive for him.

It is just this that shows impressively how much more closely the immanent Trinity and the threefold work in salvation history are interrelated in the Augustinian theology than is admitted by many even to this day. Quite apart from the doctrine of the *missiones,* in which Augustine, in the dogmatic part, expressly refers to the saving activity of the Son and the Spirit, he here clearly

---

[61a] Cf. Trin X 20, 29.

[62] Trin XV 7.11f; XV 22.42–23.43; also BAug 16, pp 645f, and A. Schindler, *Trinitätslehre,* pp 225f.

[63] Trin XV 2.2.

[64] Trin XV 7.13; also BAug 16, pp 646f.

[65] FidSymb 9.19f.

[66] Esp. note how often Augustine quotes Rom 5:5: 'because God's love has been poured into our hearts through the Holy Spirit which has been given to us.' Cf. A. M. La Bonnardière, 'Le verset paulinien Rom 5.5 dans l'oeuvre de s.Augustin', AugMag II, 1954, pp 657–65.

[67] Trin XV 19.36f.

[68] Trin XV 25.45; also BAug 16, pp 658–61, and A. Schindler, *Trinitätslehre,* pp 222f.

[69] Trin IX 12.17; X 11.17–12.19; XV 21.40f; XV 26.47.

[70] Trin XV 26.45–27.49, esp. 49.

explains the difference between the first and the second origin from the fact that the Holy Spirit has been sent by the glorified Lord and therefore must from before all creation derive not only from the Father but also from the Son.[71]

It is notable that Augustine through his teaching on the Holy Spirit as *amor Patris et Filii* without any doubt introduces a quite remarkable novelty into the doctrine of the Trinity. Even though Hilary of Poitiers had coined the formula *'Aeternitas in Patre, species in imagine, usus in munere'*,[72] it was only Augustine, who consistently worked out the comparison between the Spirit who comes from the Father and from the Son, and the love which flows from the lover and the beloved and unites them both.[73] However, he has not produced some unbiblical novelty. Even in the New Testament, especially John, the Holy Spirit appears only as confirming that love between Father and Son, which has been revealed in the cross and the resurrection. For in the experience of the primitive Church the Holy Spirit has sealed the fact that the Son loved the Father to the end, and that the Father responded to this love in justifying him.[74] In this way Augustine, precisely in his most profound trinitarian speculations, has returned to the biblical beginnings of the Church's trinitarian faith.

III. ST. AUGUSTINE'S CHRISTOCENTRISM

If we keep to the *Confessiones,* in which Augustine reproaches the Platonists with the fact that while knowing the eternal Word, the *patria,* they did not acknowledge the Word made man, the *via ad patriam,* we could get the impression that he himself as a philosopher had accepted the Trinity as a matter of course, whereas he had to wrestle with faith in the cross.[75] The immanent Trinity would then have been something taken for granted and therefore more fundamental than the recognition of the incarnation. We could confirm this by noting that he made more progress in understanding the one Christ than in his teaching, fixed from the start, of the *aequalitas personarum in una deitate.*[76] It must not, however, be forgotten that even during the time when he lived in alienation from the Church, he had nevertheless always believed in Christ, and even as a Manichean had certainly had a deep respect for him.[77] Precisely for this reason it was so important for him to show after his conversion that the *fides aeterna,* the intuition of the eternal truth, is most highly valued in the *fides*

---

[71] Trin IV 19.25–20.30; also the remarks in J.-L. Maier, *Les missions divines,* esp. pp 140f: on the connection between the historical mission and the eternal procession of Son and Spirit.

[72] Hilary Trin II 1, quoted by Augustine, Trin VI 10.11; cf. BAug 15, pp 588f, and O. du Roy, *Trinité,* pp 320ff.

[73] Cf. BAug 15, pp 587f, and A. Schindler, *Trinitätslehre,* pp 44ff.

[74] Cf. the Johannine notion of glorification in John 17:1–5, together with IJoh 4.7–19 and Trin XV 17.31: The Holy Spirit as God's love causes us to abide in God and God in us.

[75] Cf. Conf VII 20.26, also O. du Roy, *Trinité,* pp 413–66, esp. 453 and 96–106: on patria-via.

[76] Cf. T. van Bavel, *Christologie,* pp 176–80, and A. Grillmeier, *Jesus Christus,* pp 597–604 (=*Christ in Christian Tradition,* pp 407–13).

[77] Cf. W. Geerlings, *Christus Exemplum,* pp 241–58, and A. Schindler, 'Augustinus', TRE 4, 1979, pp 656–62: from childhood to conversion.

historica, the faith in the *clementia Dei* as revealed in the humility of the incarnation, than in pagan philosophy.[78]

At any rate, it can be taken for granted that Christ is at the centre of Augustinian theology. In all the different stages of his religious experience and his theological thought Augustine has to do with Christ. At his conversion he discovered him as *auctoritas* for faith and as *via* for the way home to God.[79] During the debate with the Donatists he was visibly encouraged by the presence of Christ in the Church.[80] In the Pelagian controversy, which made the greatest theological demands on him, his answer again was christological: Christ is not only *exemplum,* a model of the Christian life, but also *adiutorium,* a spring of inner grace always welling up.[81] Finally, with regard to the question of the meaning of the *tempora christiana,* which was forced upon him by contemporary history, he gave the only valid answer of the Christian faith, with Christ, the sole mediator between God and man.[82]

It is, however, not possible here to depict fully the Augustinian idea of Christ. It must suffice to go through his fundamental principles.[83] In this way those features, which show the interrelation of christology with trinitarian doctrine, will be particularly emphasized.

1. Christ's mediatorship

No reader of the *Enchiridion,* the unique dogmatic outline from the mature Augustine, can fail to notice the strong emphasis laid on Christ's mediatorship. This manual could well be summarized with the words: *'reconciliatio per sacrificium mediatoris'.* For in fact it deals chiefly with sin and reconciliation with God, or the way that leads from being far from God to being close to Him.[84]

This is in some way true of the whole of Augustine's theology. Both as *auctoritas,* and as *praesens in Ecclesia,* as *adiutorium et exemplum,* and as *via salutis universalis,* Christ proves to be above all the Son of God made man, to be mediator between God and man.[85] This general statement is confirmed by the indisputable fact that there are few New Testament texts so often and in so many different contexts cited in Augustine's works, even though only from about 395, as 1 Timothy 2:5: *'Unus mediator Dei et hominum, homo Christus Iesus.'*[86]

Yet, Augustine does not go back to the concept of Christ's mediatorship in a totally consistent way. In his effort to be faithful to the Bible, something he often

---

[78] Cf. W. Mallard, art.cit. in note 12.

[79] Cf. Conf. VII 18.24–19.25; also K. H. Lütcke, *Auctoritas,* esp. pp 123–8.

[80] Cf. TractIo 5.18; 6.8f; Bapt III 10.15; also BAug 28, pp 86–94, with other texts.

[81] Cf. NatGrat 40.47; PerfHom 20.43; also B. Studer, 'Sacramentum et exemplum', RchAug 10, 1975, pp 133–9.

[82] Civ IX 15.1–17.

[83] Cf. B. Studer, *Soteriologie,* pp 156–74.

[84] Ench 10.33; 13.41.

[85] Ench 28.108; Civ XI 2.

[86] Cf. O. du Roy, *Trinité,* pp 89f in general, and for the Pelagian writings in part, BAug 22, pp 729–32.

expressly emphasizes, he lays the stress in countless texts on the man Jesus. Typical in this regard is the formula in *De Trinitate: in forma Dei aequalis Patri, in forma servi mediator Dei et hominum.*[87] Accordingly, following the Bible, he identifies *mediator* with *redemptor,* and *reconciliator* with both *sacerdos* and *intercessor.*[88] How much the *mediator homo* matters to him, is finally evident above all in texts with an anti-Pelagian colouring, in which he speaks of the *gratia* and the *praedestinatio mediatoris,* where he has in mind of course only the human nature.[89]

Under the influence of philosophical, but surely also Christian, and especially anti-Arian traditions, Augustine in another series of texts, less numerous this time, points to the *in medio esse Christi,*[90] affirming his simultaneous participation in both Godhead and manhood.[91] Already as the principle of creation and illumination, the eternal Word mediates between the One and the many.[92] In his incarnation his mediatorship is, however, much more pronounced.[93] To become the saviour of sinful mankind, he has to participate both in human mortality and in the divine justice.[94]

The two concepts of Christ's mediatorship do not, however, in any way exclude each other, as at first sight may appear. For the man Jesus can finally exercise his mediatorship, which requires perfect sinlessness,[95] and, moreover, includes the highest authority,[96] only because he is taken up into personal unity with the Son of God.[97] The grace of mediatorship, the highest of all graces, benefits Jesus' manhood, but in its very essence it belongs to the only-begotten Son of God.[98] On the other hand, and this is even more significant, Augustine in both series of texts never takes *Deus* to mean the Father alone, but as he expressly states, always Father, Son and Spirit.[99] Certainly the quite numerous passages cannot be overlooked which seem to speak of a virtual christological reduction. They formulate Jesus' mediatorship as a christological constriction, Christ appears in them as *creator* and *recreator,* or even more pointedly, as *via* and *patria* at the same time.[100] When he in consequence simply says: *per Christum hominem ad Christum Deum,* this formulation leaves Father and Spirit unaccounted for. At the same time we get the impression that the

---

[87] Cf. Trin I 7.14: anti-Arian context. Cf. Trin IV 12.15; Conf X 43.68; Civ IX 14; XI 2.

[88] Cf. for *redemptio* Ench 28.108, and 14.48; 16.61; for *reconciliatio* Ench 10.33, and 13.41; TractIo 41.5; 110.4; for *sacerdos* Civ X 6, and Trin IV 14.19; for the theme of heavenly intercession EnPs 29.2, 4; 109.18.

[89] Cf. TractIo 82.2.4; 74.3; Praedest 12.23; 15.31; Persev 24.67.

[90] Cf. serm. 121.5.

[91] Cf. serm. 47.211; Civ IX 15 with IX 9.

[92] Cf. Conf XI 2.4 with XI 7.9 and XIII 2.3f.

[93] Cf. Conf XI 2.4; also the explanation of Gen 1:1: *In principio = in Verbo* in GenLit I 1.2, and the antitheses formare – reformare, creare – recreare, facere – reficere, e.g. EnPs 45.14; 94.10.

[94] Cf. Conf X 43.68, and Civ IX 17; XXI 16.

[95] Conf X 48; GratChr II 28.33; II 32.37; Corrept 11,30.

[96] Trin XIII 19.24; Civ XI 2.

[97] Cf. Praedest 15.31; also Conf VII 18.24: 1Tim 2:5 in connection with Rom 9:5.

[98] Cf. Trin XIII 19.24; TractIo 82.2.4.

[99] Cf. EnPs 29.2.1.

[100] Cf. notes 75 and 93.

incarnation is understood only as an historical way which will have no real significance for eternity.[101] On closer inspection it should be noted, however, that such unquestionably simplifying formulae often occur in a trinitarian context.[102] In the less clear texts, therefore, the trinitarian meaning of *Deus* cannot necessarily be excluded. As for the eternal continuation of the mediatorship of the Word made man, on the other hand, it is impossible to help noticing a tendency in Augustine, which denies it, all the more so as he has expressed himself quite negatively on this issue.[103] Nevertheless, those passages, according to which the just will live some day with Christ in the kingdom of the Father, must be recalled.[104]

2. The revelation of salvation in the incarnation of the Word

When Augustine says in *De Trinitate,* that Christ is *scientia* and *sapientia,* this does not only express that he is grace and truth (cf. John 1:14–18), and therefore able through purifying faith in his incarnation to lead to the eternal vision of God.[105] Augustine also indicates here that Christ's mediatorship mainly consists for him in the revelation of beatifying salvation.

The content of this revelation itself can be summarized in a few words: The incarnation of the only-begotten Son of God has revealed all that God desired for man, and all that God expected from man himself.[106] Moreover, the historical existence of Jesus Christ proved to be the highest revelation of the infinite love of God.[107] This entails that the divine humility be made known. In the complete humiliation of the incarnation God has shown what is meant by his love. It is a love emptying itself so much that in the man Jesus human pride has been radically overcome, thereby removing all envy which springs out of pride and is opposed to all love.[108]

Of course, this revelation of the humble love of God has at the same time taken the form of an invitation to man, encouraging him now to love God on his part and his fellow men in humility. So the incarnation of the Son of God has revealed how God has loved man in humility and how man himself should without pride or envy love God, and, for God's sake, love his neighbour, too.[109]

---

[101] Cf. TractIo 13.4; 22.8; 42.8; 69.1f; 70.1, serm. 293.7; also M. Comeau, *S. Augustin, exégète du quatrième évangile,* Paris 1930, pp 331–338, with other texts, and C. P. Mayer, 'Philosophische Voraussetzungen und Implikationen in Augustins Lehre von den Sakramenten', Augustiniana 22, 1972, pp 53–79, esp. pp 72ff.

[102] Cf. TractIo 42.8; serm. 293.7.

[103] Cf. Trin I 10.21; I 8.15ff.

[104] Cf. Civ XX 9.1f and 20.13, where Rev 20:4ff is explained by drawing a distinction between the millenarian rule of Christ and man's eternal rule together with Christ; cf. also Civ XV 1.2; EnPs 71.10; 145.20; serm. 84.2, and serm. 27.2; Civ XXII 30.4.

[105] Cf. Trin XIII 19.24.

[106] For a reinforcement of this basic statement the renowned Augustinian antitheses should be borne in mind: auctoritas – ratio, fides – visio, uti – frui, signum – res, via – patria, esp. in relation to Christ as mediator between God and man.

[107] Cf. Trin VIII 5.7.

[108] Cf. CatRud 4.8, Ench 28.108.

[109] Cf. Trin VIII 8.12.

This view of the *demonstratio* or *commendatio amoris Dei* opens up vast theological perspectives. We could expect, therefore, that Augustine would go into the question as to how on the cross there has been an exchange of love between Father and Son; all the more so as for him *sacrificium* means nothing else than union with God, love.[110] From the love proved on the cross he could have ascended to what he says of the threefold life: *amans – amatus – amor:* God loves the Son from eternity in the love of the Holy Spirit.[111] On the other hand, starting from his endeavours to interpret the incarnation as proof of the humble love of God, as against the Greek doctrine of the unchangeable God, he could have arrived at an understanding of the infinite love of God as a community of love.[112] Augustine, however, does not draw out these lines of thought.

Nevertheless, with regard to the justification of man, the *doctor gratiae* is more expressly trinitarian. The same grace, through which Jesus in the very first moment of his human existence became Son of God, makes of any man, as soon as he believes and is reborn by the Holy Spirit, a Christian, a child of God. And as Jesus by reason of his divine sonship has been anointed by the Holy Spirit, so any Christian is sanctified by the Holy Spirit, though not in the same perfect degree.[113] Hence for Augustine the incarnation of the Son of God through the Holy Spirit is in the final analysis grounded in the eternal divine sonship. And it is precisely this connection between eternal generation and temporal mission which is somehow mirrored in the justification of any man. The baptized one, too, becomes a child of God through the Holy Spirit, as Jesus through the same Spirit has become the one who has always been the Son of God.[114] It could even be maintained that the life in faith of the man who has become a child of God is like that extension of the eternal sonship of God, which through the power of the Holy Spirit in the incarnation was accomplished in the human nature of Jesus.

3. Jesus Christ, the only righteous one

It is to expected of such a theologian as Augustine, who said and wrote so much, while keeping thoroughly to the authority of Holy Scripture and to an all-embracing tradition, that he should be able to develop his basic christological concept of mediatorship not only in relation to his ideas of the revelation of salvation but also in many other ways. In fact one finds with him the theme of the teaching and example of Christ, as developed by the whole tradition from the beginning, and in particular by the Roman rhetor Lactantius.[115] Augustine has of course also broadly unfolded the Easter themes of Christ's victory (*redemptio*) and of the atoning sacrifice (*reconciliatio*).[116] Finally, his unceasing interest in the Church of Christ has moved him to speak much of the head of the Church and of

[110] Civ X 6; also B. Studer, 'Das Opfer Christi nach Augustins "De Civitate Dei" X, 5–6', StudAnselm 79, 1980, pp 93–107.

[111] Trin VIII 10.14.

[112] Cf. W. Mallard, art.cit. in note 12.

[113] Ench 11.36; Corrept 11.30; Praedest 15.30; Persev 24.67; serm. 174.1.

[114] Cf. Praedest 15.31.

[115] Cf. esp. CAcad III 19.42; Agon 11.12; VeraRel 16.32; DivQu 83.25; Trin IV 3.6.

[116] Cf. Conf IV 12.19; TractIo 12.10f; 52.6; Trin XIII 17.22f; Ench 10.33; 28.108.

the head of the whole *civitas Dei.*[117] It is impossible to deal with all this here in detail. Yet one theme at least should be brought out which in a way sums up quite a number of other themes, and at the same time is very closely related to the Augustinian doctrine of the Trinity: the theme of the 'only righteous one'.[118]

In line with the Pauline letters and the Latin tradition Augustine in fact often speaks of the just priest, of the only just sacrifice, of the justice which Christ has opposed to the devil's injustice. He is particularly fond of citing the Apostle's word: 'For our sake he made him to be sin who knew no sin, so that in him we might become the righteousness of God' (2 Cor 5:21). Certainly he usually traces the righteousness of man directly to the saving activity of God. But he connects the justification of man also with Christ's act of salvation. With this he is obviously thinking primarily the justifying resurrection of Christ (cf. Rom 4:25), nevertheless, he also reckons with the justifying death of Jesus who, as the righteous for the unrighteous, has taken on himself the punishment, thus doing away with their guilt and punishment.[119]

In the light of the main soteriological passage in *De Trinitate* the Augustinian conception of the justifying death of Jesus can be summarized as follows: in the humiliation of the cross God himself has once and for all disclosed to men the way to righteousness.[120] This therefore means the following: since Adam's sin any man is enslaved by arrogance (*praetentio*) and by egoism (*amor sui*); in his pride he can love neither God nor his neighbour; only in the humility with which he resists pride, can he return to the right order, to the *caritas ordinata*, to righteousness. Of this man was, however, incapable because of his frailty; in his place God himself had to humiliate himself to reopen the way to love; that is why the Son of God was made man; in his humiliation even to death he has countered the devil's example of arrogance and envy with the example of that humility which alone makes possible righteousness and love; at the same time he has in our place paved the way for humility, with which alone righteousness and love can be carried through to the end; in the name of all men he remained righteous to the last breath. Therefore he has assured them of that humility with which they can lovingly accept the justice of God even in the most extreme misfortunes of life, and can even give their lives for the brethren. His righteousness has, therefore, become righteousness for all men.[121]

This conception of the only righteous one, who has remained just before the others and for all others, so that they might also become and remain just, can certainly not be found in Augustine himself in such simple terms. It can, nevertheless, be extracted from his writings, from *De Trinitate* as well as in particular from his anti-Pelagian writings. The connections with the doctrine of the Trinity are not to be overlooked even though they are not expressly developed

---

[117] Cf. among other texts EnPs 30.2.1.4; 58.1.2; 148.8.
[118] Cf. B. Studer, *Soteriologie*, pp 169ff; B. Studer, 'Le Christ, notre justice selon s. Augustin', RchAug 15, 1980, pp 90–143.
[119] CEpPel III 4.13; Ench 13.41; Corrept 12.37; serm. 152.10f; 134.4.5.
[120] Trin XIII 10.13–18.23.
[121] On the issue of humility cf. O. Schaffner, *Christliche Demut. Des hl. Augustinus Lehre von der Humilitas*, Würzburg 1959.

here. On the one hand, according to Augustine, only Christ could be the only righteous one, the only man loving in humility, because he has from the very beginning been the Son of God. The perfect justice of Jesus, thanks to which righteousness has returned to earth, has its last foundation in the eternal sonship alone.[122] On the other hand, Augustine in his anti-Pelagian writings comes back time and again to the fact that justified man is able to bear the justice, the irrevocable will of the wise and benevolent God only by the grace of the Holy Spirit. He must not only be born again by the Holy Spirit in order to acquire righteousness from the death of Jesus. The Holy Spirit must also 'inspire' him with *caritas,* continually infuse him with it that he, together with Christ, may remain righteous. This he will never perfectly be in the world, but only in eternity, when he, like Jesus himself, has overcome the fear of death in the power of the Holy Spirit.[123]

IV. THE TRINITARIAN AND CHRISTOLOGICAL TERMINOLOGY

It must be evident to any attentive reader, that Augustine strives very hard in his theological masterpiece *De Trinitate* to formulate exactly the mystery of the Trinity which Christians confess at baptism. This strictly dogmatic interest will, however, not seem surprising, if it is borne in mind how much Augustine has been concerned to integrate the whole preceding theological tradition, which for decades had wrestled with the orthodox dogma, into his own efforts towards a catholic understanding of the baptismal faith.[124] There are to be found, particularly in the first part of *De Trinitate,* some very apt formulae, which suggest in diverse ways how, according to the *via media* of the reception of the Nicene faith, the one *essentia* is to be distinguished from the three *personae.*[125] In the books 5–7 Augustine even undertakes a special discussion of the trinitarian terms: *essentia, substantia, persona,* etc. Three points are to be noted here: First, it is worth observing the linguistic subtlety with which Augustine goes into the differences between the Latin and the Greek terminology: *substantia – hypostasis, persona – prosopon.*[126] Further, attention should be given to the sharpness with which he works out the concept of *relatio* for the distinction between the Persons. Not for nothing has his use of this Aristotelian category in the doctrine of the Trinity been regarded as a highpoint in its history.[127] Finally it is important to note the care with which Augustine uses philosophical terminology, in particular the

[122] Cf. Trin XIII 14.18.
[123] Cf. ep. 157.2.4, Civ XIII 5; EnPs 127.7; 118.10.6; serm. 155.13.14, other texts in B. Studer, 'Le Christ, notre justice', RchAug 15, 1980, pp 121f. Besides the trinitarian, note also the ecclesiological and sacramental implications. Cf. B. Studer, *Soteriologie,* pp 171–4.
[124] Trin I 3.5; I 4.7; III pr.; VI 1.1.
[125] Cf. Trin I 8.15; V 8.9; V 14.15; VI 8.9; VII 4.8; VIII pr. 1.
[126] Cf. Trin V 8.10; VII 4.8f.
[127] Cf. L. Scheffczyk, in MySal II, pp 203f.

concept of *persona,* with regard to the divine, essentially ineffable mystery. This third point will be the subject of further reflexion.[128]

Augustine himself does not in fact hesitate to record his reservations about the widely accepted terminology of his time. It need only be noted in passing that, for all his loyalty to the faith of Nicea, he uses the term *homoousios* quite rarely.[129] Also his predilection for the term *essentia* as against *substantia* appears in the context of his philosophical theological thinking to be rather a matter of course.[130] His reservations about the term *persona* are of considerable interest. He certainly adopts this term because it had been sanctified by tradition, but he is not very enthusiastic about it. This reservation regarding *persona* as a trinitarian term is explained by the fact that for him persona does not entail relationship. *Persona* must be able to express what distinguishes Father, Son and Spirit, and that is only 'relative', it only concerns their mutual interrelatedness. *Persona,* however, proves rather to be an 'absolute' term. In other words, Augustine identifies *persona* with the 'I', thus introducing a revolutionary novelty in the history of Western philosophy. In this 'subjective' sense *persona* corresponds rather to the *one* God than to any of the three, who are this one God. For in this single deity there do not exist three 'Is'. There are only three modes of being God, as Father, who is without beginning, as Son who derives of the Father's being, and as Spirit, who proceeds from both the Father and the Son.[131]

With his criticism of the traditional concept of person Augustine has bequeathed to modern theology an important hermeneutic insight. His reservations about the trinitarian terminology already in use at that time teach us on the one hand the need to have respect for tradition and, on the other hand, to try to see the old dogmatic language as being tied to its time, and to translate it, as far as necessary and possible, into a new form. Quite apart from the fact that Augustine in his critical perspective recalls the inability of man to grasp the mystery of God with human words. Man is able to experience only in faith, which is confirmed by the Holy Spirit himself, the way in which Father and Son in the same Spirit love each other.

It is not only the trinitarian terminology, that Augustine defined and explained in *De Trinitate* and elsewhere, that has proved vital for the history of theology. It is no less important that he has developed for christology the formula *una persona in utraque natura.*[132] Thus he distinguished in christology the terms for the unity and the duality in analogy with the terms of oneness and threeness in trinitarian doctrine. It is not, however, completely clear, in spite of the studies of Van Bavel and others, how Augustine arrived at his regulation of christological language.[133]

For the distinction between the two natures, the matter is less problematic. It lies in the distinction between the two substances, which goes back to

---

[128] Cf. B. Studer, 'Personbegriff', TheolPhil 57, 1982, pp 170–7.

[129] Cf. TractIo 97.4; CMax II 14.3; II 15.2; II 18.2.

[130] Cf. Trin V 2.3; VII 4.9–5.10.

[131] Cf. Trin VII 4.7–5.10, esp. 5.9 and 6.11.

[132] Cf. serm. 294.9.9; TractIo 99.1; CSermAr 6.7, 8; also T. van Bavel, *Christologie,* pp 13–26.

[133] T. van Bavel, *Christologie,* has hardly taken into account Augustine's exegetical method. This is, however, to be seen as the starting-point of the formula una persona.

Tertullian.[134] Of course, it must not be forgotten that in the course of the anti-Arian controversy the two births of Christ were worked out more thoroughly.[135] Augustine expresses himself very impressively on this issue in his sermons on Christmas in which he applies to the divine and human births of Christ the text of Isaiah ('Who can declare his generation?' Isa 53:8, LXX), and states both births to be miraculous (*utraque mirabilis*). In this way he correlates the two *natures* with the two *nativitates*. Because Christ is born of the Father, he possesses his nature and is *connaturalis* with him, and because he is born of the mother, he possesses her nature, too, and is *connaturalis* with her.[136]

Augustine's conception of the unity of Christ's person is more difficult to gauge. He has certainly gone through a certain development here. At first he tends to speak of the *unitas personae,* and only later of *una persona.*[137] All the same it is certain that two presuppositions behind the use of *persona* of Christ are to be considered. On the one hand, the use of *persona* emerges from exegesis. In this context we could well speak of a logical regulation of language. According to Augustine – and this is true of the whole anti-Arian tradition – two sets of statements about Christ have to distinguished: a divine and a human. Christ must not, however, be torn apart into two sons, two Christs, or two *personae.* While being God *and* man, he nevertheless is one and the same, *una persona.*[138] On the other hand, under the influence of Neo-Platonic philosophy, Augustine has considerably deepened his conception of Christ's unity. He compares, as Gregory of Nazianzus and Nemesius of Emesa had already done before him, the union of divinity and humanity with that of soul and body. Soul and body are united in one person. In the same way divinity and humanity are united to one person.[139] It has not yet, however, been satisfactorily explained how Augustine came to develop the exegetical way of speaking of one person into a more philosophical reflexion about the one Person. In particular it is not clear under what influences he did this, if indeed, as is also possible, he did not do so on his own accord.[140]

For the rest, Augustine plainly made no attempt to distinguish clearly the trinitarian and christological uses of *persona.* At any rate, he never asserts that the second person of the Trinity assumed the humanity of Jesus, thus making him a person. Even though he maintains more than once that only the Son has become man, he had not yet reached an accurate analysis of the hypostatic union. It is worth noting, nevertheless, the extent to which he brought Christology and the doctrine of the Trinity into harmony on the terminological level.

---

[134] Tertullian, Prax 27.11, also J. Moingt, *Thélogie trinitaire de Tertullien* 2, Paris 1966, pp 668–74.

[135] Cf. B. Studer, 'Consubstantialis Patri – consubstantialis matri', REAug 18, 1972, pp 87–115.

[136] Cf. serm. 184.2.3; 188.2.2; 196.1.1; also CMax I 7; II 14.1f; II 15.2, and further serm.174.2.2.

[137] Cf. T. van Bavel, *Christologie,* pp 176ff; A. Grillmeier, *Jesus Christus,* pp 597ff (=*Christ in Christian Tradition,* pp 407ff).

[138] Cf. serm. 294.9.9 (dated 413): 'ut unam demonstraret in utraque natura personam', and ep. 187.3.8ff (dated 417), Ench 10.35; further, the anti-Arian statements in TractIo 78.1–3, from which it is clearly evident that Augustine sought to balance the distinction between the substances with an emphasis on the unity, without expressly speaking of *una persona.*

[139] Cf. ep.137.3.11ff; TractIo 19.15; also T. van Bavel, *Christologie,* pp 30ff, with other texts, and A. Grillmeier, *Jesus Christus,* pp 574ff: on Nemesius (=*Christ in Christian Tradition,* pp 389ff).

[140] Cf. T. van Bavel, *Christologie,* pp 177f, where he emphasizes Augustine's originality.

There is no doubt, therefore, that Augustine worked out a magnificent and comprehensive reinterpretation of the traditional baptismal faith. In particular he arrived, as had no one else before him, at a deeper understanding of the immanent Trinity. Two points are, however, always to be kept in mind in this context. Even with Augustine the *intellectus fidei* is exercised in an entirely spiritual context; it is unambiguously a religious concern. Secondly, even his more speculative trinitarian doctrine is based on the *regula fidei,* and is therefore rooted in a salvation-historical view of the Bible. As evidence for this his teaching on the *Filioque* could be cited, which is not so much to be understood as derived from his psychological analysis of the human inner life, but rather as an interpretation faithful to scripture of the Easter mystery.

This unmistakeably salvation-historical context of the Augustinian doctrine of the Trinity is also evident in that Augustine in his properly trinitarian work *De Trinitate* gives a good deal of space to soteriology. For him the incarnation is indeed absolutely necessary for a full understanding of the eternal God as well as for complete union with him. This had already dawned upon him in his conversion, and he worked it out in a special way in the Pelagian controversy. The grace without which salvation can be neither attained nor preserved is therefore always *gratia Christi.* Augustine, however, under the influence of ancient philosophy, by and large succumbs to the temptation to understand the incarnation of God merely as *via ad patriam,* thus somewhat compromising its eternal value for salvation.[141]

Understandably enough, with his trinitarian doctrine primarily orientated towards soteriology, Augustine exerted an immense influence on later Latin theology.[142] He decisively contributed to the establishment of a technical terminology, which is in tune with both the mysteries of faith.[143] To a large extent he prepared the way for later questions, above all for that of the *relationes subsistentes.* Last but not least he laid the foundations of the Latin dogma of the *Filioque.* Even though it could be questioned whether it was right to insert into the *Credo* of the Latin Church the Filioque, and perhaps the formula *per filium* would have been preferable to the *Filioque,* it must, nevertheless, be granted – contrary to all Eastern claims – that Augustine's doctrine in this respect represents a real advance in theology.

---

[141] Cf. p 178 above.

[142] Cf. esp. the Symbolum Quicumque (DS 75f), which is inspired by Augustine, also BAug 15, p 585 note 35.

[143] Cf. B. Studer, 'Una persona in Christo. Ein augustinisches Thema bei Leo dem Großen', Festschrift A. Trapé = Augustinianum 25, 1985, pp 453–87.

PART THREE
Under the Sway of Chalcedon

BIBLIOGRAPHY

A. Grillmeier and H. Bacht, eds., *Das Konzil von Chalkedon. Geschichte und Gegenwart I-III*, Würzburg 1951–4, ⁴1973.

H. G. Beck, *Kirche und theologische Literatur im byzantinischen Reich (=Handbuch für Altertumswissenschaft* 12 section II/1), Munich 1959.

H. Jedin and J. Dolan, eds., *History of the Church*, vol. 2: *The Imperial Church from Constantine to the Early Middle Ages*, London 1981.

See also:

J. Meyendorff, *Christ in Eastern Christian Thought*, Crestwood, NY 1975; id., *Imperial Unity and Christian Divisions. The Church 450–680 A.D.*, Crestwood, NY 1989.

A. Grillmeier, *Christ in Christian Tradition*, vol. 2, pt. 1, London 1987.

K. Beyschlag, *Grundriss der Dogmengeschichte, II. Gott und Mensch, 1. Das christologische Dogma*, Darmstadt 1991.

B. Studer and L. Perrone, 'La teologia patristica posteriore', *Storia della Teologia*, pp 509–622.

15. The Beginnings of the Christological Question

BIBLIOGRAPHY

L. I. Scipioni, *Richerche sulla cristologia del 'Libro di Eraclide' di Nestorio. La formulazione teologica e il suo contesto filosofico*, Fribourg 1956.

H. M. Diepen, *Douze dialogues de christologie*, Rome 1960.

T. Šagi-Bunić, *Deus perfectus et homo perfectus a concilio Ephesino (431) ad Chalcedonense (451)*, Rome 1965.

J. Meyendorff, *Christ in Eastern Christian Thought*, Crestwood, NY 1975.

L. I. Scipioni, *Nestorio e il concilio di Efeso*, Milan 1974.

E. Mühlenberg, 'Apollinaris von Laodicea', TRE 3, 1978, pp 362–71 (with bibl.).

B. Studer, 'Soteriologie der Kirchenväter': HDG III/2a, Freiburg 1978, pp. 175–81 (with bibl.).

A. Grillmeier, *Christ in Christian Tradition*, vol. 1, 2nd ed. London 1975, pp. 345–539 (with bibl.).

The later theology of the Fathers is without doubt determined by the council of Chalcedon (451). For the first part of the fifth century is to a large extent dominated by those theological controversies that were to result in this fourth ecumenical synod. The following period, on the other hand, exhibits to a large extent, at least in the East, a deepening of its confession. This is even true of the doctrine of the Trinity itself, which was developed under the influence of the christological decisions of Chalcedon.

The Council of Chalcedon, however, never achieved the significance of that of Nicea. On the one hand it was, in a certain sense, less ecumenical. In fact, the so-called Nestorian Churches were excluded right from the beginning. Above all, its dogmatic statement resulted in the separation of the so-called monophysite Churches. On the other hand, the faith, as defined by the council, was less comprehensive. The synod itself had not intended to present an all-embracing *regula fidei*. It essentially aimed at safeguarding from all misrepresentations the *fides nicaeno-constantinopolitana*, the very base of ecumenical orthodoxy, with regard to the second, the christological article, while remaining faithful to Scripture and to the Fathers.

This limited significance of Chalcedon for the history of dogma gives no reason, however, for devoting less attention to it, quite the contrary. On the one hand, the reunion of the Latin and Byzantine Churches with the oriental Christians, to which much effort has been devoted particularly in the past few years, will depend precisely on an understanding of the faith of Chalcedon. On the other hand, there is no doubt that the faith in the one Lord Jesus Christ, true God and true man, has been called in question even by those Christians who until the most recent times held fast to Chalcedon.

It is precisely the way in which Western, and even Catholic, theologians have engaged in critical debate about the faith of Chalcedon, that demands that we should not be satisfied with the texts of the council but should seek to understand their prehistory and reception and, above all, their context. It is appropriate, therefore, in this the third part of our introduction to the faith of the Early Church, to concentrate mainly on the council of Chalcedon, its prehistory, its course, and its repercussions. As regards the prehistory, which will be dealt with first, it will be useful to go back a long way, even though some issues from our first two parts will thereby have to be repeated.

I. THE HERITAGE OF THE FIRST THREE CENTURIES

Among the christological formulae encountered in the writings of the apostolic and post-apostolic periods, there are to be found from the very beginning formulae which show the first signs of a distinction between the divine and human in Christ, without questioning the unity: Romans 1:3f; 1 Timothy 3:16; Ignatius, Ephesians 7:2. It cannot be said, however, that at that time the question concerning a God-man was already being asked. This only emerged later, in a full sense only in the fourth century.[1]

But already in the course of the second century, the presuppositions of the christological problem proper had been created, and they emerged, characteristically, out of a pastoral and spiritual concern. On the one hand, the concern to proclaim in contemporary terms the gospel of the one saviour of all people resulted in the introduction of the Logos-theology. This facilitated the explanation, not only of the way in which the history of salvation encompasses all human beings, Jews and pagans alike, even those who had lived long before Christ's advent. It also made it clear that the suffering of the Messiah in no way excluded his pre-existence. For the suffering itself fitted into the history of salvation, since the Logos had announced it through the prophets. Thus it was asserted, much more clearly than before, that the only Saviour really deserved to be worshipped by the Christians as their God.

On the other hand, at the same time, and even to some extent earlier, the reality of God's incarnation came to be emphasized more than ever. Already the later writings of the New Testament, chiefly the Johannine letters, but also the letters of the martyr bishop Ignatius, were combating docetist tendencies within

---

[1] For the following cf. B. Studer, *Soteriologie,* pp 176–81.

the Christian communities.[2] The temptation to doubt the coming of Christ in the flesh, and the real sufferings of Jesus, did not, however, abate in the course of time; quite the contrary. This becomes comprehensible, if two points are borne in mind. First, it must be remembered that ancient man had no difficulty in accepting appearances of heavenly beings; to believe in the suffering of a real God, however, was for him an impossibility.[3] Even more important: people of that time, in their need of salvation, expected it only from an entirely sinless, celestial being. If the latter were a man, then he must at least be a heavenly man, born of a virgin.[4] The antidocetic tendency itself was in turn confirmed in the following period by the development of the messianic *testimonia,* such as e.g. Isaiah 53 and Psalm 21, by which it was asserted, against the Jews, that Jesus was the Christ, promised by the prophets.[5] Above all, it was a corollary of the teaching concerning the resurrection, of the faith in the *salus carnis,* to confess unambiguously the true incarnation of Christ.[6]

Because of this double tendency in the theological development, it became imperative to distinguish sharply the divine and the human in Christ. Accordingly, in Tertullian and Origen there is found a forthright theology of distinction.[7] No wonder, therefore, that even before the Arian controversy such a simple-minded theologian as the Latin rhetor Lactantius sought to establish man's salvation expressly on both the divinity and the humanity of Christ.[8]

Under these circumstances the question had to be posed as to how the divine and the human in Christ, while remaining different, are united. This question was all the more burning, as the gnostics, who were inclined to docetism, distinguished in their speculations the upper Christ from the lower Jesus.[9] The anti-gnostic theologians, such as Irenaeus and Tertullian therefore pointed more than ever before to the unity of Christ. It is to their time that the traditional formula *'heis kai autos',* i.e. it is one and the same who is God and man, goes back.[10] They did not, however, carry very far their reflexion on this unity of the God-man. Still, Tertullian attempted to explain the incarnation as a becoming without changing.[11] Origen, with his conception of the soul mediating between the Logos and the flesh, went a step further.[12] He, however, burdened his mode of explanation, which was also important for his soteriology, with his opinion about

---

[2] Cf. I John 4:3f; Ignatius, Trall 10; Smyrn 5.1–6.1; also A. Grillmeier, *Jesus Christus,* pp 199f (=*Christ in Christian Tradition,* pp 87f).

[3] Cf. Justin, Apol I.13; Tertullian, Carn 5.1–4; Origen, Cels IV.14f.

[4] See the view of certain gnostics on this issue and Tertullian's polemics against them in Carn 23; also A. Grillmeier, *Jesus Christus,* pp 188f (=*Christ in Christian Tradition* pp 78f), and G. Söll, *'Mariologie',* HDG III/4, Freiburg 1978, pp 30 and 46f.

[5] Cf. Justin, Dial 98–106; Origen, Cels I.54.

[6] Cf. esp. Irenaeus, AHaer I 10.1; I 22.1; IV, praef 4; IV 41.4.

[7] Cf. Tertullian, Carn 1.2; Prax 29.2f; Origen, CoIo I 28.192–200; XXXII 25.321–7; Cels III 28; IV 18.

[8] Cf. Lactantius, Instit IV 25.

[9] Cf. Irenaeus, A. Haer I 7.2; I 26.1; I 15.3; also J. Liébaert, *Christologie,* HDG III/1a, pp 23f.

[10] Cf. Irenaeus, A. Haer III 16.8; III 17.4.

[11] Tertullian, Prax 27.5–9.

[12] Origen, PA II 6; also A. Grillmeier, *Jesus Christus* pp 276ff. (=*Christ in Christian Tradition* pp 146ff).

the pre-existent soul of Jesus, which had always remained faithful. It is striking then that the soul of Jesus, in any form, is excluded in many circles. At any rate, the bishops around Malchion, fearing that Jesus might be regarded as mere man, had already in 268 replaced the human soul of Jesus with the Logos, thus introducing the Logos-sarx framework, which in the ensuing period was to have fatal consequences.[13]

Even though during the second and third centuries soteriological interest in the true divinity and the true humanity of Jesus was felt to lead to the question of the one Christ, however this question was posed, it was not yet at that time posed in its full clarity. This would not happen until the Nicene faith in Jesus' divinity had been received as the common basis for orthodoxy, and the christology of distinction implicit in that had been fully accepted.

As has been shown before, the council of Nicea placed Christ entirely on the side of the creator. Thus it had, on the one hand, met all the requirements for transferring all biblical names of God, including even that of Pantokrator (*omnipotens*), to the Son.[14] On the other hand, from a more philosophical point of view, it unambiguously declared Christ to be the unchangeable God (*theos*), rather than a divine, heavenly being (*theios*).[15] It is quite clear now, that in view of these biblical, and above all, philosophical assumptions, the problem of the possibility of the incarnation, of the union of the utterly transcendent God with weak creatures, was posed far more clearly.

The Arians had facilitated the solution of this provocative question in a twofold way. Because, for them, the Word was not true God, but was liable to change, they could all the more easily accept a union of this changeable being with changeable creatures. Moreover, by taking over the Logos-sarx framework, they had less difficulty in explaining how the Logos had employed as his tool mere flesh, which was devoid of human freedom.[16]

Athanasius and the greater part of the Nicenes, by accepting the true divinity of Christ, had chosen the more difficult way. They had to explain how the unchangeable could become liable to change. However, they did not follow this more difficult route to the end. Like Eusebius of Caesarea and the Arians they also kept to the Logos-sarx framework. Because they regarded the soul as the image of the Logos, they assumed they could in the case of Jesus, in whom the Logos himself was present and the governing principle, dispense with the soul, as being a mere image.[17] Thus they were not obliged to explain in detail, how the entirely free God could act in an entirely free man; for, in their view, the Word had appropriated a tool, which was devoid of freedom. Hence, according to their doctrine, the true God really became man; in this sense it was the incarnation of

---

[13] Cf. A. Grillmeier, *Jesus Christus*, pp 295–9 (=*Christ in Christian Tradition*, pp 163–6), and R. Lorenz, *Arius judaizans?*, pp 211–34.

[14] See the typical Nicene exposition of Ps 23:7–10 in Ambrose, Fid IV 1–2.

[15] Cf. W. Maas, *Die Unveränderlichkeit Gottes*, pp 138–47.

[16] Cf. A. Grillmeier, *Jesus Christus*, pp 374–82 (=*Christ in Christian Tradition*, pp 238–45), and esp. J. Liébaert, *Christologie*, pp 63ff, with an allusion to Gregory of Naz., ep.101.7.34.

[17] Cf. A. Grillmeier, *Jesus Christus*, pp 315–18, 460–79, with bibl. (=*Christ in Christian Tradition*, pp 180–3; 308–28).

God. The true God, however, did not become true man; that is why it was no incarnation, in the sense of becoming *man.*[18]

This position certainly had the advantage that it made the eternal God himself the subject of all of Christ's saving activity. It excluded any misrepresentation of Christ as a prophet, in whom God works with his power. Athanasius certainly felt the difficulty of taking John 1:14 completely seriously, when on the one hand he supplemented the notion of indwelling ('and the Word dwelt among us') with the adjective 'real', and on the other hand identified the notion of becoming (*egeneto*) with that of 'assumption', thus correcting it.[19] Nevertheless, he did not succeed in taking Christ as man in the full sense, and correspondingly foreshortened his soteriology. For him it was sufficient that the *logos ensarkos* secured for the human soul *apatheia* and for the human body *aphtharsia.*[20] He did not need a Jesus, who with his obedience and loving surrender preceded man on the way to God. The same can by and large be affirmed of Hilary.[21]

Even though Nicene theology, apart perhaps from the group around Eustathius, did not at first fully grasp the problem of the true incarnation,[22] it nevertheless substantially contributed to the later formulation of the question. On the one hand, in applying the *regula canonica,* i.e. in distinguishing between the divine and the human attributes, it sought to safeguard the unity of subject, to which all attributes were to be ascribed.[23] On the other hand, in its concern to safeguard the concept of divine generation from all inadequacy, it resulted in the doctrine of the two natures (*physis* from *phyein* – linked with *nativitas* and *natura*). For inasmuch as the two natures were referred to as divinity and humanity in abstract terms, the whole human nature demanded to be taken into account.[24] The extent to which this development was determined by other anthropological models, and, above all, by a more historical exegesis of the gospels, particularly the passion story, cannot, however, be dealt with here.[25]

II. THE DEVELOPMENT OF THE CHRISTOLOGICAL PROBLEM FROM 360

Around 360 the lengthy debate on Christ's divinity finally came to an end. At least, at the synod of Alexandria of 362, both the formulae of the *mia ousia* and of the

---

[18] Cf. A. Grillmeier, *Jesus Christus,* pp 477ff (=*Christ in Christian Tradition,* pp 326ff).

[19] Cf. Athanasius, CAr II 47; III 30; III 47; Epict 2.

[20] Cf. Athanasius, Incarn 9.54; cf. also Vita Antonii 67: on Christ 'free from suffering'.

[21] Cf. Hilary, Trin X 21–24; also J. Liébaert, *Christologie,* p 68.

[22] Cf. A. Grillmeier, *Jesus Christus,* p 375 (=*Christ in Christian Tradition,* pp 239f).

[23] Cf. the note on the beginnings of the communicatio idiomatum in A. Grillmeier, *Jesus Christus,* pp 445, 457ff, 466f (=*Christ in Christian Tradition,* pp 300f, 306ff, 313f).

[24] Cf. Hilary, Trin II 12; VII 23, also B. Studer, 'Consubstantialis Patri – consubstantialis matri', REAug 18, 1972, pp 106–190, and esp. Athanasius, Incarn 37, and other texts with Isa 53:8; also G. M. Durand, '"La generation, qui la raconte?" (Is 53,8b)', RSPhTh 53, 1969, pp 638–57.

[25] Cf. R. A. Greer, *The Captain of our Salvation. A Study in the Patristic Exegesis of Hebrews,* Tübingen 1973.

treis hypostaseis were accepted, thus restoring ecclesiastical unity between the Nicenes and the Homoiousians, the group around Basil of Ancyra. At the same synod the christological problem was also raised for the first time.[26] To this the so-called *Tomus ad Antiochenos* of Athanasius testifies.[27] Here it is a matter of two parties. The one, the group around Eustathius, was accused of holding Jesus to be a mere prophet. This party condescended forthwith to place more emphasis on the unity of Christ (7.1). The other party, i.e. the friends of Apollinaris, was accused of denying the soul of Jesus. This party, in its turn, to some degree adopted the contrary position. It accepted the formula: 'Son of God and Son of Man are one and the same being', thus even consenting to the assumption of the human soul. On this point, however, their consent was so vague that their statement was open to an Apollinarian interpretation at a later date (7.2f). Athanasius himself, who had apparently taken part in the redaction of these two statements, did not present an open confession of the human soul. Thus christology had become a matter of public discussion.

For an understanding of this new situation it is necessary to consider more closely the position of, above all, Apollinaris, bishop of Laodicea (+ ca. 390).

While a strict Nicene and as such a friend of Athanasius and of Basil of Caesarea, he carried the unitarianism of the Logos-sarx framework to its logical end by expressly denying the existence of a human soul in Christ.[28] In this he was guided by the following concerns. First he attempted to apply trinitarian terminology to the incarnation of the Word. He not only transferred the *homoousios* to the flesh of Christ (*homoousios hemin/ metri*), but also spoke of one *hypostasis*,[29] by *hypostasis* meaning that of the Son, which, according to him, in Christ took the place of the soul. At the same time, however, he spoke of one *ousia* or *physis* thus causing terminological confusion. Behind that there were obviously his own philosophical notions, chiefly that according to which hypostasis and soul are more or less to be identified.[30] The crucial point for him, however, was his soteriological concern. With his thesis of the *logos ensarkos* he wanted to exclude any conflict between two wills, thus safeguarding the sinlessness of Christ, without which there was no redemption from sin.[31] Finally, with such a concept of the unity of Christ not only the miracles but also the suffering were attributed to the Logos incarnate. In this way it achieved its value for salvation.[32]

In spite of its splendid features this christology inevitably met with resistance. At first, the group of Eustathians, a group difficult to define, paid attention to it.[33]

[26] Cf. A. Grillmeier, *Jesus Christus*, pp 472–7 (=*Christ in Christian Tradition*, pp 318–26).

[27] Athanasius, TomAntioch 7: MG 26, 804A-805A.

[28] Cf. for Apollinaris in general E. Mühlenberg, 'Apollinaris', TRE 3, 1978, pp 362–71, with bibl., and with regard to his christology esp. A. Grillmeier, *Jesus Christus*, pp 480–94, with bibl. (=*Christ in Christian Tradition*, pp 329–40).

[29] Cf. Apollinaris Laodicensis, De unione 8: ed. Lietzmann p 188, 9–18; frag. 161; 163: ed. Lietzmann pp 254f; Fides 28: ed. Lietzmann p 177; FidIncarn 3 and 6: ed. Lietzmann pp 194 and 199.

[30] Cf. M. Richard, 'L'introduction du mot "hypostase" dans la thélogie de l'incarnation', MélSR 2, 1945, pp 5–32; 243–70.

[31] Cf. Apollinaris, frag 151 and 74: ed. Lietzmann pp 247f and 222.

[32] Cf. Apollinaris, frag 151: ed. Lietzmann pp 247f; Fides 11: ed. Lietzmann pp 170f.

[33] Cf. Athanasius, Tom Antioch 7.1; also A. Grillmeier, *Jesus Christus*, pp 473f (=*Christ in Christian Tradition*, pp 318ff).

Soon Epiphanius, Damasus of Rome and above all the Cappadocians, though not Basil, intervened in the debate.[34] Finally, there formed around Diodore of Tarsus an openly anti-Apollinarian tendency, which has entered the history of dogma as the Antiochene school.[35] In the first phase of the resistance it was primarily the integrity of the human nature of Christ, i.e. the formulation of the doctrine of the two natures, that was at stake. The intention was to take full account of the confession of the divine and the human origin of Christ, of the *ex Deo* and the *ex Maria*. This was certainly done also for a soteriological reason, namely to make clear that Jesus Christ could be only our saviour if he was consubstantial with both his Father and his mother.[36]

In this respect in particular the old axiom: *quod non assumptum – non sanatum* came into the limelight.[37] This principle, which had already been recalled in the fight against the docetic tendency of the gnostics, was given its classical formulation by Gregory of Nazianzus: 'What is not assumed is not healed; what is united with God is saved.'[38] Gregory first directed this in fact, against the Arians. Yet, later on it was also employed in opposition to the Apollinarians, who were one with the Arians in denying the soul of Jesus.[39] It is to be noted that in defending the full incarnation, they did not stop at the integrity of the human nature in the metaphysical sense. Accepting the full human nature rather involved, as Gregory of Nyssa in particular showed, all that it means to be human. As the head of the new humanity Christ has established salvation for all people.[40]

In the further development of the anti-Apollinarian controversy the serious concern which stood behind the consistent application of the Logos-sarx framework, namely the unity of Christ, could not be evaded. Otherwise the reproach of the Apollinarians would have been justly deserved: that Christ was torn apart, that two sons were postulated, a son of God and a son of Mary.[41] Hence the anti-Apollinarian theologians looked for a way of regulating the language that expressed faith in Jesus Christ. Here, too, Gregory of Nazianzus broke new ground with his formulation: *allon kai allon,* not *allos kai allos.*[42] By going back to the trinitarian formula 'not one (person) but one (thing)', he pointed to the right way of making trinitarian and christological dogma parallel, that would prove instrumental in solving the problem of Christ's unity, which had proved Apollinaris' downfall.

---

[34] Cf. J. Liébaert, *Christologie,* pp 85–92 with a note on the most important anti-Apollinarian statements: Epiphanius, Ancoratus 75 and 119; Damasus, frag. 'Illud sane': DS 146; Tomus 159: DS 159; ep. ad Paulinum: DS 148; Gregory of Naz., ep. 101 and 102; or. 22; Gregory of Nyssa, Ad Theophilum c.Apoll., Antirheticus; cf also Basil, ep 261.2. See also B. Studer, 'Der geschichtliche Hintergrund des ersten Buches Contra Eunomium' (art. cit., p 155 above), pp 144f.

[35] A. Grillmeier, *Jesus Christus,* pp 610–34, esp. 610 (=*Christ in Christian Tradition,* pp 418–39, esp. 418).

[36] Cf. Gregory of Nyssa, Antirheticus 21f; 55.

[37] Cf. A. Grillmeier, '"Quod non assumptum – non sanatum"': LThK 8, 1963, 954ff.

[38] Cf. Gregory of Naz., ep. 101.7.32.

[39] Cf. Gregory of Naz., or. 2.23 (before Easter 362).

[40] Cf. R. M. Hübner, *Die Einheit des Leibes Christi bei Gregor von Nyssa,* Leiden 1974.

[41] Cf. Apollinaris, Fides 28: ed. Lietzmann p 177.9–12; frag 163. ed. Lietzmann p 255; cf. also Jerome, ep. 120.9; Gregory of Nyssa, Ad Theophilum c. Apoll. 2.

[42] Gregory of Naz., ep. 101.4.20f.

The Cappadocians and after them the so-called Antiochene theologians went even further. They were concerned, with more or less success, to provide a more profound basis for the unity of Christ. They kept to the traditional formula of 'one and the same'.[43] They also employed philosophical models, like the Neoplatonist concept of *krasis*, which was chiefly used to formulate the unity of man, composed as he is of body and soul.[44] What is more, they bore in mind the soteriological implications of the union of God and man in Christ. So, Gregory was not simply concerned with philosophical speculations about *perichoresis*, the mutual penetration of the two natures, but rather with a truly Christian concern: 'The deification of Christ's humanity is (for him) the basis for his mysticism of the deification of man.'[45] On the other hand, the Antiochenes did not simply turn against the unity of Christ expressed in the Logos-sarx framework out of respect for the mystery of the transcendent God. They conceived of the Christian life as being less deification by the Word incarnate, a liberation of the flesh from corruptibility, than the union of the whole man with God, an inward overcoming of sin. For them the *homo assumptus*, therefore, was the pattern for union with God. Union with Christ meant for them *synapheia*, communion of love, in which the baptized participates and through which he, too, becomes united with the Father and the Son.[46]

The attempts to formulate unambiguously and to expound more profoundly the unity of the God-man saviour against the Arians, and above all against the Apollinarians, did not, however, yet lead to a final solution. The question of the one Christ was not even raised in a proper sense. Only when the two main christological parties of the East clashed in their most prominent representatives, Nestorius and Cyril of Alexandria, was the question raised at all acutely.[47] This was, without doubt, initiated by the former. He had clearly recognized that the problems of unity and duality in Christ could not be dealt with on the same level.[48] The bishop of Alexandria, however, who was endowed with a far wider theological outlook than his colleague of Constantinople, not only took up the question but, more than anyone else, promoted it.[49] So in 428 the debate was opened, which by way of the twin-councils of Ephesus (431), the Formulary of Reunion of 433 (DS 271ff), and the synods of Constantinople and Ephesus (448/49) eventually led to the council of Chalcedon (451).[50]

---

[43] Cf. Gregory of Naz., ep. 101.3.13; 101.4.16; or. 37.2; Ps.Athanasius, CApoll 1.6; Athanasius, TomAntioch 7.2.

[44] Cf. Nemesius, NatHom: MG 40, 601 AB; also A. Grillmeier, *Jesus Christus*, pp 574ff (=*Christ in Christian Tradition*, pp 389ff), and esp. L. I. Scipioni, *Nestorio*, pp 15–24; also Gregory of Naz., ep. 101.6.31: mutual penetration (perichoresis) of the divine and the human nature, and ep. 101.4.21; mingling (synkrasis).

[45] Cf. J. Liébaert, *Christologie*, p 90, with Gregory of Naz., or. 29.19; cf. also Gregory of Nyssa, Ad Theophil. c. Apoll. 7f.

[46] Cf. Theodore of Mopsuestia, HomCat 5.10ff: liberation of the soul from all sinful movements; 6.2; 6.10: the example of evangelical life; 10.18: the exemplary function of the union of Christ.

[47] Cf. A. Grillmeier, *Jesus Christus*, pp 661–86 (=*Christ in Christian Tradition*, pp 464–83).

[48] Cf. A. Grillmeier, *Jesus Christus*, pp 656, 659f (=*Christ in Christian Tradition*, pp 460, 462f).

[49] For the significance of Cyril in general cf. esp. G. Jouassard, 'Cyrill von Alexandrien', RAC 3, 1957, cols. 499–516, and E. R. Hardy, 'Cyrillus von Alexandrien', TRE 8, 1981, pp 254–60, with bibl.

[50] Cf. besides A. Grillmeier, *Christ in Christian Tradition*, esp. T. Šagi-Bunić, *Deus perfectus et homo perfectus*.

Before considering the immediate prehistory of this council, its course and dogmatic results more closely, it would be appropriate to consider in more detail the great christological traditions which led to it, in their most important representatives: Theodore of Mopsuestia for the Antiochenes, Cyril of Alexandria for the Alexandrines, and Leo the Great for the Latins. Of course, our concern will be with the soteriological aspect rather than the strictly christological point of view; for only in this way shall we succeed in comprehending the faith of Chalcedon in all its profundity.

In view of the preceding expositions we can also state: the question as to how a Christian might understand Christ to be true God and true man, or, to put it in other words, as to how this true Son of God has become one of us certainly belongs to the basic questions of Christian faith. Yet, this fundamental question was only gradually asked in its full acuteness. As it concerns the integrity of the human nature the question does not feature before ca. 360. From the point of view of the express distinction between unity and duality it does not appear before 428.

Even though the christological question proper, the problem of a divine-human Christ came comparatively late to the mind of Christian theologians, its presuppositions had, nevertheless, entered very early into the Christians' conscience. In the second century the divinity of the pre-existent Logos and equally the real incarnation from Mary had clearly been developed. Preliminary formulations of the unity of Christ were not lacking either at that time. Then, for quite a long period, until far into the fourth century, the relation of Christ with his Father dominated theological thought. It was especially with regard to this that the divine and the human had to be better distinguished. This happened chiefly in the fight with the Arians, who denied the true divinity of Christ. The distinction between the two natures, however, then had to lead to an explanation of the Son as being one. Neither Apollinaris' theology which overemphasized the unity, nor the anti-Apollinarians' defence of the integrity of the human nature led to a satisfactory result. Both sides, however, made their contribution to a clearer formulation of the question and to the solution of the problem, especially by the drawing of parallels between trinitarian dogma and the christological question by Apollinaris and Gregory of Nazianzus.

In the development of the christological question we must not lose sight of the soteriological point of view. In all the stages of the development of this question, soteriological, i.e. pastoral and spiritual, concerns stood in the foreground: the universality of salvation for the Logos-Christology; the idea of *salus carnis,* or the resurrection, for the defence of the true incarnation; deification for the theology of Christ's divinity; the imitation of Christ for the safeguarding of his full humanity; the real and at the same time loving union with God for the attempts at a more profound understanding of the unity of the God-man. Only from this soteriologically directed development can the christological question be fully understood, even though philosophical, anthropological, and even political aspects are not to be neglected.

16. The Great Christological Traditions

BIBLIOGRAPHY

Cf. chiefly B. Studer, 'Soteriologie der Kirchenväter', HDG III/2a, Freiburg 1978, pp 181–212 (with bibl.).

On Theodore of Mopsuestia: R. Devreesse, *Essai sur Théodore de Mopsueste* (=Studi e Testi 141), Città del Vaticano 1948.

R. A. Norris, *Manhood and Christ. A Study in the Christology of Theodore of Mopsuestia*, Oxford 1963.

G. Koch, *Die Heilsverwirklichung bei Theodor von Mopsuestia*, Munich 1965.

R. A. Greer, *The Captain of our Salvation. A Study in the Patristic Exegesis of Hebrews*, Tübingen 1973.

On Cyril of Alexandria: J. Liébaert, *La doctrine christologique de s.Cyrile d'Alexandrie avant la querelle nestorienne*, Lille 1951.

G. M. Durand, *Cyrille d'Alexandrie, Deux dialogues christologiques* (=SChr 97), Paris 1964.

R. Wilken, *Judaism and the Early Christian Mind. A Study of Cyril of Alexandria's Exegesis and Theology*, New Haven 1971.

E. R. Hardy, 'Cyrillus von Alexandrien', TRE 8, 1981, pp 254–60 (with bibl.).

On Leo the Great: J. P. Jossua, *Le salut. Incarnation ou mystère paschal chez les Pères de l'Église de s.Irenée à s.Léon le Grand*, Paris 1968.

B. Studer, 'Consubstantialis Patri – consubstantialis matri', REAug 18, 1972, pp 87–115.

H. Arens, *Die christologische Sprache Leos des Großen. Analyse des Tomus an den Patriarchen Flavian*, Freiburg 1982.

G. Hudon, 'Léon le Grand', DSpir 9, 1976, pp 597–611 (with bibl.).

B. Studer, 'Una persona in Christo. Ein augustinisches Thema bei Leo dem Großen', Festschrift A. Trapé = Augustinianum 25, 1985, pp 453–87.

The christological question proper, the question about the one Christ, or the nature of God's incarnation, was, without doubt, chiefly a matter of concern for the Eastern Churches, the West being less involved in this subject. In the East the christological problem was first brought to the notice of the ecclesiastical public at the synod of Alexandria (362). The antagonism between the followers of Eustathius and those of Apollinaris, who had already emerged by that time, was to grow into a lengthy controversy, which broke out fully in 428, and then led up to the council of Chalcedon. The two main tendencies, which from the beginning opposed each other, may be somewhat simplistically labelled Alexandrine (Apollinaris, Cyril) and Antiochene (Diodorus, Theodore of Mopsuestia, Chrysostom, Nestorius, Theodoret), the latter tradition including that of Constantinople, which had always been closely related to it. In political terms this involved the antagonism of the two great bishoprics of Alexandria and Constantinople. While Nicea had conceded to the former the second position after Rome, the latter at the synod of Constantinople (381) and above all at Chalcedon advanced to a position immediately subordinate to 'Old Rome'.

Even though the christological controversy for the most part occurred in the East, the West did not remain uninvolved. It was not entirely insignificant that Damasus and Ambrose dissociated themselves from the Apollinarians (cf. DS 159)[1] and that Celestine I from 430/31 took his stand alongside Cyril against Nestorius.[2] Above all Leo the Great exerted a noteworthy influence on the decision of Chalcedon. Not only had his *Tomus ad Flavianum* been accepted by the synod as in agreement with the Eastern tradition, but it was also used in the final redaction of the Chalcedonian Definition.[3] With Leo Augustine made himself felt, as it was he who had summed up the Western tradition with his *una persona in utraque natura*,[4] in this way decisively influencing the christology of Leo who can be regarded as his disciple.[5]

So in the approach to Chalcedon we encounter three great traditions, which are linked with the episcopal sees, already prominent at that time, of Rome, Alexandria, and Antioch / Constantinople. It is not possible, however, to give here a full account of these three schools. Yet, their most prominent representatives will be dealt with: Theodore of Mopsuestia, Cyril of Alexandria and Leo the Great. It will not be our task to discuss in detail the christological formulae and expositions of these three bishops, but rather to focus on the image of Christ, which they presented to believers chiefly in their sermons. This will enable us to have a better grasp of both the soteriological and kerygmatic content of their christology. It will also become clearer that the Chalcedonian Definition itself, for all its dogmatic importance, must primarily be evaluated with regard to its pastoral and spiritual significance. This can, however, only be done, if its context, that is to say, its connection with contemporary preaching is taken sufficiently into account.[6]

---

[1] Cf. C. Pietri, *Roma Christiana*, pp 791–872, esp. pp 811–18, 833–40.

[2] Cf. C. Pietri, *Roma Christiana*, pp 1347–93, and esp. M. Wojtowytsch, *Papsttum und Konzile von den Anfängen bis zu Leo I. (440–461)*, Stuttgart 1981, pp 283–99, with bibl.

[3] Cf. A. Grillmeier, *Jesus Christus*, pp 734–50, 753f (*Christ in Christian Tradition*, pp 529–39), also M. Wojtowytsch, *Papsttum und Konzile*, pp 318–49.

[4] Cf. Augustine, serm. 294.9.9; CSermAr 6.7, 8; also T. van Bavel, *Christologie*, pp 13–26.

[5] Cf. B. Studer, *Una persona in Christo*, esp. pp 475–86.

[6] Cf. for the following B. Studer, *Soteriologie*, pp 181–212, with bibl.

I. THE ANTIOCHENE TRADITION

Two points should be made in advance. The Antiochene tradition proper does not commence before the end of the fourth century with Diodore of Tarsus, and is above all represented by his pupil Theodore of Mopsuestia (+428), the great Syrian exegete.[7] Unfortunately we have scant knowledge of his writings. The same is also true of Diodore and Nestorius; we are in a better situation, as regards the sources, with Theodoret and John Chrysostom.[8]

1. Theodore of Mopsuestia's basic christological assumptions

The concern for the true faith was a matter of prime concern for Theodore. Throughout his preaching he bears in mind the polemic against Eunomius and Apollinaris. So at every point he represents a christology, which can be regarded as a doctrine of the *homo assumptus,* or rather of the *Deus assumens* and the *homo assumptus.*[9]

This is to say that for Theodore the clear distinction between the human and the divine natures stands in the foreground. Out of reverence for the transcendence of God he seeks to exclude any mingling of the divine and human. He is restrained, therefore, in his use of expressions such as 'incarnate God', 'God-bearing',[10] and prefers to call Christ Son or Lord.[11] On the other hand, Theodore is concerned to present Jesus as a whole man, with body and soul, even as *homo* in the full sense.[12]

While distinguishing the natures and placing emphasis on the complete humanity of Jesus, Theodore is still concerned not to compromise the unity of Christ. He not only rejects the accusation of two sons or two Christs,[13] but also positively expresses his conception of the unity of Christ by means of the expression of the one *prosopon.*[14] However, he sees in this *prosopon* the result of the union, rather than its origin.[15] Further, he describes the union more in moral terms, first of all as *synapheia,* a loving union.[16] Even though he emphasizes that the Word in this union does not dwell in Jesus as in a prophet, that one must rather speak of a union 'as in a Son',[17] he does not succeed in describing in a fully

---

[7] Cf. M. Simonetti, 'Antioch V. School', EEC 1, 1992, pp 50–1.

[8] Cf. B. Altaner and A. Stuiber, *Patrologie,* Freiburg [7]1966, pp 318–31, 339ff.

[9] Cf. Theodore of Mopsuestia, HomCat 8.1.5, 10.

[10] Cf. HomCat 8.5, 16, 6.3.

[11] Cf. HomCat 8.1, 4, 15.

[12] Cf. HomCat 5.11, 15ff.

[13] HomCat 8.14f.

[14] HomCat 6.3; CoIo 8.16: ed. Vosté 119; cf. HomCat 8.14; also A. Grillmeier, *Jesus Christus,* pp 624–34 (=*Christ in Christian Tradition,* pp 429–39), with a note concerning the most recent research and esp. the problem of the authenticity of certain texts ascribed to Theodore.

[15] Cf. HomCat 6.3: 'enseignant une seule personne (prosopon) à cause de la conjonction exacte qui eut lieu'.

[16] Cf. HomCat 6.3 as well as the texts with synapheia (conjonction) in R. Devreesse, *Essai sur Théodore de Mopsueste,* pp 115f.

[17] Cf. HomCat 6.3; Incarn 7: ed. Swete p 296, and HomCat 8.10: 'comme d'un seul', and HomCat 14.24; CoIo 5.37: ed. Vosté p 89.

satisfactory fashion this union, in which the Word itself took the initiative and which will never cease. It was in this sense that Nestorius was to speak of the *prosopon* of union, which joins the two natures together, including their respective *prosopa,* thus laying bare the drawbacks of the Antiochene manner of speaking.[18]

2. The soteriological consequences of the Christology of distinction

In line with his doctrine of the *homo assumptus* Theodore first fully explains his conception of the Easter mystery as marking the transition from this age of imperfection to the age of perfection. According to this the *homo assumptus,* led by the Logos, through the grace of the Holy Spirit, has changed into a new state of body and soul.[19] The transition to the resurrection life itself is understood in a double sense: as an overcoming of death and sin, which involves Jesus himself being tempted and put to the test; and all this having happened for us, for the sake of salvation. His transition to the second katastasis has, therefore, become the origin and guarantee of our transition.[20]

The significance for salvation of the assumed humanity is explained even more precisely. For Theodore final salvation is not realized before the second age, when there will be no more death and sin, and when those saved in the Holy Spirit will be children of the Father.[21] All this is, however, only possible in communion with the *homo assumptus,* who has already entered incorruptibility.[22] Further, the *homo assumptus* has become the pattern for Christians not only in his Easter mystery, but also in his whole earthly life, chiefly in his orientation in hope towards eternal life.[23] So it is most important above all that the *homo assumptus,* who in his death and resurrection has become high priest, continually intercedes for us in heaven, while believers partake through the eucharist in his heavenly liturgy.[24]

All these saving assertions without doubt apply first of all to the *homo assumptus.* For Theodore behind everything there is the fundamental idea of God, who is himself the redeemer in his Son. For the transition to the second age was essentially an act of the Word of God. The Son, the *Deus assumens,* has led the *homo assumptus* to perfection. Along these lines Theodore interprets Hebrews 2:10: 'He made him perfect through suffering', as well as John 2:19, which speaks of the temple being raised up again on the third day.[25] This activity of the Son is moreover for Theodore an activity of the whole Trinity. The Father has taken the initiative in salvation, the Holy Spirit has anointed Jesus and also continually

---

[18] Cf. A. Grillmeier, *Jesus Christus,* pp 659f, 714–26 (=*Christ in Christian Tradition,* pp 462f, 507–19).

[19] Cf. HomCat 5.20; 7.4–9.

[20] HomCat 5.11; 12.6.

[21] Cf. HomCat 10.20; 16.26; In Gal 3.26: ed. Swete I. 55, also G. Koch, *Die Heilsverwirklichung bei Theodor von Mopsuestia,* pp 141–56.

[22] HomCat 7.10f; ColO 1.16: ed. Vosté p 26; also G. Koch op.cit. p 153.

[23] Cf. HomCat 6.1, 11f; 7.9f.

[24] HomCat 15.16.

[25] HomCat 8.5–9.

nourishes Christians with his grace.[26] Above all, the Son himself works always only in communion with the Father and the Spirit for the salvation of humankind.[27] Theodore's teaching on salvation is always bound up with the anti-Arian doctrine of the joint activity of Father, Son and Spirit.

II. THE ALEXANDRINE TRADITION

In contrast to the Antiochene tradition, in the Alexandrine we encounter a tradition which goes right back to pre-Nicene times.[28] It would be one-sided, however, simply to trace it, or at least its exegetical aspect, back to Origen, even though he certainly exerted a considerable influence, mainly indirectly through Eusebius of Caesarea, on Alexandria's greatest fourth century theologian, Athanasius, who is indebted to Irenaeus and others who were influenced by the so-called Asiatic theology.[29] Athanasius himself, the great theologian of the *cur Deus homo*, did not become, however, the promoter of the authentic Alexandrine christological tradition. This honour must rather be assigned to Apollinaris of Laodicea, even though he has been deemed a heretic by posterity.[30] He was not only the first to formulate the mystery of the incarnation in terms of the trinitarian rule of faith. More than his predecessors he reflected on the fundamental basis of our salvation, the anchoring of Christ's saving act in the existence of the eternal Word.[31] At any rate, it is to him and to his school that Cyril of Alexandria owes his deepest christological insights, and it is because of this that Cyril became the leading teacher of christology not only in the Alexandrine tradition but in the whole Church.[32] It is odd that he was not influenced by another great Alexandrine, Didymus the Blind.[33] In spite of this he was able, and this to the credit of his Antiochene opponents, and even more, of his own theological genius, to free himself from Apollinaris' shortcomings, and thus prepare authoritatively for the faith of Chalcedon.[34]

---

[26] Cf. HomCat 2.10–19; 10.7–14.

[27] Cf. HomCat 8.17.

[28] Cf. C. D. G. Müller, 'Alexandrien I', TRE 2, 1978, pp 248–61, esp. pp 253f, and M. Simonetti, 'Alexandria, II School', EEC 1, 1992, pp 22f.

[29] Cf. J. Roldanus, *Le Christ et l'homme dans la théologie d' Athanase d'Alexandrie*, pp 17ff, and M. Tetz, 'Athanasius von Alexandrien', TRE 4, 1979, pp 333–49, esp. p 345.

[30] Cf. E. Mühlenberg, *Apollinaris von Laodicea;* id., Apollinaris von Laodicea: TRE 3, 1978, p 370: Nachwirkung, also C. Kannengiesser, 'Apollinaris', EEC 1, 1992, pp 58f, with bibl.

[31] Cf. esp. Cyril of Alex., Quod unus est Christus 724d-725b; 734d; 754a-757a; SChr 97, pp 334ff, 368; 434–44; for the whole problem A. Grillmeier, *Jesus Christus*, p 684 (=*Christ in Christian Tradition*, pp 481f).

[32] Cf. A. Grillmeier, *Jesus Christus*, pp 673–9, esp. p 678 (=*Christ in Christian Tradition*, pp 473–8, esp. pp 476f).

[33] Cf. G. Jouassard, 'Cyrill von Alexandrien', RAC 3, 1957, cols. 500–4, esp. 502.

[34] Cf. esp. Cyril's stand when signing, and later on defending, the union with John of Antioch in 433; also A. Grillmeier, *Jesus Christus*, pp 682, 703–7 (=*Christ in Christian Tradition*, pp 497–501), and esp. M. Simonetti, 'Alcune osservazioni sul monofisismo di Cirillo di Alessandria', Augustinianum 22, 1982, pp 493–511.

1. Cyril the follower of Athanasius and the anti-Arian traditions

Like his master Athanasius Cyril also stands under the spell of the question about the meaning of the incarnation. So he sought, among other places in his commentary on John 14:20, for an all-embracing answer. Here he explains renewal in Christ (Eph 1:10) from three perspectives: as condemnation of sin (Rom 8:3f), as overcoming of corruption (Heb 2:14f) and as divine childhood (John 1:11f). This threefold salvation he, like Athanasius, bases on the incarnation. Through the assumption of the flesh by the Logos there has been accomplished the exclusion of sin, i.e. the restoration of *apatheia,* the return to incorruptibility (*aphtharsia*), as well as a renewal of participation in the divine nature, in which we through the Spirit of the Son become children of the Father. On the last point Cyril is even more explicit than Athanasius.[35]

Granted that he draws chiefly on Athanasius' basic ideas, elements from other traditions still cannot be disregarded. So Cyril takes more seriously than ever the principle *quod non assumptum, non salvatum est,* in the course of his argument with the strictly anti-Apollinarian christology of the Antiochenes. He also comes increasingly to consider the life of Jesus as holding up an example.[36] For that reason, in the course of time, he adopts the traditional notion of the *descensus ad inferos,* and speaks of Jesus' soul, which descended to the underworld to preach there to the righteous.[37] Further, he places emphasis not only on participation in the nature of Christ on the ground of his incarnation (*kata physin*), but also on participation in the sonship of Christ (*para physin*).[38] According to him the Christian is akin to Christ physically because of a common nature, but also spiritually owing to the communication of the Spirit in faith and in the sacraments.[39] Just for this reason he also develops his incarnational theology of the eucharist.[40] Finally Cyril with his doctrine of the 'hypostatic union' traces salvation back to the assumption of the flesh by the Word far more radically and systematically than Athanasius did.[41] This doctrine, quite typical of Cyril, deserves an investigation of its own.

2. The soteriology of the real union of God and man

According to A. Grillmeier, Cyril's final christological stand can be summed up in the statement: 'God the Logos did not come into a man, but he "truly" became man, while remaining God.'[42] In this sense after 428 Cyril rejected the concept of

---

[35] Cyril of Alex., CoIo 9.14 (14.20): MG 74, 273B-281B; also G. M. de Durand, *Cyrille d' Alexandrie, Deux dialogues christologiques* (SChR 97), Paris 1964, pp 81–98.

[36] Cf. esp. Quod unus est Christus 726a; 754a-755d: SChr 97, p 340. 434–8: RectFidReg II 55: MG 76, 1412 D – 1413 B; also G. M. de Durand, SChr 97, pp 107–13.

[37] Cf. Incarn 693a-e: SChr 97, pp 234ff; also A. Grillmeier, 'Der Gottessohn im Totenreich', *Mit ihm und in ihm,* pp 76–174, esp pp 165ff.

[38] Cf. Thesaurus 32: MG 75, 561CD; also J. Liébaert, *La doctrine christologique,* pp 232ff.

[39] Cf. CoIo 6 (10.14): MG 73, 1044B-1048C.

[40] Cf. H. Chadwick, 'Eucharist and Christology in the Nestorian Controversy', JThSt NS 2, 1951, pp 145–65.

[41] CoIo 9.14 (14.20): MG 74, 280AB; J. Liébaert, *La doctrine christologique,* pp 220f.

[42] Cf. A. Grillmeier, *Jesus Christus,* p 678 (=*Christ in Christian Tradition,* p 477), with Cyril of Alex., OrDom 31: MG 76, 1228 C.

indwelling, which he had used before, or at least only used it reluctantly. At the same time he increasingly preferred the term *henosis,* and took care to avoid any terminological ambiguity.[43]

Even before 428 Cyril had been more precise with regard to Christ's unity of subject, the 'God with us', as he would say, than had earlier Alexandrians.[44] This is evident in two respects: in a predilection for an ontic understanding of Christ's mediatorship; for he is mediator between God and man, insofar as he is consubstantial both with the Father and with us.[45] In consequence, and this is the second point, he disposes of the distinction between the 'ages' (*kairoi*) in favour of the 'becoming flesh', and speaks in more abstract, no longer historical, terms of the assumption, appropriation, or of *kenosis.*[46]

This concern for a very realistic expression of Christ's unity, which was characteristic of Cyril right from the beginning, and was only confirmed in the arguments with Nestorius, also characterized the whole of his teaching on salvation.[47] It is this concern in particular, which gives the authentic basis for the elements already characterized as original. Thus the main idea of the deifying, or more precisely, life-giving incarnation appears to be most profoundly founded on the fact that the Word really has been united with the flesh in a union excluding any change.[48] The Word, as the life-giving power of God, has implanted itself in the flesh, and therefore made the grace of the Holy Spirit genuinely take root there.[49] In particular the three above-mentioned leading aspects of the restoration grounded in the incarnation of the Word – condemnation of sin, overcoming of incorruption, and divine childhood – find their final confirmation in the true union of the Word with the flesh.[50]

3. The priesthood of the God-man

Through his doctrine of the true union of the Word with the flesh, Cyril has given more importance not only to assertions about our participation in the divine nature, but also to those concerning the saving activity of the God-man. This is particularly apparent in the theme of Christ's priesthood, which with Cyril is closely linked with the themes of death and resurrection, even though it does not simply coincide with them.[51]

The historical rather than metaphysical view of the doctrine of Christ's priesthood clearly recognizes that the soteriology of the incarnation must almost necessarily lead to a soteriology of utter kenosis, of the voluntary death of Jesus.[52]

---

[43] Cf. G. M. de Durand, SChr 97, pp 128–31, 139.

[44] Cf. Quod unus est Christus 717ab: SChr 97, pp 310ff with note 1.

[45] Cf. TrinDial: MG 75, 692C-693B; CoIo 3.3 (5.46): MG 73, 429AC; CoIo 11.8 (17.9ff): MG 74, 505D-508A.

[46] Cf. J. Liébaert, *La doctrine christologique,* pp 159–69.

[47] Cf. B. Studer, *Soteriologie,* pp 195f.

[48] CoLc 5.19: MG 72, 908D; Quod unus est Christus 772c: SChr 97, p 194.

[49] CoIo 5.2 (7.39): MG 73, 756A, with the whole context.

[50] AdvNest: MG 76, 17BC; Quod unus est Christus 723ab: SChr 97, p 330, Incarn 700a: SChr 97, pp 254ff.

[51] Cf. Quod unus est Christus 763 8ff: SChr 97, p 466.

[52] Cf. Quod unus est Christus 721d–722d: SChr 97, pp 326ff; 741c–742d: SChr 97, pp 392–6.

The theme of Christ's priesthood, or rather, the mode of formulating Jesus' saving act in sacerdotal and cultic terms, certainly goes back to the New Testament and the traditions of primitive Christianity.[53] In the Arian controversies, which chiefly concerned the Origenist conception of Christ's mediatorship, and thus Christ's priesthood, the interest in this theme apparently grew.[54] Cyril himself has adopted the theme in the anti-Arian interpretation of his immediate predecessors, for example in his commentaries on the Old Testament, on the gospel of John and on Hebrews.[55] In the argument with Nestorius the theme of Christ's priesthood was, however, right from the start, one of the most controversial issues. Because Nestorius explained the passage on Jesus as 'apostle and high priest' (Heb 3:1) certainly in an anti-Arian sense, but in line with the Antiochene tradition, Cyril felt himself challenged on this point in particular.[56]

When Cyril then speaks of Christ's priesthood, or attempts to describe his saving function as mediator, he does so from several points of view.[57] He distinguishes the offering of the spotless sacrifice, the presentation of transformed humanity, and intercession for endowment with spiritual gifts. The first aspect concerns the death of an innocent on behalf of sinners. Following the Bible Cyril expressly states that the Word made flesh in dying did not sacrifice himself on his own behalf, but for us, since he had been without sin. According to the second, also in essence a biblical view, the death and the resurrection of Christ have above all the meaning of sanctification, of the presentation to God of renewed humanity, of the return to the Father, embracing all humankind. Finally, through the resurrection Christ has become eternal priest. As such he offers to the Father the faith of the justified; there is nothing good in Christian life that could be accomplished without this mediatorship.[58]

For all the diversity of these considerations of priestly mediatorship, they have nevertheless one point in common: they ascribe this priesthood neither to the Word alone, like the Arians, nor to the *homo assumptus,* like the Antiochenes, but to the Logos made flesh.[59] Cyril here obviously follows Athanasius.[60] He, however, dwells much more, especially from 428 onwards, on the personal unity of the unique and true priest. It is here especially that the basic intention of his polemic against the Antiochenes, and in particular against Nestorius, in fact of his whole soteriology, becomes evident. His ultimate point of concern is the fact that God himself has died for us. Even though he does not yet express it, as his pupils will later, in the formula *unus ex Trinitate passus,* this is fundamentally what he

---

[53] Cf. E. J. Scheller, *Das Priestertum Christi im Anschluß an den heiligen Thomas von Aquin,* Paderborn 1934, pp 106–51, with texts of the early Christian period.

[54] Cf. R. A. Greer, *The Captain of our Salvation,* where in the context of the history of the exegesis of Hebrews this issue is thoroughly discussed.

[55] Cf. R. A. Greer, *The Captain of our Salvation,* pp 307–55.

[56] Cf. ep. 17 with anathema 10: MG 76, 116D–117B, 121BC; also R. A. Greer, *The Captain of our Salvation,* p 321.

[57] Cf. CoIo 11.4 (17,2): MG 74, 480Df (summary text).

[58] CoIo 11.8 (17.9ff): MG 74, 508BC; 4.2 (6.52): MG 73, 569A; RectFidReg: MG 76, 1312A; Adorat 9: MG 68, 588A–604B (comment on John 15:5: 'Without me you can do nothing.')

[59] Cf. R. A. Greer, *The Captain of our Salvation,* pp 305f; 307–55.

[60] Cf. R. A. Greer, *The Captain of our Salvation,* pp 65–97, esp. pp 94ff.

means in speaking of the death of Christ as the summit of the incarnation.[61] Along these lines he has in fact much to say about the death of Jesus: of its universal significance for salvation, and of its quite unique dignity.[62] Yet he was not the first to present the death of the God-man as the only satisfactory ransom for the sins of all human beings. This theme is already to be found in Eusebius of Caesarea, Cyril of Jerusalem, Basil of Caesarea,[63] and also in Ambrose.[64] With Cyril, however, it has quite a different power, and all the more so, as he does not adopt the popular theories of redemption: the ransom paid to the devil, and the devil's abuse of his power.[65] Cyril is also most willing to include the trinitarian aspects in his teaching on the priesthood of the Logos made man. While the Word made flesh himself participates in the Holy Spirit, he becomes a priest, who through the Holy Spirit leads humankind to the Father.[66]

III. THE LATIN TRADITION

Like the Alexandrine tradition the Latin tradition reaches back, with Tertullian, to pre-Nicene days.[67] Like both Eastern traditions it had in the course of the fourth century taken on board, particularly through Hilary and Ambrose, strong anti-Arian traits.[68] Above all in Augustine it found a theologian, who, with his creativity, can certainly be ranked with any of the Eastern theologians, including Origen and Gregory of Nyssa. Yet the Latin tradition attains neither the originality nor the completeness of either of the Eastern traditions. Moreover, its relationship with the East is still too little investigated. This is particularly true of Augustine, whose sources are often difficult to trace.[69] In so far as we can speak of the Latin tradition having a coherence of its own, we would place it between the two Eastern traditions. On the one hand it emphasizes the distinction between the two natures,[70] on the other hand it acknowledges, in line with the Alexandrian tradition, and more than the Antiochene, the *communicatio idiomatum*.[71] This

[61] Cf. Anathem. 10: MG 77, 121B; RectFidReg II 45: MG 76, 1397D; also J. N. D. Kelly, *Early Christian Doctrines*, p 384; G. M. de Durand, SChr 97, pp 148f.

[62] Cf. CoIo 4.2 (6.52): MG 73, 564D–566A; RectFidReg I.7: MG 76, 1208B.

[63] Cf. J. Rivière, *Le dogme de la rédemption*, pp 160–73.

[64] Cf. Ambrose, Fid III 11.86ff; ExplPs 48.15; ExposPs 118.20.35; also R. Gryson, *Le prêtre selon s. Ambroise*, Louvain 1968, pp 49–60.

[65] Cf. J. Rivière, *Le dogme de la rédemption*, pp 192–9.

[66] Cyril of Alex., CoIo 10.2 (15.1): MG 74, 333Df, AdvNest III 1: MG 76, 120BC; CoPs 44.8: MG 69, 1037D–1040A.

[67] Even though Tertullian was regarded as a heretic, his influence, nevertheless, lived on among Latin authors. Cf. Jerome, VirIll 53.

[68] The trinitarian works of Hilary and Ambrose remained standard, in particular for Augustine and Leo. Cf. B. Studer, *Zur Theophanie-Exegese Augustins*.

[69] Cf. B. Altaner, *Kleine patristische Schriften*, Berlin 1967, for his various studies on the Greek sources of Augustine.

[70] Cf. B. Studer, 'Consubstantialis Patri – consubstantialis matri', REAug 18, 1972, pp 87–115.

[71] The Latin tradition ascribes the divine and the human attributes not only to Jesus Christ or the Son of God, but also to God (Deus) himself and, above all, to the Word (Verbum) Cf. esp. Augustine's position in the Libellus Leporii; also A. Grillmeier, *Jesus Christus*, pp 661–5 (=*Christ in Christian Tradition*, pp 464–7).

observation is also true of Leo the Great. It is he in particular, who is often said, as regards his soteriology, to be closer to the Eastern Fathers.[72] That this is by no means certain will also be seen below.

1. Leo the Great's doctrine of the double consubstantiality

When Leo the Great was dragged into the controversy between Flavian, bishop of Constantinople, and his presbyter Eutyches, he judged the position of the latter to be a brand of monophysitism, either denying the true humanity, or entailing theopaschism.[73] Against such 'docetism', ascribed to Eutyches, Leo developed in his *Tomus ad Flavianum* the doctrine of the double consubstantiality. Following the baptismal symbol, he showed that Christ was born of God and Mary and therefore possessed a divine and a human nature, and accordingly possessed both divine and human characteristics and ways of acting, without the unity of his person being brought into question.[74]

Even though he did not employ in his dogmatic letter the formula of the double consubstantiality, as he was intending to do, apparently under Eastern influence, he nevertheless stated the issue in clear terms.[75] This is not surprising, if the fact is taken into consideration that the Latin tradition had already long accepted, so far as content is concerned, the double consubstantiality, even without the corresponding formula.[76]

If we bear in mind that Leo the Great in his sermons, too, repeatedly proclaimed this teaching, we can conclude that he himself regarded it as an authentic statement of faith.[77] He, however, understood the formula of the double consubstantiality in a somewhat vague sense. The two parts of the formula are certainly not to be understood to be strictly symmetrical. For Leo is aware that the kinship of Christ with his Father is far more intimate than that with humankind, and that the two births which stand behind the double consubstantiality are not to be compared with each other.[78] He wanted to state by means of the formula, like the council of Chalcedon, which followed him, simply that Jesus Christ must be confessed both as true God and also as true man, according to the faith of the Fathers.[79]

2. The soteriological implications of the double consubstantiality

Following a long tradition Leo the Great was fond of separating the soteriological statements about Christ as God and about Christ as man. As true God the Lord

[72] Cf. J. P. Jossua, *Le salut, incarnation ou mystère pascal.*

[73] Cf. Leo, ep. 28.6 (Silva-Tarouca 78f), also ep. 59.3.

[74] Cf. the commentary by H. Arens, *Die christologische Sprache Leos des Großen. Analyse des Tomus an den Patriarchen Flavian.*

[75] Cf. esp. ep. 28.2 (Silva-Tarouca 16–20, 42–8).

[76] Cf. B. Studer, art.cit.: REAug 18,1972, pp 104–14.

[77] The connection between the sermons and the dogmatic letters is evident, esp. from the fact that the latter take over whole passages from the former. Cf. the references in the edition by A. Chavasse, CChL 138A, pp 612f.

[78] Cf. serm. 51.6; 75.5; 77.6.

[79] Consubstantialis is rendered most accurately by 'in solidarity with'; for it does not mean so much natural identity, but rather unity in responsibility and action.

performed miracles, as true man he took upon himself sufferings.[80] More frequent than the merely static juxtapositions of the divine and human saving activies are the dynamic statements according to the scheme: God came in order to live and die as man.[81] Such soteriological statements gain in expression insofar as they are linked with the idea of double consubstantiality; for Leo consubstantiality means unity as well as equality, closeness as well as resemblance.[82] Hence, Christ performs divine works because he stands wholly on the side of God, and at the same time performs human works and suffers, because he has entered into full solidarity with humankind. According to him, only Christ as God was able to bring salvation: to reveal the Father, and to overcome both sin and death.[83] His polemic against the Manichees and against Eutyches moved him to point even more expressly to the human qualities of Christ. Only as man was Christ able to adapt his proclamation of God to human understanding; Only as man could he give them an example of patience and humility; only as man was he able to heal his fellow human beings from their frailties and to cover their fickleness and anguish with his firm power; above all, only as man could he die, and only as a descendant of Adam he could suffer death on behalf of his posterity.[84] Along these lines the resurrection too is to be seen. Only as man was he able to show that the terrors of death could be overcome, and that humankind might hope for divine glory.[85]

3. The soteriological significance of the two natures, joined in unity

Following the Latin tradition, in particular with regard to his polemic against the 'monophysitism' of Eutyches, Leo obviously emphasized the distinction of the two natures in Christ.[86] This did not, however, prevent him from keeping in mind the unity of Christ. His expositions of the true God and the true man in the *Tomus ad Flavianum* quite unambiguously served to establish the *unitas personae*.[87] When he later had to defend this doctrine against the accusation of Nestorianism, he became even more emphatic on this score.[88]

This confession of the personal unity, which has come to pass through the union of the two natures, on the initiative of the Son of God,[89] is for Leo of enormous soteriological significance. He always presupposed that the saving act, even in its human dimension as suffering, propitiatory death and sacrifice, was to be ascribed to the Son of God.[90] Above all it is the personal union which Leo the

---

[80] Serm. 34.3; 28.3.
[81] Serm. 26.2; 25.5.
[82] Cf. B. Studer, 'Il concetto di "consostanziale" in Leone Magno', Augustinianum 13, 1973, pp 599–607.
[83] Serm. 25.2f; cf. ep. 59,3.
[84] Cf. serm. 25.2; 66.4; 54.4; 64.2f.
[85] Cf. ep. 59.2; serm. 72.2.5ff; 64.2; 95.1; 67.4; 39.4.
[86] Cf. ep. 28.2 (Silva-Tarouca 23–53).
[87] Cf. ep. 28.3 (Silva-Tarouca 54–60); also H. Arens, *Die christologie Sprache Leos des Großen*, esp. pp 338–49, and B. Studer, *Una persona Christi*, p 454, with a criticism of Arens.
[88] Cf. ep. 124.2 (=ep. 165,2); ep. 129.2.
[89] Cf. serm. 64.2.
[90] Cf. esp. the theme medicus caelestis / omnipotens, serm. 64.2; 95.1; 67.5; 39.4.

Great considered to be the foundation of Christ's mediatorship: of the rebirth in baptism and the redemption through the blood of suffering.[91] Further, he quite expressly emphasizes that human frailty was able to endure suffering only because it was linked with divine power. Even though he simplified too much the joint activity of the two natures, he unambiguously pointed to the fact that the man Jesus was able to accept the redeeming death with full freedom and obedience, only because he was God and man at the same time.[92] Finally, his exposition of the just overcoming of the devil's unrighteousness, of the infinite value of the death of a sinless man, and of the overcoming of death in the resurrection, are entirely founded on the idea of the personal unity of Christ. Only the Son of God, who has united humanity with himself, without ceasing to be God, was able to effect all this.[93]

A closer inspection of the three most important christological traditions, which in the first half of the fifth century led to the faith of Chalcedon, shows in a striking manner that, for all their faithful conformity to the gospel, they display considerable diversity. The Alexandrine tradition emphasizes the unity of subject of the whole existence of Christ, the Antiochene the integrity of the nature of the man Jesus (of the *homo assumptus*), and the Latin the double solidarity with God and humankind.

It is none the less significant that each of these christological schools of thought is always bound up with a soteriological concern: with the guarantee of the saving act through the power of God, with the model of Jesus' obedience, with solidarity with sinners, for whom God himself was made sin.

The soteriological outlook of these at first sight very abstract seeming christologies would have emerged still more clearly, if we had gone into even more detail in establishing how Theodore's christological expositions are bound up with his baptismal catechesis, those of Cyril with his commentaries on Scripture, and those of Leo the Great with his sermons on the main feasts of the liturgical year.[94] It would also have become clearer how much the mystery of the incarnation in the *Deus assumens,* in the eternal Logos, or in the *Filius Dei,* that is to say, in all three traditions, however different they are, is finally rooted in the mystery of the Trinity.

[91] Serm. 69.5; 64.3; ep. 35.3.
[92] Cf. serm. 54.1f: on the distinct activities of the two natures, also serm. 67.2ff: on the causae of the death of Christ.
[93] Cf. serm. 22.2; 23.2; 64.3; 70.3; 91.2.
[94] Cf. B. Studer, *Soteriologie,* pp 184f, 207–12.

17. The Faith of Chalcedon

BIBLIOGRAPHY

R. V. Sellers, *The Council of Chalcedon*, London 1953.

A. de Halleux, 'La définition christologique à Chalcedoine', RThLouv 7, 1976, pp 3–23, 150–170: report on research, sources, textual analyses.

B. Sesboüé, 'Le procès contemporain de Chalcédoine', RchSR 65, 1977, pp 45–80.

A. Grillmeier, *Christ in Christian Tradition*, vol 1, 2nd ed., London 1975, pp 541–68 (with bibl.).

L. R. Wickham, 'Chalkedon', TRE 7, 1980, pp 668–75 (with bibl.).

L. R. Wickham, 'Eutyches, Eutychianischer Streit', TRE 10, 1982, pp 558–65 (with bibl.).

See also:

A. Grillmeier, *Jesus der Christus im Glauben der Kirche, II/1. Das Konzil von Chalzedon (451). Rezeption und Widerspruch (451–518)*, Freiburg 1986 (cf. B. Studer, in ThR 83, 1987, pp 125–9) (Eng. tr.: *Christ in Christian Tradition*, vol. 2, pt. 1, London 1987).

Even though the council of Chalcedon is not as important as the first council of Nicea, and is rather to be seen as confirming it and complementing it in Christology, it nevertheless also deserves detailed treatment. This need is all the more urgent, as Chalcedon has actually become a matter of dispute for modern criticism today.[1] It will not be sufficient, however, to analyse the wording of its definition of faith. We must also seek to place it in the context of Church history and theology.[2]

I. THE COUNCIL OF CHALCEDON AS HISTORICAL EVENT

1. Final point of a theological controversy

The council of Chalcedon, which was held in October 451 in the vicinity of the capital of the East Roman empire, marked the end of a development, which had

---

[1] Cf. among others L. Scheffczyk, 'Chalzedon heute', IntKathZschr 8, 1979, pp 10–21; P. Schoonenberg, 'Denken über Chalkedon', TThQ 160, 1980, pp 295–305; J. Liébaert, 'Valeur permanente du dogme christologique', MélSR 28, 1981, pp 97–126, 179–93; P. Stockmeier, 'Das Konzil von Chalkedon. Probleme der Forschung', FZPhTh 29, 1982, pp 140–56.

[2] Cf. above all the monumental work by A. Grillmeier and H. Bacht, eds., *Das Konzil von Chalkedon. Geschichte und Gegenwart*, 3 vols, Würzburg 1951–54, [4]1973, with the bibiliography by A. Schönmetzer, in vol 3, pp 825–65, also L. R. Wickham, 'Chalkedon', TRE 7, 1980, pp 668–75.

been initiated in 428, and the main phases of which had been the double council of Ephesus, 431, the accord of Antioch, 433, the synod of Constantinople under Flavian, 448 and the synod of Ephesus under Dioscorus, 449, the so-called Robber Synod.

The council, which had met in Ephesus under Cyril of Alexandria, approved his position against Nestorius and rejected Nestorian criticism of Cyril. Without issuing a definition of faith – something in fact explicitly excluded – the synod pronounced in favour of the Alexandrian view, according to which the Word itself is in a mysterious way the subject of the whole of Jesus' life.[3]

The rival synod which met also in Ephesus, a few days later under John of Antioch drafted a diphysite formula, apparently under the influence of Theodoret of Cyrus, a bitter adversary of Cyril's. This formula was enlarged in 432, and then in 433 adopted as the basis of the agreement between Cyril and the Antiochenes. This so-called Formulary of Reunion of 433 (DS 271ff) is dominated by the Antiochene perspective. Yet, even though it expressly emphasizes the double consubstantiality, thus stressing duality in Christ, it nevertheless, in line with Cyril, confesses one Lord and even adopts the title *theotokos*, which Nestorius had rejected.[4]

The synod under Flavian rejected the criticisms of Eutyches, a strict Cyrillian, and others, against the diphysite views of the Antiochenes, and stated, in accordance with the christology that had been established in Constantinople under Proclus, that Christ in his incarnation exists in two natures, which are united in one hypostasis and one prosopon.[5]

Under Dioscorus of Alexandria the synod of Ephesus of 449, with the protests of the Roman delegates, finally rejected the definition of Constantinople and at the same time condemned the Antiochenes, Ibas, Theodoret and Domnus. In standing by Eutyches it practically accepted the Cyrilline equation of the one nature and the one hypostasis. The Alexandrines' monophysitism had, therefore, prevailed in a sharpened form.[6] It was opposed by the diphysitism of the Antiochenes and Flavian, and also by the more dualistic position of Leo the Great, who expressly rejected the synod of Ephesus. Therefore, the council, called by the emperor at Chalcedon, had to decide either for Dioscorus or for Leo.[7]

---

[3] Cf. A. Grillmeier, *Jesus Christus*, pp 687–91 (=*Christ in Christian Tradition*, pp 484–7), and esp. L. I. Scipioni, *Nestorio e il concilio di Efeso*. See also B. Studer, 'Il concilio di Efeso (431), nella luce della dottrina mariana di Cirillo di Alessandria', S. Felici, ed., *La mariologia nella catechesi dei Padri*, Rome 1991, pp 49–67, with bibl.

[4] Cf. A. Grillmeier, *Jesus Christus*, pp 692–707 (=*Christ in Christian Tradition*, pp 488–501), and esp. T. Šagi-Bunić, 'Deus perfectus et homo perfectus', and H. J. Vogt, 'Das gespaltene Konzil von Ephesus und der Glaube an den einen Christus', TrThZ 90, 1981, pp 89–105.

[5] Cf. A. Grillmeier, *Jesus Christus*, pp 727–33 (=*Christ in Christian Tradition*, pp 520–6), and esp. L. R. Wickham, 'Eutyches/Eutychianischer Streit', TRE 10, 1982, pp 558–65.

[6] Cf. A. Grillmeier, *Jesus Christus*, pp 734–7 (=*Christ in Christian Tradition*, pp 526–9), and esp. W. de Vries, 'Das Konzil von Ephesus 449, eine "Räubersynode"', OCP 41, 1975, pp 357–98.

[7] Cf. A. Grillmeier, *Jesus Christus*, pp 753f (=*Christ in Christian Tradition*, pp 543f).

2. A matter of ecclesiastical politics

The imperial convocation of the council was itself the result of a lengthy political controversy, in which the great bishoprics, above all the Apostolic See of Rome and the court of Constantinople, were involved. At first it was the pope who was opposed to an ecumenical synod, then Theodosius II. Only when the emperor died through an accident did the council take place, and this chiefly because the imperial court, under Pulcheria and Marcian, was now interested in gaining political backing from the pope.[8]

But even the procedures of the council were largely a political event. Under the chairmanship of the imperial commissioners, or of the imperial couple itself, the Fathers of the council proved to be entirely dependent on the civil authority. They would have simply maintained that Cyril's second letter to Nestorius and Cyril's letter to John of Antioch, containing the Formulary of Reunion, were in agreement with the *Tomus Leonis,* and that on the basis of Nicea and Constantinople. Any addition to the Nicaeno-Constantinopolitan creed was for them, in accordance with the decisions of Ephesus, out of the question.[9] Yet, under imperial pressure they gave way and had a formulary of faith drafted by a special commission. When the Roman legates, however, protested against the *ex duabus naturis,* the members of the synod once more withdrew before the imperial court, which had reached an agreement with the Roman delegates. A new episcopal commission, with Egyptian bishops however excluded, finally drafted the definitive text of Chalcedon.[10]

3. The importance of the faith of Chalcedon

The Chalcedonian definition of faith thus presents a compromise achieved in political interests. Yet it is a happy compromise in so far as in it all the great christological traditions of that time were represented. This faith of Chalcedon, which is certainly dogmatic rather than kerygmatic in character,[11] has become, after further theological and at the same time political controversies, the basis of Byzantine and Roman Catholic, and also of Protestant christology. On the other hand, this compromise has remained to the present day a stumbling block for the monophysite Churches. Also the Nestorian Church has since the fifth century opposed the council of Chalcedon, which condemned Nestorius.[12]

[8] Cf. K. Baus and E. Ewig, *Die Reichskirche nach Konstantin dem Großen:* (HDK III/1), pp 120–6, and esp. M. Wojowytsch, *Papsttum und Konzile,* pp 318–43.

[9] Cf. the prologue of the definition of faith: DS 300, also A. Grillmeier, *Jesus Christus,* pp 753f (=*Christ in Christian Tradition,* pp 543f).

[10] Cf. A. Grillmeier, *Jesus Christus,* pp 754–9 (=*Christ in Christian Tradition,* pp 544–7), and esp. A. de Halleux, 'La définition christologique à Chalcédoine', RThLouv 7, 1976, pp 3–23, 155–70.

[11] Cf. A. Grillmeier, *Jesus Christus,* pp 765–8 (=*Christ in Christian Tradition,* p 551).

[12] Cf. P. Monterde, 'Le concile de Chalcédoine d'après les historiens monophysites de langue syrienne', *Chalkedon* I, pp 581–602, and W. de Vries, 'Die syrisch-nestorianische Haltung zu Chalkedon', *Chalkedon* I, pp 603–35.

II. THE DEFINITION OF CHALCEDON (DS 300FF)

1. The structure of the document

The document, which after many setbacks was approved on 22 October 451, contains the following sections:

An introduction justifying the new Definition; the symbols of the 318 Fathers (N) and of the 150 Fathers (NC), which thus achieved ecumenical validity; consent to the aforementioned two letters of Cyril and to the *Tomus Leonis;* the Definition proper, and finally an anathema against anyone who wants to teach another faith than that of the synod.

The Definition itself consists of two parts. The first part (DS 301) may be regarded as an interpretation in a Cyrillian sense of the Formulary of Reunion of 433. It is, apart from language of body and soul and the formula of the double homoousios, very biblical in character. The second part, on the other hand (DS 302), develops in a more technical manner the doctrine of the two natures. The formula *in duabus naturis* must be seen as a correction of an earlier text.

Especially worthy of note is the grammatical structure of the whole in its main part: 'The entire confession concerns the Son, our Lord Jesus Christ', which is more precisely defined by further statements.[13] In other words, the subject which governs the second article of the *Nicaenum* is also taken up here.

2. The individual elements of the Definition

The Definition describes what, in accordance with the holy Fathers (above all of Nicea), is to be confessed about the one and selfsame Son, our Lord Jesus Christ. The first part states concerning him: He is perfect in divinity and perfect in humanity; true God and true man, i.e. he possesses body and soul; consubstantial with the Father according to his divinity, and consubstantial with us according to his humanity, i.e. like us in every way, apart from sin; begotten from eternity from the Father, and then also born for our sake of the Virgin, the God-bearer, according to his humanity.

The second part states of the one and selfsame Christ, Son, Lord, only-begotten, that he is to be confessed in two natures, without confusion and without change, without division and without separation. The difference between the two natures is, however, not cancelled by the fact that they are united. We must rather acknowledge the individual features of each of the two natures, even though they come together in one person, or one hypostasis. For we must not tear apart the one and selfsame only-begotten Son, God, Word, Lord Jesus Christ.

The Definition closes with the statement that the council in its faith wanted to keep to the prophets and to Jesus Christ himself, i.e. to Holy Scripture, but also to tradition, as laid down in the creeds of Nicea and Constantinople, and that it has finally handed down the creed of the Fathers.

---

[13] Cf. A. Grillmeier, *Jesus Christus,* p 756 (=*Christ in Christian Tradition,* pp 544f).

3. The main message

The structure of the text itself betrays that it is a compromise achieved with great effort. But the tenor of the text is clear. We have the one subject to deal with: 'One and the same' is repeated three times (DS 301 line 1f; 302 lines 1, 6). This subject is more closely defined, above all as 'our Lord Jesus Christ'(DS 301 line 2). He is also named Son, only-begotten, God and Logos (DS 302 line 6). To this one single subject all assertions are attributed: those of divinity and humanity, the double consubstantiality, the two natures, which remain distinct even after the incarnation. The relationship of the two natures is more precisely stated as being founded on the unity of the person, or hypostasis. Further, it is not to be treated as a natural unity, rather it consists in the unity of person, or hypostasis. In other words, the council wanted to define the double nature, the divine and human consubstantiality, while fully safeguarding its unity.

III. THE SOURCES OF THE FAITH OF CHALCEDON

1. The origin of the individual elements in general

It is immediately evident that the Definition of Chalcedon consists of different elements, with different origins. This does not, however, necessarily imply that a secretary has fitted together the several contributions of a redaction commission into a mosaic. The grammatical coherence and the unified line of thought rather indicate a single author, who has independently woven the different elements into a single whole. Basil of Seleucia, it has been suggested, was this author, and it has been noted that he has given the whole text a Cyrilline touch.[14]

There is no doubt thus far that the first part is in line with the Formulary of Reunion of 433, which goes back to Theodoret of Cyrus.[15] The repeated 'one and the same' at the beginning and the end of the adopted text suggests, however, an Alexandrian reinterpretation. The formula 'in two natures' in the second part and the following four adverbs (DS 302 line 1f) are apparently to be traced back to the revising commission. It must remain an open question whether the negative adverbs which are fitted into the diphysite structure are the result of a Roman suggestion, or already existed in Basil's text. The formula safeguarding the individual features of the two natures certainly comes from the *Tomus Leonis*.[16] The doctrine of the two natures tallies with the Antiochene as well as with the Latin tradition, both of which developed the two natures from the two births. But we are also dealing here with a Cyrilline reinterpretation,

---

[14] Cf. A. de Halleux, art. cit., RThLouv 7, 1976, pp 158ff, also S. J. Voicu, 'Basil of Seleucia', EEC 1, 1992, p 115.

[15] Cf. DS 271ff; also T. Šagi-Bunić, Deus perfectus et homo perfectus, pp 19–64.

[16] Cf. Leo, ep. 28.3 (Silva-Tarouca 54f); also H. Arens, *Die christologische Sprache Leos des Großen*, pp 314–21. The origin of the formula is not, however, finally traced even in this study, because it does not take account of Ps. Eusebius, Trin 9.6: CChL 9, p 160.

especially in the assertion that the difference between the natures is not cancelled.[17]

2. The origin of the phrase 'one person and one hypostasis'

The phrase 'Coming together in one person (*unam personam*)'(DS 302 line 4) comes from Leo's letter to Flavian. The addition 'and one hypostasis' (line 4f) is apparently intended to make clear the agreement between Leo's and Cyril's letters. According to de Halleux it could have been taken over from Cyril's second letter to Nestorius, where the *henosis kath' hypostasin* is mentioned, and further, a 'mere assumption of the prosopon' is rejected.[18] At any rate, this combination recalls the trinitarian importance of both these terms.[19]

If we take into account the fact that further on the single subject of all assertions is also called Logos, we might be tempted to think that the council wanted to maintain that the Son, i.e. the second person of the Trinity, is the subject also of the *oikonomia*.[20] It is not to be overlooked, however, that *et in unam personam atque subsistentiam concurrente* is a formula of Leo's, even if altered (in a Cyrilline sense?). With Leo, who here follows Augustine, the single person is nevertheless the result of the union and not its starting point.[21] In the formula itself the *una persona* is, accordingly, the goal of the *concursus*. In other words: it is true that the Definition names the subject of the attributes as the Word, but the Definition does not express, at least not positively, that the divine Word itself is the personal element of Christ, of the God-man. This only occurred later, when there was an attempt to bring the faith of Chalcedon into line with the monophysitism of the Alexandrine tradition.

IV. THE THEOLOGICAL SIGNIFICANCE OF THE FAITH OF CHALCEDON

As has already been emphasized, the faith of Chalcedon, from the point of view of ecclesiastical politics as well as of theology, must be regarded as a compromise. The great Churches with their different traditions, and certainly also political interests, all contributed to this result: a fact not to be disregarded. We must not, however, forget that this council brought with it the separation from the monophysite Churches, and that, in spite of its diphysitism, it was not acceptable to the Nestorian Churches. In saying this we have already shown that an evaluation of Chalcedon must have both negative and positive sides.[22]

---

[17] The Cyrilline reinterpretation must not, however, be overrated. The Chalcedonian definition of faith on the whole is still to be regarded as an example of the doctrine of the two natures. The duality is attributed to one single subject, not the other way round.

[18] A. de Halleux, art.cit.: RThLouv 7, 1967, p 166.

[19] On the trinitarian level, from the end of the fourth century, persona and hypostasis are taken to correspond to each other.

[20] This view is represented by, among others, P. Smulders, 'Christologie', MySal III/1, p 467.

[21] Cf. B. Studer, *Una persona Christi*, pp 483ff.

[22] Cf. A. Grillmeier, *Jesus Christus*, pp 765–775 (=*Christ in Christian Tradition*, pp 551–7).

1. The one Christ, true God and true man

Even though the faith of Chalcedon is a theological compromise, there is no doubt that it brought about an invaluable advance in christology. The fact of the compromise alone deserves a positive evaluation. Even though the result was achieved in a less than edifying way, it must, nevertheless, be conceded that the controversies between the different ecclesiastical currents finally led to an acknowledgement of the core of truth in the others, and therefore to a mutual enrichment.

On the one hand the Alexandrine view, which goes back to Athanasius and found its most mature expression in Cyril's christology, found general approval. According to this view the Son of God himself made himself present in the life of Jesus: God has saved us. On the other hand, the concern of the Antiochenes and Latins for the integrity of Jesus' human nature won the agreement of the others. As a consequence it was affirmed that it was precisely through the presence of the Word that Jesus was constituted a full man. By God's creative act a man has been created of whom it can be said that he is Son of God, and therefore also man, more perfect than any other man.[23] Hence, what has been accepted, is what Augustine and with him Leo expressed, perhaps more clearly than the others: *Natura quippe nostra non sic assumpta est ut prius creata post assumeretur, sed ut ipsa assumptione crearetur.*[24]

We have to emphasize in particular that the council of Chalcedon established the distinction between the personal and natural levels, which Nestorius had grasped somewhat intuitively without being able to formulate correctly. For in contrasting the trinitarian terms *physis* and *prosopon* (or *hypostasis*), and at the same time ascribing the function of union to the person, or hypostasis, the council opened the way for a later solution of the problem, even though it had not itself yet found the solution. According to this the unity of Christ must not be sought in that which makes the Trinity one, neither in nature, nor in essence, but rather in what distinguishes the divine persons from each other. The divine nature as such is not bearer of the divine and human attributes, neither does the Godhead as such constitute the unity, nor is it as such the principle of all action. We must rather seek for the unity in the direction of the hypostasis. Even though the council thus presented a negative rather than a positive, a tentative rather than explicit answer to the christological question proper, it has at least unambiguously excluded the false solutions of Apollinaris and Eutyches, which tended to envisage the divine Word as constituting the animating principle of Jesus' human nature, or even to understand the unifying hypostasis as the soul.

---

[23] Cf. A. Grillmeier, *Jesus Christus*, pp 772f.
[24] Leo, ep. 35.3, adapted from Augustine. CSermAr 8.2, also A. Grillmeier, *Jesus Christus*, p 771, n 6.

2. The open questions

In the third volume of the monumental work *Chalkedon,* which appeared on the occasion of the 1500th celebration of the council of Chalcedon, Karl Rahner published an essay with the title 'Chalkedon, Ende oder Anfang?'[25] Alois Grillmeier used the same title for the epilogue to the first volume of his *Christ in Christian Tradition.*[26] The answer to this question can only, however, take the form of a 'both/and'. The faith of Chalcedon must in fact be regarded not only as the final point of a long development, but also as the starting point for fresh christological discussions. Like any other statement of faith the confession of Chalcedon in particular cannot simply signify an end, but must imply continual openness to a yet deeper understanding of the gospel of Jesus Christ.

The council, accordingly, opened the way to the doctrine of the hypostatic union. For with the officially sanctioned application of trinitarian terminology to christology, it pointed the way to the solution of the christological problem. Because, however, it abstained from elucidating the questionable concepts of *physis,* and, above all, of *hypostasis,* or rather, because it had not yet realized the implications of this distinction, it could not yet define the hypostatic union itself. It had not yet determined that the divine person of the Word itself is the personal element in Jesus' humanity. It is this neglect which was also responsible for the misunderstandings, that arouse in the seventh century, as regards Jesus' human will.

There are, however, still graver criticisms of the faith of Chalcedon. According to them, the council presented the Christian message in a language too Greek and abstract; it posed the christological question only from the perspective of the God-man, and not from the biblical perspective of the Son, who entered upon a life of obedience and suffering; further, as regards soteriology, it contented itself with merely stating the *propter nos homines;* it spoke in too naive a manner of the unchangeability of God, and understood the union of body and soul in too static a way.[27]

All these objections must certainly be taken seriously, but, all the same, one may treat them with a certain reserve. Certainly the language of the Definition of Faith sounds, for the most part, very abstract; further, the starting-point of the dogmatic account of the mystery of Jesus proves to be too physical, too little personal ; it hardly mentions human freedom and personal responsibility; it hardly takes account of the salvation historical context of the Word's incarnation; it does not appear as a revelation of God's love.

But it must not be forgotten that the context determined that this Definition be understood rather as a negative defence of the Christian tradition,

---

[25] K. Rahner, 'Chalkedon – Ende oder Anfang?', *Chalkedon* III, pp 3–49, (Eng. tr. in: id., *Theological Investigations,* vol. 1, London 1961, pp 149–200).

[26] A. Grillmeier, *Jesus Christus,* p 765 (=*Christ in Christian Tradition,* p 555).

[27] A summary exposition of the various difficulties with the faith of Chalcedon is found in P. Smulders, 'Christologie', MySal III/1, p 468; cf. also P. Schoonenberg, 'Christologische Diskussion heute', ThPrQ 123, 1975, pp 106–17; P. Sesboüé, 'Le procès contemporain de Chalcédoine', RchSR 65, 1977, pp 45–80.

than as a juridical foundation of the one faith.[28] To understand its full bearing it must also be seen in the context of the whole of the christology of that time. Precisely because of this it is also important, not only to consider the pre-history of the faith of Chalcedon from the perspective of dogmatic development, but also to examine those authors to whom the most important formulae can be traced, in order to find out how they preached Christ to their faithful.

On the other hand all critics of the faith of Chalcedon have to be reminded of the fact that a Christian can hardly avoid its problematic aspects. From the first, the Nicene distinction between creator and creature with its christological implications could not be avoided; above all one would always have to acknowledge, in one way or other, two things and somehow explain them: God has in some way made himself the subject of Jesus' saving activity, so that he himself is responsible for it, without Jesus' human freedom being questioned. But, at the same time, Jesus' responsibility for his saving activity must be understood in such a way that he is nevertheless regarded not as a mere prophet, but as the Son of God himself.

[28] For the term 'dogma' cf. B. Studer, 'Dogma', EEC 1, 1992, pp 244f.

18. Post-Chalcedonian Theology

BIBLIOGRAPHY

V. Schurr, *Die Trinitätslehre des Boethius im Lichte der skythischen Kontroverse*, Paderborn 1935.

G. Bardy, 'Trinité', DThC 15, 1950, cols. 1682–1699: The end of the patristic period.

J. Lebon, 'La christologie du monophysisme syrien', *Chalkedon I*, Würzburg 1951, pp 425–580 (='Monophysisme').

C. Moeller, 'Le chalcédonisme et le neo-chalcédonisme en Orient de 451 à la fin du VIe siècle', *Chalkedon I*, Würzburg 1951, pp 637–720 (='Chalcédonisme').

A. Grillmeier, 'Vorbereitung des Mittelalters. Eine Studie über das Verhältnis von Chalkedonismus und Neu-Chalkedonismus in der lateinischen Theologie von Boethius bis zu Gregor dem Großen', *Chalkedon II*, Würzburg 1953, pp 791–839.

B. Studer, *Die theologische Arbeitsweise des Johannes von Damaskus*, Ettal 1956.

W. Elert, *Der Ausgang der altkirchlichen Christologie. Eine Untersuchung über Theodor von Pharan und seine Zeit als Einführung in die Dogmengeschichte*, Berlin 1957.

H. U. von Balthasar, *Kosmische Liturgie. Maximus der Bekenner: Höhe und Krise des griechischen Weltbildes*, Einsiedeln ²1961.

S. Otto, *Person und Subsistenz. Die philosophische Anthropologie des Leontius von Byzanz*, Munich 1968.

F. X. Murphy and P. Sherwood, *Constantinople II et III (Histoire des conciles oecumeniques 3)*, Paris 1974.

B. Studer, 'Soteriologie der Kirchenväter', HDG III/2a, Freiburg 1978, pp 212–23 (with bibl.).

E. Klum-Böhmer, *Das Trishagion als Versöhnungsformel der Christenheit. Kontroverstheologie im V. und VI. Jahrhundert*, Munich – Vienna 1979.

P. T. R. Gray, *The Defense of Chalcedon in the East (451–453)*, Leiden 1979.

F. Ake, 'Cassiodor', TRE 7, 1980, pp 657–63.

L. Perrone, *La Chiesa di Palestina e le controversie christologiche. Dal concilio di Efeso (431) al secondo concilio di Constantinopoli (553)*, Brescia 1980 (=*Palestina*).

L. Perrone, 'Il dialogo contro gli aftartodoceti di Leonzio di Bizanto e Severo di Antiochia', *Christianesimo nella storia* 1, Bologna 1980, pp 411–43.

L. Frivold, *The Incarnation. A Study of the Doctrine of the Incarnation in the Armenian Church in the 5th and 6th centuries according to the Book of Letters*, Leiden 1981.

L. Pozzi, 'Boethius', TRE 7, 1981, pp 18–28 (with bibl.).

F. Heinzer and C. Schönborn, eds., *Maximus Confessor. Actes du Symposium sur Maxime le Confesseur, Fribourg, 2–5 septembre 1980*, Fribourg 1982.

P. Piret, *Le Christ et la Trinité selon Maxime le Confesseur*, Paris 1983.

See also:

H. Chadwick, *Boethius*, Oxford 1981.

A. Grillmeier, *Jesus der Christus im Glauben der Kirche*, vol. II,1; II,2; II,4, Freiburg 1986–90.

A. Louth, *Denys the Areopagite,* London 1989.
A. de Halleux, 'Actualité du néochalcédonisme. A propos d'un accord récent', RThLouv
21, 1990, pp 23–54.

The council of Chalcedon was an 'end', insofar as it concluded with a Definition
of Faith the development of the christological question, which had become
acute in 428 with the controversy between Nestorius, patriarch of Constantinople,
and Cyril of Alexandria. Chalcedon, however, was also a 'beginning', because it
did not finally lay the christological question to rest. Its decisions, accepted by
East and West, were rather immediately subject to discussion. For although the
council with its threefold emphasis on the 'one and the same' (DS 301f) had
essentially adopted the leading intention of Cyril of Alexandria, his most
zealous adherents were not content with its Definition of Faith. It was not
anti-Nestorian enough for them, and thus amounted to a betrayal of Cyril's
christology. Immediately after the close of the synod resistance stirred among
the Palestinian monks.[1] Shortly after, a revolt occurred in Alexandria under
Timothy Aelurus.[2] Even in Rome the *Tomus Leonis,* widely debated in the East,
was called in question, and with it the authority of Chalcedon.[3] At a later stage,
after 500, the monophysite opposition under Severus of Antioch and Philoxenus
of Mabbug prevailed not only in Syria but even in Constantinople.[4] Neither were
the political endeavours for the religious unity of the empire, the survey which
Leo I carried out among the bishops, and the interventions of Zeno and Anastasius
I, able to eliminate the theological divergences.[5] Certainly Justin I (518–527)
officially restored the authority of Chalcedon,[6] but only his successor Justinian
(527–565) was able, not however without concessions to the monophysites, to
establish it throughout the whole empire.[7] Thus, from the middle of the fifth
century a lengthy controversy was dragged out between the adherents and the
opponents of the council of Chalcedon, which was to last until the seventh
century. If the so-called Iconoclast controversy is also to be regarded as a
christological issue, these controversies only came to an end in 787, at the second
council of Nicea.[9]

    Because in the decades after the council of Chalcedon it was primarily its
dogmatic decisions that were questioned, the theology of this period can be said

[1] Cf. L. Perrone, *Palestina,* pp 89–103.
[2] Cf. H. Jedin, *History of the Church,* vol. 2, pp 421–3 (The Henoticon and the Acacian Schism),
also L. Lebon, 'Monophysisme', p 428 and passim.
[3] Cf. Leo, serm. 96, also Arnobius, Conflictus: CChL 25A, 43–173; also C. Bardy, 'La repercussion
des controverses christologiques en Occident entre le concile de Chalcédoine et la mort de l'empereur
Anastase (451–518)', *Chalkedon* II, pp 779f. See also C. Pifarré, *Arnobio el Joven,* Montserrat 1988.
[4] Cf. H. Jedin, *History of the Church,* vol. 2, pp 430ff, also above all J. Lebon, 'Monophysisme'.
[5] Cf. H. Jedin, *History of the Church,* vol. 2, pp 421–33.
[6] Cf. H. Jedin, *History of the Church,* vol. 2, pp 433–6 (The Elaboration of the Church of the
Byzantine Empire in the Age of the Emperor Justinian I).
[7] Cf. H. Jedin, *History of the Church,* vol. 2, pp 436–43 (chapters 23–25: The Early Byzantine
Church), also C. Moeller, 'Chalcédonisme', pp 679f.
[8] Cf. the various contributions in *Chalkedon* I and II.
[9] Cf. C. von Schönborn, *L'icóne du Christ,* Fribourg 1976, also H. G. Beck, *Kirche und Literatur,*
pp 296–306.

to be dominated by christology. This is especially true of the East. In the West, in so far as the difficult political situation, which resulted in isolation, allowed any serious theological work at all, other concerns came to the fore. Nevertheless, at the same time christological interest had not totally evaporated, as the witness of Arnobius the Younger, Vigilius of Thapsus and Avitus of Vienne shows.[10] The further, very demanding development of the doctrine of the one Christ, true God and true man, was by no means insignificant for the history of trinitarian doctrine. There are two reasons for this.

On the one hand discussion of the person of Christ has always somehow involved his relation to the Father. As the working out of a trinitarian terminology, initiated chiefly by the Cappadocians, had proved very significant for the faith of Chalcedon, so, vice versa, a deeper understanding of the christological terminology taken over from Chalcedon was not without importance for a more profound understanding of trinitarian doctrine. As Nestorius had already fought Arians and Apollinarians alike,[11] and a whole range of theologians had developed their christological reflection from the traditional anti-Arian polemic,[12] the discussion of the theopaschite formula *Unus de Trinitate passus est* was bound to be of considerable significance for a theological understanding of the mystery of the Trinity.[13]

On the other hand, after Chalcedon, largely in connection with the christological controversy, there was a far reaching development in the understanding of theological work in general.[14] Not only did the theologians place far more weight on the authority of the Church Fathers,[15] they also adopted Aristotelian logic, as propagated especially by the Neoplatonist philosophers of Alexandria.[16] Even theologians like Severus of Antioch,[17] who relied on the ideas of the Fathers rather than on the categories of teachers 'from outside', could not avoid a confrontation with the latter. It was especially on this level that a balance had to be achieved between trinitarian doctrine and christology.[18] The development of theological method, which began about 500, was bound to have repercussions on both fields.

As regards the special problem of the *Filioque*, it was not yet in the post-Chalcedonian period an issue for discussion; it was only after 800 that it became

---

[10] Cf. M. Simonetti, 'Letteratura antimonofisita d'Occidente', Augustinianum 18, 1978, pp 487–532.

[11] Cf. A. Grillmeier, *Jesus Christus*, p 647 (=*Christ in Christian Tradition*, pp 451f).

[12] Cf. esp. the first part, trinitarian in character, of Arnobius' Conflictus: CChL 25A, 43–86, as well as the beginning of the second part: CChL 25A, 87–90, with New Testament proof texts of the anti-Arian tradition; and Vigilius, CEutych, esp. 5.2–5, where he points to the coherence with earlier heresies; also M. Simonetti, art.cit., Augustinianum 18, 1978, pp 489f, 505f.

[13] Cf. A. Grillmeier, 'Vorbereitung des MA', *Chalkedon* II, p 801, on the treatises I and II by Boethius.

[14] On the question in general see B. Studer, *Johannes von Damaskus;* also esp. C. Moeller, 'Chalcédonisme', pp 637–48.

[15] Cf. the studies by M. Richard on the dogmatic florilegia, esp.: 'Les florilèges diphysites du Ve et du VIe siècle', *Chalkedon* I, pp 721–48.

[16] Cf. C. Moeller, 'Chalcédonisme', pp 638–43, also L. Perrone, *Palestina*, pp 234–60.

[17] Cf. J. Lebon, 'Monophysisme', pp 545f, with Severus Ant., CGram 2,1: ed. Lebon p 44.

[18] Cf. e.g. Leontius of Byz., Epilysis: MG 86, 1920D–1921B, and later Maximus Conf., op 13: MG 91, 145A–149A.

a matter of controversy, the heat of which has still not cooled down today.[19] Nevertheless, the first signs were already evident. In the West the procession of the Holy Spirit from Father and Son had already been adopted in credal formulations, and thus made into dogma to some degree.[20] On the other hand, the Nicene distinction between *theologia* and *oikonomia,* which even today could prove fundamental for the solution of this disputed question, was further developed.[21] The connection between the eternal processions of the Son and the Holy Spirit and their missions in time had not yet, however, come to bear on the controversy between Cyril of Alexandria and Theodoret of Cyrus, although it was about the Holy Spirit sent by Christ.[22]

I. THE UNFOLDING OF CHALCEDONIAN CHRISTOLOGY UP TO 553

The faith of Chalcedon had been established as a theological compromise in 451 under pressure of the imperial court. It is not, therefore, surprising that it met with only partial acceptance.[23] By distinguishing between *physis* and *hypostasis* the fourth ecumenical council had provided only a stopgap measure. It had certainly gone further than Nestorius' application to christology of the Cappadocian trinitarian terminology. As it had not, however, fully defined the above-mentioned distinction, there inevitably arose a demand to make up for this with all precision. While Cyril of Alexandria had explicitly made the Logos the subject of all christological statements, the fathers of Chalcedon with their formula of faith seemed to draw too much into parallel the two natures in Christ. Such an impression would particularly emerge if the Chalcedonian faith were interpreted by means of the formula of Leo the Great: *agit utraque forma quod proprium est.*[24] What is more, the synod of 451 had hardly tackled the soteriological implications of the doctrine of the one Lord Jesus Christ. It did not speak of Jesus' personal inner life, of his human knowledge and striving. The concepts of the one hypostasis and the one person,

---

[19] Cf. the numerous studies which were published on the occasion of the centenary of the second ecumenical council in 1981, e.g. B. Schultze, 'Die Pneumatologie der Synode von Konstantinopel als abschließende Formulierung der griechischen Theologie (381–1981)', OCP 47, 1981, pp 5–54; and esp. L. Vischer, ed., *Spirit of God – Spirit of Christ. Ecumenical reflections on the Filioque Controversies,* London 1981.

[20] Cf. above all the Symbolum Quicumque (DS 75), where the a Patre et Filio stands in the first, theological part, which is clearly different from the economic part.

[21] Cf. A. Grillmeier, 'Fulgentius von Ruspe's "De fide ad Petrum" and the Summa Sententiarum', *Mit ihm und in ihm,* pp 637–79.

[22] Cf. A. de Halleux, 'Cyrille, Théodoret et le Filioque', RHE 74, 1979, pp 597–625.

[23] Cf. for the following section A. Grillmeier, *Jesus Christus,* pp 768ff (=*Christ in Christian Tradition,* pp 551ff).

[24] Cf. Leo, ep. 28.4 (Silva-Tarouca p 94): ML 54, pp 767AB; also A. Grillmeier, *Jesus Christus,* pp 743–6 (=*Christ in Christian Tradition,* pp 533–6). Leo's christology is criticized above all by Timothy Aelurus, Refutation 81, CPG III, 5475 (cited in J. Lebon, 'Monophysisme', p 466, note 34), but also by Severus of Antioch, ep. ad Oecumenium: Mansi X, p 444 (cited in J. Lebon, 'Monophysisme', p 557, note 68).

therefore, necessarily appeared to be empty conceptual frameworks. This abstraction was bound to prove fatal, the more so as the biblical texts concerning the soul's life were generally not taken seriously enough, even in diphysite circles.

In the christological development, which now inevitably began, the Antiochene tradition was, unfortunately, repressed more and more.[25] In the East the monophysites everywhere sensed the Nestorian danger, and, therefore, rejected all that smacked of Nestorianism. In the West, the Eutychians and monophysites were opposed by a rather artificial Nestorianism. The Nestorian tradition proper had already been eliminated in the course of the second half of the fifth century, and in 553 was finally written off in favour of orthodoxy; it lived on only outside the Byzantine empire. Hence, the balance in christology, which the Chalcedonian solution had made possible, was disturbed; in particular many insights into the links between the mystery of Christ and its realization in the liturgy and the following of Christ were lost.[26]

The controversies resulting from Chalcedon, which were, accordingly, fought only between more or less strict adherents of the council and the so-called monophysites, were at first, during the century from 451 to 553, about a full recognition of Cyril of Alexandria's christology.[27] Hence, in Palestine and Egypt, immediately after the close of the synod of Chalcedon, a violent reaction against it set in. Because the most zealous adherents of Cyril felt his authority compromised by the decisions of the council, they launched an attack on these as well as against Leo's letter to Flavian.[28] To oppose this tendency various endeavours were initiated to show that Cyril and the debated documents were compatible. This is confirmed by the *Conflictus* of Arnobius[29] and certain episcopal statements in the *Codex Encyclius*.[30] The question, however, turned almost exclusively on Cyril, because he had been acknowledged by the fathers of Chalcedon, and even before by the agreement of 433.[31]

In the ensuing period the monophysite movement, partly because of encouragement on the part of the political power, increasingly got the upper hand. Opposing the rather timid efforts of such as Nephalius and others to defend Chalcedon,[32] Severus of Antioch and Philoxenus of Mabbug worked out a strictly

[25] Cf. C. Moeller, 'Chalcédonisme', pp 651–8, also W. de Vries, Die syrisch-nestorianische Haltung zu Chalkedon: *Chalkedon* I, pp 603–35.

[26] Cf. A. Adam, *Dogmengeschichte,* pp 342–53.

[27] Cf. esp. J. Lebon, 'Monophysisme', pp 425–580, and C. Moeller, 'Chalcédonisme', pp 637–720; also L. Perrone, *Palestina.*

[28] Cf. esp. Timothy Aelurus, Refutation (CPG III, 5482); also J. Lebon, 'Monophysisme', pp 428f. 461–7.

[29] Arnobius, Conflictus; also O. Bardenhewer, *Geschichte der altkirchlichen Literatur* IV, p 604.

[30] Cf. A. Grillmeier, *Jesus Christus,* pp 765ff, cf. *Mit ihm und in ihm,* pp 283–300; also C. Moeller, 'Chalcédonisme' pp 659f, 667f.

[31] Cf. C. Moeller, 'Chalcédonisme', p 658.

[32] Cf. C. Moeller, 'Chalcédonisme', pp 652f, with a note on Macedonius, patriarch of Constantinople (495–511), and certain diphysite florilegia, also pp 670ff on Nephalius who already regarded the Cyrillian formula of the one nature as necessary addition to the faith of Chalcedon; on this issue cf. also L. Perrone, *Palestina,* pp 234–40.

Cyrilline christology.[33] Hence, from 509 to 512, monophysitism gained a complete victory. There could not fail to be a reaction. Between 512 and 519 an acceptance of the Chalcedonian faith developed, which is today labelled with the term of Neo-Chalcedonianism. This consists in an equal acceptance of the formula of Chalcedon and typical Cyrilline credal formulae: *henosis kath' hypostasin, mia physis tou Logou sesarkomene, unus de Trinitate passus est.*[34] This version, regarded as a *via media*, was represented above all by John of Caesarea,[35] John of Scythopolis,[36] the emperor Justinian[37] and Leontius of Jerusalem.[38] Parallel to this Neo-Chalcedonianism a christology developed, which went much less far in acknowledging Cyril, but, in analysing the Chalcedonian concepts of *physis* and *hypostasis,* nevertheless took more seriously than the synod of 451 Cyril's overriding concern to identify the single hypostasis with the eternal Son of God.[39] Among the most prominent representatives of this Chalcedonian christology are Leontius of Byzantium, who mainly on grounds of tactics condemned the 'Three Chapters',[40] Theodore of Raithou[41] and the author, perhaps identical with him, of the treatise *De Sectis,* a summary of the christology of that time.[42]

In these lengthy discussions, in which not only the results of detailed study in the Fathers,[43] but also the categories of contemporary philosophy[44] played a part, the doctrine of the hypostatic union came gradually to be shaped. For the Chalcedonians, who simply sought a deeper philosophical understanding of the concepts of 451, as well as for the Neo-Chalcedonians, who strove to reconcile the Chalcedonian dogma with the concern for unity

---

[33] Cf. the compilation of the most important writings by Severus of Antioch and by Philoxenus of Mabbug in J. Lebon, 'Monophysisme', pp 429f. In the following section Lebon gives a detailed exposition of their doctrine of the incarnation.

[34] Cf. C. Moeller, 'Chalcédonisme', esp. pp 666f; also the critical continuation by A. Grillmeier, 'Der Neu-Chalkedonismus', *Mit ihm und in ihm,* pp 371–85, and in L. R. Wickham, 'Chalkedon', TRE 7, 1981, pp 673–5, with bibl.

[35] Cf. C. Moeller, 'Chalcédonisme', pp 672–5; L. Perrone, *Palestina,* pp 249–60, also CPG III, 6855–62.

[36] Cf. C. Moeller, 'Chalcédonisme', pp 675f; L. Perrone, *Palestina,* pp 240–9, also CPG III, 6850ff.

[37] Cf. C. Moeller, 'Chalcédonisme', pp 679f, also CPG III, 6865–93.

[38] Cf. C. Moeller, 'Chalcédonisme', pp 686f; L. Perrone, *Palestina,* pp 260–75, also CPG III, 7911f.

[39] Cf. C. Moeller, 'Chalcédonisme', p 658.

[40] Cf. C. Moeller, 'Chalcédonisme', pp 662ff; L. Perrone, *Palestina,* pp 275–85, also CPG III, 6813–15.

[41] Cf. C. Moeller, 'Chalcédonisme', pp 685f, also CPG III, 7600ff.

[42] Cf. C. Moeller, 'Chalcédonisme', pp 664ff, also CPG III, 6823.

[43] That these studies in the Fathers were very diligently pursued, is shown, not only by the florilegia, but also by the fact, that the so-called Apollinarian forgeries were detected as such; cf. the treatise Adv. fraudes Apollinaristarum, CPG III, 6817; also C. Moeller, 'Chalcédonisme', p 644, note 23; Severus of Antioch proves to be particularly well informed about the theology of the Fathers, cf. J. Lebon, 'Monophysisme', pp 454f; note, however, also the florilegium of the Fathers which Leontius of Byz. added to his CNestEutych; also M. Richard, 'Les florilèges diphysites du Vᵉ et du VIᵉ siècle', *Chalkedon* I, pp 739f. See also B. Studer, 'Una teologia patristica', *Storia della Teologia,* pp 583–98, with bibl.

[44] Cf. e.g. Theodore of Raithou, Praeparatio: MG 91, 1484–1504, also Ps. Leontius, De Sectis, 1.1 and 7: MG 86/1, 1193A–1196B and 1204A–1252A, also, with certain qualifications, M. Grabmann, *Die Geschichte der scholastischen Methode* I, Freiburg 1909, pp 92–116. See also B. Studer, 'Una teologia scolastica', *Storia della Teologia,* pp 599–611, with bibl.

expressed in Cyril's formulae, the single hypostasis, in which divinity and humanity were united, coincided with the Logos, the second hypostasis of the Trinity. While the divinity was identical with the Logos itself, the humanity, therefore, did not subsist in itself but wholly in the Logos and was only through that hypostatic. Cyril's *henosis kath' hypostasin* was therefore not only a real union at the level of being, but a union which was grounded in the subsistence of the Logos and equally in the enhypostasis of the human nature.[45]

This doctrine of the hypostatic union did not just remain a *theologoumenon,* rather it became a criterion of Byzantine orthodoxy. Even though Justinian's decrees, as well as the condemnation of the Three Chapters by the second council of Constantinople (553), did not remotely achieve unanimous consent, their essential core was adopted as the norm of faith.[46] This is confirmed, first, by Ephrem, patriarch of Antioch (526–544),[47] and Leontius of Byzantium,[48] who had developed their ideas independently of Justinian. But it is chiefly later authors, like the author of *De Sectis*[49] and Anastasius, patriarch of Antioch (559–599),[50] who reveal how much the doctrine of the hypostatic union had become the common property of Byzantine orthodoxy.

This basic observation can also be applied to the Latin Church.[51] Already in 534 John II at Justinian's request approved the long-debated formula *Unus de Trinitate passus est* (DS 401f), which gave the faith of Chalcedon not only an ambiguously anti-Nestorian interpretation, but at the same time brought out what was fundamentally to be understood by the dogma of the one hypostasis.[52] In a less edifying manner Vigilius later took his stand for, and then against, the synod of 553.[53] His regrettable inconsistency, however, only touched the question as to whether it was opportune or not to condemn the Three Chapters, not the further deepening of the Chalcedonian faith.[54] The same is true of the later bishops of Rome, who not only accepted the formerly disputed council as ecumenical, but

---

[45] Cf. John of Scythopl., Scholia: MG 4, 68A, on the hypostatic union; MG 4, 196C, on the theopaschite formula; John of Caesar., ApolConcChalc IV 3 and 6: CChG I, p 55, 181–7, 205–8, on the term enhypostatos; Leontius of Byz., CNestEutych: MG 86/1, 1348D, on the hypostatic union; TrigCap 25: MG 86/2, 1909 CD; Epilysis: MG 86/2, 1933AB; Leontius of Jerus., AdvNest I 20 and III 8: MG 86/1, 1485C and 1629A; Ps.Leontius, De Sectis 8: MG 86/1, 1249AC.

[46] DS 421–41, esp. can 5: DS 426; also W. de Vries, 'Das zweite Konzil von Konstantinopel (553) und das Lehramt von Papst und Kirche', OCP 38, 1972, pp 331–66, where the notion of reception is, however, given too narrow an interpretation.

[47] Cf. the fragments of Ephrem in Photius, Bibliotheca: MG 103, 993AB, 1001B; also C. Moeller, 'Chalcédonisme', pp 680–3.

[48] Leontius of Byz., CNestEutych: MG 86/1, 1336D-1337A; Epilysis: MG 86/2, 1944C-1945A.

[49] Ps.Leontius, De Sectis 7.1: MG 86/1, 1240A–1241C.

[50] Anastasius of Antioch, in: *Doctrina Patrum,* ed. Diekamp pp 125f, no.6; also C. Moeller, 'Chalcédonisme', pp 690f.

[51] Cf. G. Bardy, art.cit., *Chalkedon* II, pp 771–89; A. Grillmeier, 'Vorbereitung des MA', *Chalkedon* II, pp 791–839.

[52] Cf. L. Perrone, *Palestina,* p 179; cf. also Agapitus, ep. ad Justinianum: Coll.Avell. no. 91.

[53] Cf. H. Jedin, *History of the Church,* vol. 2, pp 451–6 (The controversy over the Three Chapters and the Fifth General Council); also A. Grillmeier, 'Vorbereitung des MA', *Chalkedon* II, pp 823f, with further literature on the question of Vigilius.

[54] Cf. C. Moeller, 'Chalcédonisme', pp 687–90.

also consented to the reception of Chalcedon which it had established.[55] Particularly relevant here is the position of Gregory the Great, who compared the first four ecumenical councils to the four gospels, but at the same time testified to his respect for the fifth council, including its condemnation of the Three Chapters.[56] It remains to say that the later councils in which the West participated, the Lateran synod of 649 (DS 500-522) and the third council of Constantinople of 681 (DS 553–559), moved along the same lines.[57]

The general acceptance of the dogma of the hypostatic union had without doubt presented no problem for the Latin Church, the more so as from the first years of the sixth century the authority of Cyril of Alexandria had also been established in the West. Even though the Roman synod of 512 had little understanding of the question of the validity of the christological formula *ex duabus et in duabus naturis,* a question which the bishops of the Danubian lands had brought before Symmachus,[58] this inquiry was taken seriously by Boethius (+524), who had also taken part in that synod.[59] In reply he drafted his treatise *Contra Eutychen et Nestorium,* in which he presents his renowned definition of person as *naturae rationalis individualis substantia.*[60] Even though this scholastic definition as such was difficult to apply to the christological problem, such that any Nestorian interpretation would be excluded, it was nevertheless to prove of far-reaching significance for the future.[61] When the Scythian monks also propagated their formula *Unus de Trinitate passus est* in Rome, they met with the opposition of the authorities.[62] In the long run things could not remain this way. Dionysius Exiguus, a Scythian monk, with his translation of a number of Cyril's writings, provided a better knowledge of his christology, and Fulgentius of Ruspe (+533) contributed to a change in the Roman position with regard to Alexandrine theology.[64] In his answer to the Scythian monks he went beyond his anti-Arian Christology and came close to the Byzantine teaching on the enhypostasis.[65] In the following decades Facundus of Hermiane and other African theologians, together with Rusticus, the nephew of pope Vigilius, with a quite formidable ecclesiology opposed the condemnation of the Three Chapters.[66] Nevertheless, they appropriated on their side the doctrine of the Word as subsisting in the human nature. Thus Facundus, by 550, in his work *Pro defensione trium capitulorum,*

---

[55] Cf. A. Grillmeier, 'Vorbereitung des MA', *Chalkedon* II, pp 824–34.

[56] Cf. A. Grillmeier, 'Vorbereitung des MA', *Chalkedon* II, pp 833f, with the Professio fidei: ACO IV/2, pp 136f (=DS 472).

[57] Cf. p 231 below.

[58] Cf. A. Grillmeier, 'Vorbereitung des MA', *Chalkedon* II, pp 792f.

[59] Cf. A. Grillmeier, 'Vorbereitung des MA', *Chalkedon* II, pp 792–6, also V. Schurr, *Trinitätslehre.*

[60] Boethius, Tract 5,3: ML 64, 1343C.

[61] Cf. A. Grillmeier, 'Vorbereitung des MA', *Chalkedon* II, pp 795f, esp. notes 13 and 19.

[62] Cf. A. Grillmeier, 'Vorbereitung des MA', *Chalkedon* II, pp 797–805.

[63] Cf. A. Grillmeier, 'Vorbereitung des MA', *Chalkedon* II, pp 798f, also esp. M. Richter, 'Dionysius Exiguus', TRE 9, 1982, pp 1–4.

[64] Cf. A. Grillmeier, 'Vorbereitung des MA', *Chalkedon* II, pp 799 and 802f, also P. Langlois, 'Fulgentius', RAC 8, 1972, cols. 632–61: analysis of these writings.

[65] Cf. Fulgentius, ep. 17; also A. Grillmeier, 'Die Rezeption des Konzils von Chalcedon in der römisch-katholischen Kirche', *Mit ihm und in ihm,* p 363, note 62.

[66] Cf. A. Grillmeier, 'Vorbereitung des MA', *Chalkedon* II, pp 807–22.

took his stand for the faith of Chalcedon, yet simultaneously adopted the theopaschite formula in an anti-Nestorian sense.[67] Above all, Rusticus in his *Contra Acephalos disputatio,* following Boethius and Leontius of Byzantium, strove after a concept of person, which would be capable of being applied in christology, too. Through his concept of 'standing on its own' (*manere in semetipso*) he anticipated the way in which the too strict symmetry of Chalcedonian faith would be transcended.[68] So in the sixth century Latin theologians paved the way for the reception of the fifth ecumenical council by the Church of the West. That it entailed a comprehensive deepening of the Chalcedonian faith, Western theologians were, however, to appreciate only in the Middle Ages, when the sources of Eastern christology and the acts of the councils of 451 and 553 were made more accessible.[69]

II. THE CHRISTOLOGICAL CONTROVERSIES OF THE SEVENTH CENTURY

The concerns of the first main phase of the christological controversies in the late patristic age also for the most part dominated the second phase from 633 to 681: the objections against the Definition of 451 and the *Tomus ad Flavianum,* and, in particular, the concern to integrate as rigorously as possible Cyrilline christology.[70] Two issues, however, mark off the new controversies. First, the issue of *energeia theandrike,* which had already occupied Severus of Antioch and other theologians of his time, was taken up, particularly in the context of the gospel accounts of Jesus' agony.[71] Secondly, also at this time, the Cyrilline formula, though now interpreted in Chalcedonian terms, of the *henosis kath' hypostasin* formed the central issue of the discussions. If it were possible with certainty to identify Theodore of Raithou, who stands at the end of the neo-Chalcedonian movement, with Theodore of Pharan, to whom is ascribed a decisive role in the rise of monenergism, we would have one further reason to emphasize the close connection between the christological controversies of the sixth and the seventh centuries.[72] By then, however, no longer was it a matter of rigorous monophysites opposed to strict adherents of the *Chalcedonense.* The issue at stake was not the problem as to whether faith in the one Christ was to be expressed by means of the formulae *mia physis,* or *mia hypostasis,* respectively; certain monastic circles rather felt the need to express Christ's unity in more concrete terms.[73]

[67] Facundus, DefCapit I.3: ML 67, 534C–540C.

[68] Rusticus, CAcephDisp: ML 67, 1238A–1241A, esp. 1239B.

[69] Cf. A. Grillmeier, 'Vorbereitung des MA', *Chalkedon* II, pp 837ff.

[70] On the history of the christological controversies in the seventh century in general see H. G. Beck, *Kirche und Literatur,* pp 292–5 and 430–49, also A. Grillmeier, 'Vorbereitung des MA', *Chalkedon* II, pp 834–7.

[71] Cf. J. Lebon, 'Monophysisme', pp 443–559, with texts by Severus, and L. Perrone, *Palestina,* p 247, with a note on John of Scythopolis; *Doctrina Patrum,* ed. Diekamp pp 86, 7ff.

[72] Cf. H. G. Beck, *Kirche und Literatur,* p 292, and W. Elert, *Altkirchliche Christologie.*

[73] Cf. H. G. Beck, *Kirche und Literatur,* pp 449–54; B. Studer, *Soteriologie,* pp 216–19, and L. Perrone, *Palestina,* pp 223–333, for the sixth cent. See also B. Studer, 'Una teologia monastica', *Storia della Teologia,* pp 613–22.

The outward impulse for this new wave of christological controversy was given by the Persian occupation of Syria and Egypt and the ascendency of monophysitism, which was bound up with this. In order to protect the empire more effectively against the East, the emperor Heraclius and Sergius, Patriarch of Constantinople, felt it politically necessary to seek an agreement with the monophysites. With this in view Cyrus, patriarch of Alexandria, in 633 signed a treaty of union, in which he spoke of one divine-human 'energy', through which the one Christ performed divine and human works alike.[74] After a first protest against this, Sophronius, later patriarch of Jerusalem, agreed to consent to a compromise. According to this neither one nor two energies should be postulated, but rather one single agent.[75] When Sophronius, however, had become bishop of Jerusalem in 636, he renounced the agreement. In a great encyclical he proposed his own teaching of the two 'energies' corresponding to the two natures, and of one hypostasis of Christ.[76] Sergius, however, saw in this the danger of Nestorianism. In rejecting this, he not only sought the backing of pope Honorius, but also had his opinion confirmed by an imperial edict in 638.[77] The answer of the pope, which therefore also became important, had already finally transferred the problem of the one 'energy' to the level of the one will.[78] Thus the discussions about Chalcedon took a new turn. As the criterion for an authentic understanding of the two natures, united without confusion, or division in the one hypostasis, there stood in question no longer the mere antitheses – infinite-finite, unchangeable-changeable – nor the mere contrast between the miracles of the Son of God and the sufferings of the Son of Man,[79] what was of concern here was rather what is most inward in man: the interplay of divine and human freedom, and thus also the final meaning of Christ's redeeming death.[80]

In this controversy between the monotheletes and dyotheletes there were all the time concerns of imperial and ecclesiastical politics at stake. Not only the emperors but also the patriarchs who co-operated with them always had in view orthodoxy as the religious foundation of the empire's unity.[81] On the other hand, the patriarchates involved, those of Constantinople and Jerusalem, at the same time fought for their jurisdictional privileges.[82] This aspect must not, however, be overrated; for the religious and theological motives were at any rate much stronger here. On the one hand, in the dogmatic decision of Chalcedon an inner dynamic was inherent, which necessitated further clarification. The formula of the one hypostasis in two natures required closer definition, not only as regards the

---

[74] Mansi XI, 563–8, esp. 565D.

[75] Mansi XI, 533D.

[76] Mansi XI, 461–510, and MG 87/3, 3147–3200; also C. von Schönborn, *Sophrone de Jérusalem. Vie monastique et confession dogmatique*, Paris 1972.

[77] Mansi X, 992–7, 1000f.

[78] DS 487f; for the question of Honorius, which is bound up in this see H. Jedin, *History of the Church*, vol. 2, pp 211f, with a note on recent studies on this issue.

[79] Cf. similar antitheses in Ps. Leontius, De Sectis 7.6: MG 86/1, 1245AB.

[80] Cf. W. Elert, *Altkirchliche Christologie*, pp 241ff.

[81] Cf. H. G. Beck, 'Die Erben Justinians. – Monergismus und Mono-theletismus', HKG II/2, pp 37–43, with bibl.

[82] Cf. W. Elert, *Altkirchliche Christologie*, pp 185–229: on Theodor of Pharan and his ecclestiastical affiliation.

unity of Christ, but also with respect to correct faith in the Trinity, and not least the essential meaning of salvation. It was this inner dynamic which finally and in the broadest sense determined the controversy about the divine-human activity and the one will in Christ. For it had to be more clearly shown, precisely in this quite existential perspective, how the union of true divinity and true humanity, without division and without confusion in the one hypostasis of the Logos, is to be conceived. On the other hand, this dogmatic concern, significant as it was, would never have been fought for with such passion and pertinacity, if there had not been a still stronger, deeply religious concern, which stood behind it all. The discussion about the unity of Christ did not take place without a vivid longing for an inner union with God, which had always rendered Alexandrine theology so attractive, and to which all monophysite tendencies, on their part, owed their whole vigour. Above all, the one side as well as the other could not evade the picture of the suffering Son of God, which the readings of the gospel and the celebration of the great liturgical feasts always recalled anew. No Christian could, finally, be indifferent to the question as to how God himself had saved humankind in the suffering and death of Jesus.[83]

The controversies about the divine-human activity, or the divine-human will of Christ, led first of all to the decisions of the Lateran council of 649.[84] Apparently under the influence of the monk Maximus, who had already at an early stage sided with the patriarch Sophronius, and who at that time was to be found at Rome, the synod declared that it could not be accepted that there was one will and one energy in Christ. There were rather two wills in him, the divine and the human, so closely bound together that one and the same person through both his natures had freely willed our salvation (DS 500–522, esp. 510f). This definition of the two wills and the two energies was at last, after lengthy political and theological controversies, also accepted by the third council of Constantinople (DS 553–559).[85] Maximus the Confessor's main concern, the autonomy of the human will, was, however, taken too little into account. Nevertheless, in its final session the synod to some extent redressed the balance. For in the so-called *Sermo acclamatorius* it declared the integrity of the human being to be constituted by nothing else than the essential will, which also characterized the power of human self-determination.[86]

The rather vague, too generally pronounced, dogmatizing of the two wills in Christ by the sixth ecumenical council was surely echoed in the christology of the Confessor himself. Even though it represents the summit of post-Chalcedonian development, it does not, however, prove satisfactory in every respect.[87] In denying

---

[83] Cf. B. Studer, *Soteriologie,* pp 216f, 223.

[84] Cf. R. Riedinger, 'Die Lateransynode von 649 und Maximus der Bekenner', *Maximus Confessor,* Freiburg 1982, pp 111–21.

[85] Cf. C. von Schönborn, '681–1981: ein vergessenes Konzilsjubiläum – eine versäumte ökumenische Chance', FZPhTh 29, 1982, pp 157–74.

[86] Mansi XI, 664D; also W. Elert, *Altkirchliche Christologie,* p 258.

[87] Cf. the critical reflections on Maximus' soteriology in R. Schwager, 'Das Mysterium der übernatürlichen Naturlehre', ZKTh 105, 1983, pp 32–57, esp. pp 38–44 (reprinted in *Der wunderbare Tausch,* Munich, 1986, pp 135–60).

to Jesus the will to deliberate (*gnomikon*) and to choose (*proairetikon*), that is to say the capability of free choice, Maximus clearly meant to exclude from him any error, any hesitation, and thus any kind of sinfulness.[88] In his hesitation concerning such self-determination, he did not at all mean to content himself with the natural will, i.e. the ability to strive for what is in accordance with nature.[89] In fact, he very clearly acknowledged Jesus' free volition, his consent to and his subordination under the divine will.[90] It is not surprising either that this consent of the human will is achieved through the influence of the divine will, not simply through the hypostasis of the Logos;[91] for Maximus was interested in the full consent of Christ's human will to the divine will rather than in its causally effective dependence on it, quite apart from the fact that he surely never forgets the traditional principle of the common activity of all three divine persons externally.[92] Yet, we have to concede that he did not bother to explain how the role of the second hypostasis of the Trinity in the execution of human freedom is to be conceived.[93] In other words: Maximus contented himself with a general safeguarding of Jesus' human autonomy.[94] For all his emphasis on the free act of salvation, he does not discuss any further the way in which the suffering, freely accepted by the Word of God in Jesus, was free human suffering, and therefore the origin and example for any free human self-surrender in love. Further, this is true also of John of Damascus, whose christology was to a high degree normative for the scholastic theology of the Middle Ages.[95] Even though he kept more to the main lines of Maximus' christological thought rather than to the dogmatic decisions of the third council of Constantinople, he did not, however, take it any further.

III. THE REPERCUSSIONS OF THE CHRISTOLOGICAL CONTROVERSIES ON THE DOCTRINE OF THE TRINITY

Already on the face of it christology appears to be linked with trinitarian doctrine in the history of late patristic theology. So the synodal documents,

[88] Cf. Maximus, op 1: MG 91, 32A; op 15: MG 91, 164C; op 20: MG 91, 236BD; DispPyr: MG 91, 308Df (Because Christ subsists divinely, he has a natural tendency to the good and a natural aversion to evil).

[89] Cf. Maximus, op 3: MG 91, 45C–48A (definition of the natural will); op 15: MG 91, 157AB (founding the human will on the human nature); op 16: MG 91, 192AB (anti-Nestorian rejection of two hypostases); DispPyr: MG 91, 294BC.

[90] Cf. esp. Maximus, op 6: MG 91, 65BC and 68A, and op 3, MG 91, 48C; op 7: MG 91, 80A–81B; op 16, MG 91, 197A; also F. M. Léthel, *Théologie de l'Agonie du Christ*, Paris 1979, esp. pp 50–54, and F. Heinzer, 'Anmerkungen zum Willensbegriff Maximus' Confessors', FZPhTh 28, 1981, pp 372–92, esp. p 391.

[91] Cf. Maximus, op 3: MG 91, 45C–48D; op 7: MG 91, 80D and 81D.

[92] Cf. Maximus, op 3: MG 91, 37B–D.48A; op 7: MG 91, 77BC; also Ambig I 5: MG 91, 1056A.

[93] Cf. Maximus, op 3: MG 91, 29BC; op 6: MG 91, 65A–68D; op 7: MG 91, 81AD.

[94] Cf. the quite general explanations in Maximus, Ambig MG 91, 1056AC, also op 7: MG 91, 84BC; op 13: MG 91, 517AC.

[95] For the christology of John of Damascus see K. Rozemond, *La christologie de s. Jean Damascène*, Ettal 1959.

which provide statements concerning the debated christological problems, set out with a confession of true faith in Father, Son and Spirit, the one God.[96] In the same way the theologians of the fifth century did not simply deal now with christological and now with trinitarian problems. Rather they published works which were concerned with both *theologia* and *oikonomia,* or at least, in their presentation of the doctrine of the Trinity introduced christological issues.[97] Such writings survive in the East from Theodoret of Cyrus,[98] Philoxenos of Mabbug,[99] John Philoponus,[100] the author of *De Sectis,*[101] as well as from Ps. Cyril, whom John of Damascus was to follow in his *Expositio fidei.*[102] The Western authors by no means lagged behind in this respect, as the writings of Arnobius,[103] Vigilius of Thapsus,[104] Fulgentius of Ruspe,[105] and also Dionysius Exiguus[106] prove.

At that time there was also a very close connection between *theologia* and *oikonomia.* It should be noted from the outset that a great many theologians developed their christological conceptions from the doctrine of the Trinity, as can be seen from the anti-Arian controversy. This is the case not only with the leading theologians such as Cyril of Alexandria and Nestorius,[107] but also with Arnobius and Fulgentius.[108] With Cyril, the teacher of the *Verbum incarnatum,* the connection is still closer, as the biblical notion of the divine glory revealed in the incarnation of the Word runs through the whole of his theology.[109] Still, the close connection of the doctrine of the Trinity and Christology is most obvious in the terminology which has already to a certain extent become dogma.

Nestorius, following Theodore of Mopsuestia, is known to have attempted to employ the trinitarian terminology of the Cappadocians to tackle the problem of the one Christ.[110] The trinitarian-christological 'exchange', which Gregory of Nazianzus with his still rather general formula 'the one and the other (masculine), not the one and the other (neuter)' had introduced,[111] by then increasingly

---

[96] Cf. DS 421; 501ff; 525–33; 542f; 554.

[97] Cf. A. Grillmeier, 'Vom Symbolum zur Summa', *Mit ihm und in ihm,* pp 585–636.

[98] Theodoretus, De theologia sanctae trinitatis et de oeconomia (CPG III, 6216).

[99] Philoxenus of Mabbug, De Trinitate et incarnatione: ed. Vaschalde, CSCO 9/10.

[100] John Philoponus, Diaietes (CPG III, 7260, cf 7268 and 7270); also H. G. Beck, *Kirche und Literatur,* pp 391f.

[101] Ps.Leontius, De Sectis (CPG III, 6823). This work represents, according to C. Moeller, 'Chalcédonisme', p 665, a résumé of the theology of the time.

[102] Ps.Cyril, De sancta Trinitate (CPG III, 5432); also B. Studer, *Johannes von Damaskus,* p 23.

[103] Cf. p 223, note 12 above.

[104] Cf. p 223, note 12 above.

[105] Fulgentius of Ruspe, De fide ad Petrum (CPL 826).

[106] Dionysius Exiguus, Praef in ep Procli ad Armenios: ML 67, 407–10; also A. Grillmeier, 'Vorbereitung des MA', *Chalkedon* II, pp 798f.

[107] Cf. Cyril's works on the Trinity (CPG III, 5208, 5215, 5216), which followed the preceding anti-Arian tradition; also J. Liébaert, *La doctrine christologique,* and A. Grillmeier, *Jesus Christus,* pp 647–52: on Nestorius (=*Christ in Christian Tradition,* pp 651–6).

[108] Cf. M. Simonetti, 'Letteratura antimonofisita d'Occidente', Augustinianum 18, 1978, pp 487–532.

[109] Cf. A. Dupré-la-Tour, 'La doxa du Christ dans les oeuvres éxegétiques de s. Cyrille d'Alexandrie', RchSR 48, 1960, pp 521–43; 49, 1961, pp 68–94.

[110] Cf. A. Grillmeier, *Jesus Christus,* p 713, esp note 10 (=*Christ in Christian Tradition,* pp 506f).

[111] Gregory of Naz., ep. 101: MG 37, 180AB.

assumed a technical form.[112] In both areas *physis* and *hypostasis,* or *ousia* and *prosopon* were distinguished. While in trinitarian doctrine the unity was expressed with concepts of *physis* or *ousia, hypostasis* or *prosopon* were generally regarded as being the principle of unity on the christological level. What still remained to be dealt with was to determine more precisely the concepts in question, thus justifying, or even eventually rejecting, their twofold use. Unfortunately the fathers of Chalcedon did not provide the necessary clarification. Even though basically distinguishing *physis* and *hypostasis,* they had not yet sufficiently defined them. With their emphasis on the one hypostasis they nevertheless made it clear where the focus of further development had to lie.

An approach to a more exact definition of the principle of christological unity is found immediately after the council of Chalcedon in Theodoret, who in his letter to the Nestorian John of Aegae, clearly with reference to the Cappadocians, distinguished more clearly *physis* and *hypostasis,* while identifying *hypostasis* with *prosopon.*[113] The discussion, however, did not get fully under way before 500.[114] In opposition to the already philosophically orientated defence of the Chalcedonian faith by the grammarian, John of Caesarea, Severus of Antioch based himself on the authority of the Fathers, on Athanasius and Basil.[115] Unlike John, who thought of the hypostasis simply as something existing on its own,[116] he called the individual reality that exists on its own both *hypostasis* and *physis,* and distinguished them from *ousia* as universal being.[117] Thus he objected to the defenders of Chalcedon that the identification of *physis* with *ousia* would lead to the assumption that the whole Trinity has become man.[118] Further, according to him, his opponents could decide for one of two options: a universal, or an individual *ousia.* In the first case the Word would have assumed the whole of humankind, in the other case they would arrive at two hypostases and two sons.[119] Despite all these difficulties Leontius of Byzantium kept fast to the Chalcedonian distinction. Further, he emphasized more than had been done before,[120] the *kath' heauto einai* in the concept of hypostasis.[121] Neither did he neglect to distinguish the different meanings of *hypostasis* in the Fathers' linguistic usage.[122] As he did not, however, conclusively enough distinguish the *kath' heauto einai* from the *idiomata* of the Cappadocian concept of hypostasis,

---

[112] Cf. Leontius of Byz., CNestEutych: MG 86/1, 1309AB.

[113] Theodoret, ep. ad Ioannem Aegeatem (CPG III, 6278); also C. Moeller, 'Chalcédonisme', p 658.

[114] Cf. J. Lebon, 'Monophysisme', pp 454–67; C. Moeller, 'Chalcédonisme', pp 696–704.

[115] Severus of Antioch, CGramm 2.33: ed. Lebon 197f; cf. J. Lebon, 'Monophysisme', pp 454ff.

[116] Cf. John of Caes., frag.: *Doctrina Patrum* 27.3, ed. Diekamp pp 197. 25–198.20; also L. Perrone, *Palestina,* p 254, note 71, bibl.

[117] Cf. J. Lebon, 'Monophysisme', pp 460f, with notes 24 and 26.

[118] Cf. John of Caes., ApolConcChalc III 1: CChG 1, pp 50f; also Leontius of Jer., CNest I 23; II 6; VII 5: MG 86/1, 1498BC, 1544CD, 1768AC.

[119] Cf. Leontius of Jer., CNest II 6: MG 86/1, 1544C–1545B.

[120] A first approach to the *kath' heauto einai* can be traced as early as the anti-Arian authors of the 4th cent., who, accordingly, are repeatedly cited. Cf. Athanasius, Ad Afros 4; Basil, ep. 226.6; Gregory of Naz., or. 33.16; Ps.Basil ep. 38.2, and esp. John of Caes., ApolConcChalc IV 6: CChG 1, pp 55.205–56.211; Leontius of Byz., CNestEutych MG 86.1, 1309AB.

[121] Cf. Leontius of Byz., Epilysis: MG 86/2, 1917CD, 1945AB.

[122] Cf. Leontius of Byz., CNestEutych: MG 86/1, 1309AB; Epilysis: MG 86/2, 1945AB.

he was not able to counter effectively Severus' objections.[123] Leontius of Jerusalem, however, surpassed his namesake. He introduced the concept of individual nature, of the *physis idike'*,[124] thus ruling out all natural properties from the hypostasis. Even though he, on his part, with his concept of the composite property (*idioma syntheton*) did not fully dissociate himself from the old concept of hypostasis,[125] with him the hypostasis nevertheless appears as the reality, which exists and also acts on its own.[126]

This development, which was concerned with transferring trinitarian terminology, in line with Chalcedon, to christology, and simultaneously drawing a distinction between the concepts taken over from the Fathers and those of contemporary dialectics, was bound to result in tensions between *theologia* and *oikonomia*. One could either maintain, more or less, the *hypostasis charakteristike*, as it had been employed from the time of the Cappadocians for the divine Persons; or one could simply consider the *kath' heauto einai*. The latter had the advantage, as far as christology is concerned, that any natural perfection was excluded from the hypostasis.[127] To the extent that the aspect of union, that is of the subsistence, on which the union rested, was safeguarded, however, there emerged for trinitarian doctrine the difficulty of applying such a concept of hypostasis to Father, Son and Spirit, without speaking of three realities, and therefore three gods. This danger could be avoided only if the *kath' heauto einai*, in so far as it expressed being, was understood as the common *ousia*, in which all three hypostases participate, and with which they are at the same time identical.[128] When, however, emphasis is put on the aspect of individuation, as was the case with the original Cappadocian concept of hypostasis, and as it was understood by the monophysites, as well as more or less by the Neo-Chalcedonians, that involved the risk of speaking of a single nature-hypostasis, or of accepting two hypostases. The hypostasis as such was thus no longer the principle of union. For this difficulty there was only one solution: to exclude any idea of natural perfection from the hypostasis. This was basically the aspiration of those who pleaded for the *hypostasis synthetos*, i.e. for an hypostasis of the Word, which was identical with the divine nature, but which was united with a new nature, the human nature, without suffering any change.[129] It was not impossible in this way

---

[123] Cf. Leontius of Byz., Epilysis: MG 86/2, 1920D–1921B, 1944CD; CNestEutych MG 86/1, 1308C; CSev 24: MG 86/2, 1909BC; also C. Moeller, 'Chalcédonisme', pp 700f; cf. also John of Caes., frag.: MG 86/2, 2953C.

[124] Cf. Leontius of Jer., AdvNest I 20: MG 86/1, 1485AD; also C. Moeller, 'Chalcédonisme', pp 701ff, esp. note 18 with other texts; cf. also Severus of Antioch, frag.: MG 86/1, 920.

[125] Cf. Leontius of Jer., AdvNest I 20: MG 86/1, 1485BD.

[126] Cf. Leontius of Jer., AdvNest I 1: MG 86/1, 1412C; I 20: MG 86/1, 1485BD; also C. Moeller, 'Chalcédonisme', p 702, note 19, with other texts.

[127] Cf. Leontius of Jer., AdvNest I 6: MG 86/1, 1420B–1421C; Ps.Leont, De Sectis VII 2: MG 86/1, 1240C–1242A.

[128] Cf. Leontius of Byz., Epilysis: MG 86/2, 1945AB; also S. Otto, *Person und Subsistenz*, pp 56–60; cf also Maximus Confessor, Ambig I 1: MG 91, 1034D, 1036C, and ep. 15: MG 91, 553CD: with the distinction between being and subsisting.

[129] Cf. John of Caes., CMonoph 7: CChG 1, 63; Leontius of Byz., Epilysis: MG 86/2, 1928A; Leontius of Jer., CNest I 24: MG 86/1, 1585CD; also H. U. von Balthasar, *Kosmische Liturgie*, pp 219–24, 232–53, with texts by Maximus; and P. Piret, *Maxime*, pp 157–201. For the connection of this term with monophysite views cf. J. Lebon, 'Monophysisme', pp 486–90.

to understand the hypostasis as the principle of union as well as the principle of distinction.[130] For if the hypostasis of the Word, the mode of being Son of God, is so understood, it does not only mark the distinction from Father and Spirit, it also distinguishes Christ from any other human being. Through it Jesus' humanity is linked to God like no other human being. At the same time it constitutes the form of existence, by virtue of which the individual human nature *in actu*, i.e. in reality, is distinct from any other realization of humanity. In this way the two basic aspects of the traditional concept of hypostasis could be upheld, subsistence and manifestation, the principle of union founded in an autonomous existence and the principle of individuation resting on the manifestation: the two aspects, therefore, that had always made up the concept of hypostasis.[131]

To get a better grasp of the bearing of this theological development and of the tension involved in it between *theologia* and *oikonomia*, it will be useful to give a fuller account of its connection with contemporary philosophy. In the fifth century Proclus of Athens (412–485), the main representative of Neoplatonism, which had by then become the only school of philosophy, was mainly concerned with the problem of the relation of the One to the many.[132] In particular he was occupied with the question as to how the Forms are at the same time one and distinct.[133] Inspired by him, Pseudo-Dionysius went further than Cappadocian trinitarian doctrine, as expressed chiefly in the letter of Gregory of Nyssa, attributed to Basil (ep. 38), and sought to explain with such considerations the oneness and the threeness in the mystery of God.[134] He, however, was guided by the tendency to reduce the divine hypostases to the multiplicity of the divine forms, thus dissolving the Trinity into unity.[135]

The same context in the history of philosophy is shared by John Philoponus (+ after 565).[136] While opposing Proclus' opinion on the eternity of the world, he, on the other hand, depended on him in other respects. At any rate, he attempted to justify, by means of the Aristotelian categories, as understood by the Neoplatonists, the Cyrilline formula of *mia physis tou Logou sesarkomene*. In order to exclude a second nature in Christ, he identified the concrete nature, Aristotle's first substance, with the hypostasis. He was, however, forced in his understanding of the Trinity to contrast the hypostases as *ousiai merikai* with the one common substance.[137] This is why he was opposed as a

[130] For the twofold function of the hypostasis cf. Leontius of Byz., Epilysis: MG 86/2, 1917CD; also S. Otto, *Person und Subsistenz*, p 60.

[131] Cf. B. Studer, 'Hypostases', HistWPhil 3, 1974, pp 1255–9, with bibl.

[132] Cf. R. Beutler, 'Proklos', PWK 45, 1957, pp 186–247, esp. pp 210.21–211.63; 216.1–217.60; and W. Beierwaltes, *Proklos. Grundzüge seiner Metaphysik*, Frankfurt a. M. ²1979, esp. pp 39–48.

[133] Cf. Proclus, Instit.theol., prop 176: ed. Dodds 154,3f; and also R. Beutler, art.cit., pp 229.60–230.43.

[134] For Ps.Dionysius in general cf. S. Lilla, 'Introduzione allo studio dello Ps.Dionigi l'Areopagita', Augustinianum 22, 1982, pp 533–77, and for his trinitarian doctrine in particular art.cit. 552ff, and S. Lilla, 'Terminologia trinitaria nello Ps. Dionigi l'Areopagita', Augustinianum 13, 1973, pp 609–23.

[135] Cf. esp. Ps.Dionysius, DivNom 2.3–5: MG 3, 640C–644B.

[136] Cf. H. G. Beck, *Kirche und Literatur*, pp 391f, with bibl.; and G. A. Lucchetta, 'Aristotelismo e cristianesimo in Giovanni Filopono', Studia Patavina 25, 1978, pp 573–93.

[137] Cf. Ps.Leontius, De Sectis: MG 86/1, 1233AB, John of Damasc., Haer 83.

tritheist by Anastasius of Antioch (559–590),[138] by the author of *De Sectis*[139] and others.[140]

In the West Boethius (+524) had earlier already employed a philosophical method similar to that of the Neo-Chalcedonians and monophysites, who had been influenced by the Alexandrine commentaries on Aristotle.[141] The inquiry of the Danubian bishops, as to whether it was correct to use the formula *ex et in duabus naturis,* gave him, as we have already mentioned, the opportunity of defining other concepts besides, chiefly that of person as *naturae rationabilis individua substantia.*[142] He thereby also brought to expression the two aspects of the original concept of hypostasis, stating that hypostasis, regrettably rendered by him as *substantia,* meant manifestation, or individual characteristics, as well as independent existence. Even though this definition was to become the accepted one, it does not rule out a Nestorian interpretation.[143] Above all, it was not easy to employ it in the doctrine of the Trinity, for it seemed to represent the divine essence as non-individual, thus endangering the divine unity, all the more so as Boethius applied the concept of *subsistentia* to the one God.[144] The propaganda of the Scythian monks in favour of the formula *Unus de Trinitate passus est* moved Boethius in the ensuing period to clarify his trinitarian conceptions. His understanding of the *communicatio idiomatum* posed no difficulty for his acceptance of the formula.[145] In this context he also developed the concept of *relatio.* Following Augustine he explained the mode of being of Father, Son and Spirit as being *ad aliquid. Relatio multiplicat Trinitatem* is the concise expression which he coined for it.[146] He avoided, however, attributing to the divine persons as such too high a degree of being. Because he regarded *relatio* as a mode of being rather than as being itself, he was, accordingly, able to show that the 'individualities' within the Trinity could be understood in such a way that the unity of the divine being was not jeopardized. Following Boethius scholastic theology was to speak of *relatio subsistens* and thus of the three persons as subsisting not *substantialiter* but *relative.*[147]

The whole development of the Chalcedonian concept of hypostasis, with not only its christological, but also its trinitarian complications, had taken place during the debate between the adherents and the opponents of the council of 451 in the sixth and seventh centuries. This development can be even better illustrated

---

[138] Cf. Anastasius of Antioch, frag.: *Doctrina Patrum,* ed. Diekamp, p 263.13; also H. G. Beck, *Kirche und Literatur,* p 380.

[139] Ps.Leontius, De Sectis V 6: MG 86/1, 1232D–1233B.

[140] Cf. among others John of Damascus, Haer 83.

[141] Cf. in general M. Grabmann, *Die Geschichte der scholastischen Methode* I, pp 148–77, and L. Pozzi, 'Boethius', TRE 7, 1981 pp 18–28; and esp. V. Schurr, *Trinitätslehre,* and M. Baltes, 'Gott, Welt, Mensch in der consolatio philosophica des Boethius', VigChr 34, 1980, pp 3131–340, with bibl. and note on books and philos. context. See also B. Studer, 'Una teologia scolastica', *Storia della Teologia,* pp 604–6.

[142] Cf. p 228 above.

[143] Cf. A. Grillmeier, 'Vorbereitung des MA', *Chalkedon* II, p 801.

[144] Cf. Boethius, CNestEutych 3: ML 64, 1345AB.

[145] Cf. A. Grillmeier, 'Vorbereitung des MA', *Chalkedon* II, p 801.

[146] Boethius, Tract I (Trin) 5 and 6: ML 64, 1253D–1256A.

[147] Cf. Thomas Aquinas, *Summa Theologica* I 28.

in the theology of John of Damascus (+ after 750), the 'last of the Church Fathers'.[148] An analysis of this would reveal, too, that the influence of contemporary Neoplatonist philosophy was time and again corrected by a faithfulness to Scripture and in particular to the patristic tradition.[149] Further, it would be confirmed by the monk of Mar Saba near Jerusalem that all those speculations, often so subtle in appearance, were entirely subservient to the spiritual life. They were designed for nothing else than the consummation of the *theoria*, the contemplation of the trinitarian God, who in the incarnation of his Word had revealed his glory.[150]

It may seem somewhat one-sided if the whole wealth of late patristic theology, usually too little regarded, is considered under the aspect of the development of the concept of hypostasis. Yet, after what has been said, it could hardly be doubted that the decisive contribution of the theologians of that time consisted in the clarification of this concept, dogmatized by Chalcedon. They sought to bring the Definition of that synod into accord with the whole of Cyril of Alexandria's theology. They were, however, subject to the influence of contemporary philosophy, in which the reinterpretation of the Aristotelian categories and the clarification of the principle of individualization found widespread interest.

The essential dogmatic result of these concerns for the concept of hypostasis may be regarded as being the doctrine of the hypostatic union, but also the definition of the two wills, through which the hypostasis of the Word accomplished the work of salvation. From a theological perspective, in these lengthy and somewhat painful controversies, a concept of hypostasis was worked out which was capable of being applied both to the Trinity and to the incarnation. In this way too the *Unus de Trinitate passus est* could be explained. Still, some attempted to produce explanations of the mystery of the Trinity which grazed the borders of orthodoxy. This whole further development of Chalcedonian theology can hardly be underestimated in its importance for the later history of theology and philosophy.

[148] Cf. B. Studer, *Johannes von Damaskus*, summary in DSpir 8, 1974, cols. 452–66. The same can be said, perhaps with even better reason, of Maximus Confessor; cf. P. Piret, *Maxime*.

[149] Cf. John of Damascus, Dial: ed. Kotter: PTS 7, 1969, pp 51–146, and also G. Richter, *Die Dialektik des Johannes von Damaskus*, Ettal 1964.

[150] Cf. B. Studer, *Johannes von Damaskus*, pp 31–56.

Retrospect and Prospect

At the end of this introduction to patristic theology it may be useful briefly to go over its main aspects again. This will be done from three points of view, which may be summarized in propositional form as follows. First, the doctrine of the Early Church on 'God and our salvation in Jesus Christ' developed in a very complex history. Secondly, in so far as the result of this historical development is the expression of the one catholic faith, the Christian believer today cannot remain indifferent to it. Thirdly, the gospel, the 'Good News', which lies behind this faith, has been understood anew in each new period of Church history, but has not essentially changed.

More precisely, it may be useful in *retrospect* to indicate clearly again what theological and historical concerns were at the forefront in the preceding exposition. It was necessary first of all to show how much the proclamation of the mystery of God, revealed in Christ, has at all times been bound up with what happened to and challenged the Christian communities. Secondly, it was our particular concern to show how, from a salvation historical perspective of God's activity, questions of a more metaphysical nature emerged: the question about Christ's eternal pre-existence, the question about his inner-divine relation to the Father and the Holy Spirit, the question about the one Lord Jesus Christ, who is at the same time true God and true man. Finally, it was a matter of showing how the whole development of doctrine in the Early Church has always been inspired by pastoral and existential motives. Even in the philosophically orientated considerations of that time, there was always in the background the question: *cur Deus homo?,* i.e., how has humankind in the cross and in the resurrection of the Son of God through the power of the Holy Spirit experienced the salvation of the eternal God, the creator of all things?

As this retrospect is also to serve as a prospect, it will, on the other hand, be necessary to allude at least to the questions which have remained open in this introduction: open, because they have not been considered owing to the restriction which is naturally imposed on any study, or because they have not yet found a valid answer in recent research, or have perhaps hardly been noticed at all, or because above all, as divine mysteries, they reveal themselves only to the inner experience of faith, and therefore have had to be left open.

I. A COMPLEX HISTORY

1. A continuing reinterpretation of the baptismal faith

As it is maintained at the end of St. Matthew's gospel (Matt 28:19f), as well as in the earliest of the yet preserved Church orders, in the *Didache* (ch. 7), according to the will of Jesus himself no one belongs to the Church who has not been baptized in the name of the Father, the Son and the Holy Spirit. For a full understanding of this ordinance of baptism we may recall the letter to the Romans, one of the oldest documents of the New Testament. The Apostle here not only treats baptism as a participation in the death and resurrection of Christ (Rom 6), but in the same context points to the union with Christ, established in baptism, by virtue of which a Christian can exclaim through the Holy Spirit: Abba, Father (Rom 8:14ff). In view of this Pauline theology of baptism it is certainly justifiable to regard Christian existence as union with God through Christ in the Holy Spirit, or, more in keeping with the language of the gospels, as the kingdom of God in Jesus Christ.[1]

This baptismal faith always remained the central core of the Church's proclamation, and constantly formed the centre of Christian theology. The baptismal creed, given to all baptismal candidates, developed out of this,[2] as well as the *regula fidei,* on which all theological endeavour was founded, as the examples of Irenaeus, Tertullian and Origen bear witness.[3] It was the baptismal faith to which Justin and others pointed, when they began to expound to outsiders the meaning of the Christian life and of the Church's liturgy.[4] It was again the baptismal faith that led Athanasius, Basil and other fourth-century Fathers in particular to affirm that the Son and the Holy Spirit, together with the Father, were to be acknowledged as the source of all salvation and therefore as God.[5]

Admittedly the baptismal faith was regarded in the course of time in a more ontological context. On the one hand Christ's pre-existence and his eternal relation to the Father and the Holy Spirit were emphasized here, on the other hand the true humanity was maintained as the presupposition for the death and resurrection of Christ, through which in baptism the believer receives salvation. Yet even in this hellenic, metaphysical rather than historical, understanding of the baptismal faith, its basic idea, that God through Christ in the Holy Spirit wrought salvation was not neglected. It was perhaps no longer thought of as the establishment of God's kingdom, nor as the pouring out of the Spirit in the fulness of time, but rather as deification, union with God in the Spirit of Christ. But even this essentially meant nothing else than what Christians had from the beginning confessed in their baptismal faith.

---

[1] Cf. R. Kerst, '1K 8,6 – ein vorpaulinisches Taufbekenntnis?', ZNW 66, 1975, pp 130–9.
[2] Cf. p 28f above.
[3] Cf. pp 56, 70, 78f above.
[4] Cf. p 53f above.
[5] Cf. pp 148ff above.

2. The inculturation of the baptismal faith

The historical development of the Church's doctrine of the Trinity and the incarnation may, therefore, be regarded as involving continually fresh interpretation of the primitive Christian baptismal faith. For a full account of this fairly complex process it needs to be made more precise how this continual reinterpretation was achieved under perpetually changing cultural conditions. This undeniable phenomenon may be described in the modern slogan of *inculturation*, by which is understood the reception of the gospel of Christ by the various cultures of mankind.

In this so-called inculturation the following elements can be distinguished: first of all the linguistic transitions, from Aramaic to Greek, from Greek to Latin and Syriac, etc.[6] This of course entailed an adaptation to new cultures. We need only recall the change in meaning of Christ's titles, Son of God and Son of Man,[7] the connection between name and person, the rendering of the term *hypostasis* by *substantia*, or *physis* by the Syriac *kyana*.[8] Further, the Christian faith had to become accessible to a more intellectual milieu, to the Jewish rabbis, the Greek philosophers, to the Roman aristocracy with their political ideals. The contrast between the 'simple-minded' and the 'intellectuals', between proclamation to the believers and a *théologie savante*, was indeed time and again to play an important role, not only in the Alexandrine Church of the third century, or among the Eastern monks of the fourth and sixth centuries.[9] Finally, the Christians' attitude to public life too has at all times been of more or less importance. When they lived with the Jews in the 'ghetto', they were inspired by a different image of Christ than later, when Christianity became the official religion of the Roman empire. In the imperial Church itself they not only increasingly expressed their theological conceptions in political and juridical terms, but also linked their concern for the true faith with responsibility for political unity. This in fact meant that they presented Christ as the true emperor, and formulated orthodoxy after the pattern of imperial legislation with the help of dogmas and edicts.[10]

In assessing this inculturation, in particular in evaluating the so-called hellenization of ecclesiastical language and theological thought, one should not be guided by any notion of the deformation of the gospel or by a model of decadence. It is true that the Good News of Christ could lose some of its original power under the manifold influences of the political and social environment. This was not, however, at all inevitable; for the apostolic proclamation of the mystery of Christ could actually gain ground in terms of universality, clarity and conclusiveness. In each case one has, therefore, to investigate whether the reception of the proclamation, the use of technical expressions in the creeds, the use of

---

[6] Cf. A. Adam, *Dogmengeschichte* I, pp 92–105: linguistic presuppositions of ecclesial and dogmatic reflexion.

[7] Cf. p 18 above.

[8] Cf. A. Grillmeier, *Jesus Christus*, p 449 (=*Christ in Christian Tradition*, pp 216f).

[9] Cf. A. Grillmeier, 'Vom Symbolum zur Summa', *Mit ihm und in ihm*, pp 589ff, with bibl., also A. Guillaumont, *Les 'Kephalaia Gnostica' d'Évagre le Pontique*.

[10] Cf. p 128ff above.

anthropological models that were unknown to the Bible, such as the Platonist-Stoic conception of body and soul, the Stoic idea of *ratio* as the ruler of inner life etc., had a positive or negative effect. Simply to speak of a falling away would at any rate be a gross simplification, if not a misjudgement of human openness to the Word of God.

II. DOGMA AS THE RESULT OF 'NEGATIVE' DEMARCATION

A presentation of the historical development of the doctrine of the Early Church will time and again be determined by the fact that the teaching authority of the Church felt obliged to summarize the mystery of God and the experience of divine activity in the world in simple propositions and slogans and therefore to formulate dogmas which possessed binding authority like the state laws, and the acceptance of which was regarded as prerequisite for the *communio fidei*. So the mystery of the Trinity was defined by the phrase *mia ousia – treis hypostaseis,* and that of the incarnation of the Son of God by the phrase *una persona in duabus naturis.* For a genuine understanding of such dogmatic formulae, but also for the assessment of the longer confessions of faith, the following criteria may prove helpful.

1. Dogma as a demarcation of the true faith

It should be remarked how often from the time of the first ecumenical council of Nicea (325) the common faith has been fixed in negative terms, in anathemas.[11] Even before this time, at least from the second century onwards, we encounter disciplinary proceedings, which ended with the exclusion of those who did not comply, or with the condemnation of heretics.[12] Thus from the earliest times compilations of errors, and catalogues of heretics, have played a large part in Christian literature.[13] Even when addressing simple believers preachers not seldom listed heretics schematically: Paul of Samosata, Arius, Photinus, Eunomius, the Manichees and many others. They did not fail to remark that the latest heresy, the one they were about to fight, was the worst of all.[14]

It appears that the formulations of a common faith on the part of the teaching authorities, the dogmas, should rather be understood as being a negative linguistic ruling. They laid down ways in which it was *not* permissible to speak of God or of Christ. Borders were defined, outside which a Christian believer was not allowed to practise theology. Faithfulness to Scripture and to the Fathers, a matter of course for all, was more exclusively delineated.

[11] Cf. DS 126; 151, 153–77 etc. Also H. Vorgrimler, 'Anathema', LThK 1, 1975, 494f.
[12] Cf. C. Andresen, *Die Kirchen der alten Christenheit*, pp 173–8.
[13] Cf. K. Rahner, 'Häresiengeschichte', LThK 5, 1960, 8–11.
[14] Cf. e.g. Leo, serm. 24.5; 28.4f.

2. Dogma as a merely approximate expression

As a negative and demarcating linguistic ruling, dogma does not affect the essential core of the matter. Yet, even in so far as it possesses a positive sense of marking out a framework, it does not exactly define the matter itself. Early Christian theologians were in fact largely aware of this. At any rate, as can easily be shown, they sought time and again for convergence in the forms of expression of the basically common faith. Hence, Athanasius, the leader of the Nicene party, was prepared to accept dogmatic compromise. He not only tolerated, as the *Tomus ad Antiochenos* bears witness, two credal formulae: *mia ousia* and *treis hypostaseis,* but was even satisfied with the *homoiousios kata panta.*[15] Basil avoided, at least in part, out of consideration for his opponents, calling the Holy Spirit God.[16] The Council of Constantinople (381) followed suit, obviously in order not to provoke the Macedonians.[17] Cyril of Alexandria in the negotiations about the union in 433 was prepared to speak of two natures, without giving up his main idea of the incarnation of the Logos.[18] The Neo-Chalcedonians, finally, gave up their resistance to the *Unus de Trinitate passus est.*[19] It must, however, be admitted that after 400 the requirement of faithfulness to a formula, once it had been coined, became enforced more strictly than before. So Leo the Great was inexorable with Eutyches.[20] Yet, as the above-mentioned instances show, theologians even in later times proved to be adaptable. The best proof of this is finally the Chalcedonian Definition, which must be regarded as a dogmatic compromise.[21]

At bottom, therefore, there was an awareness that ecclesiastical dogma rendered only inadequately the mysteries of faith. For all the joy to be found in a well-constructed formula, the inadequacy of the linguistic expression was fully taken into account. Such a point of view is relevant even today, as it is vital to integrate early Christian dogma into modern proclamation. Unshakeable faithfulness in the matter is always required here, as well as respect for traditional forms of expression, but not sterile intransigence with regard to traditional formulae, which are certainly not immutable.

3. The mystery of faith

In tracing the tenacious struggle for linguistic expression in which the Fathers engaged in order to demarcate the true faith from error, one is not surprised to note that the same Fathers time and again speak with unconcealed reverence of the mysteries of Christian faith, of the divine mysteries. Even in times when precise dogmatic formulation received more authority, a sense was preserved of the ineffability of God and his activity in the world.

---

[15] Cf. p 140f above.
[16] Cf. p 151 above.
[17] Cf. p 157 above.
[18] Cf. p 212 above.
[19] Cf. p 225f above.
[20] Cf. Leo, epp 28.1f; 31.1; 35.3.
[21] Cf. p 213 above.

Basil brusquely rejected the position of Eunomius, who hoped to discover in *agennesia* the essence of God himself,[22] as did, if not more strongly, his brother Gregory.[23] John Chrysostom, who was more a practical than a speculative theologian, wrote on his part on the 'incomprehensible God',[24] and in his sermons made the faithful aware of the *mysterium tremendum*.[25] Further, Augustine seemed to make it a point in his profound expositions to show God's incomprehensibility.[26] Even Leo the Great, who was very concerned to define unambiguously in juridical terms the Catholic faith, acknowledged that man should really be satisfied precisely when it dawns on him how much God transcends his thought, and when he can find no words for God's ineffability.[27]

How many mysteries there are which the Fathers were not able to fathom, and did not even want to fathom: the mystery of Jesus' resurrection, in which God confirmed the mission of his anointed one, and in which the resurrection of all mankind has already commenced; the mystery of the Father, who from eternity is not without the Son, and of God, who 'has done something' without himself 'having become something new'; the mystery of Jesus, who, because he is Son of God, has accepted in full human freedom the will of his Father; the mystery of the cross, in which the love of God has been revealed through all-destroying death; the mystery of Christ the head, who, in his earthly existence, included in himself the whole of mankind, and who now from heaven replenishes his believers with the Holy Spirit; the mystery of the Church, which after the pattern of Mary, the mother of Jesus, in the grace of the Holy Spirit and in the darkness of faith travels towards eternal perfection.

When the Christian theologians of the first centuries were therefore inclined to develop a rather negative theology, they were certainly largely inspired to do this by ancient piety, and most of all by the Greek philosophy of the imperial period.[28] They were, however, even more moved by the insight, according to which the love of the all-surpassing Creator and the compassion of the eternal Father for his sinful creatures is incommensurable. In this respect let us simply cite Augustine, who in his *Confessiones* and in his theological masterpiece *De Trinitate*, not simply as a Neoplatonist, but also and far more as a Christian believer, only reflected on God with reverence, and only spoke of him to fellow human beings with holy awe.[29]

---

[22] Basil, CEunom I, esp. 18–23.

[23] Gregory of Nyssa, CEunom I 151–4: MG 45, 297A–C; II 25: MG 45, 917BC.

[24] John Chrysostom, De incomprehensibili Dei natura (CPG II, 4318).

[25] Cf. G. Fittkau, *Der Begriff des Mysteriums bei Johannes Chrysostomus*, Bonn 1953.

[26] Cf. p 175f above.

[27] Cf. Leo, serm. 70.3; 75.3.

[28] Cf. A. Gouhier, 'Néant', DSpir 11, 1982, cols. 64–80, with bibl.; also esp. V. Lossky, *The Mystical Theology of the Eastern Church*, London 1957, pp 23–43, and J. Hochstaffl, *Negative Theologie. Ein Versuch zur Vermittlung des patristischen Begriffs*, Munich 1976.

[29] Cf. Augustine, Trin XV 28.51: concluding prayer.

III. THE EVER–FRESH REINTERPRETATION
OF THE BAPTISMAL FAITH

For all the negative character of Church dogma and the reverence which the Church Fathers showed for the mysteries of God described in dogma in their day, it should not be overlooked that they also arrived at new insights, that they succeeded in placing the baptismal faith in ever new perspectives. They not only adapted the gospel to their time, but they thereby also opened up to faithful knowledge depths of the divine mysteries unknown until then. It would, however, be just as one-sided to speak, instead of decadence, of a continually expanding advance. There is always a history of forgetting, of loss of original freshness. We for example could point to the difference between Irenaeus and Hilary of Poitiers.[30] All the same, in many respects early Christianity in the course of time acquired a more comprehensive vision of the revelation of the divine love, which was finally declared in the cross and the resurrection. At any rate, it is possible today continually to gain new insights into the mystery of Christ from the inexhaustible riches of the patristic interpretation of the baptismal faith. Such an enrichment is subject to one condition: one must take account of the way in which the Fathers appropriated ever anew the gospel.

1. The change in categories and patterns of thought

The fact that Christianity has encountered various conditions of life, renders a certain changeability in the baptismal faith inevitable. The message of salvation in Jesus Christ has each time called forth a different echo and different reactions. It has had to be made accessible to Greeks in Greek, to Latins in Latin, and to Syrians in Syriac. That is to say, it has been clothed in various languages, different imagery, different forms of expression.

In recent research this process of transformation has been differently evaluated.[31] There are still authors who speak of a wholesale alienation. Others represent the view that what has been changed only affects the forms of expression, but not the content. So Heinrich Dörrie compares the hellenization of Christianity to a 'hermit crab', which makes itself at home in the shell of another snail. For him hellenism is, accordingly, only the shell of the gospel, now proclaimed in Greek.[32] The legitimate question will be raised here as to whether such an explanation does not tear apart content and form too much. For with new words and modes of expression human beings also grasp the content of their thinking in another way. To evade the difficulties of a too sharp distinction between the form of tradition and the traditional heritage itself, it will be better

---

[30] Cf. p 120 above.

[31] Cf. A. Grillmeier, '"Hellenisierung" – "Judaisierung" in der Erforschung des Urchristentums seit A. von Harnack', *Mit ihm und in ihm*, pp 458–88, with bibl.

[32] Cf. H. Dörrie, 'Die andere Theologie. Wie stellten die frühchristlichen Theologen des 2.–4. Jahrhunderts ihren Lesern die "Griechische Weisheit" (=den Platonismus) dar?' TheolPhil 56, 1981, pp 1–46. See also C. J. Vogel, *Der sog. Mittelplatonismus, überwiegend eine Philosophie der Diesseitigkeit?* Festschrift H. Dörrie (Münster 1983), pp 277–302.

to distinguish the experience of faith from its forms of expression. Such a distinction will prove very helpful above all for the beginnings of Christianity. For the Easter event was experienced in faith by the first Christians, and only then interpreted in the categories of the Old Testament and contemporary Judaism. In a similar way later Christians, following this original experience, have experienced their own baptismal faith and have expressed it similarly and also differently. It should at any rate be accepted that everyone encounters their saving God in a different manner. Even though he or she believes together with others, every individual nevertheless experiences their own faith. And yet each person senses the same mystery of the divine love. Origen understood this well, when he spoke of the accommodation to all humankind of the Logos,[33] or when he maintains that the Holy Spirit is received only by the holy, while he himself always stays the same.[34]

2. New scientific demands

The transformation of the baptismal faith was not only dependent on the transposition into new forms of expression, it was also conditioned by the new methods employed in order to try to understand it better. When in the second century the Christian religion was conceived of as the true philosophy, metaphysical ways of thinking increasingly gained significance in theology. God was understood less in his historical activity, remembered less in his *memorabilia*, theologians sought to integrate him into the order of being. In this way the generation of the Son was explained in terms of the immutability of a God, transcendent over all being. This, however, happened not just in the second century, but in the whole patristic age, as we could doubtless have shown more clearly.[35] A little later Alexandrine exegesis was introduced into Christian theology. Holy Scripture was, accordingly, not only referred to in the *testimonia*, but also came to be commented on with all the skill available.[36] Along these lines the christological titles were developed far more systematically than before.[37] In the fourth century, when the divinity of the Son and the Holy Spirit was debated, contemporary logic was employed. Basil and his friends undertook to make understandable in some way the paradox of the One and the Three using the methods of the Stoics and Neoplatonists.[38]

In this whole development of scientific theology we shall have to bear in mind that certain theological problems were in the air. The need for a more profound penetration of certain truths of faith has in many instances arisen from relevant philosophical ways of questioning. Hence the debate about the Origenist conception of Christ as the mediator between the One and the many cannot fully be appreciated without taking into account the contemporary philosophical

[33] Cf. Origen, PA I 2.7f; CoIo I 20.119–24; also M. Harl, *Origène*, pp 229ff.
[34] Cf. Origen, PA I 3.5–8; I 8.3.
[35] Cf. for the early period W. Maas, *Unveränderlichkeit Gottes*.
[36] For exegesis of Origen cf. R. Gögler, *Zur Theologie des biblischen Wortes bei Origenes*.
[37] Cf. Origen, CoIo I 21.125–39.291.
[38] Cf. pp 141–5 above.

discussion about the eternity of the world. Nicea must therefore be regarded as the crisis of 'Christian Platonism'.[39] In a similar way the question about the unity of Christ was connected with the contemporary discussion of the union of man in body and soul, as it can be seen above all in Nemesius of Emesa's *De natura hominis*.[40] Finally the problems of the hypostatic union can hardly be separated from Proclus' discussion of the problem of individuation.[41] Unfortunately these interrelations in the history of ideas have even to this day been too little clarified.

3. The ever-new gospel

The translation of the Good News into other languages and patterns of thought, the formation of a scientific theology, and also the consideration of ever-changing needs of pastoral care have without doubt resulted in a transformation of the gospel itself. The incessant concern of preachers and theologians to remain faithful amidst all the changes to the apostolic tradition should not be underestimated. As can be shown from their faithfulness to the Bible and the Fathers who went before them, they adapted even their most profound philosophical concerns to the baptismal faith, not the other way round. So, for example, Origen in his teaching on the Holy Spirit,[42] Augustine in his teaching on the incarnation of the Word.[43] It is above all evident that the Fathers even in their most sublime speculations were guided by faith in the only Saviour Jesus Christ, true God and true man. It was precisely in this way that they ensured that the true, authentic and original gospel should be proclaimed at all times. Such a continuity is in the final analysis based on the unique nature of the gospel itself. For it is so inexhaustibly rich that it can present to all people at all times something new. It is granted to every believer to make for himself or herself their own idea of Christ, without thereby abandoning the message, entrusted to the one catholic and apostolic church, of the immeasurable love of God, revealed in Christ through the Holy Spirit. 'Jesus Christ is the same yesterday and today and for ever'(Heb 13:8).

---

[39] Cf. pp 95f and 104 above.

[40] Nemesius, De natura hominis (CPG II, 3550); also A. Grillmeier, *Jesus Christus*, pp 574ff (=*Christ in Christian Tradition*, pp 389ff), and A. Kallis, *Der Mensch im Kosmos. Das Weltbild des Nemesios von Emesa*, Münster 1978.

[41] Cf. p 236 above.

[42] Cf. Origen, PA I.3.1f.

[43] Cf. pp 177ff above.

Bibliography

In the following general bibliography a number of handbooks of the history of dogma, summary expositions of the patristic doctrine of the Trinity and of the incarnation, and other aids are referred to, which are especially appropriate for a fuller understanding of this introduction to early Christian theology, *Trinity and Incarnation*. In the special notes on books those works are cited which are fundamental especially for the relevant parts and paragraphs. Further studies in the fields in question are quoted only in the footnotes, but can also be found through the index of modern authors. The Fathers' writings are generally not recorded bibliographically; they can, however, be easily verified in patrologies as well as in the *Clavis Patrum Latinorum* (=CPL), Steenbrugge [2]1961, and in the *Clavis Patrum Graecorum* I-IV (=CPG), Turnhout 1974ff.

1. General introduction to the history of dogma

R. Seeberg, *Lehrbuch der Dogmengeschichte* I-IV, Leipzig [3]1922ff, reprint 1953.

M. Schmaus, A. Grillmeier, Leo Scheffczyk, M. Seybold, eds., *Handbuch der Dogmengeschichte* (=HDG), Freiburg 1952ff.

B. Lohse, *Epochen der Dogmengeschichte*, Stuttgart 1963.

A. Adam, *Lehrbuch der Dogmengeschichte I. Die Zeit der alten Kirche*, Gütersloh 1965.

J. Pelikan, *The Emergence of the Catholic Tradition (100–600) = (The Christian Tradition. A History of the Development of Doctrine*, I), Chicago 1971.

J. N. D. Kelly, *Early Christian Doctrines*, London [5]1977.

C. Andresen, ed., *Handbuch der Dogmen- und Theologiegeschichte* I, Göttingen 1982.

K. Beyschlag, *Grundriß der Dogmengeschichte* I and II, Darmstadt 1982 and 1991.

See also:

F. M. Young, *From Nicaea to Chalcedon*, London 1983.

S. G. Hall, *Doctrine and Practice in the Early Church*, London 1991.

B. Ramsey, *Beginning to Read the Fathers*, London 1986.

E. Villanova, *Historia de la teología cristiana, I. De los orígenes al siglo XV*, Barcelona 1987.

I. Hazlett, ed., *Early Christianity. Origins and Evolution to AD 600*, London 1991.

B. Studer, *Dominus Salvator, Studien zur Christologie und Exegese der Kirchenväter* (Studia Anselmiana 107), Rome 1992.

A. di Berardino and B. Studer, *Storia della Teologia, I. Epoca patristica*, Casale Monferrato 1993 (with bibl.).

2. Expositions of patristic trinitarian doctrine

Bibliographical notes are to be found in the periodical Estudios Trinitarios 1ff, Salamanca 1967, esp. in EstTrin 5, 1971, pp 3–114, as well as in V. Venanzi, 'Dogma e linguaggio trinitario dei Padri della Chiesa. Un panorama bibliographico', Augustinianum 13, 1973, pp 425–53.

G. Bardy, 'Trinité', DThC 15/1, 1946, cols. 1545–1702.
L. Scheffczyk, 'Lehramtliche Formulierungen und Dogmengeschichte der Trinität', Mysterium Salutis (=MySal). II, J. Feiner and M. Löhrer, eds., Einsiedeln 1967, pp 146–220 (with bibl.).
B. de Margerie, La Trinité chrétienne dans l'histoire (=Théologie historique 31), Paris 1975.
G. Kretschmar, Der Heilige Geist in der Geschichte: Grundzüge frühchristlicher Pneumatologie (=Quaestiones Disputatae 85), Freiburg 1979, pp 92–130.
Y. Congar, I believe in the Holy Spirit, New York and London 1983.
See also:
F. Courth, Trinität in der Schrift und Patristik (HDG II/1a), Freiburg 1988 (cf. B. Studer, in ThR 86, 1990, pp 458–64).

3. Expositions of patristic christology and soteriology

Bibliographical notes are given in C. Kannengießer, 'La christologie comme tâche au champs des études patristiques', RchSR 65, 1977, pp 139–68, and M. Serentha, 'Cristologia patristica: per una precisazione dell'attuale "status quaestionis"', La Scuola Cattolica 106, 1978, pp 3–16.

J. Rivière, Le dogme de la rédemption. Études critiques et documents, Louvain 1931, cf. DThC 13/2, 1937, cols. 1912–2004.
J. Liébaert, Christologie. Von der apostolischen Zeit bis zum Konzil von Chalcedon, 451 (=HDG III/1a), Freiburg 1965.
H. E. W. Turner, The Patristic Doctrine of Redemption. A study of the development of doctrine during the first five centuries, London 1952.
C. Andresen, 'Erlösung', RAC 6, 1966, cols. 54–219 (with bibl.).
J. Plagnieux, Heil und Heiland. Dogmengeschichtliche Texte und Studien, Paris 1969.
H. Kessler, Die theologische Bedeutung des Todes Jesu. Eine traditionsgeschichtliche Untersuchung, Düsseldorf 1970.
P. Smulders, 'Dogmengeschichtliche und lehramtliche Entfaltung der Christologie', Mysterium Salutis III/1, J. Feiner and M. Löhrer, eds., Einsiedeln 1970, pp 389–467.
J. Barbel, Jesus Christus im Glauben der Kirche. Die Christologie bis zum 5. Jahrhundert, Aschaffenburg 1976.
L. I. Scipioni, 'Il Verbo e la sua umanità. Annotazioni per una cristologia patristica', Teologia 2, 1977, pp 3–51.
B. Studer, Soteriologie der Kirchenväter (=HDG III/2a), Freiburg 1978 (with bibl.).
A. Grillmeier, Christ in Christian Tradition, I. From the Apostolic Age to Chalcedon (451), 2nd revised ed., London 1975 (fuller German edition: Jesus der Christus im Glauben der Kirche. I. Von der Apostolischen Zeit bis zum Konzil von Chalcedon (451) (=Jesus Christus), Freiburg 1979).
G. Moioli, Cristologia. 'Momento' storico – Lettura delle 'fonti'. Gesù di Nazareth secondo il NT e nella feda e teologia dell' epoca 'patristica' – Secoli II-VIII, Milan 1980.

4. Related fields and aids

O. Bardenhewer, *Geschichte der altkirchlichen Literatur* I-V, Freiburg 1913–1932.

J. Quasten, *Patrology* I-III, Utrecht 1950–1960; IV, ed. A. di Berardino (Eng. tr., Westminster, Maryland, 1986).

G. L. Prestige, *God in Patristic Thought*, London 1952.

C. Mohrmann, F. van der Meer, H. Kraft, *Bildatlas der frühchristlichen Welt*, Gütersloh 1959.

J. N. D. Kelly, *Early Christian Creeds*, London ³1972 (German edition: Göttingen 1972).

H. Jedin, ed., *Handbuch der Kirchengeschichte* (=HKG), Freiburg 1962ff. Eng. tr., H. Jedin and J. Dolan, eds., *History of the Church*, 10 vols., London 1980ff.

J. Daniélou and H. I. Marrou, *The First Six Hundred Years* (*The Christian Centuries* I), London and New York, 1964.

B. Altaner and A. Stuiber, *Patrologie. Leben, Schriften und Lehren der Kirchenväter*, Freiburg ⁷1966 ⁹1978.

B. Altaner, *Kleine Patristische Schriften*, Berlin 1967.

C. Andresen, *Die Kirchen der alten Christenheit*, Stuttgart 1971.

B. Studer, *Zur Theophanie-Exegese Augustins*, Rome 1971.

H. Karpp, *Textbuch zur altchristlichen Christologie*, Neukirchen 1972.

J. Maier, *Geschichte der jüdischen Religion*, Berlin 1972.

A. Grillmeier, *Mit ihm und in ihm. Christologische Forschungen und Perspektiven*, Freiburg 1975.

A. M. Ritter, *Alte Kirche. Kirchen- und Theologiegeschichte in Quellen*, Neukirchen 1977.

R. Hübner, *Der Gott der Kirchenväter und der Gott der Bibel*, München 1979.

H. J. Sieben, *Die Konzilsidee der Alten Kirche*, Paderborn 1979.

H. Dörrie, 'Die andere Theologie. Wie stellten die frühchristlichen Theologen des 2.-4. Jh. ihren Lesern die "Griechische Weisheit", (=Platonismus) dar?' TheolPhil 56, 1981, pp 1–46.

A. di Berardino, ed., *Dizionario Patristico*, 2 vols, Turin 1983 and 1984. Eng. tr., *Encyclopaedia of the Early Church* (=EEC), 2 vols, Cambridge 1992.

See also:

A. H Armstrong, ed., *Cambridge History of Later Greek and Early Medieval Philosophy*, Cambridge 1967.

G. Reale, *Storia della filosofia antica*, 5 vols, Milan 1976–80.

Index of Modern Authors

Italicized references indicate the location of bibliographical information.

Index of Names

Subject Index

(including selected Greek and Latin concepts)

theology (cont.)
    4. theology of history 17–18, 44, 54,
      58–9, 63–4, 79–80, 121, 128, 171
    5. political theology *see also* Church: 5.
      imperial Church; Roman empire 8, 74,
      110, 115–16, 127–32, 136, 156–7, 159,
      213, 216, 222–3, 224, 241
theopaschism 208, 223, 229
theophanies 37, 50, 85, 104, 170, 173
theotokos (God-bearer) 201, 212, 214
Tomus ad Antiochenos 110, 140–2, 148, 149,
    194, 196, 243
Torah see Law
Traditio Apostolica (Hippolytus) 27
tradition 4, 5–7, 9, 10, 36–8, 39–41, 44, 45,
    49, 51, 56, 85, 86, 96, 116, 119, 152, 156,
    158, 161, 162, 168, 172, 174–5, 180,
    182–3, 185, 225, 232, 236, 238, 243, 245,
    247
Trinity
    1. general *see also* God-man; Logos,
      theology of; *oikonomia;* pneumatology;
      procession; *theologia* 1–2, 4–8, 9, 22,
      26–7, 51, 54, 60–4, 70–5, 78–9, 84,
      86–7, 90–1, 95, 96, 97, 103, 107–10,
      112, 113, 116, 123, 124, 125, 139–53,
      156, 158, 161–3, 167–85, 217, 223,
      231, 232–8, 239–42, 246
    2. trinitarian formulae
      general 38, 53–4, 70–3, 96, 108,
        140, 141, 145–8, 176

mia ousia – treis hypostaseis 87,
    141–5, 152, 193–4, 242, 243
una substantia – tres personae
    97–8, 161, 182–3
unitas – trinitas 174
unus ex Trinitate passus est see
    under Christology: 2.
    christological formulae
    3. economic and immanent 1, 8, 29, 70–5,
      96–7, 109, 152, 164, 175, 176, 185, 232
    4. and salvation history 1–3, 5, 22–4, 29,
      56, 60–4, 66, 73–5, 147, 164, 176,
      202–3, 207
    5. trinitarian spirituality 2–3, 5–6, 8–10,
      29, 40, 53, 54, 90, 233, 240
tritheism 73, 144, 145, 150, 156, 237
Tropici 108, 118, 148
two hands, doctrine of the 39, 62–3, 67
two natures, doctrine of *see also* diphysitism
    87, 193, 195, 207, 214, 215–16, 231

unction 53, 117, 180
unitarianism *see also* modalism; Sabellianism
    73, 78, 89, 90, 92, 106, 109, 140–1

virgin (out of the virgin) 49, 59, 68, 70, 82,
    191, 214

will of Christ 69, 194, 218, 231–2, 238, 240,
    244
worship *see* adoration